Connecting

A Culture-Sensitive Approach to Interpersonal Communication Competency

Second Edition

Roy M. Berko
George Washington University

Lawrence B. Rosenfeld
University of North Carolina at Chapel Hill

Larry A. Samovar
San Diego State University

Harcourt Brace College Publishers

Fort Worth   Philadelphia   San Diego   New York   Orlando   Austin   San Antonio
Toronto   Montreal   London   Sydney   Tokyo

Publisher	Christopher P. Klein
Senior Acquisitions Editor	Carol Wada
Developmental Editor	Laurie Runion
Project Editor	Elizabeth Cruce Alvarez
Art Director	Melinda Welch
Production Manager	Jessica Wyatt
Cover Design	Nick Welch/Design Deluxe

ISBN: 0-15-503227-5

Library of Congress Catalog Card Number: 96-75216

Harcourt Brace & Company may provide complimentary instructional aids and supplements or supplement packages to those adopters qualified under our adoption policy. Please contact your sales representative for more information. If as an adopter or potential user you receive supplements you do not need, please return them to your sales representative or send them to: Attn: Returns Department, Troy Warehouse, 465 South Lincoln Drive, Troy, MO 63379.

Address for Editorial Correspondence: Harcourt Brace College Publishers, 301 Commerce Street, Suite 3700, Fort Worth, TX 76102.

Address for Orders: Harcourt Brace & Company, 6277 Sea Harbor Drive, Orlando, FL 32887-6777. 1-800-782-4479, or 1-800-433-0001 (in Florida).

This book is dedicated
to the memory of Joshua Lee Warren.

PREFACE

This is a textbook about interpersonal communication—a process that requires self-understanding, recognizing the influence of a setting on an encounter, and a realization that each person's unique background is reflected in her or his communication. While the way we communicate expresses individual cultural uniqueness, it also bridges the gaps between individuals. That bridge unites us in the common struggle for individual and social meaning—the struggle to work, live, and play together, while retaining our individual identity.

Connecting: A Culture-Sensitive Approach to Interpersonal Communication Competency, Second Edition, is based on the recognition that many people have improved their personal, social, and work lives by becoming competent communicators—by changing ineffective interpersonal communication patterns to productive, creative, and thoughtful ones. To be a competent communicator requires three things: first, it requires an understanding of communication in general and interpersonal communication in particular; second, it requires developing skills that reflect the most current thinking on effective communication behaviors; and third, it requires motivation, the desire to communicate competently. Your motivation provides the encouragement you need to put your understanding and skills together as you interact with others.

The second edition of *Connecting* emphasizes materials intended to provide an understanding of the field—its research and theories—and provides opportunities to develop important communication skills. The goal is to help you develop personal understanding and useful skills—to become a competent interpersonal communicator.

ABOUT THE AUTHORS

Since this is a textbook about interpersonal communication, it is important for us, the authors, to introduce ourselves to you. This textbook reflects who we are—our beliefs about what is important to understand when studying interpersonal communication, our personal and educational experiences that help us determine which communication skills seem most effective in particular settings and with certain people, and our thoughts about what makes a textbook interesting, engaging, and motivating.

Roy M. Berko is a faculty member in communication at George Washington University. He was formerly an associate director of the Speech Communication Association. He also served on the faculty of Towson State University, and as a professor and administrator at Lorain County Community College.

Dr. Berko holds an Ed.D. from Pennsylvania State University, an M.A. from the University of Michigan, and a B.A. from Kent State University. He is the author or co-author of eight books in the areas of public speaking, interpersonal communication, business communication, and education. He also is the editor or co-editor of five books about communication education. He was selected as the first recipient of the Speech Communication Association's Outstanding Community College Teacher award, and was named a "Teacher on Teaching" by that organization. He was designated a Master Teacher by the National Institute for Teaching and Learning, and was given the Teacher Recognition Award several times by the Consortium for Higher Education.

A certified counselor, Dr. Berko has been in private practice and serves as a consultant for educational institutions, businesses, and governmental agencies. In addition, he has performed on television and served as an entertainment critic for public radio.

Lawrence B. Rosenfeld is a professor of Communication Studies at the University of North Carolina at Chapel Hill. He was formerly on the faculty of the University of New Mexico. He holds a Ph.D. from Pennsylvania State University in human communication, an M.A. from the University of Iowa in play writing and theatre history, and a B.A. from Hunter College of the City University of New York in mathematics and chemistry.

Dr. Rosenfeld's recent honors include receiving the Robert J. Kibler Memorial Award for Life Time Achievement from the Speech Communication Association, the Johnston Award for Teaching Excellence from the University of North Carolina at Chapel Hill, serving as the editor of *Communication Education* and the *Western Journal of Communication,* and being recognized as one of the most published authors in the field of communication. He is the author or co-author of nine books on interpersonal, small group, and nonverbal communication; over eighty articles for journals in communication, social work, education, psychology, and sports psychology; and thirteen chapters in books on self-disclosure, family communication, support groups, and teleconferencing. He has presented more than seventy papers at national and international conferences.

Larry A. Samovar is a professor in the School of Communication at San Diego State University. He is a leading researcher and writer in the field of intercultural communication. He is the author or co-author of thirteen books on human communication. Four of his books dealing with intercultural communication have been translated into Japanese and are widely used in Japan. In addition, three of his textbooks on intercultural communication have been adopted by universities in eleven countries. He has presented over one hundred papers at national and international conferences and has been a consultant to numerous private and governmental organizations in the United States,

Mexico, and Japan. Dr. Samovar hosted a weekly television series for KPBS and was a guest commentator for the program "Profile."

Dr. Samovar holds a Ph.D. and an M.A. from Purdue University, where he also taught, and a B.A. from California State University at Los Angeles. He was one of the founders of the Society for Intercultural Education, Training and Research, and is also an active member of many other professional organizations.

INSTRUCTIONAL FEATURES

This new edition of *Connecting* contains many of the same features found in the first edition that instructors and students indicated were useful. In addition, some new features have been added—and others expanded—to facilitate your becoming a competent communicator.

- Each chapter begins with a list of the Communication Competencies addressed in the chapter. This provides you with an introduction to the chapter that should help you read more efficiently and effectively.

- Each chapter contains Knowledge Checkup activities, which help you apply your understanding of the material covered in the text or gain information about yourself, and Skill Development activities, which help you practice or develop a specific skill. Together, Knowledge Checkup and Skill Development activities bridge theory and research with practice. Knowledge and skill are not separate but work together to provide you with a firm basis to become a competent communicator.

- At the end of each chapter is a Communication Competency Checkup, an activity that presents you with a problem to solve using the material in the chapter. Whether you are asked to describe a real teacher-student conflict and make recommendations for how it may be resolved, or analyze Calvin and Hobbes' cartoon family, you will need to integrate the material of the chapter as you solve the problem. The Communication Competency Checkup also helps you evaluate your progress in becoming a competent communicator.

- Each chapter contains endnotes that you may use to pursue topics covered in the chapter.

- New to this second edition is a glossary of terms used in the textbook. This feature should help you overcome any problems you may have with the special vocabulary of communication scholars.

- A number of marginal quotes are inserted throughout the textbook. Each quote is a "food for thought" that should help stimulate your thinking about the material in the chapter.

CHANGES IN THE SECOND EDITION

Changes throughout *Connecting* are designed to ensure that the text reflects the most recent thought on competent communication. New sources, new and expanded topics, and new Knowledge Checkup and Skill Development activities all guarantee an up-to-date introduction to the topic of interpersonal communication. Greatly expanded is consideration of the role of gender and culture in understanding communication processes. Material on gender and culture is integrated throughout *Connecting* to reflect the reality that these two topics cannot be separated from other communication topics.

Here are some of the important changes made to each chapter, in addition to the increased coverage of issues related to gender and culture.

Chapter 1, "Foundations for Communication Competency," has a new section on models of communication, which ends with a model to help you visualize the complex process of communication. A list of characteristics of communication has been added, including: the meaning of any message depends on the situation in which the message is communicated, communicators can only infer what their partners are thinking or feeling, and communicators are self-reflective as they think about their messages.

Chapter 2, "Conceiving the Self," introduces consideration of impression management strategies that people use to influence how others view them.

Chapter 3, "The Self and Others," has two new sections: the problems associated with the perception process and the relationship between gender and emotions. Material has been added on primary emotions (those chief, deeply felt emotions) and secondary emotions (those often communicated instead of the primary emotions).

Chapter 4, "Listening," has three new sections: the effects of global and linear learning styles on listening, poor listening habits, and how to prepare yourself to listen effectively.

Chapter 5, "Nonverbal Communication," now includes consideration of the effects of climate on communication, as well as the effects of peoples' different conceptions of time on their interaction.

Chapter 6, "Verbal Communication," includes a new section on the characteristics of language and a detailed consideration of gender differences in communication goals and style.

Chapter 7, "Stress and Communication Anxiety," offers meditation as an additional method for coping with stress, and an expanded discussion of social support that includes technical and emotional challenge support as dimensions of the social support process.

Chapter 8, "Interpersonal Relationship Processes," now describes a hierarchy of types of relationships, ranging from role relationships to intimate relationships.

Chapter 9, "Beginning, Maintaining, and Ending Interpersonal Relationships," includes two additional bases for attraction—Self-Esteem Enhancement and Attempting to Overcome Family-of-Origin Problems. A new section on the Johari Window graphically conceptualizes self-disclosure, and a new section on compliance gaining strategies describes how people get others to do what they want.

Chapter 10, "Interpersonal Relationships in the Family," contains a large number of new features: a section on how culture helps determine what a family is like; an approach to defining "family" that accounts for the contemporary changes and configurations in family structure; a presentation of material on the family life-cycle, beginning with separating from a family-of-origin and ending with separation, divorce, and death; and a consideration of the characteristics of less and more functional families.

Chapter 11, "Managing Relational Discord," has four new sections, three related to conflict and culture: the relationship between conflict and culture, cultural differences as a source of conflict, and how to respond to conflict between members of different cultures. The fourth section considers the health consequences of conflict.

Chapter 12, "Creativity, Power, and Interpersonal Satisfaction," has an expanded discussion of gender differences in powerful and powerless speech and cultural differences in perceptions of powerful speech.

SUPPLEMENTS

The second edition of *Connecting* has several valuable resource materials available for instructors. A completely revised and restructured instructor's manual and test bank, by Joan E. Aiken of the University of Missouri-Kansas City, contains multiple choice, true-false, and essay questions for each chapter; a series of activities, many of which were first published in the Speech Communication Association's publication, *The Speech Communication Teacher;* and additional teaching and learning tools. Also available are a computerized version of the test bank; overhead transparency masters; instructional videos; *Communication in Film,* a book of film reviews with instruction on how to teach using films; and *Cinemania,* a CD-ROM software that provides film reviews, video and audio clips, and cinema insights.

ACKNOWLEDGMENTS

Connecting, Second Edition, is the result of a team effort, including the three authors and the students with whom they had the opportunity to test the textbook in the classroom. Valuable critiques and suggestions were provided by communication teachers throughout the nation, and we want to thank them and acknowledge their help: Joan Aitken, University of Missouri-Kansas City; Vincent Bloom, California State University-Fresno; Deems Brooks, Central Missouri State University; Brant R. Burleson, Purdue University; Jamie Comstock, University of West Florida; Charity Granata, Fresno City College; Richard Halley, Weber State University; Thomas E. Jewell, University of New Mexico; Marylin Kelly, McLennan Community College; Shirlee A. Levin, Charles County Community College; Preston Ni, Foothill College; Alexia Olds, California Polytechnic State University; Terry Perkins, Eastern Illinois University; Susan Richardson, Prince George's Community College; Edwina Stoll, DeAnza College; Gail Whitchurch, Indiana University-Purdue University at Indianapolis; and Steve Wilson, Michigan State University.

We also want to thank the editors and production people at Harcourt Brace College Publishers, who made writing this second edition more enjoyable than any of the authors expected: Carol Wada, senior acquisitions editor; Laurie Runion, developmental editor; Beth Alvarez, project editor; Melinda Welch, art director; Jessica Wyatt, production manager; Julie McBurney, marketing manager; Barbara Moreland, copy editor; and Aimé Merizon, proofreader.

CONTENTS

Chapter 1 FOUNDATIONS FOR COMMUNICATION COMPETENCY 2

Communication Competencies 3
Key Words 3

DEFINING COMMUNICATION 5
Elements of the Communication Process **5**
Messages Are Simultaneously Sent and Received **8**
Messages Cannot Be Erased **8**
Communication Is Proactive **8**
Meaning Depends on Context **9**
Communicators Can Only Infer What Their Partners Are Thinking and Feeling **10**
Messages That Are Received Have a Consequence **10**
Communication Is Self-Reflective **10**

THE ROLE OF CULTURAL DIVERSITY IN INTERPERSONAL COMMUNICATION 10
Characteristics of Culture **12**

KNOWLEDGE CHECKUPS AND SKILL DEVELOPMENT ACTIVITIES 14

DEFINING INTERPERSONAL COMMUNICATION 16
Predicting Responses **16**
Defining Roles **17**

THE COMPONENTS OF INTERPERSONAL COMMUNICATION COMPETENCY 18
Knowledge **19**
Skills **19**
Motivation **22**

THE QUALITIES OF COMPETENT INTERPERSONAL COMMUNICATORS 23
Competent Interpersonal Communicators are Appropriate **23**
Competent Interpersonal Communicators Effectively Balance Opposing Communication Goals **24**
Competent Interpersonal Communicators are Adaptable **24**

Competent Interpersonal Communicators Recognize Obstacles to Effective Communication 26
Competent Communicators are Ethical 27

YOU AS AN INTERPERSONAL COMMUNICATOR 28
Communication Competency Checkup 29
Notes 30

KNOWLEDGE CHECKUP EXERCISES
1.1 Recognizing the Elements and Characteristics of Human Communication 15
1.2 How Competently Do You Communicate? 20

SKILL DEVELOPMENT EXERCISES
1.1 Assessing Relationship Interpersonalness 18

Chapter 2   CONCEIVING THE SELF   32

Communication Competencies 33
Key Words 33

WHO YOU ARE: YOUR SELF-CONCEPT 35
The Person You Are 36
Social Identity 37
Personality Characteristics 38
Values 41
Physical Characteristics 43
The Sources of Self-Concept 43
Reflected Appraisal 43
Social Comparison 46
Organizing the Elements of Your Self-Concept 47
The Person You Wish You Were 48
The Idealized Self 48
The Actual Self 48
The Should Self 49
The Person You Present to Others 50
The Requirements of a Situation 50
Others' Expectations 51
The Goals for Communicating 52

HOW YOU FEEL ABOUT YOURSELF: YOUR SELF-ESTEEM 53

ENHANCING YOUR SELF-ESTEEM 57
Confronting Your "Should" Messages 57
Focusing on the Positive 58
Eliminating Your Self Put-Downs 59

Communication Competency Checkup   60
Notes   61

KNOWLEDGE CHECKUP EXERCISES

2.1 Who Am I?   **36**

2.2 Bem Sex-Role Inventory   **38**

2.3 Discovering Your Values   **41**

2.4 Identifying Your Significant Others and Their Appraisals of You   **44**

2.5 Identifying Your Social Comparison Groups   **46**

2.6 Identifying Your "Should" Statements   **49**

2.7 Analyzing Your General Self-Esteem   **53**

2.8 Analyzing Your Specific Self-Esteem   **55**

SKILL DEVELOPMENT EXERCISES

2.1 Confronting Your Should Messages   **58**

Chapter 3   THE SELF AND OTHERS   64

Communication Competencies   65
Key Words   65

PERCEPTION   **66**

Selective Perception   **67**

External Forces   **67**

Internal Forces   **68**

The Selection Process   **68**

Selective Organization   **69**

Ways of Organizing Perceptions of Others   **70**

Selective Interpretation   **74**

The Self-Fulfilling Prophecy   **77**

COMMON PROBLEMS IN PERCEPTION   **78**

INCREASING PERCEPTUAL ACCURACY   **79**

Stretch Yourself   **80**

Remain Open-Minded   **81**

Increase Empathy   **82**

EMOTIONS AND PERCEPTION   **84**

Failure to Express Emotions   **86**

Gender and Emotions   **89**

Expressing Your Emotions   **90**

Identify Your Feelings   **90**

Accept Responsibility for Your Feelings   **91**

Select a Good Time and Place to Share Your Feelings   **92**

Share Your Feelings Clearly   **92**
Helping Others Express Their Emotions   **93**
Communication Competency Checkup   95
Notes   96

KNOWLEDGE CHECKUP EXERCISES
3.1 Analyzing Your Perception Process   **76**
3.2 Assessing Empathy in Friendship   **83**
3.3 Identifying Your Emotions   **85**
3.4 Identifying Your Emotional Reactions   **88**

SKILL DEVELOPMENT EXERCISES
3.1 Developing Alternative Interpretations   **75**
3.2 Increasing Sense Awareness and Sense Imagination   **80**
3.3 Expressing Your Feelings   **93**

Chapter 4   LISTENING   98

Communication Competencies   99
Key Words   99

WHAT IS LISTENING?   100

THE REASONS FOR LISTENING   102

INVESTIGATING YOUR LISTENING PATTERNS   103
The Effect of Global and Linear Learning Styles on Listening   **106**
The Levels of Listening   **108**
Level 3 Listening   **109**
Level 2 Listening   **109**
Level 1 Listening   **110**

BARRIERS TO EFFECTIVE LISTENING   110
Nonlistening Cues   **111**
Overloading   **111**
Poor Listening Habits   **111**
Responding to Emotionally Loaded Words   **113**
External Distractions   **115**
Internal Distractions   **115**

MAKING LISTENING WORK FOR YOU   116
Being Prepared to Listen   **116**
Focusing Attention   **117**
Paraphrasing   **118**
Taking Notes   **119**

Repeating **120**
Staying Alert Physically **120**
Organizing Material **121**
Chunking **121**
Ordering **121**
Reordering **121**

PROVIDING FEEDBACK **122**

LISTENING RESPONSE STYLES **124**
Active Response Style **126**
Recommendation Response Style **127**
Information Seeking Response Style **127**
Critical Response Style **128**

LISTENING TO HELP **128**
Communication Competency Checkup **131**
Notes **132**

KNOWLEDGE CHECKUP EXERCISES
4.1 Paying Attention? Take This Listening Self-Evaluation Test and See **104**
4.2 Left/Right, Linear/Global Brain Dominance **107**
4.3 Your Nonlistening Signals **110**
4.4 Sending Up Your Red and Green Flags **114**
4.5 Assessing Your Listening Responses **124**

SKILL DEVELOPMENT EXERCISES
4.1 Recognizing Effective Paraphrasing **118**
4.2 Chunking, Ordering, and Reordering **122**
4.3 Providing Feedback to Indicate You Are Listening **123**

Chapter 5　NONVERBAL COMMUNICATION　134

Communication Competencies **135**
Key Words **135**

FUNCTIONS AND CHARACTERISTICS OF NONVERBAL COMMUNICATION **137**
Functions of Nonverbal Communication **137**
Characteristics of Nonverbal Communication **138**

PHYSICAL APPEARANCE **139**
Body Shape **140**
Body Image **140**
Clothing and Other Artifacts **142**

FACE AND EYES **144**

CONTEXT OF INTERACTION   149
  Physical Context   150
  Psychological Context   152

TOUCH   156
  Uses of Touch   160
  Expectations for Touch   160

VOICE   163

BODY MOVEMENTS   168
  Types of Body Movements   169
  Uses of Body Movements   170

TIME   172

NONVERBAL CLUES TO DECEPTION   174
Communication Competency Checkup   175
Notes   177

KNOWLEDGE CHECKUP EXERCISES
  5.1 Appearance Satisfaction   140
  5.2 Clothing Preferences   142
  5.3 Analyzing Your Territorial Defense   154
  5.4 Analyzing the Use of Space in a Common Setting   156
  5.5 Assessing Your Touch Avoidance   159
  5.6 Analyzing Your Touch Behavior   161
  5.7 Using Vocal Cues to Regulate Conversations   167

SKILL DEVELOPMENT EXERCISES
  5.1 Increasing Your Skill at Interpreting Facial Expressions   148
  5.2 Assessing Two Environments   151
  5.3 Expressing Your Emotions Effectively   165
  5.4 Increasing Perceptions of Similarity   172

Chapter 6   VERBAL COMMUNICATION   180

Communication Competencies   181
Key Words   181

THE IMPORTANCE OF VERBAL COMMUNICATION   182

CHARACTERISTICS OF LANGUAGE   185

LANGUAGE AND MEANING   187
  Abstract and Concrete Symbols   187
  Denotation and Connotation   190

Denotations   **190**
Connotations   **191**
Private and Shared Language   **192**

FEMININE AND MASCULINE LANGUAGE   194
Communication Goals   **194**
Characteristics of Women's and Men's Talk   **195**

BARRIERS TO SUCCESSFUL COMMUNICATION: OUR IMPERFECT LANGUAGE   **197**
Polarization   **197**
Indiscrimination   **198**
Fact-Inference Confusion   **200**
Allness   **202**
Static Evaluation   **202**
Bypassing   **203**

USING LANGUAGE EFFECTIVELY   203
Unclear Language   **204**
Relative Words   **204**
Euphemisms   **205**
Clichés   **206**
Emotive Words   **206**
Distortions   **207**
Qualifiers   **207**
Oxymorons   **207**
Sexist Language   **209**
Nonsexist Communication   **209**
Racist Language   **211**
Communication Competency Checkup   **211**
Notes   **213**

KNOWLEDGE CHECKUP EXERCISES
6.1 Distinguishing Facts from Inferences   **200**
6.2 Recognizing Unclear Language   **208**

SKILL DEVELOPMENT EXERCISES
6.1 Constructing a Ladder of Abstraction   **189**
6.2 Communicating Differences   **199**
6.3 Eliminating Static Evaluation   **203**
6.4 Eliminating Sexist Language   **210**

Chapter 7   STRESS AND COMMUNICATION ANXIETY   216

Communication Competencies   **217**

Key Words   217

STRESS AND COMMUNICATION   218
Verbal and Nonverbal Reactions that Reflect Feeling Stressed   218
Stages of Stress Reactions   222
The Alarm Stage   222
The Adaptation or Resistance Stage   223
The Exhaustion Stage   223
Recognizing Your Stressors   223
Responding to Your Stressors: Self-Help Techniques   225
Attitude Changes   225
Perfection   226
Speed   226
Pleasing Others   226
Winning   227
Physical and Emotional Strength   228
Time Management   229
Exercise   233
Meditation   233
Repeating a Word, Sound, or Phrase   234
Paying Attention to Your Breathing   235
Responding to Your Stressors: Seeking the Help of Others   235
Professional Help   239
Self-Help Groups   240

COMMUNICATION ANXIETY   240
Communication Anxiety and You   243
Private and Public Communication Anxiety   243
Situational Communication Anxiety   244
Causes of Communication Anxiety   244
The Effects of Communication Anxiety   245
Dealing with Communication Anxiety   246
Communication Skills Training   246
Systematic Desensitization   247
Positive Visualization   247
The Stress Management Model   248
Communication Competency Checkup   249
Notes   250

KNOWLEDGE CHECKUP EXERCISES
7.1 Self-Assessment of Your Stress Reactions   220
7.2 Your Nonverbal Signs of Stress   221
7.3 Your Stress Analysis   224
7.4 Communication Apprehension in Generalized Contexts Questionnaire   241

SKILL DEVELOPMENT EXERCISES
7.1 Developing Coping Responses to Self-Defeating Attitudes   228

7.2 Time Management Model   **230**
7.3 Providing Social Support   **237**
7.4 Practicing Positive Visualization   **248**

Chapter 8   INTERPERSONAL RELATIONSHIP PROCESSES   252

Communication Competencies   **253**
Key Words   **253**

RELATIONSHIP DIMENSIONS   254

CULTURE AND RELATIONSHIPS   257

THE FRAMEWORK FOR INTERACTION   258
    Goals   **258**
    Structure   **261**
    Rules   **268**

QUALITIES AND RESOURCES OF RELATIONSHIPS   271
    Commitment   **272**
    Intimacy   **274**
    Resources   **277**
Communication Competency Checkup   **278**
Notes   **279**

Knowledge Checkup Exercises
    8.1 What Are Your Relationship Goals?   **258**
    8.2 Relational Structure Analysis   **264**
    8.3 Your Relationship Rules   **271**
    8.4 Commitment Probe   **272**
    8.5 Intimacy Probe   **276**

SKILL DEVELOPMENT EXERCISES
    8.1 Ascertaining Your Relationship Goals   **260**

Chapter 9   BEGINNING, MAINTAINING, AND ENDING INTERPERSONAL RELATIONSHIPS   282

Communication Competencies   **283**
Key Words   **283**

RELATIONAL DEVELOPMENT: BEGINNING, MAINTAINING, AND ENDING RELATIONSHIPS   284
    Beginning a Relationship   **284**
        Attraction   **286**

Attractiveness   286

Proximity   288

Personal Rewards   289

Complementarity   289

Similarity   290

Personal Motives   292

Self-Esteem Enhancement   292

Attempting to Overcome Family-of-Origin Problems   292

Objectives   294

Initiating Contact and Gathering Information   294

Creating a Favorable Impression   297

Maintaining a Relationship   299

Objectives   299

Achieving Your Objectives   300

Supportiveness and Confirmation   300

Self-Disclosure   303

Affinity Seeking   312

Compliance Gaining   314

Electronic Mail   316

Ending a Relationship   317

BUILDING RELATIONAL AWARENESS   322

Communication Competency Checkup   322

Notes   324

KNOWLEDGE CHECKUP EXERCISES

9.1 Desired Characteristics in a Long-Term, Intimate Partner   285

9.2 Comparing Your Preferences with the General Population   291

9.3 Your Bases of Attraction   293

9.4 Disclosure and Feedback in Two Relationships   304

9.5 Assessing Your Affinity-Seeking Strategies   312

9.6 Assessing Your Compliance-Gaining Strategies   314

SKILL DEVELOPMENT EXERCISES

9.1 Probing for Information   297

9.2 Creating a Favorable Impression   298

9.3 Giving Supportive and Confirming Responses   302

9.4 Increasing Your Self-Disclosure and Receptiveness to Feedback   311

Chapter 10   INTERPERSONAL RELATIONSHIPS IN THE FAMILY   328

Communication Competencies   329

Key Words   329

A DEFINITION OF FAMILY   330

THE IMPORTANCE OF THE FAMILY   331

CULTURE AND THE FAMILY   333

WHAT FAMILIES TEACH   334
    Images   **335**
    Family Themes   **336**
    Boundaries   **337**
    Biosocial Attitudes   **338**
    Social Skills   **340**
    Concepts of Self   **341**

THE FAMILY AS A COMMUNICATION SYSTEM   342

STAGES IN THE FAMILY LIFE CYCLE   344
    Establishing a Family   **345**
    Addition of Family Members   **346**
    Children's Development of Independence   **349**
    Launching the Children   **350**
        Recoupling   **350**
        The Redeveloped Family   **351**
        The Launched Family Member   **351**
    Post-Launching the Children   **352**
    Marital Dissolution   **354**
        Divorce   **354**
        Death   **354**

LESS FUNCTIONAL VERSUS MORE FUNCTIONAL FAMILIES   355
    Cohesion and Adaptability   **356**
    Family Conflict   **358**
        Physical and Verbal Aggression in Families   **362**
        Family Conflict Should be Confronted   **362**

OPENING FAMILY LINES OF COMMUNICATION   363
Communication Competency Checkup   365
Notes   366

KNOWLEDGE CHECKUP EXERCISES
    10.1 The Contemporary Family in the United States   **332**
    10.2 Identifying Your Family Images   **335**
    10.3 Identifying Your Family's Themes   **337**
    10.4 Identifying Your Gender Role Attitudes   **339**
    10.5 Your Grandparents' Grandparenting Style   **353**
    10.6 Cohesion and Adaptability in Your Family   **356**
    10.7 Use of Parental Authority   **359**

SKILL DEVELOPMENT EXERCISES
    10.1 Observing What Families Teach   **341**
    10.2 Applying the Workshop Process of Change   **364**

Chapter 11   MANAGING RELATIONAL DISCORD   370

Communication Competencies   **371**
Key Words   **371**

CONFLICT   372
    Conflict and Culture   **373**
    Characteristics of Conflict   **374**
        Frustration   **375**
        Interdependence   **375**
        Sources of Conflict   **376**
            Limited Resources   **376**
            Individual Differences   **376**
            Cultural Differences   **377**
            Differences in Defining Your Relationship   **377**
            Competition   **377**

PERCEPTIONS OF CONFLICT   378
    Family   **378**
    Educational Institutions   **379**
    Media   **379**

CONSEQUENCES OF CONFLICT   380
    Effects on Work   **380**
    Effects on Relationships   **381**
    Personal Effects   **381**
    Health Effects   **382**

CONFLICT STRATEGIES   383
    Avoidance and Compromise   **386**
    Smoothing Over and Dominance   **387**
        Usual Outcomes of Lose-Lose and Win-Lose Conflicts   **389**
    Integration   **390**

NONASSERTION, DIRECT AGGRESSION, AND ASSERTION   392
    Nonassertion   **393**
    Aggression   **394**
    Assertion   **395**
        Assertive Skills for Simple Situations   **395**
        Assertive Skills for Complex Situations   **396**

GENDER DIFFERENCES AND CONFLICT   398
  Sexual Harassment   **399**

DEALING WITH DIFFICULT PEOPLE AND DIFFERENT CULTURES   400
  Dealing with Difficult People   **401**
  Conflict Resolution with People from Different Cultures   **403**

OPTIONS FOR RESOLVING CONFLICT   404

ASSESSING CONFLICT PROCESSES AND OUTCOMES   405
Communication Competency Checkup   408
Notes   409

KNOWLEDGE CHECKUP EXERCISES
  11.1 Analysis of Relationship Discord   **373**
  11.2 Conflict Consequences   **382**
  11.3 Your Conflict Strategies   **383**

SKILL DEVELOPMENT EXERCISES
  11.1 Stating Simple Assertions   **396**
  11.2 A*S*S*E*R*T Yourself   **397**
  11.3 Dealing with Difficult People   **402**
  11.4 Assessing the Process and Outcomes of Your Conflicts   **406**

Chapter 12   CREATIVITY, POWER, AND INTERPERSONAL SATISFACTION   412

Communication Competencies   413
Key Words   413

CREATIVITY   414
  Obstacles to Creativity   **416**
    Cultural Obstacles   **417**
    Personal Obstacles   **418**
      Habitual Ways of Doing Things   418
      Beliefs   420
      Fear of Failure   421
  Developing Your Creativity   **422**
    Forming New Associations   **423**
    Analytic Breakdown   **424**
    Manipulating Details   **426**

POWER   427
  A Definition of Power   **428**
  Sources of Power   **430**
    Expert Power   **433**

Referent Power **433**
Associative Power **434**
Reward Power **434**
Coercive Power **434**
Legitimate Power **435**
Choosing Your Power Base **436**
Powerful and Powerless Language **437**
Communication Competency Checkup 440
Notes 441

KNOWLEDGE CHECKUP EXERCISES
12.1 Examining the Habit of Saying No **419**
12.2 Overcoming Beliefs **420**
12.3 How Powerful Do You Feel? **429**
12.4 Assessing Your Sources of Power **430**

SKILL DEVELOPMENT EXERCISES
12.1 Forming New Associations **423**
12.2 Doing an Analytic Breakdown **425**
12.3 Creating New Gift Ideas **427**
12.4 Recognizing and Eliminating Powerless Language **439**

GLOSSARY **443**

PHOTO CREDITS **450**

LITERARY CREDIT **450**

INDEX **451**

Connecting

A Culture-Sensitive Approach to
Interpersonal Communication Competency

Second Edition

CHAPTER 1

FOUNDATIONS FOR COMMUNICATION COMPETENCY

COMMUNICATION COMPETENCIES

This chapter defines what *communication* and *interpersonal communication* are and explains the characteristics of competent communication. It also provides the background you need to understand and apply the material presented in the rest of the book. Subsequent chapters focus on both presenting principles of effective communication and developing your communication competencies. Specifically, the objective of this chapter is for you to learn to:

● Define the characteristics of communication and interpersonal communication.

● Appreciate the role of culture in interpersonal communication.

● Understand the components of interpersonal communication competency.

● Understand the functions of competent interpersonal communication.

● Define the qualities of a competent interpersonal communicator.

KEY WORDS

The key words in this chapter are:

communication
sender
message
receiver
context
purpose
linear process
feedback
adaptation
interactive process
transactive process
proactive
culture
acculturation
ethnocentrism
interpersonal
   communication
interpersonal
   communication
   competency
dialectical tensions
flexibility skills
cultural obstacles
environmental obstacles
personal obstacles
relational obstacles
language obstacles
ethics

A sign hanging on the bulletin board in our office reads, "I know that you believe you understand what you think I said, but I am not sure you realize that what you heard is not what I meant." To which, one day, a student added, "Are you sure?"

In any communication process, the degree to which the communication is effective depends on the communicators' mutual understanding of their messages. Have you ever found yourself in situations where you acted as if you understood what someone else was saying—to be polite, perhaps—when you did not? And how often do you think other people have done this with you? Are you and others involved in a game of "let's act like we understand each other even though we don't"?

Perhaps next to breathing, communication might well be one of our most basic activities. And yet, much like breathing, we tend to take communication for granted, seldom pausing to ask ourselves why human communication is important or what it is. Communication is meaningful in all of our lives because, first of all, it is how we know ourselves: we talk to ourselves continuously, using labels to describe for ourselves who and what we are and to determine what we should do and why we should do it. In addition, communication is the basis for all human contact. It is the way we share our internal states with other people. We tell others how we feel, what we know, what we want to know, and how the world appears to us. In turn, others can tell us how they feel, what they know and want to know, and how they see the world. Without this contact we would live in a kind of emotional and spiritual isolation, what the philosopher Aldous Huxley referred to as a "perpetual solitary confinement." But because of communication, our realities can be shared with other people.

The average person spends 30% of his or her waking hours in conversation.

You probably have been giving and getting messages about communication most of your life yet have rarely stopped to think what communication is really all about. Phrases you've probably heard are:

"If we could just learn to communicate better, we could solve all of our problems."

"If you don't have something nice to say, don't say anything at all."

"Speak when you're spoken to."

"Silence is golden."

"They really must be in love, they seem to have no trouble communicating."

"What we have here is a breakdown in communication."

When you say that communication has taken place, what do you mean? How would you define *communication,* and what would you list as its important characteristics? Would you care how many people were involved? Would it matter where the activity took place? Is it important to accomplish some specific goal? Does it matter, as part of your definition, whether the participants are face-to-face or communicating through some electronic medium? Does it matter whether the messages are spoken or communicated without words? Is it important to consider what roles the participants assume— for example, whether one is a sender and the other a receiver? Is it relevant that the participants are from the same or different cultures? Before considering what interpersonal communication is, it is necessary to define the term *communication.*

DEFINING COMMUNICATION

Regardless of the culture of the participants or the location of their interaction, communication is a distinctly human process composed of elements that combine to create a number of unique characteristics. Although we may say that computers "talk" to other computers and that thermostats "communicate" electronically to switch on air conditioners, communication for our purposes is a human process, not a mechanical one. **Communication,** the process of sending and receiving messages through a channel, can include six elements: senders, receivers, messages, a context, a purpose, and feedback.

ELEMENTS OF THE COMMUNICATION PROCESS

An early view of the communication process—and one still in use—describes a **sender** (the person who devises and encodes the message) sending a **message** (the information the sender devises for the other person to achieve some **purpose,** the goal of the communication) through a **channel** (the medium the speaker chooses, such as writing a letter, talking on the telephone, using electronic mail) to a **receiver** (the person who takes in and decodes the message). Also part of this communication equation is a **context,** the characteristics of the situation in which the communication takes place, such as the physical environment and the other people present. These elements may be put together in a **linear process** model (Figure 1.1). Models are useful for visualizing a complex process, for clarifying abstractions into something concrete.

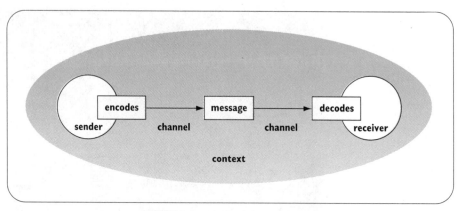

FIGURE 1.1   Linear Process Model

Although useful for pointing out important elements of the communication process, the model is too simple to describe something as complex as communication when two or more people are interacting directly with each other. For instance, the model suggests that communication flows in one direction, from a sender to a receiver, and that there is one context that describes the communication situation for both the sender and receiver. While some communication may seem like this, such as broadcast messages and electronic mail, rarely are there instances that do not allow some opportunity for a response, even if delayed, or in which the contexts for the sender and speaker are identical.

Communication is typically more than just sending and receiving messages. **Feedback** in communication is the process of sending information about the effect of a message—information the speaker uses to adjust her or his message based on feedback in a continuous process of **adaptation.** For example, a teacher, noting that her message received either blank stares or raised eyebrows, could offer some new examples to clarify her message. Adding feedback and adaptation (recognizing that senders and receivers occupy different contexts) changes communication from a linear process that flows from sender to receiver to an **interactive process** model, one that flows from sender to receiver, then receiver to sender, and so on. Our model changes to resemble Figure 1.2. This model demonstrates that the communication process entails sending and receiving messages, and receiving and sending messages, by people who occupy different contexts, which can be physical (a speaker may be standing behind a lectern with lights in her eyes, while listeners may be seated in a darkened auditorium) and psychological (a speaker may be anxious while audience members may be relaxed).

To get a fuller view of human communication we need to examine yet another model. Communication may be more than one person sending a message to another person, and more than having the other person send a message back. Consider this dialogue:

Laura: Carmen, hand me one of those sheets of paper on the desk. (*Carmen assumes she knows which sheet Laura is talking about and hands Laura a sheet of paper.*)

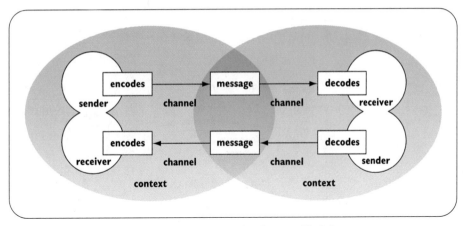

FIGURE 1.2   **Interactive Process Model**

Laura:	Not that one, the yellow one. (*Carmen puts her hand on a yellow sheet of paper.*)
Carmen:	This one?
Laura:	Not that one, the yellow one with the flowers in the margin. (*Carmen hands Laura the desired paper.*)
Laura:	Thank you.

Laura and Carmen have participated in an interaction in which, presumably, one served as the sender, the other as the receiver, and they switched roles several times until the desired outcome was achieved. In other words, based on the feedback, Laura and Carmen made adjustments in the cooperative pursuit of accomplishing their joint goal. In the process, they demonstrated seven key characteristics of human communication:[1]

1. Messages are simultaneously sent and received—people cannot be classified as "senders" or "receivers," but only as *communicators,* simultaneous senders and receivers.

2. Messages cannot be erased or taken back.

3. Communicators respond to messages proactively—that is, they respond based on their unique backgrounds.

4. The meaning of any message depends on the situation.

5. Communicators can only infer what their partners are thinking or feeling.

6. The messages that are received have a consequence.

7. Communicators are self-reflective.

Adding these seven characteristics to the definition of communication changes it from an interactional to a **transactive process,** one in which each characteristic of the communication process affects and is affected by the others. This process is represented by Figure 1.3. Now let us examine each of the seven elements separately.

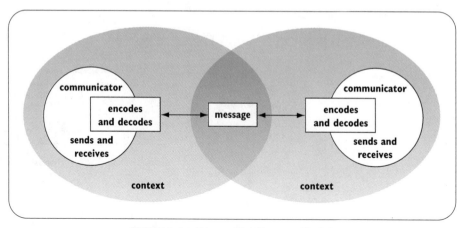

FIGURE 1.3   Transactive Process Model

Messages Are Simultaneously Sent and Received

In this model, the communication process doesn't mechanically alternate between sender and receiver. In reality, as Laura was making her initial request, she was simultaneously functioning as a receiver by watching Carmen's reactions. She functioned as a sender and a receiver at the same time. Carmen, while functioning initially as a receiver, was simultaneously functioning as a sender by giving Laura feedback. The word *communicator* is used to indicate this simultaneity—Laura and Carmen were neither senders nor receivers exclusively, but communicators.

Messages Cannot Be Erased

Notice that each message in Carmen's and Laura's conversation is built on what preceded it. Messages cannot be erased, but they can be modified and adjusted with subsequent messages. Laura continued to deal with Carmen's lack of understanding by modifying her directions until she accomplished her goal. She did this by clarifying.

Suppose that, in the heat of an argument with a friend, you blurt out the one insult that you know will hurt the other person most. And, as soon as you complete the offending message, you want to plead, "I take it back, I didn't mean it!" However, there is no such thing as "taking it back." You and your partner may choose to behave as if the message were erased, but, in reality, you both know that it exists and continues to exist in your memories.

Communication Is Proactive

Carmen and Laura's dialogue shows that communication is a **proactive** process—that is, you respond to any message based on your total history. If Carmen had not understood English, or had not recognized the color yellow, or had not cared to cooperate, then her reaction would have been different. Carmen's reaction to Laura's request demonstrated that she was not merely a passive recipient of Laura's messages; she selected what to hear, amplified and ignored portions to suit her taste, and remembered what she considered relevant based on her past experiences.

Meaning Depends on Context

The meaning of a given act of communication cannot be separated from its context. The context has three aspects: the people who are interacting, their physical surroundings, and their social relationships.

The context depends on the people communicating. If Carmen is only five years old, Laura will probably adapt her message to that age level, perhaps by using simpler language. If, in describing the yellow-toned sheets of paper, Laura had said, "Hand me the canary paper," a five-year-old Carmen might have looked for paper in the shape of a bird because of her literal understanding of the word *canary.*

The link between people and meaning becomes even clearer when we add the component of culture. What happens when a foreign language is spoken or culture-bound idioms are used? Imagine having English as a second language and hearing someone say, "Give me a buzz," or "I think Jim is spacey." In these instances the background of the participants, more than the language they are using, determines meaning.

The number of people present also affects how a message is interpreted. For example, if Laura and Carmen are surrounded by other people, Carmen might comply with the request rather than question why. If they are alone, however, Carmen might be more willing to refuse or to question why she should do what Laura requests. If Carmen comes from a culture that stresses politeness when in the company of strangers, she would be less apt to confront Laura unless they were alone.

Where you are located further affects the meanings you attribute to the messages you receive. If Carmen and Laura are at home, Carmen would probably assume Laura wants the paper to write on; however, if they were in a stationery store, she might assume that Laura wants to look at the paper to consider buying it.

Different social situations have different rules, and communication messages are interpreted based on the rules. If Carmen and Laura are taking a test and one of the rules is "No talking," Carmen might interpret Laura's request as an invitation to cheat. In contrast, if they are in a classroom working together on a project, Carmen might interpret the request as part of the normal process of sharing. How Carmen responds depends on the rules she has learned from her cultural conditioning.

Some acts of communication derive their meaning totally from the context. If taken literally, the message "Hi, how are you?" is an inquiry about the state of your health. You know, however, that within the context of passing an acquaintance on the street, it usually means "Hello," or "I see you're still here." It is not really asking for a health-related response. In fact, if you were actually to describe how you felt, you might startle the other person. In a physician's office, however, the same message would have a totally different meaning. In this context, your doctor would think you were strange if you had called for an appointment because you were ill and then gave the automatic response, "Fine, thanks, and how are you?" instead of a detailed, health-related one.

Communicators Can Only Infer What Their Partners Are Thinking and Feeling

This characteristic is perhaps at the very core of the communication process, for it reminds us of the inescapable fact that we can never have direct access to what is going on inside another human being's mind. Because there can be no direct mind-to-mind contact, we can only assume what the other person is experiencing. We are forced to use others' verbal and nonverbal symbols as representations for what they are thinking and feeling—for example, that their use of the word "hungry" corresponds to a feeling they are experiencing or that their head nod means "I agree." In some instances, our inferences are correct—our friend may, indeed, want to get something to eat because she is hungry. However, our communication partner may have something else in mind—her remark that she's hungry may actually mean she wants to stop talking with you and go home.

Messages That Are Received Have a Consequence

When Laura and Carmen interacted they had an effect on each other. What was true of these two is true for everyone: all of our messages, to one degree or another, do something to someone else (as well as to ourselves). This is not a philosophical or metaphysical theory, but a biological fact. Try as you may, it is impossible not to respond to the actions of others. While these responses may vary from outward signs, such as smiling, to inward thoughts, such as "This is crazy," you are reacting to the messages you are receiving. Even not reacting is a reaction. It should be easy for you to appreciate the ethical implications imbedded in this communication characteristic: because our communication behavior produces a response, we should think about the consequences of our messages on other people.

Communication Is Self-Reflective

This characteristic of communication points out that humans have the ability to think about themselves, their partners, their messages, and the results of those messages all at the same time. "Because of self-reflectiveness, we are able to think about our encounters and our existence, about communication and human behavior."[2] This unique characteristic lets us be participant and observer simultaneously. We are the only species that can be at both ends of the camera at the same time.

THE ROLE OF CULTURAL DIVERSITY IN INTERPERSONAL COMMUNICATION

Now that we have defined communication in broad terms and looked at some of its elements and characteristics, we are ready to narrow our focus and examine interpersonal communication and some specific issues related to the influence of culture on interpersonal communication. Your culture can affect how you interact with others, how

SIBLING REVELRY
by Man Martin

SIBLING REVELRY copyright 1990 Lew Little Ent. Reprinted with permission of UNIVERSAL PRESS SYNDICATE. All rights reserved.

you interpret your physical surroundings, and how you form your social relationships. Understanding your culture—and the diversity of cultures with which you come into contact—provides a basis for deriving meaning from your communication interactions.

More than ever before, your interpersonal relationships involve people from cultures different from your own. Some of those cultures might be as near as across the street, while others might be contacted only when you travel to other countries. Regardless of the location and setting, people are members of a "global village," interacting with new "villagers" whose perceptions and communication styles differ from those of the dominant culture. For example, you find that some people talk in whispers while others use loud voices. Why? Some people paint their entire bodies while others only apply color to their lips. Why? Some people touch their friends when they greet them while others bow their heads. Why? Some people enjoy arguing while others find it distasteful. Why? The answer to all of these questions is the same. People learn to think, feel, communicate, and strive for what their culture considers appropriate. Whether or not the other person is from your own culture or one that is alien to you, her or his cultural experiences greatly influence how she or he responds to you and your message. For example, if you were born into a culture that does not display outward signs of emotion in public, you probably do not display outward signs of emotion in your interpersonal relationships.[3]

Culture mandates who talks to whom about what and for how long. You were not born knowing a language, how to select "in" clothing, how to spend your time, or the most appropriate ways to show respect. Your culture presented you with a blueprint for how you should live your life and how you should communicate about it.

The inseparable nature of communication and culture is perhaps most manifest in the definition of culture. "**Culture** is the deposit of knowledge, experience, beliefs, values, attitudes, meanings, hierarchies, religion, timing, roles, spatial relations, concepts of the universe, and material objects and possessions acquired by a group of people in the course of generations through individual and group striving."[4] What this indicates is that people acquire their culture through various channels of communication and express their culture through these same channels.

People who share a common culture also usually share similar meanings. And, as cultures differ from one another, the communication practices and behaviors of individuals reared in those cultures also differ. For example, in one culture people may believe that deep affection and feelings of love need not be expressed verbally, yet in another culture verbal expression of one's feelings is expected: two different cultures, two different styles of interpersonal relationships. To better understand the powerful influence of culture on communication requires examining the characteristics of culture.

CHARACTERISTICS OF CULTURE

Culture is not innate, it is learned. You were not born knowing how to speak your native language or whether you should kiss on the mouth or the cheek—you had to be taught.[5] What is fascinating about cultural learning is that it takes place on so many levels. For example, you may have learned part of your gender role by *seeing* who is given a doll to play with and who is given a truck. You learned rules of proper behavior when your parents *told* you to say "thank you" when you received a compliment. In both of these examples learning took place, yet the methods of learning—one by observation and the other by lecture—were quite different.

The messages and behaviors that a culture deems most important come from a variety of sources and are constantly being reinforced. Parents, schools, peers, the media, religious leaders, folktales, and even art repeat the same message. If you were brought up in the United States, think for a moment of the many times and numerous ways you were "told" the importance of being popular and well-liked. Your culture even supplied you with the specific behaviors you needed to accomplish these two goals, such as buying the "right" car or using the "right" toothpaste.

Another characteristic also has its roots deep in the communication process—*culture is transmissible from person to person, group to group, and generation to generation.* Because we use symbols we can pass on both the content and patterns of a culture. For example, North Americans can use spoken words as symbols and tell others about the importance of winning and being "number one"—they can use car phones, fine wine, clothing, and jewelry as symbols to show others about success and status.

Each person, regardless of individual culture, is born to a massive battery of information and behaviors just waiting to be mastered. In the United States each generation is told that individualism is a key value. For the Japanese and Mexican cultures the message is that the group supersedes the individual. In the United States culture one is expected to be assertive ("If you don't stand up for your rights, others will walk all over you"). In Asian cultures interpersonal harmony is stressed ("The nail that sticks up is the first to feel the blow of the hammer"). In the United States some forms of touching in public are considered normal behavior. In many Asian cultures touching in public is considered highly inappropriate.[6] Examples are endless and each leads to the same conclusion: The content and communication patterns of a culture are subjective and transmissible.

Although it may seem paradoxical, *culture is a dynamic system that changes over time; however, the deep structure of a culture resists change.* As cultures come in contact with each other they are bound to change. As Japan and the United States have

Human nature is the same
everywhere, the modes only
are different.
LORD CHESTERFIELD

more commerce, we observe Americans borrowing Japanese methods of quality control while the Japanese use North American marketing practices. When Mexicans come to the United States for work they often have to alter their use of time. In their country people work hard and for long hours but treat themselves to an extended rest period during the middle of the day. Once in the United States, they often find that lunch is brief and the work day ends much earlier. In both examples, you can see how people can be forced to adapt to new cultures. However, you need also to remember that the deep structure of culture is less susceptible to change. The Japanese and Mexicans might alter their work environment, but it is doubtful if they are going to change their view of the family or their notion of obligation.

Acculturation, the transfer of culture from one group to another, commonly refers to a process of change experienced by members of a minority group as they adapt to a majority group's culture.[7] Changes, however, may occur in some areas and not others as subsequent generations of immigrants both accept and avoid adaptation to their "new culture." For example, the role of the family for Chinese immigrants and Chinese Americans changes with increases in acculturation[8]—decreases in traditionalism may be found in each new generation, as well as differences in how sons and daughters are treated. On the other hand, not all elements of family structure change with subsequent generations, and in many ways Chinese immigrants and subsequent generations of Chinese Americans are very much alike. For example, the strong feelings of obligation many Chinese individuals have for their family are unaffected by acculturation, and family taboo topics related to sexuality, romantic relationships, and parental authority—topics that family members are not allowed to discuss in the family—remain taboo for many generations, although they are not taboo for many European-American families.[9] (Although "European American" may seem to be an awkward term, as yet, there is no general term to define Caucasians of European descent.)

From what has been said so far, it should be clear that *culture is highly selective*. Every culture represents a limited choice of behavior patterns from the total human experience. If you are born in one location you eat with metal utensils, in another it might be chop sticks, and in yet another you might eat with your hands. This selection, whether it be to wear or not to wear shoes, to believe in reincarnation or in life after death, is made according to the basic assumptions and values that are meaningful to each culture. Because each of us has only limited experiences (we only know what we are exposed to), what we know is but an abstraction of what there is to know. Our culture helps in that selection process. Put in slightly different terms, culture defines the boundaries of different groups.[10]

This characteristic is important to students of interpersonal communication for two reasons. First, it is a reminder that what a culture selects to tell each generation is a reflection of what that culture deems important. When Mexican Americans want their children to respect the elderly, they will isolate messages and experiences that teach this lesson. In the United States, being competitive is highly valued, so messages related to that idea are isolated. Second, the notion of selectivity also suggests that cultures tend to separate one group from another. If one culture stresses the past as being important—for example, Chinese culture—while another stresses the future—for example, United States culture—we tend to have separation. On an interpersonal level, we can observe this division when one culture values formality (Japanese) while another sees merit in being informal (United States).

Another characteristic is that *members of a culture tend to be ethnocentric*. **Ethnocentrism** is a tendency to put a person's own culture and societal patterns at the core of all evaluations.[11] Feelings of "we are right" and "they are wrong" infect nearly every aspect of our interpersonal relationships with others. For example, how do you regard people who are different from you? In most instances you evaluate people by applying the standards of your culture to their culture. While this is a very natural tendency, it also means that many of your evaluations are limited, arbitrary, and possibly false and misleading. It is truly a naive view of the world to believe and behave as if one culture, regardless of what it might be, has discovered the true, ultimate, and only set of norms. It is important as you encounter people from other cultures to avoid letting nearsighted views overshadow rationality.

KNOWLEDGE CHECKUPS AND SKILL DEVELOPMENT ACTIVITIES

Throughout this text you will be asked to complete a variety of self-evaluation checkups. Keep two things in mind as you respond to each. First, the value of the results depends on the honesty of your responses. Second, the results are pieces of information that will help you understand yourself and assess your knowledge and skills. They should alert you to the additional information and skills you need to become a more competent communicator.

The Knowledge Checkups help you apply your understanding of the material covered in the reading or gain information about yourself, while the Skill Developments help you practice or develop a specific skill. Knowledge and skill are not separate but work together to provide you with a firm basis to become a competent communicator. Knowledge Checkup 1.1 will help you apply your understanding of the elements and characteristics of human communication to a dialogue between two people.

Knowledge Checkup 1.1

RECOGNIZING THE ELEMENTS AND CHARACTERISTICS OF HUMAN COMMUNICATION

Read the following dialogue and identify the elements and characteristics of human communication.

(Roberto and Sylvia are standing in line at a movie theater, waiting to purchase tickets.)

Roberto: I'm really glad we got the chance to get out of the house tonight. The kids were driving me crazy.

Sylvia: After spending all day at the hospital examining children, I was more than ready to relax.

Roberto: Just because you're an intern on thirty-six hour shifts doesn't make you any more tired than I am!

Sylvia: Don't let your male chauvinist attitude about my being a doctor get in the way of our seeing the movie!

Roberto: Don't give me that male chauvinist garbage! That's just your easy answer! I'll see you at home!

1. Who is the original sender?
2. Who is the original receiver?
3. Describe the effects of the context on the creation and interpretation of each person's message.
4. Describe the feedback in the dialogue.
5. What possible effect might the nonerasability of language have on this conversation?
6. Given the proactive nature of human communication, what assumptions can you make about Roberto and Sylvia?
7. How can the outcome of the argument be attributed to the fact that we can only infer what other people are thinking and feeling from our perception of their verbal and nonverbal language?

8. What are the consequences of the messages Sylvia and Roberto communicate?

9. Because communication is self-reflective, what do you think Roberto and Sylvia are saying to themselves, internally, during the dialogue? How might each reflect later on what was said?

10. What recommendations would you make to Roberto and Sylvia to help them communicate more competently with each other?

11. What influences from your own culture can you trace in your answers to these questions, for example, what you consider appropriate marital or male-female relationships, and what may or may not be done in a public setting?

DEFINING INTERPERSONAL COMMUNICATION

Once you are familiar with the basic elements of communication and appreciate the role of culture in human interaction, you can begin to observe how in a very specific way interpersonal communication operates in your daily life. **Interpersonal communication** is communication that is based on communicators' recognition of each other's uniqueness and the development of messages that reflect that recognition. The more communicators use personal information about each other (Dale knows that Pat's favorite food is Mexican) and define interaction styles based on their individual characteristics (Dale is usually too enthusiastic about new ideas, so Pat asks questions that bring Dale "back to reality"), the more strongly interpersonal their relationship becomes. A relationship is not interpersonal or noninterpersonal, but *tends toward* one or the other.[12]

As individuals communicate in an interpersonal relationship, they make predictions about each other's responses based on their understanding of the other, and define their roles based on their own unique characteristics.[13]

PREDICTING RESPONSES

The tendency in interpersonal relationships is for people to use distinguishing information about each other to predict the effects of what they say. This information may be cultural, sociological, or psychological. *Cultural information* includes the values, attitudes, and beliefs that are part of the culture the person comes from. For example, if you know that someone is from the dominant culture of North America and do not know anything else, you may predict that the person believes in democracy, equality, striving for a decent standard of living, and the importance of individualism. Once you learn about other cultures you can begin to make the same sort of predictions concerning what is important to the members of that particular culture. For instance, knowing that, in general, Japanese people tend to value formality, hard work, group loyalty, and interpersonal harmony, when you meet someone from that culture you might assume the person holds many of these values.

Admittedly, cultural information is but one factor people use in making predictions; however, because it provides the overall context for sociological and psychological information, it is of crucial importance in interpersonal communication. The assumption behind *sociological information* is that the groups to which we belong or with which we identify—such as our religious, social, work, political, and gender groups—provide us with values, norms, ways of perceiving the world, and, of course, patterns of communication. For example, teachers are thought to place more value on education, the importance of ideas, and their work, and to put less value on financial rewards. Democrats are stereotyped as "caring for the common person," and Republicans "look out for the rich." Women are stereotyped as "nurturing, caring, and sharing," and men are "task-oriented, emotionally controlled, and interested in sports." Whereas cultural information is the broadest type of information available and, therefore, may not "fit" the specific person with whom we are communicating, sociological information is narrower, more specific to our communication partner. The most specific information available, however, is psychological.

Psychological information concerns the character traits that make an individual unique and special. Knowing an individual's self-concept, temperament, background, interests, ethical standards, feelings, attitudes, beliefs, values, personality characteristics, and typical emotional responses can assist you in adapting your messages to *this* person and *this* setting. For example, among a man's psychological traits may be his love for his children, his enjoyment of detective novels, his compulsive dedication to jogging, and his need to be respected. Although a great many men may love their children, enjoy detective novels, and so on, it's the unique combination of this particular person's traits that may be used most effectively to predict his responses to what you have to say.

The more you possess and use cultural, sociological, and psychological information to make predictions about a relational partner, the more interpersonal your communication and the greater the degree of interpersonalness of your relationship. You see the other person as unique—as more than a representative of a particular culture or particular groups—and you deal with her or him as a unique individual. You may even be capable of seeing the individual's real self—without the smoke screens and facades.

Also, the more you possess and use cultural, sociological, and psychological information to make predictions about a relational partner, the higher the probability that the rules for communicating in your relationship will tend to be unique to that relationship. Rules may be set by cultural tradition or established by groups to which the communicators belong; they also may be set by the participants in the relationship. As people share more and more psychological information, they learn the other's likes, wants, and idiosyncrasies, and they use this information to develop their own rules for interacting.

DEFINING ROLES

In an interpersonal relationship, the roles tend to be defined by individual choices. Although roles in a relationship may be defined by the situation—as when your manager appoints you to form a task group or the task group chooses you to be its leader—they also may be defined by the individuals in the relationship. The more the roles are defined by the individuals based on their unique characteristics, the more personal the communication and the greater the degree of interpersonalness in the relationship. For example, noninterpersonal communication—communication based on generalizations from cultural and sociological information, with very little use of psychological information—is common in families in which the roles of parent and child are set by cultural stereotypes, in which, "the parent is always right and the child must always obey." In such families parent-child communication tends to be noninterpersonal because the uniqueness of both individuals is not taken into consideration when they attempt to communicate.

Skill Development 1.1 will help you use the defining characteristics of interpersonal communication to assess where a relationship falls on a continuum, with "noninterpersonal" as one endpoint and "interpersonal" as the other. With this skill, you can assess the interpersonalness of your relationships and use that information for relational decision making.

Skill Development 1.1
ASSESSING RELATIONSHIP INTERPERSONALNESS

Select three important relationships to assess—these might include your work or school relationships, friendship relationships, or family relationships. For each relationship, answer the following questions.

1. To what extent do you and your relationship partner use psychological information as the basis for predicting each other's responses?

2. To what extent are the roles in your relationship defined by you and your partner's individual characteristics.

3. Is one of your relationships more interpersonal than the others? In what ways is it more interpersonal?

4. Does the other person's cultural background affect how she or he responds to you and your messages?

5. Beyond these three examples, how many, if any, of your relationships do you think are characterized by a high degree of interpersonal communication?

THE COMPONENTS OF INTERPERSONAL COMMUNICATION COMPETENCY

Each time you communicate you have a purpose, and you are most likely to accomplish your purpose if you communicate competently. **Interpersonal communication com-**

petency is the ability to use your knowledge, skills, and motivation to achieve your interpersonal goals appropriately and effectively. For example, if your goal is to gain information, you will increase your likelihood of success if you do a good job of listening, asking questions, and summarizing information. If your goal is to form a relationship, influence attitudes or behaviors, or understand yourself or the world in which you live, the degree to which you are knowledgeable, skillful, and motivated to initiate conversations and express your opinions and feelings will influence your success.

Interpersonal communication competency, the ability to achieve your interpersonal communication goals, has three components: knowledge, skills, and motivation.[14] To reach competency, first you need to understand the situation, yourself, and the skills it takes to be effective. Second, you need to harness your knowledge and put the skills to use; doing so takes practice and experience with the appropriate behaviors. Third, you must be motivated to communicate competently: Knowing what to do and developing the appropriate skills are not enough—you must want to put them to use.

KNOWLEDGE

Once you decide to communicate, you need to analyze the who, what, and where of the situation. Who are the participants? Are they like me? What are their cultural backgrounds? What are my objectives for the interaction? Where is the communication taking place? To answer these questions you must know who you are, who the other person is—including cultural, sociological, and psychological information that makes her or him unique—how anxiety-arousing the situation is for both of you, the nature of your relationship, and the various means available for presenting your ideas.

For example, assume a friend asks what you are doing in your communication class. You believe your relationship has a high level of interpersonalness and you decide to tell your friend about the defining elements of interpersonal communication. What you know about the topic and what you think your friend knows about the topic will determine, in part, what you choose to say. Where you talk will affect how softly or loudly you speak (hushed tones are required if you talk in the library, but a normal tone is possible if you are in the student lounge). Your relationship also affects the choices you make. For instance, if your friend shares your caring feelings, you might use your relationship for examples; otherwise, you might choose examples from relationships with which you are both familiar but in which neither of you is an active participant.

Knowing *who, what,* and *where* forms the basis for deciding what skills are necessary to communicate competently. *Knowing* what skills are necessary is not the same as *being able to perform* them. Knowledge and skills are separate aspects of communication competency, although the skills you employ will be based on your knowledge of what the situation requires.

SKILLS

How competent do you think you are in using communication skills? Knowledge Checkup 1.2 will help you determine what communication skills you already have and what skills need further development.

Knowledge Checkup 1.2

HOW COMPETENTLY DO YOU COMMUNICATE?

Carefully consider the following list of communication skills.[15] Your self-assessed communication competence is most accurate if you are able to think back over past situations in which you communicated with others and generalize from those situations to derive your answers. To establish further the validity of your self-analysis, it may be helpful to get feedback from people who know you well and with whom you communicate often. Then, based on the scales, indicate how often you use each skill and how satisfied you are with your ability.

How Often

Write **5** if you use the skill all or most of the time (91–100 percent of the time).
Write **4** if you use the skill often (71–90 percent).
Write **3** if you use the skill sometimes (31–70 percent).
Write **2** if you use the skill rarely (11–30 percent).
Write **1** if you use the skill never or almost never (0–10 percent).

How Satisfied

Write **5** if you are very satisfied with your ability.
Write **4** if you are somewhat satisfied with your ability.
Write **3** if you are neither satisfied nor dissatisfied with your ability.
Write **2** if you are somewhat dissatisfied with your ability.
Write **1** if you are very dissatisfied with your ability.

	How Often	How Satisfied
1. I listen effectively.	_____	_____
2. I use appropriate words for the situation.	_____	_____
3. I use appropriate pronunciation for the situation.	_____	_____
4. I use appropriate grammar for the situation.	_____	_____
5. I use effective eye contact.	_____	_____
6. I speak at a rate that is neither too slow nor too fast.	_____	_____
7. I speak fluently (avoiding "uh," "like, uh," "you know," awkward pauses, and silences).	_____	_____
8. My movements, such as gestures, enhance what I say.	_____	_____
9. I give appropriate spoken and unspoken feedback.	_____	_____
10. I use vocal variety when I speak (rather than speaking in a monotone).	_____	_____
11. I use appropriate facial expressions.	_____	_____

12. I understand my communication partner's main ideas. _____ _____

13. I understand my communication partner's feelings. _____ _____

14. I distinguish facts from opinions. _____ _____

15. I distinguish between speaking to give someone information and speaking to persuade someone to think, feel, or act a particular way. _____ _____

16. I recognize when my communication partner does not understand my message. _____ _____

17. I express ideas clearly and concisely. _____ _____

18. I express and defend my point of view. _____ _____

19. I organize messages so others can understand them. _____ _____

20. I use questions and other forms of feedback to obtain and clarify messages. _____ _____

21. I respond to questions and other forms of feedback to provide clarification. _____ _____

22. I give understandable directions and instructions. _____ _____

23. I summarize messages in my own words. _____ _____

24. I describe another's viewpoint. _____ _____

25. My communication is usually descriptive, not evaluative. _____ _____

26. I express my feelings and opinions to others. _____ _____

27. I initiate and maintain conversations, moving smoothly from topic to topic. _____ _____

28. I recognize and control my anxiety in communication situations. _____ _____

29. I involve the other person in what I am saying. _____ _____

30. I accomplish my communication goals. _____ _____

TOTALS _____ _____

> If you continue to do what you have always done, you will continue to get what you have always gotten.
> ANONYMOUS

Compare your totals with these ranges:

How Often

    135–150 = Communicate skillfully all or most of the time
    105–134 = Often communicate skillfully
     75–104 = Sometimes communicate skillfully
     45–74 = Rarely communicate skillfully
     30–44 = Never or almost never communicate skillfully

How Satisfied

135–150 = Very satisfied with my communication skills

105–134 = Somewhat satisfied with my communication skills

 75–104 = Neither satisfied nor dissatisfied with my communication skills

 45–74 = Somewhat dissatisfied with my communication skills

 30–44 = Very dissatisfied with my communication skills

Each item in the self-analysis describes a skill that is a component of communication competence. Your effective performance of these behaviors increases your potential for being a competent communicator.

Even if you scored close to 150 on both parts of the quiz, you will find there is still much to learn and put into practice! And, don't be discouraged if you scored lower than you would have liked. The purpose of this text and of your communication course is to help you develop the knowledge and skills you need to improve your competency as a communicator.

MOTIVATION

To be a competent interpersonal communicator, you must want to communicate competently. You may be motivated by such possibilities as forming a new relationship, gaining desired information, influencing someone's behavior, engaging in joint decision making, or solving a problem.

In addition to potential benefits, every communication encounter has potential drawbacks. To communicate competently, you must be motivated to overcome such drawbacks. For example, you may have learned from past experiences to fear certain communication situations. Talking with a friend may pose no problem, but talking with an authority figure, such as a boss or professor, may cause you to fidget and show other signs of nervousness. To compensate for negative feelings, you must be strongly motivated to take the necessary action to communicate.

The amount of confidence you have in your ability to communicate will determine, in part, the strength of your motivation to communicate. If, for example, you think of yourself as shy, you are unlikely to initiate conversations with strangers. The reward for interacting may be clear to you, but your self-perceived lack of social skills decreases your motivation.

How motivated are you to communicate competently? Without some motivation to communicate competently, neither this book nor a course in communication will be useful. Look back at each of the thirty items in Knowledge Checkup 1.2 and ask yourself how motivated you are to perform the behavior described by each item at a high level of proficiency. For example, how motivated are you to "listen effectively," "use appropriate words," and "use appropriate pronunciation"?

Look at those items in Knowledge Checkup 1.2 for which you indicated low satisfaction (ratings of 1 or 2). Now examine the *how often* scores for those items. You may find that the skills with which you are most dissatisfied are the same ones you avoid using. You may be saying to yourself, "If I haven't developed that skill enough, I'm not going to risk using it."

By studying the information presented in this text, including the activities, you will begin to understand the components of competent interpersonal communication and develop the necessary skills. This combination should increase your motivation to communicate and to communicate competently.

THE QUALITIES OF COMPETENT INTERPERSONAL COMMUNICATORS

Competent interpersonal communicators have five qualities:

1. Competent interpersonal communicators act appropriately—they follow the rules.
2. Competent interpersonal communicators effectively balance opposing communication goals.
3. Competent interpersonal communicators are adaptable—they adjust their communication to the situation.
4. Competent interpersonal communicators recognize roadblocks to effective communication—they note potential obstacles and work to overcome them.
5. Competent interpersonal communicators are ethical—they adhere to standards of right and wrong based on their culture, personal views, and circumstances.

COMPETENT INTERPERSONAL COMMUNICATORS ARE APPROPRIATE

For interpersonal communication to be appropriate, a communicator must recognize and follow the rules that guide interaction in a particular circumstance.[16] Every culture has rules for how to greet, interact within and leave interpersonal situations. These vary from a greeting and departure procedure of handshaking, to bowing, to kissing on the cheek. Cultural interaction rules may dictate no direct eye contact, or short durations of looking at each other, or staring. A person who fails to follow the rules is often perceived as abrasive or bizarre and may be subject to negative reactions. Of course, because different situations call for different rules, what may be appropriate in one situation may be inappropriate in another. For example, a rule in your family may have been "No foul language." Thus, if you tripped over a bicycle when your family was around, it would have been inappropriate to scream out a four-letter obscenity. In contrast, if the same thing happened with a group of friends, your swearing might not break any rules and would therefore be acceptable. Similarly, a male job hunter might be refused employment in a clothing store for traditional businessmen if he came to an interview wearing jeans and an earring, but a store aimed at upscale, fashion-conscious youth might be very pleased to hire him.

Many of the rules of appropriateness that you have learned stem from your cultural experiences. For example, in North American culture the interpersonal rules for doing business often call for a relaxed, friendly, and casual manner. First names may be used and status differences discouraged ("Just call me Nancy"). These rules do not hold for all cultures. The Japanese culture, for example, typically maintains a protocol of high respect for formality.[17] First names are seldom used and small talk is avoided. The Latin American and Arab rules for the business context usually include small talk on non-business matters as part of business dealings. It is considered bad manners to "get down to business" before friendships have been developed, pleasantries exchanged, and coffee drunk.[18]

COMPETENT INTERPERSONAL COMMUNICATORS EFFECTIVELY BALANCE OPPOSING COMMUNICATION GOALS

Very often incompatible and opposing communication goals exist simultaneously. These opposing goals, called **dialectical tensions,** may make it difficult to communicate successfully.[19] For example, the desire to be approved by others may be in opposition to the desire to be personally effective. Consider that although you want to speak your mind and let your relational partner know how you feel about something, you also know that your partner may respond angrily. Do you let your partner know what you are feeling, or do you keep quiet?

Another dialectical tension concerns the opposite goals of being close (becoming more intimate) and being distant (becoming more separate, independent). You know that sharing secrets is a way of getting close, but sometimes maintaining your privacy keeps you feeling safe. Do you share—and get closer—or not share—and stay safe and distant?

A third important tension comes from the opposing goals of satisfying your own needs versus satisfying your partner's needs. Do you stop your work on a term paper to talk with your friend who is having relationship problems and wants to "talk them out," or do you finish your work?

Balancing these opposing goals is difficult; indeed, there may be no satisfactory solution in a particular situation. Competent interpersonal communicators recognize these dialectical tensions and strive to balance them in ways that help them remain satisfied with their interpersonal communication.

COMPETENT INTERPERSONAL COMMUNICATORS ARE ADAPTABLE

Adaptable communicators recognize the requirements of a situation and adjust their communication to their goals.[20] For example, when asked what competent communication is, a professor usually would use one set of examples in speaking to a student and a different set when speaking to a colleague.

Adaptation has three components. The first two—recognizing the requirements of a situation and adapting your communication behavior to suit the setting—have already been discussed. The third component is realizing that your values affect the way you adapt.

You may strongly believe that people should accept you as you are. But if you are inflexible in such beliefs, you will limit the number of contexts in which you can communicate competently. As long as you stay in situations that do not require adapta-

With thee conversing,
I forget all time.
JOHN MILTON

tion, everything will be fine. But outside those situations—whether you are searching for a job, attempting to influence others, or meeting someone for the first time—your unwillingness to adapt will make it more difficult to accomplish your goals.

Being competent means having the ability to adjust and fashion your communication behavior to fit the setting, the other person, and yourself.[21] Knowing that you act differently in a classroom than you do at work, or that one culture may value time while another values activity, is but the first step in the adaptive process. The real key is being able to take this information and use it to alter the way you present yourself. This is what we mean when we say competent interpersonal communicators are adaptable.

Being able to adapt moves from the simple to the complex as we move from close friends to strangers. The reason is obvious: We have more information about and clearer profiles of our friends than we do of strangers. Adaptation also is more intricate as we progress from members of our own culture to individuals from other cultures. The reason for this difficulty is often a lack of information about our communication partner. A competent communicator has the necessary information so that he or she can adapt to individuals from a variety of cultures. For example, if you know that your communication partner is from a culture that values a calm, serene, and quiet communication style, and that is not your usual pattern, you can adapt your personality to meet this behavioral requirement.

As illustrated in Knowledge Checkup 1.2, competent communicators have a large repertoire of behaviors available to them. They learn to pick and choose appropriate techniques based on the situation (including its participants) and their intentions for the interaction. Especially important for competency are **flexibility skills,** skills that enhance your versatility and resourcefulness, such as being aware that people from various

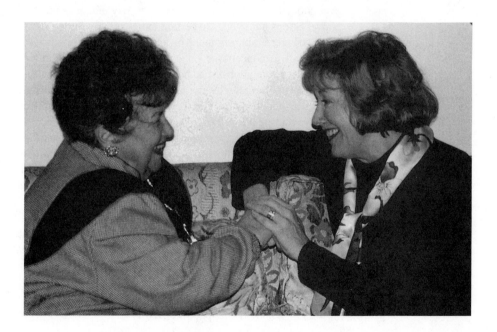

cultures hold various beliefs and you may have to adjust. These include *empathy*—seeing things from the other person's point of view; *role taking*—engaging in behaviors that fit a situation and do not conflict with your sense of self; and *problem solving*—analyzing a problem and generating appropriate solutions.

COMPETENT INTERPERSONAL COMMUNICATORS RECOGNIZE OBSTACLES TO EFFECTIVE COMMUNICATION

An obstacle that keeps you from accomplishing your communication goal may take one of five forms: cultural, environmental, personal, relational, or language.

Cultural obstacles are the result of people's differences in background and experience. You have been taught rules for communicating within your family, in school, at work, and in society at large. When your rules and someone else's rules clash, there is a cultural obstacle. For example, you might believe each member of a family should have a say in making the rules that affect all of them, whereas the person you're speaking with believes that the father is the rule maker. Consider the problems that could arise if you were discussing career choices. You might not fully understand your friend's statement, "My father would never let me become a flight attendant."

Environmental obstacles occur when something in the physical surroundings impairs your ability to send or receive messages. For example, loud, piped-in music may make it difficult to hear what your friend is saying, or on a hot, humid day you may find it difficult to concentrate.

Personal obstacles stem from your likes and dislikes, what you think is important and unimportant, what you do and do not want. When your personal attitudes, values, and beliefs get in the way of your listening, they become personal obstacles. Have you ever noticed that who is speaking to you may matter as much as what is said? Do certain conversations bore you? Do certain topics set your thoughts off on a tangent? Do certain words trigger embarrassment or anger? Do you sometimes have too many things on your mind to concentrate on communicating? If you answered yes to any of these questions, personal obstacles have created barriers to effective communication.

Relational obstacles may result from differences in status and power, differences in the way people define their roles in a relationship, and differences in the ways people perceive their relationships. The titles *boss, parent, professor, police officer, judge,* and *president* all connote status and power. Unless you are one boss talking to another boss, or one parent talking to another parent, status differences exist. There even may be a status difference between two bosses or two parents. Status differences may determine who has the right to initiate conversations, give directions, make decisions, and reward or punish.

Each person in a relationship may define his or her own role differently. For example, a student who defines a teacher's role as "authoritarian" in a class where the teacher defines her role as "guide" will encounter relational obstacles because the student will expect to be told what information he is responsible for, while the instructor will want the student to ask questions about course content.

Individual participants also may define their relationship differently. For instance, in the case of two persons who are dating, one individual may see the relationship as more of a friendship, while the other may consider the relationship to be more intimate. Their different definitions will affect any discussion of the relationship, such as future plans, and conflict is likely to occur.

The different meanings people give to words and the way they organize those words create **language obstacles.** Meaning is not inherent in a word but in the person who interprets the word. What does the word *gross* mean to you? To a shipper it means 144 of an item. To a teenager it may mean obnoxious or offensive. To a surveyor it may mean imprecise. And yet to another person, it may mean that someone's language is foul or that someone is unattractive.

Grammatical structure may either help or hinder you in communicating ideas. Say the following two sentences aloud:

> What's the latest, dope?
> What's the latest dope?

In the first question, by pausing at the comma, you insult the other person while asking for information. In the second question, by not pausing, you merely ask for information.

COMPETENT COMMUNICATORS ARE ETHICAL

Ethics are rules for conduct that distinguish right from wrong. Competent communicators endeavor to be ethical—that is, they strive to adhere to their standards of right and wrong. Your definition of what is right or wrong, what is ethical or unethical, depends on at least three considerations. The first is the culture in which you were raised. Your culture has taught you what your standards should be. For example, North American culture stresses the importance of honesty above most other values.[22]

Second, who you are and how you have interpreted "should" messages from your family, school, religion, friends, television, and movies also determine your personal code of right and wrong. If you have been taught that cheating is wrong, you won't do it, no matter how desperate you are for a good grade on a test. But if you have been taught that, above all, you should always get high grades, you may not think of copying from a neighbor's exam as right or wrong, but only as another means of obtaining your goal.

If all you had to work with were cultural and personal "shoulds," it would be relatively easy to make ethical choices. However, a third consideration, the situation in which you find yourself, complicates matters. For example, if a job interviewer asks whether you have ever been fired, should you admit that you were once dismissed from a position? One "should" message tells you to get a good job, while another says not to lie. If you believe that you won't get the job if you tell the truth, what will you tell the interviewer?

Because the range of variables that influence an individual's ethics is so wide, there are very few absolutes when it comes to communicating ethically. Perhaps the only one may be: Don't purposely hurt others or limit their choices.[23] Give others, regardless of their background and culture, what you would want for yourself—freedom from external restraint and the ability to decide your own course of action. This is a point of view that stresses a belief in the intrinsic worth of the human personality, a view that maintains that all people have the same rights. Ask yourself this question: Are your actions diminishing or contributing to the fulfillment of those rights? Remember, your words and actions create a response in other people—you have the potential to influence them. The significance of this act is clear when we remember that "change means an interposing or interference with the autonomy of the other person or persons. And the tampering with personal drives and desires is a moral act."[24]

YOU AS AN INTERPERSONAL COMMUNICATOR

Interpersonal communication competency refers to both particular behaviors and overall impressions. You may be perceived as competent in a particular situation or at performing particular skills.[25] For example, you may communicate well with your coworkers (a particular situation) and you may also have been told by one of your instructors that you are a good listener (a particular skill). This does not automatically mean that you are equally competent in other situations or equally skilled in other areas of communication.

Your overall impression of your own or someone else's interpersonal communication is based on three factors: observation of behaviors (you note what someone else does), judgment of the appropriateness of the behaviors (you apply your notions of right and wrong and good and bad to judge what you observe), and past shared experiences (you include in your understanding of the other person's behavior your shared background, including what you have done together, talked about, and so on). These factors must be dealt with simultaneously. No single behavior, judgment, or aspect of the history of an interaction by itself creates the overall impression.[26] Rather, the combination of all the behaviors, judgments, and history leads to the conclusion that someone is a competent communicator.

Take another look at your answers to Knowledge Checkup 1.2. Now that you have a general understanding of the defining characteristics of the interpersonal communication process, the importance of communicating competently, and the qualities of competent interpersonal communicators, see if there are any answers you would like to change. What are your strengths? What are your weaknesses? What goals will you set for your knowledge, skills, and motivation as a communicator?

As you progress through this book, you will gain the understanding and skills you need to communicate appropriately and effectively in interpersonal relationships. As your understanding and skills increase from reading the text and completing the activities in this book, so will your chances of being perceived as a competent interpersonal communicator.

Communication Competency Checkup

Communication Competency Checkups will help you summarize the material in each chapter. The goal of this communication competency checkup, as well as those at the end of other chapters, is to guide you in putting your skills and knowledge to use.

Each person is a potential partner for your interpersonal communication.

1. Describe your communication strengths and weaknesses using the results of Knowledge Checkup 1.2. Based on your description and the information in this chapter, formulate goals for increasing your effectiveness as an interpersonal communicator.

2. Define *communication* and *interpersonal communication.*

3. Explain each component of competent interpersonal communication and illustrate each with personal examples.

NOTES

1. Several of these characteristics are based on work by C. David Mortensen, first published twenty-five years ago: C. David Mortensen, *Communication: The Study of Human Interaction* (New York: McGraw-Hill, 1972). Classic works on defining communication include: David K. Berlo, *The Process of Communication: An Introduction to Theory and Practice* (New York: Holt, Rinehart and Winston, 1960); Frank E. X. Dance, "The 'Concept' of Communication," *Journal of Communication* 20 (1970): 201–10; Gerald R. Miller, "On Defining Communication: Another Stab," *Journal of Communication* 16 (1966): 88–98; and Paul Watzlawick, Janet H. Beavin, and Don D. Jackson, *Pragmatics of Human Communication: A Study of Interactional Patterns, Pathologies, and Paradoxes* (New York: Norton, 1967).

2. Brent D. Ruben, *Communication and Human Behavior,* 3rd ed. (New York: Macmillan, 1988), 107.

3. David Matsumoto, "Cultural Influences on Facial Expressions of Emotion," *Southern Communication Journal* 56 1991): 128–137.

4. Larry A. Samovar and Richard Porter, *Communication between Cultures* (Belmont, CA: Wadsworth, 1991), 51. For an extensive discussion on culture as it relates to communication, see Larry A. Samovar and Richard E. Porter, *Intercultural Communication: A Reader,* 7th ed. (Belmont, CA: Wadsworth, 1994).

5. E. Adamson Hoebel and Everett L. Frost, *Culture and Social Anthropology* (New York: Wiley, 1974), 58.

6. Peter Andersen, "Explaining Intercultural Differences in Nonverbal Communication," in *Intercultural Communication: A Reader.* 7th ed., ed. Larry A. Samovar and Richard E. Porter (Belmont, CA: Wadsworth, 1994).

7. C. Negy and D. J. Woods, "The Importance of Acculturation in Understanding Research with Hispanic-Americans," *Hispanic Journal of Behavioral Sciences* 14 (1992): 224–47.

8. M. K. Ho, *Family Therapy with Ethnic Minorities* (Beverly Hills, CA: Sage, 1987).

9. Valaya L. Tanarugsachock, *The Relationship between Levels of Acculturation and Descriptions of Taboo Topics in Chinese Immigrant and Chinese-American Families-of-Origin,* (Thesis, University of North Carolina at Chapel Hill, 1994); L. C. Yu and E. Harburg, "Stress of Chinese-Americans," *International Journal of Group Tensions,* 11.4 (1981): 47–58.

10. Edward T. Hall, *Beyond Culture* (Garden City, NY: Anchor, Doubleday, 1977), 13–14.

11. Robley D. Rhine, "William Graham Sumner's Concept of Ethnocentrism: Some Implications for Intercultural Communication," *World Communication* 18 (Spring 1989): 2.

12. Gerald R. Miller and Mark Steinberg, *Between People* (Chicago: Science Research Associates, 1975).

13. Miller and Steinberg, *Between People.*

14. Brian Spitzberg and William Cupach, *Interpersonal Communication Competence* (Beverly Hills, CA: Sage, 1984); Brian H. Spitzberg, "An Examination of Trait Measures of Interpersonal Competence," *Communication Reports* 4 (1991): 22–29.

15. These communication skills were determined by a task force of the Speech Communication Association (SCA), and endorsed by the organization's Educational Policies Board, to be minimal competencies for communicators. They were stated as an SCA guideline in "Speaking and Listening Competencies for High School Graduates." The full report on these competencies appears in Ronald E. Bassett, Nilwon Whittington, and Ann Staton-Spicer, "The Basics in Speaking and Listening for High School Graduates: What Should Be Assessed?" in *Communication Education* 27 (1978): 293–303. These competencies were further refined and expanded in Richard L. Quianthy (Project Director), *Communication Is Life: Essential College Sophomore Speaking and Listening Competencies* (Annandale, VA: Speech Communication Association, 1990). For additional information on communication competency assessment and other measurement instruments, see Rebecca B. Rubin and Matthew M. Martin, "Development of a Measure of Interpersonal Communication Competence," *Communication Research Reports* 11 (1994): 33–44; Brian H. Spitzberg, "Communication Competence: Measures of Perceived Effectiveness," in *A Handbook for the Study of Human Communication,* ed. Charles H. Tardy (Norwood, NJ: Ablex, 1988), 67–105; and Brian H. Spitzberg and H. Thomas Hurt, "The Measurement of Interpersonal Skills in Instructional Contexts," *Communication Education* 36 (1987): 28–45.

16. M. V. Redmond, "The Relationship between Perceived Communication Competence and Perceived Empathy," *Communication Monographs* 52 (1985): 377–82.

17. Diana Rowland, *Japanese Business Etiquette* (New York: Warner Books, 1985), 12.

18. Susan A. Hellweg, Larry A. Samovar, and Lisa Skow, "Cultural Variations in Negotiation Styles," in *Intercultural Communication: A Reader* 7th ed., ed. Larry A. Samovar and Richard E. Porter (Belmont, CA: Wadsworth, 1991), 187.

19. William R. Cupach and Brian Spitzberg (eds.), *The Dark Side of Interpersonal Communication* (Hillsdale, NJ: Lawrence Erlbaum, 1993).

20. Brian H. Spitzberg and H. Thomas Hurt, "Measurement of Interpersonal Skills in Instructional Contexts," *Communication Education* 36 (1987): 28–45; and Spitzberg, "An Examination of Trait Measures."

21. Rod Hart, R. E. Carlson, and William F. Eadie, "Attitudes toward Communication and the Assessment of Rhetorical Sensitivity," *Communication Monograph* 47 (1980): 1–22.

22. Milton Rokeach and Sandra Ball-Rokeach, "Stability and Change in American Value Profiles, 1968–1981," *American Psychologist* 44 (1989): 775–84.

23. Theodore E. Zorn and Lawrence B. Rosenfeld, "Between a Rock and a Hard Place: Ethical Dilemmas in Problem-Solving Group Facilitation," *Management Communication Quarterly* 3 (1989): 93–106.

24. Ordway Tead, *Administration: Its Purpose and Performance* (New York: Harper and Row, 1959), 52.

25. Spitzberg, "An Examination of Trait Measures."

26. Brian H. Spitzberg, "Communication Competence: Measures of Perceived Effectiveness."

CHAPTER 2

CONCEIVING THE SELF

COMMUNICATION COMPETENCIES

This chapter defines and examines self-concept, and the relationship between self-concept and communication. Specifically, the objective is for you to learn to:

- Identify the important elements that make up your self-concept, including your social identity, personality characteristics, values, and physical characteristics.
- Describe two principles of self-concept development—reflected appraisal and social comparison.
- Distinguish the person you *are,* the person you *wish you were* or think you *should be,* and the person you *present to others.*
- Assess how you feel about yourself—your level of self-esteem.
- Recognize the effects that high and low self-esteem have on communication.
- Use several techniques for increasing your self-esteem.
- Appreciate cultural differences as they relate to the concept of self.

KEY WORDS

The key words in this chapter are:

individual cultures
collective cultures
self-concept
social identity
androgynous
values
reflected appraisal
significant other
generalized others
social comparison
idealized self
actual self
should self
impression management
self-esteem

Dump the contents of your purse or wallet on the table in front of you. Spread the items out so you can look at each one separately. Now, pretend you found the purse or wallet—that it is not yours—and you're trying to figure out what kind of person owns it.

Look at the driver's license. How does the picture look? Would you want to have this person for a friend? Is this an attractive person?

Are there any family pictures? If so, what do they tell you about this person? If there are none, what might this suggest?

Are there any membership cards from social or work groups? Can you guess the person's leisure activities and job? Is there a college identification card?

Are there receipts? If there are, to what stores, for what goods or services, and for how much?

How much money is there? How many credit cards? What can you conclude about this person's financial state?

What other items are there to examine as clues to who this person is?

Take your time and consider each item. See how much you can find out about this person. Then ask yourself: Am I the person these items suggest I am?

Imagine you just received a telephone call from a famous film director who has indicated plans to make a movie about your life. The screenwriter wants your input on several facets of the script. You are asked the following questions and told that since the director and producers are interested in the *real* you, you should answer spontaneously without pausing to think of the "best" answers.

What should be the title of this film epic?

The director asks you to describe yourself so she will understand you better. How do you describe your physical appearance and how you feel about it, how you get along with other people, your usual emotional states, and what you believe in and value?

Who should play you?

Who should play some of your immediate family members?

Where should the production be filmed?

What four or five major events in your life are the most significant and must be included in the film?

What kind of background music, if any, should be used?

You hang up the receiver, lean back, close your eyes, and visualize the film. How do you feel about the final product? What did you learn about yourself from watching the movie of your life?

As you probe your sense of who you are, keep in mind that in Western cultures a preoccupation with self is very natural. Western media, art, literature, government, and psychology all focus on the importance of the individual, and a great deal of time is spent thinking about and pursuing personal happiness. Most conversations are about the self. In fact, the word *I* is used more than any other word. This emphasis on the "I," however, is not common to all cultures, just **individual cultures,** those that stress the importance of being identified as an individual. In **collective cultures,** those that subjugate the self to the group, people will not have the same model of self as those from individual cultures. For example, much of Asia is composed of collective cultures, and the concept of "self" is not as important as the concept of "group." In these cultures, the "us," not "I," is the predominant personal concept.[1]

WHO YOU ARE: YOUR SELF-CONCEPT

Your self-concept is one of the most important of all those traits that composes your personality. So, it should not be surprising that we begin this chapter with a detailed analysis of the *self*. As simple as it may sound, the self is always the main subject of communication. As you move from place to place and from person to person, you take yourself along. Or, as the philosopher Emerson stated, "Wherever we go, whatever we do, self is the sole subject we study and learn." Therefore, you should be able to see that who you are is the foundation for all your communication—the individual needs, interests, and strengths that distinguish you from others are revealed in your communication.[2] Although English probably is your common language, you and the people around you often use different words to express similar experiences. These differences reveal something about how each of you sees the world. For instance, you may see a sunset and comment that it is getting late, while a photographer may see it and notice the stunning contrast between light and dark.

The meanings you attribute to the words you hear are also slightly different from others' interpretations—again reflecting your uniqueness. You may even use a special vocabulary to express who you are and what you do. For example, if you are a computer enthusiast, you may use the words *input* and *output* to explain things unrelated to computers.

Who you are includes how you feel about yourself, and, in turn, how you feel about yourself is reflected in how you communicate. If you think of yourself as shy, you may avoid raising your hand in class or speaking at a meeting; if you think of yourself as a good listener, you may encourage others to talk to you.

Who you are (the *I-am* me), what you would like to be (the *I-wish-I-were* me), and the person you present to others (the *here-I-am* me) form the foundation for how you communicate. Thus, improving your communication competency begins with an examination of who you are, how you came to be that person, and how your self-perception affects how you communicate.

THE PERSON YOU ARE

Your self-exploration in this chapter began with an examination of your purse or wallet and the production of the movie of your life. What did you learn about who you are? Now, continue the process by answering the question "Who am I?" in Knowledge Checkup 2.1. Asking yourself "Who am I?" and "What am I?" and "What would I like to be?" provide the basis for discovering the elements of your self-concept.

Knowledge Checkup 2.1

WHO AM I?

Complete each sentence:

1. When I look at myself in a full-length mirror, I see
2. My friends would probably describe my relationships with them as
3. As a family member, I see myself as
4. My talents include
5. My greatest strengths are
6. My weaknesses or inabilities that bother me are
7. I was
8. I was
9. I was
10. I am
11. I am
12. I am

Be yourself, that's all
there is of you.
RALPH WALDO EMERSON

13. I would like to be

14. I would like to be

15. I would like to be

You are the sum total of your past, present, and future. It may be said that you are what you are based on your verb "to be"—your *I have been, I am,* and *I shall be.* Knowledge Checkup 2.1 provided you with the opportunity to recount your perceptions of these three tenses. The varied responses you gave describe who you are and provide information about your **self-concept**—the totality of your thoughts concerning who you are. Your responses most likely describe the *content* of your self-concept—your social identity, values, personality characteristics, and physical characteristics.[3]

Social Identity

Your **social identity,** the groups or categories to which you belong or aspire, begins with your birth. You are classified by gender, race, culture, religion, and family role (brother, sister, only child, youngest, firstborn), and given a name. Your birth certificate discloses the categories into which you were placed—the categories that provided you with an immediate social identity. For example, birth certificates typically identify your sex, race, whether you're a single-born, twin, or triplet, when and where you were born, your parents' names, and your parents' birthplaces. All this demographic information provides a social context for knowing who you are.

As you grow up, you add new classifications for yourself. You become a member of various groups and clubs. The groups to which you belong reflect your cultural identity (based on shared language, history, values, or territory), your religious beliefs, your political ideology, your interests, your work, and other aspects of how you view yourself.

What you are also includes what you were but are not now, such as an athlete, a baby sitter, or an officer of a club. Some former social identities you may want to conceal; others you may want to use to gain status. For example, you may not want your current friends to know that you were once married, or you may seek recognition by referring to your past activities as a manager of a local health club.

Different cultures place different emphasis on defining ourselves by our social affiliations. Cultures such as those of North America that value individualism place less stock in social organizations than do collective cultures. In collective cultures, a person's identity is defined by the group and not by the "I." The Japanese, for instance, often judge others and themselves by their company affiliations.[4] Most are so proud of whom they work for that they will wear company pins attached to outer garments. In China there is a saying that "If you know the family you need not know the person." The culture of many Mexican Americans presents yet another perspective on the "I." Whereas the European-American culture stresses that "I will achieve mainly because of my ability and initiative," Mexican-American culture tends to stress that "I will achieve mainly because of my family, and for my family, rather than myself."[5]

Personality Characteristics

The content of your self-concept is more than your social identity. The many personality characteristics you use to describe yourself also contribute to your self-concept.

Personality characteristics are the qualities constituting a person's character that are relatively stable across a lifetime and that make him or her distinctive.[6] For example, you may consider a friend "happy and easygoing" and a teacher "stern." Before looking at some of the more than twenty thousand identified personality characteristics, complete Knowledge Checkup 2.2.

Knowledge Checkup 2.2

BEM SEX-ROLE INVENTORY[7]

Indicate the degree to which each statement is true of you.

Write **1** if the statement is never or almost never true of you.

Write **2** if it is usually not true of you.

Write **3** if it is sometimes but infrequently true of you.

Write **4** if it is occasionally true of you.

Write **5** if it is usually true of you.

Write **6** if it is always or almost always true of you.

_____ 1. I am self-reliant.

_____ 2. I am cheerful.

_____ 3. I am independent.

_____ 4. I am affectionate.

_____ 5. I have a strong personality.

_____ 6. I am sympathetic.

_____ 7. I act as a leader.

_____ 8. I am eager to soothe hurt feelings.

_____ 9. I am analytical.

_____ 10. I am warm.

The ten personality characteristics you just considered describe two types of personalities. The odd-numbered items represent a stereotypical "masculine" personality and the even-numbered items represent a stereotypical "feminine" personality. Add your responses to the odd items to obtain your masculine score, then add your responses to the even items to obtain your feminine score. Total scores above 22 in either category are considered high and scores below 22 are considered low.

If you scored high on masculine and low on feminine, you would be classified by this instrument as having those personality characteristics that research shows are indicative of a person called "masculine." If you scored low on masculine and high on feminine, you would be classified by this instrument as "feminine." High scores on both lead to classification as "androgynous," a balance of both masculine and feminine personality characteristics; low scores on both lead to classification as "undifferentiated." It is important to note that both males and females fall into all four personality categories and that these classifications exist apart from your biological-sex categorization.

A person who describes herself or himself as **androgynous**—both highly masculine and highly feminine—has the largest repertoire of communication behaviors to call upon. For example, this person may behave both empathically and objectively, and both assertively and cooperatively, which increases the person's adaptability—one of the qualities of the competent communicator. Gender-typed individuals—masculine or feminine—exhibit a smaller range of communication behaviors and, therefore, are less adaptable than androgynous individuals.

Masculinity and femininity are only two of the many different personality characteristics that affect communication. For example, several others that have been studied
and found to be important for understanding an individual's communication are:[8]

Self-monitoring—sensitivity to one's communication out of concern for being
appropriate. For example, high self-monitors are more likely than others to
initiate conversations (the appropriate response to awkward silences) and
reciprocate intimacy (the appropriate response to another's intimate behaviors)
than are low self-monitors.

Extroversion-introversion—outgoing and focused on the world outside the self
versus focused on the inner world of the self. Extroverts speak more than
introverts and spend less time pausing. Introverts tend to display fewer
nonverbal actions, such as gestures, than do extroverts.

The notion of extroversion-introversion is quite interesting when placed
in a cultural context. In many cultures extroversion, at least as we know it in
North America, hardly exists. In most Asian cultures, and even among many
Native American cultures, children are raised to be compliant and docile. Signs
of extroversion are shunned as a communication style. When Asians or Native
Americans confront a North American, they are often uncomfortable if that
person is emotionally open and shares ideas about himself or herself easily.
And, of course, the reverse is true, resulting in many North Americans
perceiving Asians as standoffish and emotionally distant.

Dominance-submissiveness—controlling and authoritarian versus yielding and
obedient. People with a dominant personality communicate more assertively
and confidently than those with a submissive personality. They also participate
more in groups and interrupt more.

Need for affiliation—concern with being included in others' activities. People
with a high need for affiliation prefer to interact at closer distances and
maintain more eye contact than those with a low need for affiliation.

Need for approval—concern with receiving praise and other positive feedback.
People with a high need for approval pay attention to others' nonverbal
vocal characteristics, such as pauses, more than do those with a low need
for approval.

Other examples of personality characteristics include the extent to which you desire
social relationships (e.g., some people prefer many friends; others prefer few friends or
even to be alone), concern with making a good impression (e.g., some people are very
concerned with acting properly and politely so that others see them as well mannered;
others care little about following society's rules of etiquette), relaxed versus tense (e.g.,
some people exhibit few nonverbal indications of anxiety; others may seem to fidget
constantly, bite their fingernails, and stammer when they speak, thus displaying their
apprehension), conservative versus experimenting (e.g., some people are prone to conform to established habits; others try new things and are risk takers), and trusting versus
suspicious (e.g., some people are willing to trust others until that trust is proven wrong;
others are suspicious until the trust is earned).[9]

It is important to keep in mind that the personality characteristics discussed reflect a strong Western orientation. Because personality characteristics are reflective of a given culture, they shift from culture to culture. For example, not all cultures teach their members to seek approval. In fact, cultures that stress introspection over interaction, such as in India, believe that happiness is found in meditation, not in interaction. In fact, at times turning to others for satisfaction can be perceived as a sign of weakness.

Values

Values reflect the importance you attach to different ways of behaving, such as being honest, as well as the goals to which you aspire, such as a peaceful world. Values motivate you to behave and to communicate one way or another. Knowledge Checkup 2.3 is designed to help you clarify several values.

Knowledge Checkup 2.3

DISCOVERING YOUR VALUES[10]

Rank the items within each set of values from most important to you (1) to least important to you (9).

It is important to be:

_____ ambitious (hardworking, aspiring)

_____ broad-minded (open-minded)

_____ capable (competent, effective)

_____ clean (neat, tidy)

_____ courageous (standing up for your beliefs)

_____ forgiving (willing to pardon others)

_____ helpful (working for the welfare of others)

_____ honest (sincere, truthful)

_____ loving (affectionate, tender)

_____ responsible (dependable, reliable)

It is important to have:

_____ a comfortable life (a prosperous life)

_____ a world at peace (free of war and conflict)

_____ equality (brotherhood, equal opportunity for all)

_____ family security (taking care of loved ones)

_____ freedom (independence, free choice)

_____ happiness (contentedness)

_____ salvation (being saved, eternal life)

_____ self-respect (self-esteem)

_____ sense of accomplishment (lasting contribution)

_____ wisdom (a mature understanding of life)

Which values are most important for you? Your important values affect how you communicate. In national surveys conducted over a period of thirteen years, people across the United States were asked to rank these values.[11] For the "important to be" values, *honest,* on the average, was ranked first, *responsible* second, *ambitious* third, *forgiving* fourth, *broad-minded* fifth, *courageous* sixth, *helpful* seventh, *loving* eighth, and *capable* ninth. For the "important to have" values, *a world at peace,* on the average, was ranked first, *family security* second, *freedom* third, *self-respect* fourth, *happiness* fifth, *wisdom* sixth, *sense of accomplishment* seventh, *a comfortable life* eighth, and *salvation* ninth. A few differences between males and females were found. Males ranked *capable* and *a comfortable life* higher than females did, and females ranked *salvation* higher than males did.

These results—stable over the thirteen years—are averages; each value received every possible ranking. How you compare with the national results isn't important. What's important is for you to realize what values are important for you, understand how they help define who you are, and know how they affect the way you communicate.

The values you selected were, of course, the result of your cultural and social background; individuals from other cultures would probably not have selected the same factors. An understanding of your own and others' cultural values can help you make predictions about how your interpersonal partner might respond to you and your messages. Knowing, for instance, that much of Latin America values patience and an unhurried pace to life, might enable you to slow down and be calm when you are interacting with a person from those cultures.[12] The Irish also prize an easygoing manner, and even have a proverb that notes, "Life is a dance, not a race." The idea of knowing the values of other cultures and adjusting to those values holds true when you are dealing with individuals who typically demand punctuality, such as the Swiss or the Germans—you must be on time for appointments and meet deadlines or you will be perceived negatively, no matter your intentions.[13] You also might be perceived negatively if you were unaware of the importance of interpersonal harmony when communicating with someone from the Filipino culture. Filipinos generally value smooth interpersonal relations and avoid stressful confrontations.[14]

What is the relationship between your ranking of particular values and your behavior? For example, if you ranked *honesty* first, ask yourself if you have ever cheated on a test or kept extra change you received by mistake from a cashier.

If you value honesty highly, you are more likely to communicate directly and openly, especially if you also value being courageous. Of course, if you value being ambitious more highly than being honest, you might stretch the truth during a job interview to increase your chances of getting hired. The issue gets more complicated if you consider how much you value self-respect. Will you respect yourself if you stretch the truth during the job interview?

Completing questionnaires like Knowledge Checkup 2.3 and observing your communication behavior should help you determine what your values are and which are most important to you. Knowing your values is the first step toward analyzing them and their relationship to how you behave and communicate. You will then be better equipped to modify your values or your behavior as you see fit.

Your social identity is relatively unambiguous—you know the groups to which you belong; personality characteristics and values, however, are less discernible. You may be certain you're a student, but unsure about your warmth, true intelligence, or honesty. Your social identity is more easily verified than your psychological one. You may have a driver's license that clearly identifies you as a driver, but where in your wallet or purse is a document to prove that you're gentle, humorous, or forgiving?

Physical Characteristics

Your *physical characteristics,* your body's traits, make up another category of elements that contribute to your self-concept. While the characteristics may be clear—indeed, you are a certain height and weight and have eyes a particular color—how you feel about individual body parts, and your body in general, may be less certain. Born without a notion of self, your first identity was a physical one. Lying in your crib, you noticed hands that came and went from view. One day, you realized that the hands were *you*—and, still without your being aware of it, your physical self-concept began to form. Your physical self remains important even now, which may be why you diet, lift weights, run, or apply makeup. How you feel about yourself affects whether you do these things or not, and whether or not you do these things also affects how you feel about yourself.

Your self-concept is complex, containing your social identity, personality and physical characteristics, and values. How is it that your particular self-concept came to be what it is?

THE SOURCES OF SELF-CONCEPT

Two primary theories explain how particular elements come to form your self-concept—reflected appraisal and social comparison.[15] The first, reflected appraisal, suggests that you are influenced by the communication you receive from others, especially when it focuses on you. The second, social comparison, contends that you learn about yourself by comparing yourself to others.

Reflected Appraisal

Reflected appraisal holds that your view of yourself is consistent with the view others hold of you and that you have come to view yourself as you do *because* of the views of others. Some consistency between your self-perceptions and others' perceptions of you is essential for getting along in society.[16] Think of the problems you would encounter if you wanted to lead a team project because you thought of yourself as intelligent, outgoing, and an effective communicator, but the group members saw you as below average in intelligence, withdrawn, and a poor communicator.

At the root of reflected appraisals are the messages others send you about yourself. Not all messages carry the same weight, however. An appraisal from your best friend probably matters more to you than an appraisal from a relative stranger. To take someone's opinion seriously, you must usually perceive the person as a **significant other,** that is, someone whose opinion of you matters or whose judgment you trust. Friends normally exert more influence than strangers, and members of your family usually exert more influence than outsiders because you consider friends and kin qualified appraisers who should have your best interests at heart.[17]

For an appraisal to be accepted as true, it must first be personal. The other person must know a great deal about you and adapt an appraisal specifically to you. Second, an appraisal must be consistent with past appraisals so that you do not dismiss it as a mistake or an anomaly.

Part of reflected appraisal is the notion of imagining another's appraisal, without the other person present, you can *imagine* what her or his evaluation will be. The "little voice" that warns what your professor will say if you fail a test, or what your religious leader will think if you act improperly, exists because you can assume another's point of view, see yourself as that person sees you, and imagine and use a reflected appraisal.[18]

Who are your significant others? What are their messages of appraisal for you? The first part of Knowledge Checkup 2.4 will help you identify your significant others. The second part will help you begin the process of discovering how you perceive their appraisals of you.

Knowledge Checkup 2.4

IDENTIFYING YOUR SIGNIFICANT OTHERS AND THEIR APPRAISALS OF YOU

You can recognize your reflected appraisals and examine who your significant others are by completing four sentences:

1. Two people who know me best and have my best interests at heart are

2. Two people who, in my opinion, are competent to judge me are

3. The two persons whose comments seem to have the greatest influence on how I think about myself and how I behave are

Your answers to questions 1, 2, and 3 identified six of your significant others (there may be others you could identify). Now, consider question 4.

4. If each person identified in your responses to 1, 2, and 3 described you to someone, each would say:

Person 1 who knows me best and has my best interests at heart:

Person 2 who knows me best and has my best interests at heart:

Person 1 who is competent to judge me:

Person 2 who is competent to judge me:

Person 1 whose comments seem to have the greatest influence on how I think about myself and how I behave:

Person 2 whose comments seem to have the greatest influence on how I think about myself and how I behave:

Your answers to question 4 are the reflected appraisals that helped form your self-concept.

If you grew up in a traditional family setting, it is likely that you identified your parent or parents, or whoever brought you up, as part of your group of significant others. This is logical since they most likely know you well, probably have your best interests at heart, and may be perceived by you as competent to judge you (after all, they were probably your first heroes—the strongest, smartest, able-to-do-anything magical giants with whom you lived). To begin to assess their influence on your self-concept, consider the family sayings with which you were brought up—any sentence, phrase, colloquialism, question, or command that was communicated to you over and over again. For example, maybe a family saying was, "If you're going to do something, do it right, or don't do it at all." What do the family sayings tell you about how your family significant others viewed you? For example, if you were constantly told to clean up your room, is it possible they saw you as a slob, or lazy, or unmotivated to be clean? If you were constantly told to use your own judgment to solve a problem, is it possible they saw you as competent and intelligent? Whatever your family sayings were (and they were probably a mixture of "positive" and "negative" ones), do you see yourself in ways consistent with the messages you received?

Another way to begin to assess the influence of your parents or guardians on your self-concept is to imagine that you are one of your parents or guardians and that you meet one of your friend's parents. You stop, say hello, and then talk about your child (you). *Speaking as your parent or guardian,* what do you say about yourself? How does your "parent's" or "guardian's" conversation relate to how you see yourself now?

In addition to the appraisals of your significant others, reflected appraisal also includes what you think **generalized others**—people in general—consider correct or proper. In other words, your interpretation of the attitudes of your society. From years of watching television, for example, you may have formed the belief that conflicts are unhealthy unless they can be resolved in thirty or sixty minutes (with commercial breaks). Consequently, when you are involved in a real conflict—one that takes more than thirty or sixty minutes to resolve—your self-appraisal may be: "I am a bad person for engaging in unhealthy conflict. I had better run away or give in, or shout so loudly that I get my way, and end this problem immediately." How you communicate will be based, in part, on an appraisal from generalized others.

Social Comparison

According to the principle of **social comparison,** you compare yourself to others to learn about yourself, and you evaluate how you measure up by the standards set by those others.[19] For example, suppose you compare your height to that of your friends. If you are taller, and if being tall is valued by your friends, you can make two appraisals: You are taller than some people, and that is good.

Comparisons take at least two forms: *better or worse* and *same or different.* Assessments of traits such as intelligence, strength, and creativity typically define whether you are better or worse, while comparisons of religious background, social class, and home region typically tell whether you are the same or different.

Comparisons let you see yourself as smart or stupid, attractive or ugly, popular or unpopular, depending on to whom you compare yourself. To compare better, change your source of comparison—you don't always have to change yourself!

With which groups do you compare yourself? Knowledge Checkup 2.5 provides you with four questions useful for discovering the groups you use for making your social comparisons, and for understanding what those comparisons reveal about yourself.

Knowledge Checkup 2.5

IDENTIFYING YOUR SOCIAL COMPARISON GROUPS

You can recognize your social comparison groups by answering four questions:

1. Select one area in which you compare yourself to others. In what area is the comparison made? (For example, is the comparison based on wealth, intelligence, or social skill?)

2. In the selected area, ask yourself, "Which people am I better or worse than?"

3. In the selected area, ask yourself, "Which people am I the same as or different from?"

4. Finally, ask yourself, "What do my comparisons tell me about who I am?" (For example, do you put yourself down or inflate your ego by selecting unrealistic people with whom to compare yourself?)

The information you gather through reflected appraisals and social comparisons becomes the content of your self-concept. Because you are a complex, multifaceted, multidimensional being, the elements of your self-concept are voluminous. Once you have amassed your self-perceptions, you need to organize them.

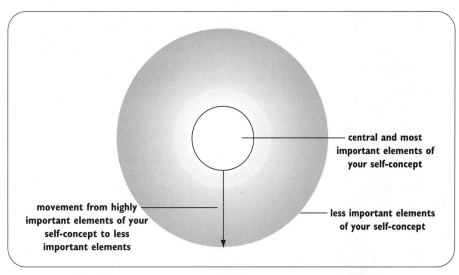

central and most
important elements of
your self-concept

less important elements
of your self-concept

movement from highly
important elements of your
self-concept to less
important elements

FIGURE 2.1 Organizing the Elements of Your Self-Concept

ORGANIZING THE ELEMENTS OF YOUR SELF-CONCEPT

The elements of your self-concept are not random and disorganized. Rather, they are ordered in a way that makes it possible for you to behave relatively consistently. The order can be pictured as a circle with elements that are most important to you at the center and ones that are less important toward the outside (see Figure 2.1). For example, thinking of yourself as a loyal friend may be more central to your self-perception than thinking of yourself as a conscientious student. Consider the following situations:

1. You have to stay on campus over spring break to research a term paper. Your parents call to remind you that a family gathering is taking place and that you're expected to attend. Your mother asks whether you will be coming home. Going home means not getting your research done. What would you tell her?

2. You apply for a job and get called for an interview. Two of the questions you're asked concern your prior work experience and your academic performance. You believe that if you tell the truth the odds are you won't get the job—which you need to pay for your college fees. What do you do?

You can determine the relative importance of the elements in your self-concept by examining your responses to hypothetical situations *as well as by observing your behavior in real-life situations.* In the first scenario, if you tell your mother you're coming home, you may value family security more than individual accomplishment. In the second scenario, if you tell the interviewer that you have a lot of experience and did very well in school, you may value ambition above honesty.

Communication problems may arise when two people who have the same elements in their self-concepts rank the elements differently. For example, you and a friend may

hold honesty as an important value, but you may believe in "honesty at all costs" while your friend believes in being honest as long as honesty doesn't hurt anyone. Right versus wrong is not the issue as you communicate. Rather, difficulties arise because you have honesty at different places in your circle of self-perceptions—such as when you want to share your real feelings with a third person about her behavior, and your friend suggests you withhold the truth because it could hurt her.

THE PERSON YOU WISH YOU WERE

The extent to which you think of yourself as a failure or a success, a good person or a bad one, depends largely on your notion of who you would like to be. At least three images form your desired self-concept: the idealized self, the actual self, and the should self.

The Idealized Self

Your **idealized self** is how you perceive yourself as "perfect." Elements of this image emerge when you say, "If I were _____, then everything would be OK." When you feel overwhelmed by problems, you may temporarily invoke your idealized self. If you feel the need to be successful, you may dream that you can do anything and accomplish anything. And if you feel the need to be loved, you may dream of being attractive and desirable. Although the idealized self is not obtainable, it influences how you judge your own and others' abilities to communicate.[20]

The idealized self that a person wants to be, like many goals, has its roots deep in our culture. For example, if you have "being attractive and desirable" as an objective, realize that people from Japan, China, and Mexico believe that the family is the primary value and the idealized self might seek to become a better son or daughter. For someone from an Arab culture, the idealized self might include being able to memorize and recite the entire *Koran* (the Islamic holy book).

The Actual Self

Your **actual self,** a more realistic image than your idealized self, conforms more to your capabilities and the restrictions of your environment. Even young children know the difference between an idealized image and the actual one. They clearly recognize the self-picture that is possible and, therefore, worth striving for. Thinking about an idealized image, such as being a basketball star, may be fun (if sometimes frustrating), but many children's real efforts are spent pursuing an actual image, such as becoming a teacher, a lawyer, or a businessperson. A child who is asked, "If you could be anything, what would you want to be?" may answer "Superman" or "Wonder Woman," but that same child would probably admit that being Superman or Wonder Woman isn't really possible because it is understood that the idealized self is simply a pleasant dream.[21]

Comparing yourself to your idealized image is bound to leave you feeling inadequate. Comparing yourself to your actual image, however, is more fruitful because the actual self may possibly be achieved.

The Should Self

The third component of the desired self-concept is the **should self,** which contains all the "oughts" and "shoulds" that serve as your moral guidelines. These standards, against which you constantly measure yourself, come from your family, culture, school, friends, and the mass media. Your "shoulds" represent the moral standards of society; transgressing them usually results in guilt or anger with yourself.

"Shoulds" result not merely from your socialization, but also from the unique demands you place on yourself. Getting A's may not be a society-wide "should," but *you* may think that there is no alternative, that anything less than an A represents failure. You may be convinced that eating more than one scoop of ice cream is disgustingly self-indulgent, or that sleeping for more than eight hours is inexcusably lazy, or that watching television is a waste of time. In addition to all the "shoulds" you acknowledge, you may generate hundreds more. Every "should" increases the likelihood that you will view yourself as a bad person at some time.

The should self is another area where you need to be aware of cultural differences. For example, in cultures where religion determines a complete way of life, such as Hinduism, Islam, and Orthodox Judaism, the "should" list might include feelings of guilt for not spending more hours each day praying.

Because of the extreme effect "shoulds" have on self-concept, it is important for you to look at the contents of your should list. Knowledge Checkup 2.6 will help you recognize some beliefs you have about what "should be."

Knowledge Checkup 2.6

IDENTIFYING YOUR "SHOULD" STATEMENTS[22]

Read the following statements and indicate the extent to which you agree or disagree with each.

If you strongly agree, mark the statement **5.**

If you agree, mark the statement **4.**

If you neither agree nor disagree, mark the statement **3.**

If you disagree, mark the statement **2.**

If you strongly disagree, mark the statement **1.**

_____ 1. It is important that others approve of me.

_____ 2. I hate to fail at anything.

_____ 3. I want everyone to like me.

_____ 4. I avoid things I cannot do well.

_____ 5. I find it hard to go against what others think.

_____ 6. It upsets me to make mistakes.

Sum up your responses to items 1, 3, and 5: _____. This is your *everyone should approve of me* score. Sum up your responses to items 2, 4, and 6: _____. This is your *I should be perfect* score. Scores of 12 and higher are high, indicating strong belief in the should statement; scores of 6 and below are low, indicating little if any belief in the should statement; and scores of 7 through 11 indicate moderate belief in the should statement.

Believing that everyone should approve of you, when this is clearly impossible, and believing that everything you do should be perfect, another clear impossibility, guarantees that you will dislike yourself at some time. Later we'll look at how to combat illogical should statements.

THE PERSON YOU PRESENT TO OTHERS

Regardless of the person you are and the person you would like to be, the only person others know is the one you present to them. Most of us distinguish actors from the characters they play; however, others do not distinguish you from the person you portray. As Kurt Vonnegut wrote in his novel *Mother Night,* "We are what we pretend to be, so we must be careful about what we pretend to be."[23]

The person you think you are and the person you would like to be, together with your "shoulds," form the foundation for all your behavior. Acting in ways that do not fit your conception of yourself is difficult and often uncomfortable. If you must behave in ways that contradict how you see yourself, you are likely to distance yourself from the image you are presenting. For example, if you consider yourself shy, you might offer a toast at a dinner party by saying: "Well, gee, this isn't something I do a lot. In fact, this is the first time. I feel really awkward about standing up here." You would reflect that being the center of attention is not part of how you see yourself.

Additional factors influence the person you present to others: the perceived requirements of the situation, others' expectations, and your goals for communicating.

The Requirements of a Situation

Your perceived requirements of a situation stem from the situation's immediate demands, the rules governing the situation, the demands of similar past situations, and the implications of your behavior for similar situations in the future. For example, one rule of thumb for child rearing is, "Be consistent in what you tell your child—don't change from situation to situation." Consider the following dialogue:

Child: I want some ice cream.

Parent: No. You know that one of our rules is no junk food before dinner.

Child: I want ice cream. I want ice cream! I want ice cream!!

The immediate demand for the parent is to respond to the child's request for ice cream. Should an exception to the rule be allowed, or should a firm *no* be repeated? Situations that parallel the current one include the many times the child asked for cookies, cake, or candy and was refused. If the parent refuses the child's request for ice cream, this behavior would be consistent with past situations and the child might eventually learn to accept the house rule. But if the child is allowed to have some ice cream, then this probably opens the door to a flood of future requests and nagging for snack-time goodies.

The parent's message to the child reflects his or her definition of a good parent: "A good parent should not allow a child to eat junk food before dinner." In addition, this message reflects his or her analysis of the implications of responses for future interactions. The result may not please the child, but it is appropriate from the parent's perspective.

Others' Expectations

What you think people expect of you also affects how you behave. "People" includes both those with whom you are interacting and significant others who are now absent but who helped form your self-image. Your goal may be to be consistent with what both groups expect of you. Those expectations may be unclear, especially for a new situation, and the expectations of one group may differ from the expectations of the other group. For example, ambiguity and conflict commonly mark dating situations, especially when dating first begins. Consider these inner thoughts of two young teenagers on a first date:

He: She wants me to put my arm around her shoulder—she expects that.

She: My mother knows his mother and she told me that he's a nice guy. I'm sure he won't try anything.

He: Should I put my arm around her?

She: I get the feeling he wants to put his arm around my shoulder. That's OK with me!

He: If I put my arm around her and she slaps me, what will I do? But if she expects me to put my arm around her and I don't, what will she think? And if I do and she slaps me, what will happen? And if I don't and she thinks I'm the village idiot, will that mean I'll never see her again? And what will my mother think if it gets back to her that I put my arm around her friend's daughter and she slapped me? And what if it gets back that I didn't, and should have, and my mother's only son is an idiot?

She: I think he thinks that I think he shouldn't put his arm around me. Then he must think I'm a prude.

And so the evening goes. No one is sure what to do. No one knows what image to live up to, what expectations to fulfill, or even what the expectations are.

People from different cultures often have different and sometimes conflicting expectations. These expectations can result in misunderstandings. For instance, a female student from Japan went out on a date with a North American student. After a lovely evening at a concert the Japanese student was sitting *silently,* respectfully enjoying the company of her date and thinking about the concert. He, however, *expected* her to talk—to make conversation to show she was having a good time. Not understanding the differences in cultural expectations, he said to her, "I'm very sorry you didn't have a nice time tonight." She expected silence, he expected to talk.

The Goals for Communicating

Several objectives also determine the self you present to others, which further complicate the issue of how to behave. First are the goals you have for interacting: You may want to get hired for a particular job, impress a professor with your intelligence, or have your love reciprocated. There are as many goals as there are people and interactions—and these goals require **impression management,** strategies to communicate in particular ways in order to influence how others view you.[24] You use a large vocabulary and serious tone of voice with the interviewer so that she sees you as a strong candidate for the job; you ask the professor probing questions about material in the textbook to increase your chances of being seen as smart; you disclose important feelings to your relational partner—say "I love you"—so that you will be seen as open and caring, worthy of being loved in return. How you communicate reflects what you want, either directly or indirectly.

Second is your objective to remain consistent with your image of yourself and avoid doing anything that might lower (or raise) your self-evaluation:[25] If the teenage boy does put his arm around the teenage girl and she slaps him, his view of himself as a nice guy will be challenged and he may well lose some respect for himself. On the other hand, if he doesn't try to put his arm around her and later finds out that she wouldn't have screamed, he will probably feel just as downcast.

Third may be your objective of "trying on" a social identity. Almost all of us test new behaviors and experiment with new elements of our self-concept throughout our lives, although adolescence is the heyday for such testing. Is the teenage male too forward? The only way he can find out is to try on the behavior and see how it feels. If it's comfortable and others seem to approve, he may decide to keep it as an element of his self-concept. Is the teenage girl assertive? The only way she can find out is to tell her date that she wants him to put his arm around her and see how it feels to have communicated assertively.

Not all cultures have the same goals in mind when they engage in acts of communication. For example, cultures that value "talk," such as African American, Arab, Italian, Jewish, and Mexican, will engage in much more communication than cultures that value silence, such as Japanese, Chinese, and Korean. "Talking" cultures take great delight in communication, and their communication goal might simply be pleasure. In "silent" cultures there are often specific goals that motivate conversation. A Japanese proverb that states "A flower does not speak" only serves to underscore the importance of silence in this culture.

HOW YOU FEEL ABOUT YOURSELF: YOUR SELF-ESTEEM

Whereas self-concept focuses on *who you are*—your social identity, values, personality characteristics, and physical characteristics—**self-esteem** refers to your evaluations of yourself, *how you feel about who you are.* To get a quick idea of how you feel about yourself, answer the questions in Knowledge Checkup 2.7.

Knowledge Checkup 2.7
ANALYZING YOUR GENERAL SELF-ESTEEM[26]

Indicate the extent to which you agree or disagree with each statement.

Write **1** if you strongly disagree with the statement.
Write **2** if you disagree.

Calvin and Hobbes   by Bill Watterson

Write **3** if you neither agree nor disagree.

Write **4** if you agree.

Write **5** if you strongly agree.

_____ 1. I am generally satisfied with myself.

_____ 2. I feel that I have a number of worthy qualities.

_____ 3. I am able to do things as adequately as most people.

_____ 4. I think of myself in mostly positive ways.

_____ 5. I have few regrets about my life.

_____ 6. I wouldn't change much if I had the chance to live my life over again.

_____ 7. I feel like a useful person.

Add up your responses to the seven items. The higher your score, the higher your self-esteem. Scores of 21 and higher suggest positive self-esteem, while scores below 21 suggest lower self-esteem.

Although the test is short, it should give you a general idea of how you feel about yourself. You may disagree with the results and say something like, "Sure, I have a high score, but so what? I still hate the way my nose hooks and I don't do well in foreign language courses," or "My low score doesn't take into account that I'm a great pianist and play guard on the varsity basketball team." Such statements reflect the relationship between your general attitude toward yourself, as measured by the test, and your attitude toward parts of yourself. You may like some elements of your self-concept and not others. Thus you may take pride in your social abilities yet be embarrassed by your math deficiencies.

Knowledge Checkup 2.8 will help you analyze how you feel about yourself by posing specific, as opposed to general, questions.

Knowledge Checkup 2.8

ANALYZING YOUR SPECIFIC SELF-ESTEEM[27]

Indicate the degree to which each item is true or false for you.

If it is completely false, mark the item **1.**

If it is mostly false, mark the item **2.**

If it is partly false and partly true, mark the item **3.**

If it is mostly true, mark the item **4.**

If it is completely true, mark the item **5.**

_____ 1. I am satisfied with my weight.

_____ 2. I am satisfied with my looks.

_____ 3. I am satisfied with my height.

_____ 4. I am satisfied with my moral behavior.

_____ 5. I am satisfied with the extent to which I am religious.

_____ 6. I am satisfied with my relationship with a Supreme Being.

_____ 7. I am satisfied with my family relationships.

_____ 8. I am satisfied with how well I understand my family.

_____ 9. I am satisfied with how I treat (treated) my parents.

_____ 10. I am satisfied with how sociable I am.

_____ 11. I am satisfied with the extent to which I try to please others.

_____ 12. I am satisfied with the way I treat other people.

> The most terrifying thing is to accept oneself completely.
> CARL JUNG

SCORING:

Add items 1, 2, and 3: _____ This is your *physical self-esteem score.*

Add items 4, 5, and 6: _____ This is your *moral-ethical self-esteem score.*

Add items 7, 8, and 9: _____ This is your *family self-esteem score.*

Add items 10, 11, and 12: _____ This is your *social self-esteem score.*

Scores between 12 and 15 in any category indicate high self-esteem; scores between 3 and 6 indicate low self-esteem; scores from 7 through 11 indicate moderate self-esteem.

Is your self-esteem higher in some areas than others? How are differences in your scores reflected in how you interact with other people?

Whether you should focus on the overall evaluation or the individual assessments depends on what you want to know about yourself. Regardless of where you focus, keep in mind that generalizing from smaller parts to the whole or from the whole to smaller parts can mislead you: If you feel good about your work in school, avoid the generalization that you feel good about yourself in general. If you are upset with yourself in general, avoid concluding that you do not think highly of your singing ability. Instead, consider the whole and its parts together to gauge how justifiable is your self-esteem.

Your level of self-esteem tends to be reflected in your communication.[28] As you might suspect, communicators with high self-esteem, at least in North American cultures, are at a distinct advantage. Individuals who like and accept themselves tend to remain open-minded when they encounter new ideas, opinions, and beliefs. They also tend to change their minds more easily than people with low self-esteem because they are confident and unthreatened by others' ideas. As a result, their interactions are more supportive and friendly, which leads to greater involvement with other people and the possibility of more intimate relationships. Consider the following dialogue between an employee who has low self-esteem and the employee's boss.

Boss: I'd like you to tackle the Long account.

Employee: I already worked on it.

Boss: I'd like you to try out some new ideas. I have some suggestions that you might consider.

Employee: What's wrong? Didn't you like what I did?

Boss: It's not that. I just think a new approach . . .

Employee: Well, I just don't see how to go about it any other way. I'm sorry you have a problem with me.

The employee's reactions indicate an inability to accept change and an unwillingness to consider alternatives. The request for change was perceived as a personal attack, and rather than talk with the boss to discover what was desired, the employee responded defensively and created a poor impression.

People with high self-esteem also tend to show sensitivity toward others and have empathy, the ability to see things from another's perspective. Both of these characteristics hone the accuracy of a person's perceptions and contribute to effective conflict resolution. The ability to see a conflict from the other person's perspective strongly influences whether a mutually agreed-upon solution will be found.

Self-esteem also directly affects language. People with high self-esteem tend to have rich vocabularies and confident-sounding voices, whereas people with low self-esteem tend to use language filled with clichés and jargon. When things go wrong, the person with low self-esteem may say, "It never rains but it pours," or "Why does it always happen to me?" whereas the person with high self-esteem will probably give a clear description of the situation and its consequences. Language reflects feelings about the world, whether it is a place to trust others, act spontaneously, and be happy, or a place to withdraw, act defensively, and feel unhappy.

What gives a person high self-esteem in one culture may not be the rule for all cultures. Indeed, the entire concept of self and of self-esteem has its roots deep in one's culture. People who belong to collectivist cultures, such as in China, Japan, and Mexico, perceive the self quite differently than do people from individualistic cultures, such as in the United States. Self-esteem for those in collectivist cultures—unlike those in individualistic cultures—is connected to their relationship with other people; it does not emerge from the individual alone.[29] In short, self-esteem, like most of the communication variables we look at throughout this book, is related to culture.

ENHANCING YOUR SELF-ESTEEM

Your communication reflects how you feel about yourself. The discussion so far reveals that one sure way to improve your communication is to increase your self-esteem. Among the methods of raising your self-esteem are confronting your "should" messages, focusing on the positive, and eliminating your self put-downs.

CONFRONTING YOUR "SHOULD" MESSAGES

A prime source of low self-esteem is the "should" image you hold. If your self-esteem is low, you can boost it by discovering your "should" messages, assessing their reasonableness, and then refuting unreasonable ones. For example, to confront the message "I should get A's in all my classes" you might say: "Earning A's in all my classes is desirable, but expecting to may be unreasonable. I am better at some things than others. I can reasonably expect to get A's in some courses and not others. I can't reasonably expect to earn all A's, although I will strive for them."

Analyzing and refuting unreasonable "should" messages, such as those uncovered in Knowledge Checkup 2.6, provides information that clarifies your strengths and weaknesses and the demands you place on yourself. It also lays the foundation for enhancing your self-esteem because you begin to set realistic goals.

Because "should" messages reflect a culture's values, they are bound to differ from culture to culture. The message "I should be more assertive" is generally out of place in many Asian cultures; and, "I should have more friends" is not common in cultures that stress solitude over interaction. Therefore, in setting interpersonal expectations, you must recognize that your "should" messages may not be the same as someone else's.

Skill Development 2.1 will help you identify several of your specific should messages, note which appear to have unreasonable demands, and then begin the process of changing them.

Skill Development 2.1

CONFRONTING YOUR SHOULD MESSAGES

1. Complete each of the following sentences.
   a. To be a good family member, I should
   b. To be a good friend, I should
   c. To be a good student, I should
   d. To be a good person, I should

2. What unreasonable or reasonable demands does each "should" statement in question 1 make?

3. How do the unreasonable demands prevent you from feeling better about yourself?

4. Refute each "should" statement in question 1 and substitute a more realistic goal. (Discover the incorrect thinking that supports each should statement and replace it with more reasonable thinking.)

Nobody can make you feel
inferior without your
consent.
ELEANOR ROOSEVELT

FOCUSING ON THE POSITIVE

All communication is open to interpretation, and your interpretation of a specific event can either increase or decrease your self-esteem. Assume that you are asked to lunch by a coworker, Jamie. You could say to yourself, "I guess Jamie likes my company and would enjoy having lunch with me—perhaps to discuss something important." You could also say, "Jamie probably needs a favor and thinks I'm the sucker who will do it. That schemer probably doesn't care about me at all and is using lunch to set me up." The first interpretation enhances your self-esteem; the second decreases it.

The next time you find yourself in an ambiguous situation, try to analyze how much your interpretation reflects or affects your self-esteem. Do you tend to interpret situations positively or negatively? If you tend to interpret situations negatively or make negative statements, your self-esteem is likely low. If your interpretations or statements are predominantly positive, your self-esteem is likely high.

If you want to change, you must first recognize your problem.

To determine whether you are interpreting a situation negatively, the next time you find yourself in an ambiguous situation, ask yourself these questions:

1. Is what I am saying really true?

2. Am I being unfair?

3. Is there something bothering me that has nothing to do with this issue?

4. Am I responding to the other person or using her or him as a scapegoat?

If your analysis indicates that you view matters negatively, consider focusing on the positive. Make the choice to change your interpretation.

ELIMINATING YOUR SELF PUT-DOWNS

A third method for enhancing your self-esteem is to attack your self put-downs. We are all experts at putting ourselves down. We know all our weaknesses, including the ones most vulnerable to attack. The book *Vulture: A Modern Allegory on the Art of Putting Oneself Down* describes self put-downs in terms of vultures.[30] Consider, for a moment, the real vulture, an unattractive bird with sharp claws and a pointy beak whose favorite activity is picking on the weak, the helpless, and, preferably, the dead. It dives into the flesh and picks away at it.

The imaginary, psychological vulture, is similar to that bird: It is ugly and hungry, eager to pounce on its psychological food—your self-concept. Every self put-down is a call to the bird to attack. It screams to the bird that you are weak, helpless, and ailing in self-concept. What do you call yourself when you lock your keys in the car? What do you call yourself when you trip over the edge of the carpet? Every self put-down— "Idiot!" "Klutz!"—summons the vultures.

Put-downs may be either obvious or subtle. The obvious ones have a clear physical referent, like the keys dangling in the ignition of the locked car or the frayed edge of the carpet on which you tripped. The subtle put-downs impose limitations on you that, though not obvious, are destructive. Some typical ones are:

"I could never jog five miles a day."

"I could never write a paper longer than ten pages."

"I could never stick to a diet for more than a week."

"I just can't stop smoking."

Vultures tend to congregate in six areas. There are *intelligence vultures* ("I'm dumb," "I'm terrible in math," "I'm no good at foreign languages"); *creativity vultures* ("I'm not imaginative," "I can't draw as well as she can," "I can't sing like he sings"); *family vultures* ("I'm the odd-ball in the family," "I should do more for my parents," "My brother is the favorite child"); *relationship vultures* ("I'm no good at meeting people," "I can't make friends," "I'm boring"); *physical vultures* ("I'm too short/tall/fat/thin," "My fingers are fat," "My teeth are crooked"); and *sexual vultures* ("I'm not sexy," "I'm boring in bed").

The results of self put-downs are obvious: You avoid the areas where the vultures lurk. Math vultures keep you out of math classes, creativity vultures stop you from sharing your drawings, family vultures may keep you from visiting your family, relationship vultures inhibit you from speaking to people at parties, and physical vultures ensure that you wear clothes to hide this or that part of your body. You act and communicate how you feel.

To kill off your vultures, follow this five-step process:[31]

1. Pat yourself on the back by saying something good and true about yourself. You can surely think of something for which to compliment yourself.

2. Pat someone else on the back by saying something good and true about her or him. Not only will you feel good about yourself for complimenting another person, but you'll also find that compliments beget compliments.

3. Recognize your self put-downs. This is hard because you probably utter so many put-downs every day. To make sure you catch them all, you may want to ask a friend for help. Be sure to identify both the obvious and the subtle ones (and don't argue when your friend points them out). This step is crucial: You can't change what you don't recognize!

4. Block each put-down. As you hear it coming out, put your hand over your mouth (literally, if you have to). Soon you'll feel a negative statement coming and you'll be able to head it off before you say it.

5. Turn the put-down around. Put it in the past tense and eliminate its evaluative component. For example, when you trip over the edge of the carpet, say, "I used to be *clumsy,* but I'm not anymore. I *tripped,* that's all, and that's human."

As you work on raising your self-esteem, remember to be realistic: Don't expect too much too soon! Plan on some hard work. You view yourself as you do because you get some payoff, some desirable outcome, even if it doesn't *seem* desirable; for example, you get to sulk, or you get to feel sorry for yourself because people ignore you, or you get an excuse for being a poor student. Changing your self-concept and self-esteem means giving up the old rewards for new and better ones.

Communication Competency Checkup

The goal of this Communication Competency Checkup is to guide you in putting your skills and knowledge about conceiving the self to use and to help you summarize the material in this chapter.

Imagine that the person standing off to one side, who seems to be avoiding interaction with the other party-goers, complains to you that he doesn't like himself and thus avoids people.

1. What can you do to help him identify the elements of his self-concept that may be responsible for his problem?

2. With an understanding of the thoughts and feelings he has about himself, how would you identify his idealized self, his "should" self, and the self he presents to others? How would an understanding of these different aspects of self help him understand the present situation and his problem?

3. Develop three strategies (specific behaviors) for helping him improve his self-esteem: one for helping him confront his "should" messages and replace them with more realistic goals, one for helping him recognize the unreasonableness of his negative interpretations and focus instead on the positive aspects of the situations in which he finds himself, and one for eliminating his self put-downs by substituting statements that recognize being human means accepting imperfection.

4. Assume people at the party are from a variety of cultures. What specific advice could you give him to ward off possible culture shock?

NOTES

1. Akbar Javidi and Manoochehr Javidi, "Cross-Cultural Analysis of Interpersonal Bonding: A Look at East and West," *Howard Journal of Communications* 3 (Summer/Fall 1991): 131.

2. Mary Ann Scheirer and Robert E. Kraut, "Increasing Educational Achievement via Self-Concept Change," *Review of Education Research* 49 (1979): 131–50.

3. For detailed descriptions of the various ways the content of self-concept has been described, see Ronald B. Adler, Lawrence B. Rosenfeld, and Neil Towne, *Interplay,* 6th ed. (Fort Worth, TX: Harcourt Brace, 1995), chapters 2 and 3; William H. Fitts, *The Self-Concept and Self-Actualization* (Nashville, TN: Counselor Recordings and Tests, 1971), chapters 1 and 2; Morris Rosenberg, *Conceiving the Self* (New York: Basic Books, 1979), chapter 1; and L. Edward Wells and Gerald Marwell, *Self-Esteem: Its Conceptualization and Measurement* (Beverly Hills, CA: Sage, 1976), especially chapter 3.

4. Diana Rowland, *Japanese Business Etiquette* (New York: Warner Books, 1985), 91.

5. John W. Santrock, *Life-Span Development,* 4th ed. (Dubuque, IA: Wm. C. Brown, 1992), 261.

6. Thomas M. Steinfatt, "Personality and Communication: Classical Approaches," in *Personality and Interpersonal Communication,* ed. James C. McCroskey and John A. Daly (Newbury Park, CA: Sage, 1987).

7. Adapted from Sandra L. Bem, "The Measurement of Psychological Androgyny," *Journal of Consulting and Clinical Psychology* 42 (1974): 155–62. The original inventory developed by Bem contains sixty items: twenty masculine, twenty feminine, and twenty neutral (neither masculine nor feminine exclusively).

8. For a summary of research conducted on communicator characteristics, see Howard Giles and Richard L. Street, Jr., "Communicator Characteristics and Behavior," in *Handbook of Interpersonal Communication,* ed. Mark L. Knapp and Gerald R. Miller (Beverly Hills, CA: Sage, 1985), 205–62. Another useful source is Don E. Hamachek, *Encounters with the Self,* 3rd ed. (Fort Worth, TX: Harcourt Brace, 1992).

9. Harrison G. Gough, *Manual for the California Psychological Inventory* (Palo Alto, CA: Consulting Psychologists Press, 1956); Allen L. Edwards,

Manual for the Edwards Personal Preference Schedule (New York: The Psychological Corporation, 1959); Raymond B. Cattell, *16PF* (Champaign, IL: The Institute for Personality and Ability Testing, 1969).

10. Adapted from an instrument developed by Milton Rokeach in *Understanding Human Values* (New York: Free Press, 1979). The original questionnaire contains eighteen "to be" and eighteen "to have" values.

11. The values here were those ranked one through nine by the national samples from 1968 through 1981. See Milton Rokeach and Sandra Ball-Rokeach, "Stability and Change in American Value Profiles, 1968–1981," *American Psychologist* 44 (1989): 775–84.

12. Edward T. Hall, *The Dance of Life* (New York: Doubleday, 1983), 66–67.

13. Hall, *The Dance of Life,* 106–7.

14. Theodore Gochenour, *Considering Filipinos* (Yarmouth, ME: Intercultural Press, 1990), 23.

15. I. Burkitt, *Social Selves: Theories of the Social Formation of Personality* (Newbury Park, CA: Sage, 1992); Rosenberg, *Conceiving the Self.*

16. William B. Swann, Richard M. Wenzlaff, Douglas S. Krull, and Brett W. Pelham, "Allure of Negative Feedback: Self-Verification Striving among Depressed Persons," *Journal of Abnormal Psychology* 101 (1992): 293–306.

17. Fitts, *The Self-Concept and Self-Actualization.*

18. According to George Herbert Mead, an important prerequisite for developing a concept of self is the ability to take the perspective of others and view yourself as others view you. George Herbert Mead, *Mind, Self, and Society* (Chicago: University of Chicago Press, 1934).

19. Rosenberg, *Conceiving the Self.*

20. Charles Pavitt, "Biases in the Recall of Communicators' Behaviors," *Communication Reports* 2 (1989): 9–15.

21. Rosenberg, *Conceiving the Self.*

22. Items are based on descriptions of several of the irrational beliefs discussed in Albert Ellis and Robert Harper, *A New Guide to Rational Living* (North Hollywood, CA: Wilshire Books, 1977).

23. Kurt Vonnegut, Jr., *Mother Night* (New York: Dell Books, 1966), v.

24. In two books—*The Presentation of Self in Everyday Life* (Garden City, NY: Doubleday, 1959) and *Relations in Public* (New York: Basic Books, 1971)—Erving Goffman describes "facework," the verbal and nonverbal behaviors in which we engage to maintain a particular presenting image and that we also use to help others maintain their own presenting images. According to Goffman, each of us "scripts" our behavior, much like a playwright scripts a play, to achieve certain goals. Also see M. R. Leary and R. M. Kowalski, "Impression Management: A Literature Review and Two-Component Model," *Psychological Bulletin* 107 (1990): 34–47.

25. According to Swann et al.'s research, "Allure of Negative Feedback," maintaining low self-esteem may be as important a goal as maintaining high self-esteem. The point is to be stable and consistent, whether with low or high self-esteem.

26. Adapted from the Rosenberg Self-Esteem Scale, in Morris Rosenberg, *Conceiving the Self.*

27. Adapted from items presented in the *Tennessee Self-Concept Scale* (Nashville, TN: Counselor Recordings and Tests, 1964).

28. Don E. Hamachek, *Encounters with Others: Interpersonal Relationships and You* (New York: Holt, Rinehart, and Winston, 1982). For an argument *against* the importance of self-esteem, especially as it relates to academic achievement, see Randall Edwards, "Is Self-Esteem Really All That Important?," *APA [American Psychological Association] Monitor* (May 1995): 43–44.

29. William B. Gudykunst and Stella Ting-Toomey, *Culture and Interpersonal Communication* (Newbury Park, CA: Sage, 1988).

30. Sidney B. Simon, *Vulture: A Modern Allegory on the Art of Putting Oneself Down* (Niles, IL: Argus Communications, 1977).

31. The steps to killing off vultures are adapted from those presented by Simon in *Vulture,* 34–44.

CHAPTER 3

THE SELF AND OTHERS

COMMUNICATION COMPETENCIES

This chapter examines the self and others. Specifically, the objective of this chapter is for you to learn to:

- Describe how you perceive objects and people.
- Explain the role of self-fulfilling prophecies in your interactions with others.
- Apply several techniques for increasing your perceptual accuracy.
- Learn how to express your emotions.

KEY WORDS

The key words in this chapter are:

perception
selective perception
selective organization
selective interpretation
self-fulfilling prophecy
self-serving bias
empathy
emotion
labeling
stuffing

Read the following events concerning graduation at Somewhere State College.

When it came to graduation ceremonies, Dale was not interested in wearing a cap and gown. A call to the Dean of Students' office confirmed that a cap and gown were not required to attend graduation. In order to be sure, Dale called back a second time, spoke to another person, and was given the same information. Dale attended graduation wearing nice clothes, but without a cap and gown. Shortly before Dale got in line for the march into the stadium, the Dean of Students came up and asked if there was a problem. Learning that Dale did not intend to wear a cap and gown (and agreeing that there was no rule requiring one), she offered to supply one—free. Dale said, "Thank you, this is not a matter of money, I just prefer not to wear one." A few minutes later the college's Vice President approached Dale, offered a cap and gown, and pointed out the possible embarrassment to everyone when Dale went on stage to accept the diploma without the traditional collegiate garb. "I understand," Dale said, "but I consider a cap and gown the symbol of what's wrong with education: pomp and ceremony without a real concern for learning." After some discussion, the Vice President offered to get Dale's diploma and present it before the regular ceremony began. Dale, indicating no desire to embarrass anyone, agreed. The Vice President gave Dale the diploma and Dale went off to sit in the stands and watch the ceremony.

If you were a member of the administration, how would you interpret the events? How would you interpret the events if you were a member of the planning committee? If you were a campus protester? A parent? A member of a minority culture? A member of a culture that valued collectivism? A member of a culture that valued individualism?

How do *you* interpret the story, and what does that interpretation of the story tell about how you perceive specific events? How you perceive the particular events of the story—and, in an important sense, all the "stories" in your life—is reflected in how you communicate about the story, including your interpretation of it.

What the questions concerning Dale's story are alluding to, of course, is the entire process of perception. More specifically, how your perceptions of people and events influence how you communicate in your world. To better understand the perception process, this chapter examines (1) the constituents of perception, (2) how you can increase your perceptual accuracy, and (3) the role of emotional expression in perception.

PERCEPTION

Perception is the process of becoming aware of objects and events, including yourself and others. How you perceive yourself forms the basis for your perception of the world, and how you perceive the world both affects and reflects how you communicate.

Perception is an *active* process; the world may offer an infinite variety of details, but it does so passively. You need to make sense of the random pieces of information presented: You need to determine what you will perceive, how you will organize it, and how you will interpret it. *You* are the *cause* of what you perceive; you are the one in control, the one who determines what you perceive.

The physical dimensions of perception are pretty much the same for all people. Sensations that bombard us move through our nervous system to our brains and there are given meaning. However, the meaning also is affected by our *individual* and *cultural* differences. A careful reading of the sentence just before this one should bring to mind many examples that make the point that meaning and perception are different for different people because of their individual and cultural differences. Take the simple instance of a dog. While one person might see a dog and be frightened because of past experiences, another person, who breeds dogs, will have a different internal response to seeing a dog. There are cultural variations for this example, too. In much of North America dogs are pets; however, in some parts of the world people eat dogs. And moving from the perception of dogs to the perception of people, greater variations may be found. In North American culture, for example, people might respond positively to those who "speak their mind," yet this same behavior would produce an unfavorable interpretation in most Asian cultures that value cooperation and politeness more than individual assertiveness.

Based on this understanding of the concept of perception, on what features of Dale's graduation ceremony did you *choose* to focus? How did you *choose* to put those pieces together to make a coherent story? What meaning did you *choose* to derive from the story? Your answers to these questions reflect your individual and cultural perceptions. So that you might be able to appreciate the complexity of those perceptions, we now consider the perception process, including selective perception, selective organization, and selective interpretation.

SELECTIVE PERCEPTION

We are bombarded with information from television, radio, magazines, friends, family, and teachers. The data available to your senses are too many to be grasped in their totality. You, therefore, need to engage in **selective perception;** that is, you need to choose what to focus your attention on. What you choose to perceive—whether that choice is conscious or not—determines the subject matter of your communication.

What you choose is usually contingent on two factors. First, forces *outside* of us greatly influence what we select to focus on. Second, there are determinants that reside *within* us. An examination of these factors will help you understand why you experience and react to the world the way you do.

We see things not as they
are, but as we are.
H. M. TOMLINSON

External Forces

Stimuli, whether objects or people, that are brighter, more intense, moving, larger or easily distinguishable from their surroundings in some other way are more likely to attract your attention than are objects that seem to fade into the background. You focus

on the Hawaiian shirt at a formal party, the tallest building on a street, the loudest person in a room, or Dale without a cap and gown—because these things stand out. Of course, the choice to pay attention is yours. You can choose to concentrate on the sea of black tuxedos instead of the colorful shirt, the entire skyline instead of one skyscraper, the hum of voices instead of the loudest one, or the uniform caps and gowns instead of the lone person without academic garb.

Internal Forces

An object's distinctiveness is one determinant of selection. Another is *you.* Think for a moment. Isn't it true that if you're hungry, restaurant signs attract your attention; if you're in a bad mood, possible insults receive your focus; and if you want company, people passing by may draw your notice? Your interests, motives, emotions, and needs help determine what part of the outside world you let inside. It is also important to keep in mind that what you select and give meaning to may not be the same as that of the person standing next to you: None of us can ever truly "see" what another person sees, feel what another person feels.

The Selection Process

The selection process is essentially the same whether you choose to focus on people or objects. What the person or object looks like in comparison to the context, together with your own needs, wants, and desires, determines where you focus your attention and what you select to perceive.

If the focus of your attention is a person or a personal characteristic, something else happens—you make a *snap judgment*. When the Hawaiian shirt grabs your attention at a formal party, you may immediately decide that its wearer is either a jerk or an individualist you want to know better.

Snap judgments—conclusions reached rapidly with little forethought, which usually relate to liking or disliking—are based on your past experiences with similar people or characteristics or on cultural stereotypes. Snap judgments help you decide whether to continue focusing your attention on the person. If your initial judgment is positive, you'll choose to gather more and more clues from the person; if your judgment is negative, you'll dismiss the person from your attention and move on to other aspects of your environment.

The speed with which you make these judgments is often a reflection on your culture. Cultures that tend to be impulsive, such as those of North America, are quick to reach conclusions and take action. North Americans often admire characters played by Clint Eastwood and Sylvester Stallone because they are swift in taking action when faced with problems, yet in many Asian cultures people frequently learn to be reflective and arrive at a course of action at a slower pace. For example, if a teacher asks her kindergarten students to draw pictures of their families, the Japanese-American children probably would think about their pictures before they began sketching, whereas the European-American children most likely would start drawing immediately.

SELECTIVE ORGANIZATION

Once you've chosen what to attend to, your next task is to organize the information in a way that makes it possible to interpret. To understand the information you amass, you must be able to see how parts relate to each other and how the parts interrelate to form the whole. **Selective organization** is the process of fitting together the information you selectively perceive to form a whole. Just as what to perceive is your choice, so is how to organize it.

General tendencies guide how you organize what you perceive. You tend to accentuate details that you consider essential and minimize those that seem less important to you, to fill in gaps so that details relate easily and logically to each other and eliminate details that don't fit or make sense, and put all the information you gather into a context that facilitates a recognizable pattern.

You would organize the material you heard while listening to a speech on affirmative action quotas in one way if you were a lawyer specializing in affirmative action cases, in another way if you were a person discriminated against, and yet in a different way if you were a student writing a term paper on affirmative action. If you were a lawyer, you would selectively perceive data related to legal issues and organize them into a coherent speech, filling in gaps left when the speaker handled other topics. You would probably place the information into a recognizable pattern such as "arguments in favor of X," or "arguments against X." If you were a victim of discrimination, you would focus on information related to your particular problem and, like the lawyer, fill in gaps and eliminate anything that seemed irrelevant; you also might create a pattern out of the pieces you accumulate, such as "useful" versus "useless" information. If

FIGURE 3.1   Perception and Context

you were a student new to the topic, you might take notes quickly, not sure what to focus on, but hoping that the speaker's tone of voice and method of organization would offer clues about what to report on later. Regardless of your purpose, you must organize the speaker's words—often without consciously thinking about it—so that meaning can be attributed to them. If a speaker does not organize a speech in a way that is meaningful to you, all you reap is a collection of unrelated, irrelevant facts.

The goal of filling in details (or eliminating them) is to create a unified whole of the information you receive. Hold your hand over the bottom line of Figure 3.1. What do you see? Now cover the top line and read the bottom one. What do you see?

Although the letters are fully formed, you probably have no trouble organizing the top line into A, B, and C, and the bottom line into 12, 13, and 14. If you take another look at the middle figures of both lines, however, you may notice that they are the same. Because you created a context out of the surrounding figures, you determined that the middle figure is a B in the first line and a 13 in the second line. The other possible sequences—A, 13, C, and 12, B, 14—seem illogical because you have been raised in a culture where A's, B's, and C's, like 12's, 13's, and 14's, come in packages. The selective organization process is essentially the same for a person as it is for objects, letters, or numbers. For example, you commonly add details to people who are the focus of attention. Research shows that if you perceive someone as attractive, you add positive traits such as *kind, friendly, smart,* and *happy.* And you tend to add negative traits to complete the picture of someone who is less attractive.[1]

Ways of Organizing Perceptions of Others

There are two primary approaches to organizing impressions of other people. The first assumes that *traits interact with each other* to form the total picture of a person.[2] Traits are not independent of each other; rather, they combine and assume relative importance to form the overall impression. Consider these characteristics you might perceive of someone:

intelligent

skillful

industrious

cold

determined

practical

cautious

What would be your overall impression of a person who possesses these traits? How do the traits interact to form your impression? One way to determine the answer to this question is by simple substitution. Consider these characteristics you might perceive of someone:

industrious

skillful

intelligent

warm

practical

cautious

determined

This second list substitutes *warm* for *cold* and rearranges the characteristics. Did your impression change dramatically? Some traits are central to an overall impression, so changing any or all of them changes the impression. Your response to the first list might have been that this is an unhappy, stingy person who is unpopular. But after substituting *warm* for *cold,* as in the second list, you might think that this is a generous, happy, good-natured person.

Although the warm-cold trait is central when you evaluate a person's sociability, it becomes less important when you evaluate honesty. In such cases, the blunt-polite trait probably is more central. Which traits are central depends on the nature of the evaluation.

The second approach to organizing your impressions takes form from *your ideas about the behaviors that characterize particular types of people or how people should behave in certain situations.* You have ideas about how certain types of people, such as extroverts, introverts, students, teachers, parents, and children should behave. You also have ideas about what certain events, such as lectures, wedding ceremonies, and football games, should be like. You use these ideas to organize what you see and to make predictions about what else you should or should not see. You therefore evaluate what you see according to how well it fits your idea of what the person or event should be like. For example, if you think graduation ceremonies are very serious and important events, you might attribute characteristics such as "immature" and "closed-minded" to Dale for not wanting to wear the traditional graduation costume. If you think of them

THE CHRONICLE OF HIGHER EDUCATION   MISCHA RICHTER AND HARALD BAKKEN

Reprinted from *The Chronicle of Higher Education.* By permission of Mischa Richter and Harald Bakken.

as frivolous and unimportant, you might attribute "strong-willed" and "clear-thinking" to Dale.

Perceiving people is different from perceiving objects, if for no other reason than that you normally have many more things in common with another person than you do with an object. When the focus of perception is a person, you attribute qualities to the person that, for you, seem to go together. For example, *happy* and *independent* may be related in your mind, so that someone you perceive as happy you also perceive as independent. As with everything else, who you are determines what you attribute to another person. In someone you like, you see characteristics that you value for yourself; in someone you dislike, you see characteristics that you find objectionable for yourself. If you are proud of your ability to run long distances, you'll admire this trait in others. If you dislike your tendency to shout when you're angry, you'll dislike this trait in others.

It is important to keep in mind that most of the traits you value are those that stem from your cultural background. If, for example, you like people who act young, behave aggressively, are competitive, and like to keep busy, it is because you learned that those were traits to be admired. On the other hand, if you had been brought up in another culture, you might not admire those traits.

Selective perception and selective organization are not static events—events that occur and then stop, fixed. Rather, they are ongoing, dynamic processes that change and grow as new information is acquired and old information is discarded. Indeed, the process of perceiving another person is a complex one. It requires gathering bits and pieces of information from the other's appearance and behavior and assuming those bits and pieces represent who and what the other person is. We gather information about another person—and continue gathering information—in several ways.

First, it may be the case that you form an impression of another person before meeting her or him. Personal experience tells you that you can construct an image of another person based on what someone else tells you. Think for a moment of the profile you draw of a person if a friend tells you, "I think you'll like Marta. She's on the debate team, active in campus politics, an A student, and just finished an internship with the Honor Court." This material alone tells you something about Marta.

Second, perceptions of another person are influenced by nonverbal data. The notion of "first impressions" refers to inferences drawn immediately about another person from nonverbal information. It takes little time to ascertain another's gender, approximate age, physical characteristics (tall/short, thin/stout), and clothing. With the briefest visual encounter a mental picture can be drawn in seconds and decisions can be made—whether accurate or not—about a person's neatness, temperament, attractiveness, trustworthiness, integrity, and a host of other traits. Of course, nonverbal information continues to be used while interacting with the other person. How often does the person smile? Is the person's handshake positive? How does the person smell? What is the person's posture? Answers to these and a hundred other questions help us decide who our partner is and what she or he is like.

Third, what the person says also contributes to our continuously developing impression of her or him. Go over this list of sentences and imagine how your picture of the person would be influenced by the comments:

"I'm a brain surgeon."

"I don't like following rules. In fact, rules are for fools!"

"Actually, I own two cars, a BMW and a Mercedes."

"When I really want good food I go to McDonald's."

"I think singles' bars are disgusting."

"I hate it when men call women 'girls.' "

Fourth, we draw our perceptions of other people from a variety of additional sources that may be either intentional and unintentional. For example, people provide clues to their character by the bumper stickers on their cars and the decorations in their offices. An anonymously written poem reminds us of all the subtle ways people provide us with information we use in forming perceptions of them.

You tell on yourself by the friends you seek,
By the very manner in which you speak,

By the way you employ your time,
By the way you make a dollar and a dime.

You tell what you are by the things you wear,
By the spirit in which your burdens you bear,

By the kinds of things at which you laugh,
By the records you play on your phonograph.

You tell what you are by the way you walk,
By the things in which you take delight while you talk.

You tell on yourself by the manner in which you bear defeat,
By even simple things, such as what you eat,

By the books you choose from a well-filled shelf,
In these ways, and more, you tell on yourself.

SELECTIVE INTERPRETATION

Interpreting what you perceive is just as much your choice as what you perceive and how you organize it. In **selective interpretation,** you choose how to explain the information you selectively perceive and selectively organize. How you interpret what you perceive depends on who you think you are, who you would like to be, and who you think you should be. It also depends on your knowledge and expectations of the people and objects in your environment as well as how you feel at the moment.[3] How involved you are with the other person and how happy you think your relationship is are additional influences on how you interpret what you perceive.[4] Many variables enter into your interpretation of what you perceive, which is why two individuals' perceptions are never the same. Just as no two people are identical, no two interpretations are identical.

How do you think the member of the college administration interpreted the "problem" with Dale (even using the word *problem* implies an interpretation)? Would the administrator think, "Why does this have to happen to me? Why can't these kids just cooperate?"

How do you think a member of the Student Planning Committee for Graduation would interpret the event? Would the committee member think, "This gives all students a black eye. Why can't some people just go along with graduation traditions, even if they think they're stupid?"

How do you think a campus radical would interpret Dale's behavior? Would the radical think, "Finally, someone stood up to the fascist administration!"?

And what about Dale's parents? Would they sigh and think, "What did we do wrong raising Dale?" (or, conversely, "What did we do right?").

What might the school administrators have done if Dale were a member of a racial minority, an active member of the school's Gay and Lesbian Society, or an international exchange student? And, how might Dale as a minority or other-culture person have interpreted the administrator's behavior?

Because different people perceive things differently, it is important to realize that how you perceive things reflects who you are, just as how others perceive things reflect who they are—the point is that perceptions are "different," and not, necessarily, "right or wrong." One way to understand this is to develop the ability to generate alternative perspectives of any given person, idea, or event. Skill Development 3.1 provides you with the opportunity to develop alternative interpretations for the same event.

Skill Development 3.1

DEVELOPING ALTERNATIVE INTERPRETATIONS

You have just finished working on a class project and Sandy tells you, "I had a great time working with you. I hope we can work together again sometime." Briefly explain how you would interpret Sandy's remarks in each of the following circumstances.

1. You see yourself as a desirable person.

2. You see yourself as desirable, but you assume that Sandy says something nice because doing so is just good etiquette.

3. You see yourself as desirable, assume Sandy says something nice because it is polite, but you have a bad stomach ache.

4. You feel that your interpersonal skills are weak and that you are boring.

5. You perceive that Sandy's remark is a prelude to a sexual advance.

> Some things have to be believed to be seen.
> RALPH HODGSON

After you selectively perceive and organize cues from another person— whether they are nonverbal or verbal—you attribute a motive to the person, make a general judgment, and finish by making a prediction. For example, here are possible answers to Skill Development 3.1:

1. "Sandy wants to work with me again because Sandy thinks I'm a nice person. I can expect Sandy to like me more and more as we continue to get to know each other."

2. "Sandy acted politely because Sandy is a polite person who can be expected to behave politely in the future."

3. "Sandy kept talking because Sandy could see I was in pain and wanted to inflict further pain on me. Sandy is a cruel person who can be expected to try to hurt me whenever the opportunity arises!"

4. "I know I'm boring, so it's obvious Sandy is lying and I can expect Sandy to lie to me in the future—except we'll probably never work together again."

5. "Sandy was nice to me as a prelude to sexual advances! What kind of fool does Sandy think I am?" (Or, "I must really be desirable if Sandy is interested in me.")

What determines what you select to perceive? What determines how you organize what you select to perceive? What determines how you interpret what you selectively perceive and organize? With answers to these questions, you can learn a great deal about yourself and your own perception process. Knowledge Checkup 3.1 will help you begin to understand your own perception process and what it reveals about you by focusing on your perception of an ambiguous picture.

Knowledge Checkup 3.1

ANALYZING YOUR PERCEPTION PROCESS

Describe what you see in the picture. The picture is ambiguous. Because it presents a great deal of information that is unorganized and uninterpreted, there is no right or wrong way to perceive it.

1. What details of the picture do you select to perceive?
2. How do you organize the details you select to create a whole story?
3. How do you interpret the details that you select to perceive and organize?
4. What does your description of the picture—what you selectively perceive, selectively organize, and selectively interpret—tell you about yourself and your perception process? Do you believe that others will perceive the picture in the same way?

What you chose to see in the picture, how you chose to put the details together, and how you chose to make sense of the details reflect what is important to you. Were you more concerned with the two people than where they were? Did you describe their physical characteristics? Did you go into detail about their relationship, and, if you did, how did you describe it? Did you perceive the scene as calm or tense? What does your perception of this picture tell about who you are?

THE SELF-FULFILLING PROPHECY

What you believe about yourself and others has a tendency to come true. This notion is called the **self-fulfilling prophecy.**[5] Consider, for example, the likely outcomes of the earlier interactions with Sandy. If you believe that you are a good person and that Sandy recognizes this (as in the first situation), you are likely to behave nicely the next time you two are together, which should increase the probability that Sandy will, indeed, treat you nicely. If you believe that Sandy was simply polite and didn't care about you as a person (the second scenario), you might treat Sandy distantly and politely the next time you are together, which should increase the probability that you will be treated likewise. If you believe that Sandy intends to harm you (the third case), you might be suspicious of Sandy's every move, convinced that danger lurks in every behavior; if you continue behaving accordingly, Sandy just might treat you unkindly. If you believe that you are boring, you might avoid talking or enthusiastically listening to what Sandy says, and Sandy just might think you're boring. And if you felt Sandy was making sexual advances that you were not interested in, you might avoid Sandy in the future; if you were flattered by Sandy's advance, you might seek Sandy out in hopes of fulfilling your fantasy.

People behave in ways that increase the probability that their beliefs about themselves and others will come true. Consider how the self-fulfilling prophecy applies to the man in the following conversation. His basic belief was that he couldn't get any love. He was asked, "From whom can you get love? Anyone?" His responses, and the prompting questions, went like this:

"No, not anyone. The person needs to be a woman."

"Any woman?"

"No, she needs to be between eighteen and forty years of age."

"Any woman between eighteen and forty?"

"No, she needs to have long red hair."

"Any woman between eighteen and forty with long red hair?"

"No, she needs to have blue eyes."

"Any woman between eighteen and forty, with long red hair and blue eyes?"

"No, she also needs to be between 5'3" and 5'7"."

"Any woman between eighteen and forty, with long red hair and blue eyes, between 5'3" and 5'7"?"

"No, she also needs a college degree."

"Any woman between eighteen and forty, with long red hair and blue eyes, between 5'3" and 5'7", with a college degree?"

"No, she needs to have a degree in the helping professions, such as teaching, nursing, or social work."

"Any woman between eighteen and forty, with long red hair and blue eyes, between 5'3" and 5'7", with a college degree in the helping professions?"

"No, there's one more requirement. She has to love me—first."

"And what's the problem?"

"I'm unlovable."

This man created his own experience of "getting no love" by making his requirements so strict that few women could possibly meet them. But if even one person matched his description, the final obstacle *guaranteed* that his prophecy would come true: He was unlovable. He could never perceive being loved because he *saw himself as unlovable.* So before his experiences could change, his self-perception needed to change. He was the cause of his experience.

Similarly, *you* are the cause of *your* experiences.

COMMON PROBLEMS IN PERCEPTION

There are common tendencies in perception that may cause problems as people interact. Four of these tendencies are that we judge ourselves less harshly than we judge others, we focus on what is most obvious, we adhere to first impressions, and we assume other people are like us.

The tendency to judge ourselves less harshly than we judge others is called the **self-serving bias.** This tendency typically manifests itself in our attribution of blame when something goes wrong. For example, when someone else fails to complete an assignment, it's because he didn't understand what to do (read: stupid) or was unmotivated (read: lazy), but when we fail to complete an assignment, it's because we had an emergency to attend to. The same reasoning applies when the perception is a self-perception and not an other-perception. Consider that when you build a complex electronic piece of equipment, you will tell anyone who will listen how smart, capable, and brave you are (for attempting the project in the first place). However, when the equipment fails to work, you are quick to blame "those idiots who can't write decent instructions!" The point is the same: To be charitable—especially to ourselves—we attribute failures to "outside forces," and when we judge more harshly, we attribute failures to personal inadequacies.

Being influenced by the obvious—what stands out most from its surroundings because it is brighter, more intense, louder, repetitious, unusual, and so on—is a problem when it curtails your seeking more information, such as more details of an event. For example, focusing exclusively on the graffiti on a wall because it is intense may keep you from seeing the beautiful skyline behind it or the colorful sunset reflected in the tall buildings beside it.

The fundamental delusion of humanity is to suppose that I am here and you are out there.
YASUTANI ROSHI

To keep our world stable, once we form an impression we tend to allow that impression to guide our selection, organization, and interpretation of new information. We try to confirm our first impression by fitting new information into it because that's easier than creating a new impression. People and events are complex, and accounting for each new piece of information is a difficult task. A first impression, by creating the context for all subsequent information, makes complex people and events easier to understand. If your first impression of Carlos is that he is self-centered, you may miss the fact that he is willing to help friends, to share his ideas freely, and to work hard on group projects, or you may interpret this information as an "exception" to how Carlos "really is." Complex people and events may be made simple and less complex by first impressions, but this may mean the loss or distortion of much potentially useful information.

Because the person we know best—indeed, the only person we *know*—is ourself, we tend to assume other people are like us. You like to read detective novels, so you assume other people do, too. You like to exercise, so you assume other people do, too. Of course, you know there are people who do not like either detective novels or exercising, but you *assume* they do until you are told otherwise.

By being aware of these four tendencies, you are a giant step toward avoiding them. Recognize when you judge yourself less harshly than you judge others, and avoid being quick to make judgments; instead, gather information and avoid boosting your own ego at others' expense. Instead of focusing on what is most obvious, take the time to look at other information available to you. First impressions are useful because they make life easier, but be careful not to avoid new and possibly conflicting information—remain open-minded and ready to alter your impression. Assuming other people are like you is a natural tendency, but problems may occur if you fail to test your assumptions, and you can do so simply by listening to what others tell you and by asking questions.

INCREASING PERCEPTUAL ACCURACY

Many issues need to be addressed before you can increase the accuracy of your perceptions. Given that *who you are determines what you perceive,* you may need to change even who you are in order to perceive things more accurately.

What you perceive is limited by what you believe. Picture yourself as a tube. At one end is a mesh screen through which you perceive your environment. If each thin wire in the screen were a belief, accumulating enough beliefs would mean that eventually nothing could get through. From the inside, all you could see would be your own screen. You would be trapped in your beliefs and they would cloud your view of reality. From inside the tube, everything would seem orderly, stable, and logical, resulting in the most dangerous of all beliefs: *What I see is what there is, and that is all there is.*

There are several things you can do to increase your perceptual accuracy. You can increase your imagination, stretch yourself, and expand what you are capable of perceiving. You can develop your ability to remain open-minded, and this will ensure you are ready to receive new information. And you can increase your ability to empathize with other people, to see things from their perspective.

STRETCH YOURSELF

Increasing your imagination expands what you are capable of perceiving. The more you can imagine, the more you can perceive. Begin with your senses, because it is through your senses that you perceive things. Skill Development 3.2 will help you develop your sense awareness.

Skill Development 3.2

INCREASING SENSE AWARENESS AND SENSE IMAGINATION

Increasing Sense Awareness

1. Close your eyes.
2. Sit quietly for two minutes. Be aware of your surroundings, such as the sounds and smells.
3. Open your eyes.
4. What did you hear?
5. What did you smell?
6. What did you taste?
7. What were you touching or what was touching you?
8. What did you see?
9. Close your eyes again for two minutes. Again concentrate on what each of your senses is taking in.
10. Open your eyes.
11. What did you notice as you sat with your eyes closed the second time? How did you perceive things as you focused on each of your senses?

Increasing Sense Imagination

1. What does winter *taste* like?
2. What is the *color* of worry?
3. What does time *feel* like?
4. What does a rainbow *sound* like?
5. What is the *smell* of silence?

To increase the accuracy of your perceptions, you need to break the habit of using your senses in usual ways and stop making common, automatic associations. Expand your imagination!

REMAIN OPEN-MINDED

To ensure accurate perceptions, you must be receptive to new information, assumptions, beliefs, and opinions, even when they seem to contradict your own positions. Increasing your perceptual accuracy requires, above all else, open-mindedness.

Being open-minded means recognizing that there may be more to see than you see, more to touch than you touch, more to hear than you hear, more to smell than you smell, more to taste than you taste—more to know about one subject, one person, or one world than you alone could ever know.

Being open-minded also means recognizing that you may perceive things that aren't there, eliminate inconvenient pieces of information, and otherwise push, pull, stretch, and bang the world to fit your preconceived notions.

Finally, being open-minded means recognizing that you may draw conclusions too quickly, state them too assuredly, and assume that if an answer works for you, it must work for everyone.

You can increase your open-mindedness by making yourself available to new and varied experiences. Your objective is to gain additional information about your world. The following are suggestions to help you increase your open-mindedness.

> When we describe what the other person is really like, I suppose we often picture what we want. We look through the prism of our need.
> ELLEN GOODMAN

1. *Talk to people.* The more you interact with others, the more you will learn and the greater your personal storehouse of varying perceptions will grow. Because each person sees the world differently, talking to others and listening to what they say provides you with a new perspective to consider.

2. *Share your perceptions and listen to the feedback you receive.* Avoid being defensive when you check your perceptions. Keep in mind that your view is a personal interpretation. You are entitled to your perception just as others are entitled to theirs. Your perception is right for you as others' perceptions are right for them. Be aware, however, that others may work very hard to make their perceptions your own, and you may also try to make your perceptions theirs.

3. *Deal with contradictions—don't ignore them.* Contradictions are often predictable once you recognize their origin, that is, that you are different from others as each of us is different from everyone else—so gather the contradictions, look at them, reconcile them when you can, and understand why you can't when you can't.

4. *Continue gathering information on a subject,* even after you have reached a decision. Recognize that what you know is only a fraction of what there is to know. Stay open to new information.

To be open-minded, you must accept change and be willing to adjust your thoughts and beliefs. There is no point in gathering new information if you don't intend to evaluate it and act on it.

INCREASE EMPATHY

To improve your perception of other people, you must strive to increase your **empathy,** your ability to experience the world as others do. Researchers in the area of interpersonal and intercultural communication competence believe that our success as communicators depends, to a large extent, on our skill at identifying with our communication partner.[6] When you empathize with another person, her or his experience becomes clearer to you, you begin to understand her or his reasons for behaving and feeling in particular ways, and you start to develop an understanding of these things as *the other person under-stands them.* The goal, although unachievable, is something like the Vulcan mind-meld that Mr. Spock performed occasionally on "Star Trek." Placing his fingertips on anoth-er's head, he and the other become one, and Spock comes to know the other person as the other person knows *himself or herself.*

Although earthbound creatures cannot perform a Vulcan mind-meld, attempts to achieve empathy may be made in other ways. For example, groups of students with physical disabilities have invited those who can walk to "spend the day paralyzed from the waist down," or those who can see to "spend the day blind," or those who can hear to "spend the day hearing impaired." With the help of wheelchairs, blindfolds, and earplugs, the participants enlarge their own perception of the world.

Incorrect assumptions about another person also may be revealed by engaging in role reversal. Switch positions with someone with whom you have an ongoing argu-ment, regardless of what the argument is about, and try to see the situation from the other's perspective. What does this person think, feel, and want? How does this person see you in the situation and interpret your behaviors? Empathy for the other person's position should provide insights that allow you to resolve your differences.

You might well imagine how difficult it is when the other person is from another culture. Empathy demands that we be able to infer the feelings and needs of another person. To do this we must, of course, know something about the other person. If the person is your best friend you have a great deal of knowledge about the ways he or she expresses himself or herself. Should that person be from another culture, one that is very or even slightly different from your own, it is difficult to know the meaning of many specific actions. If your friend is Italian, and you're not, you might consider him very talkative when he gets upset, and you can use that data to engage in role reversal and imagine how you feel when you are upset. If your friend is from a culture where silence has meaning, such as Korea, and you are not Korean, you can still strive to understand that behavior and, therefore, take on a particular role. Some people find it easier to empathize than others.[7]

To overcome some of the problems associated with empathizing with someone from another culture, you need to develop these five skills.[8] First, recognize that there are differences in the way people express themselves. Some individuals might shout in the company of strangers while others have learned to keep their emotions in check. Second, know yourself and how you respond to the unknown. Do you feel comfortable when confronted with ambiguous situations or do you work to overcome feelings of frustration? Third, try to gather information about the other person so you can under-stand the meaning behind his or her actions. Do members of the other's culture value openness or is the person part of a culture that values privacy? Fourth, using the information you have, try to put yourself in the other's place—from the point of view of his or her culture. Finally, take some action that demonstrates empathy. For example, if touching is acceptable behavior for the other person, you might consider touching him or her; if touching is not acceptable, you might consider refraining from any touching but telling the other person you care.

Unless you are a member of a helping profession—perhaps a psychologist, social worker, or nurse—your ability to empathize may not extend too far beyond the people with whom you share your most personal relationships. Empathy requires open-mindedly gathering information about the other person over long periods of time, while at the same time being aware of your own life experiences. Experiencing the death of a parent, a life-threatening illness, or a serious car wreck may arouse new emotions in you, emotions that may help you better empathize with others.

Too often people say, "I know how you feel," when a better reaction might be, "I can try to imagine . . . ."

How much empathy is there in one of your important friendships? Knowledge Checkup 3.2 should help you gather the information necessary to assess the degree of empathy in one of your friendship relationships.

Knowledge Checkup 3.2

ASSESSING EMPATHY IN FRIENDSHIP

The following questions can help you determine the degree to which empathy is part of a friendship. Select the closest personal friendship you have and respond to the questions based on that friendship.

1. Does your friend understand most of what you say?
2. Does your friend understand how you feel?
3. Does your friend appreciate what your experiences feel like to you?
4. Does your friend try to see things through your eyes?
5. Does your friend ask you questions about what your experiences mean to you?
6. Does your friend ask you questions about what you're thinking?
7. Does your friend ask you questions about how you're feeling?

Have your friend answer the same questions. Compare your answers. The results might well contribute to greater empathy in your relationship.

You may find the questions in Knowledge Checkup 3.2 useful as a guide for increasing your ability to empathize because they specify particular questions to consider.

Each question relates to the goals of increasing your understanding of what your communication partner says and how he or she feels, increasing your appreciation for what your partner's experiences feel like to him or her, increasing your ability to see things as your relational partner sees them, increasing the frequency with which you ask your partner what his or her experiences mean to him or her and what he or she is thinking and feeling.

As you would suspect, developing empathy is not an easy assignment. One of the most common obstacles is a constant self-focus. There is a German saying that "Everyone thinks that all the bells echo his own thoughts." Put in slightly different terms, most of us are somewhat self-absorbed and spend a great deal of time thinking about ourselves. It is difficult to gather information about another person if we are consumed with thoughts of ourselves. And remember, we need information about other people if we are to understand and respond to them appropriately.

Another obstacle to empathy is our tendency to note some features to the exclusion of others. If, for example, we notice a person's skin color or his family name, and from this limited data assume we know all there is to know about him, we are likely to do a poor job empathizing. While color and surname may provide some information about the other person, that information is extremely limited.

A third obstacle to empathy is our stereotyped notions concerning gender, race, and culture. If we believe that a *stereotype* (an unsupported generalization) is true, we may fail to see the person with whom we are communicating as a unique human being for whom the stereotype may not apply. People are much more complex than the stereotypes used to label and categorize them.

EMOTIONS AND PERCEPTION

Perhaps the most important determinant of your perceptions and reactions are your emotions. How you feel at a given moment—whether you're feeling confident or insecure, happy or sad—has more influence than other possible determinants on what you select to perceive, how you choose to organize it, and how you decide to interpret it. Although time and reflection, as well as new information, may alter your perception, your immediate response is based to a large extent on how you feel at the moment. For instance, if you feel confident, the reprimand from your boss may be seen as containing some positive remarks (selective perception), on the whole containing about half negative and half positive comments (selective organization), and, in the end, a call for improvement rather than a threat of being fired (selective interpretation). Of course, if you're feeling insecure, positive elements of the reprimand may be "unheard," and the message may be interpreted as, "One more problem and you're out of here!"

Emotions are feelings accompanied by physiological changes, such as increased respiration, and overt nonverbal manifestations, such as crying, shrugging, or smiling. Although physiological changes and overt manifestations are the primary components of emotions, a third aspect often is found: labeling. **Labeling** takes place when someone experiences particular physiological changes and overt manifestations and verbally declares the feelings being felt or displayed.[9] For example, "I'm feeling angry" may be declared when experiencing increased respiration, flushed face, tense and blaring voice, and a raised fist.

All human beings experience a wide range of emotions, although many choose to express a very limited number of them. Knowledge Checkup 3.3 provides you with the opportunity to acknowledge those emotions you express most often. What are some of your most-used or expressed emotions? (Your most-used or expressed emotions are those you *do,* not necessarily those you would *like* to do, *can* do, or *will* do.)

Knowledge Checkup 3.3

IDENTIFYING YOUR EMOTIONS

Check the emotions that you use or express—and so communicate—most often.

affectionate	alienated	angry
anxious	apathetic	ashamed
beaten	bewildered	brave
calm	caring	compassionate
confident	confused	creative
cruel	curious	defeated
depressed	desperate	disappointed
disgusted	eager	embarrassed
envious	evil	excited
exhilarated	fearful	fixated
flirtatious	frightened	frustrated
generous	gentle	glad
grateful	guilty	gutless
happy	hateful	hopeful
hopeless	hostile	hurt
hyper	impatient	incompetent
indecisive	inferior	insecure
insincere	isolated	jealous
joyful	lively	lonely
lovable	loving	lovestruck
melancholy	misunderstood	needy

_____ optimistic	_____ overwhelmed	_____ paranoid
_____ passionate	_____ peaceful	_____ phony
_____ playful	_____ pleased	_____ possessive
_____ preoccupied	_____ prejudiced	_____ pressured
_____ quiet	_____ rejected	_____ remorseful
_____ repulsed	_____ repulsive	_____ restrained
_____ sad	_____ sadistic	_____ secure
_____ seductive	_____ self-pitying	_____ self-reliant
_____ shy	_____ silly	_____ sincere
_____ sinful	_____ smug	_____ sorry
_____ stubborn	_____ stupid	_____ superior
_____ suicidal	_____ supported	_____ surprised
_____ suspicious	_____ sympathetic	_____ tender
_____ terrified	_____ touchy	_____ triumphant
_____ two-faced	_____ ugly	_____ unsure
_____ useless	_____ vindictive	_____ violent
_____ weary	_____ weepy	_____ youthful
_____ zany	_____ zippy	_____ zonked

If one or more of your most-used or expressed emotions isn't on this short list of all the possibilities, add it here:

_____

FAILURE TO EXPRESS EMOTIONS

How many emotions did you check in Knowledge Checkup 3.3? Although there are a large number of emotions that may be expressed, people typically express very few.[10] If you have one emotion you like to express often, it may be your "tool," your proven way to get things you want. For example, when you were a child and you were angry, you may have acted on your feelings by crying. If crying helped you then to release your anger, now, many years later, you may find that when you are angry you tend to cry.

If you have a small number of emotions you express, you are limiting the ways you can communicate the many and complex feelings you can experience. Limiting yourself this way poses a roadblock to communicating effectively.

Some people may limit themselves almost exclusively to one or two emotions, such as feeling angry and disappointed or happy and energetic, and some may strive to eliminate the expression of their emotions altogether. There are several reasons why people limit which emotions they experience and how often they express them. These reasons typically reflect a cultural attitude. For example, North Americans, the English, and Scandinavians tend to contain their emotions, while Italians and Spaniards tend to be emotionally expressive. Let's examine six concepts about emotions—which typically reflect a North American and Western European attitude—that should help you understand why you do or do not express your emotions.

First, emotions are hard to understand. They aren't logical. Rather, they are felt, and feelings often can't be diagnosed, analyzed, or fully understood. Because of the nature of emotions, many people are afraid of them, just as they are afraid of other things they have difficulty understanding and being logical about. This fear of emotions leads to a decrease in how often and how strongly they are expressed.

Second, people are often unaware of their emotions because they are taught to desensitize themselves to how they are feeling. For example, you may be feeling anger, but your companion convinces you that you're only "upset," or you may be feeling overjoyed, but your friends label your emotion as "happy." Eventually, if you accept others' perceptions, you become less sensitive to the extremes of your emotions, and this decreased sensitivity may lead to decreased awareness of them.

Third, many of us are taught, as part of the socializing process conducted by our parents, religious institutions, schools, and the media, that many of our emotions are bad and must be controlled. You may even have been taught to stuff your feelings. **Stuffing** is the process of pushing emotions inside rather than confronting and expressing them. For example, many North American boys are taught that it is not manly to cry, and many North American girls are conditioned to believe that it is "unladylike" and "improper" to overtly express anger. Holding back these strong emotions often has unfortunate consequences, including masking the feelings with food, alcohol, or drugs.

Fourth, people may fail to express their emotions for fear of exposing themselves. The reasoning goes like this: "If you know how I feel, you may use this information against me, or think I'm bad or stupid or wrongheaded." In order to protect yourself, you control your honest feelings so you do not give yourself away.

Fifth, many social and career roles limit the honest expression of feelings. In some cases the social expectations even describe which feelings are OK and which aren't— for instance, crying is OK at a funeral but not at a Jim Carrey movie. Certain professions limit the emotions that may be expressed. Doctors and nurses who are too sad or happy, and police officers who are anything but cool and detached run the risk of being perceived as unprofessional.

Sixth, many people are told not to embarrass others by displaying their feelings, feelings that would naturally be expressed through hearty laughter, loud vocal expressions, and physical touching. Ironically, if you constantly stuff your feelings your body often rebels. If you store up the hurts, the angers, and the glee, eventually the feelings will come out in other ways. Unexpressed feelings can manifest themselves physically through headaches, neck tightness, ulcers, heart attacks, high blood pressure, impotence, and insomnia. The need for an emotional outlet can lead to eating binges, physical and verbal abuse, and excessive sexual activity. These reactions are your body's way of saying, "I don't like what you're doing to me. You are denying me my natural right to feel. I won't be denied!" They are the body's way of warning, "By repressing my talent for expressing emotions, you're killing me."

Besides the physical reactions, the failure to experience emotions and to express felt emotions leads to an ever-increasing emotional incapacity. If you have been brought up in a family where you were restricted from letting out your felt emotions—"Stop being a sissy," "Be brave, keep up that stiff upper lip," "Stop that whining"—eventually, the denying and ignoring leads to your being desensitized to your own and others' emotions and you become unable to identify your own and others' feelings. The problem feeds on itself, growing larger and larger until a potentially rich emotional life becomes emotionally bleached and stagnant. With emotions, as with many other aspects of life, the problem is that you must "use it or lose it."

Finally, it should be clear that nearly all of the reasons why we often fail to express our emotions can be traced to our cultural, social, and psychological background. And it also should be clear that these reasons are multiple and complex. That is, a reluctance to let others see what is going on inside of you could stem from a cultural value that stresses self-restraint or from cultural definitions of sex roles that allow certain people to do one thing and deny that role to members of the opposite sex. A few concrete examples will help clarify this point. In the Korean culture people learn to conceal outward signs of emotion and, therefore, seldom project their emotions onto other people.[11] The Chinese also do not readily show emotion for reasons that are rooted deeply in their culture—the Chinese concept of "saving face" being one of the most important. For the Chinese, displaying emotion violates face-saving norms by disrupting harmony and causing interpersonal conflict.[12] For examples related to gender we need only turn to North American culture, where a woman can cry in public, but a man who cries in public is likely to get surprised looks and stares from passers-by.

How do you react emotionally to events you experience? Do you express what you feel, or do you attempt to stuff your feelings, cut them off, deny them—"control" them? Knowledge Checkup 3.4 provides you with the opportunity to examine your emotional reactions and to determine how you deal with the emotions you feel.

Knowledge Checkup 3.4

IDENTIFYING YOUR EMOTIONAL REACTIONS

Place a check mark before any of the following ways you deal with your emotions:

_____ 1. I react immediately if I feel a strong emotion, such as happiness, anger, or hurt.

_____ 2. I withdraw rather than tell someone how I feel, whether positive or negative.

_____ 3. I feel like crying, but I don't.

_____ 4. I get so mad I can't think straight.

_____ 5. I find someone I feel comfortable with and talk out my feelings.

_____ 6. I talk to myself and try to get rid of my feelings.

_____ **7.** I go and do something—physical exercise, write poetry—to get my mind off what's affecting me.

_____ **8.** I avoid expressing my feelings for fear of hurting other people's feelings or getting negative reactions.

_____ **9.** I physically or verbally attack the person whom I feel is causing my emotional hurt.

_____ **10.** I find someone to aggress against whether or not she or he is the person I feel is causing my emotional hurt.

_____ **11.** I determine whether this is a matter that must be dealt with now or can be put off until later.

_____ **12.** I recognize that I am in control of myself and I don't have to get angry, feel out of control, or show my feelings to others.

Review your answers. What did you learn about yourself as an expresser of emotions? Are you a stuffer (for example, did you check item 2, item 3, or item 8?)? Do you express your anger in hurtful ways—hurtful to yourself (did you check item 4?) and others (did you check item 9 or item 10?)? Do you attempt to cut off your emotions (did you check item 6, item 7, or item 11?)? Have you been desensitized to your emotions (did you check 12?)? Do you express your emotions at the time you feel them (did you check item 1?) or, if that is not possible, deal constructively with them in some other way (did you check item 5?)?

Dealing with your emotions by stuffing them, avoiding them, or cutting them off is not automatically "wrong." Rather, what matters is whether these methods of dealing with your emotions are *typical* or part of a *pattern.* Used now-and-again, none of these methods is "wrong," just as always expressing your emotions when you feel them is not always "right." Guidelines for expressing your emotions are covered later in this chapter.

GENDER AND EMOTIONS

There appear to be no differences in how women and men feel emotions.[13] Both are likely to feel nervous at job interviews and on first dates, get angry when someone is disrespectful, and feel lost and lonely when a relationship ends. However, even though the feelings may be similar, women and men often express their emotions differently.[14] Many North American males *do* fit the stereotype of "inexpressive," and many North American females *do* fit the stereotype of "demonstrative."

In the North American culture, women and men seem to have their own short-list of most-expressed emotions. Women, for example, are more likely to express feelings of vulnerability, sadness, loneliness, and embarrassment; men are unlikely to express these emotions, especially to their male friends, although they may express them to women with whom they share an intimate relationship. Men, on the other hand, are more likely to express positive emotions about their strengths; they also are more likely to express anger.

When it comes to recognizing others' emotions, most men and women differ in their detection ability. Research focusing on emotions portrayed in facial expressions, body movements, and vocal cues found that women were consistently more sensitive to these nonverbal cues and better able to determine the emotions expressed.[15] Differences in emotion detection are affected by several considerations. First, men are better able to recognize emotions in other men, and women are better able to recognize emotions in other women. Second, the more you know someone, the more sensitive you become to her or his particular expressions of emotion. Courting and married couples, for example, are better at recognizing each others' emotional states than they are at recognizing the emotional states of strangers. And third, when there is a power difference between communicators, as in a job interview, the less powerful person is better able to read the signals of the more powerful person, regardless whether the communicators are the same or opposite sex.[16]

EXPRESSING YOUR EMOTIONS

There is ample evidence that expressing emotions appropriately often promotes physical health,[17] greater relational intimacy,[18] and effective conflict resolution.[19] The key word, however, is *appropriately.* Some general principles for expressing your emotions provide the basis for the following six guidelines.

Identify Your Feelings

"I feel angry," "I feel wonderful," "I feel embarrassed," "I feel frustrated"—whatever the feeling, it is impossible to share what you feel unless you are aware of what you feel. In order to accomplish this, notice your physiological changes (what's happening in your body), your nonverbal behaviors (what your face looks like, what your voice sounds like, your posture, your gestures), your self-talk (what you tell yourself), and what you say to others (for example, telling someone you do not like something may help you get to the emotion behind "not liking," such as boredom, nervousness, or anger).

Realize that emotions do not always come in neat packages, allowing for easy classification. Often, we experience several emotions simultaneously, some more important than others.[20] Jealousy, for example, may be a combination of distress, anger, disgust, contempt, fear, and, perhaps, shame.[21] Disappointment is probably a combination of sadness and surprise, and love is probably some combination of joy and acceptance. Expressing one emotion without acknowledging or expressing the others is unfair to those with whom you are sharing—they do not get all the information they need—and may not allow you to deal with your feelings effectively.

Distinguishing your *primary,* or main, emotion from your *secondary,* or lesser, emotion provides you with the opportunity to share what is really most important to you. For example, consider the parent who, expecting his daughter home at midnight, greets her at the door at two in the morning when she finally arrives. The parent yells, threatens, and lectures for fifteen minutes, giving vent to the felt anger. Is anger the primary emotion? The primary emotion is probably relief or even happiness—the daughter, presumed hurt, is home safely. Expressing the primary emotion, "I was so worried, I thought you were hurt!" can lead to a dialogue. Of course, it also makes the parent vulnerable. Expressing the anger may be easier (many of us were taught how to express anger and not how to express worry), but it results in the daughter stomping off to her room and the parent fuming for the rest of the night.

Finally, it also may be useful for you to ask yourself what you get out of having the feeling. Feelings have a reason for being, and knowing the reason can help you clarify the emotion. For example, you may "be angry" (actually, you *choose* to be angry) to get out of having to accomplish something, to keep from being vulnerable, to create the opportunity to leave a boring situation, or to hurt someone. Your anger may be related to fear (ask yourself, "Am I actually afraid of something?"), an unexpressed demand (ask yourself, "Is there a specific behavior I expect or need from the other person?"), or perhaps depression (ask yourself, "Am I justifiably angry at the other person, or am I angry at myself?"). Whatever the reason, knowing it may be useful as an aid to helping you identify why you act as you do.

However you determine what your feeling is, the prerequisite to sharing your emotion is recognizing it. You cannot share what you do not know.

Accept Responsibility for Your Feelings

Assess your emotion and its intensity, and then admit to yourself that you are angry, hurt, anxious, happy, or euphoric. Also, admit to yourself that others cannot *cause* your feelings; rather, you *choose* how to feel. You, and no one else, are responsible for how you feel. Two simple questions should help clarify this important point. First, have you ever noticed that you can respond to essentially the same event different ways at different times? For example, you may respond angrily on Monday to your roommate's loud radio and respond indifferently on Tuesday when it is just as loud. The noise is the same both days—your response is different because *you* are the person who determines how you respond, not the noise. Second, have you ever noticed that different people respond differently to the same event? For example, you may feel happy about the concert you and friends are attending, whereas one friend is sad because he hears a song that reminds him of a past relationship, and another is angry because he thinks the lead singer is not singing well. If the music was the cause of the responses it gets, all three of you would have the same response. However, you each respond differently because each of you chooses your own response.

Other people may "invite" you to feel a particular way (for example, the person ignoring your question may be inviting you to feel angry or frustrated), but how you feel is, in the end, your choice. You can choose to feel angry at being ignored, or you can be sad, or frustrated, or weary, or stupid, or self-pitying ... the choice is *yours*. Although it may be easier to assume that others cause our feelings and that we are not responsible for them, the truth is that we are the ones in control, and the responsibility is all ours.

Select a Good Time and Place to Share Your Feelings

At the time your feelings are strong may not be the best time to share them. Your immediate angry response to your roommate's loud radio, for example, may include saying things you'll regret later. It is probably wiser to wait and think about how you feel (to make sure you know how you feel) and to put your feelings into words the other person will understand. Rushing into a conversation before you are clear about how you feel and how you can best express your feelings may feel good at the moment as you relieve yourself, but the end result may be a damaged relationship.

Also, avoid sharing how you feel when you are tired or rushed or when your partner feels tired or rushed. Sharing feelings takes time and energy, and you should make sure you and your partner have both before proceeding.

Where you share your feelings also is important. A quiet place that affords privacy may be the best setting. A place with few distractions helps focus your and your partner's attention on sharing.

Share Your Feelings Clearly

It is difficult sometimes to find the right words to express how you feel. After all, feelings are not easy to understand and, because of this, are not easy to translate into words. It may be helpful to express your feelings in similes and analogies: "I feel stepped on," "I feel like a cloud floating on air," "I feel squelched," "I feel like a raging river." Expressing your feelings this way helps you understand them and communicate them in ways that may help others understand how you feel.

It also may be helpful to indicate what kind of action the feelings urge you to do: "I'm so happy I feel like hugging you," "I'm so angry I'd like to slap your face," "I'm feeling so frustrated that I'd like to get up and walk out." Sometimes people have a hard time indicating the action their feelings urge them to do because they confuse acting with feeling. Keep in mind that expressing your emotion as an action is not the same as engaging in the action—"I feel like hugging you" is not the same as actually hugging your partner. Indicating what kind of action your feelings urge you to do helps to acknowledge the consequences of your emotions, which are a key to understanding the emotion's intensity.

Another way to indicate intensity is with qualifiers: "I'm *pretty* happy" is less intense than "I'm ecstatic!" "I'm *somewhat* confused" is less intense than "I'm totally baffled!" Don't discount how you feel by making it less intense than it really is, and don't make a less intense emotion seem more intense than it is. The object is to be clear about what you feel and how intensely you feel it.

With the use of a particular event as an example, Skill Development 3.3 will help you identify your feelings, accept responsibility for them, select an appropriate time and place to share them, and express them clearly.

Skill Development 3.3

EXPRESSING YOUR FEELINGS

Three days before the start of the new semester, your apartment mate and best friend for the past three years tells you of plans to leave to move in with someone else. You don't know who the other person is and what their relationship is. This means that you will be left alone to pay the total apartment rent or to find a new roommate quickly. All the people you know have already made their living arrangements for the new semester.

1. *Identify what you are feeling.* What are your primary and secondary emotions? This is a complex situation, and it is likely you have several different feelings regarding your friend and your friend's new apartment mate, as well as your situation.

2. *Assume responsibility for how you feel.* Keep in mind that you have full responsibility for how you feel and that your friend's announcement is, at most, an "invitation" for you to feel a particular way. Accept responsibility for how you feel about your friend, your friend's new apartment mate, and your situation.

3. *Select a good time and place to talk with your friend.* Are you too angry to talk with your friend right away? Is talking in your apartment likely to increase hostility? Consider several possible alternative times and places, and think about the advantages and disadvantages of each.

4. *Express what you are feeling clearly.* Express your feelings in similes, analogies, or figures of speech. What kind of actions do the feelings urge you to take? Think about your friend and how you can express yourself in a way that will be clearest for her or him.

HELPING OTHERS EXPRESS THEIR EMOTIONS

When those around us are expressing emotions, or turn to us for assistance in expressing emotions, we often are at a loss as to how to act. What do you tell someone who is disappointed, depressed, or unhappy? Typically, rather than allowing the person to feel as she or he wishes, advice is given such as, "Cheer up," "Every cloud has a silver lining," "Tomorrow will be a better day," "Things will get better." When someone is angry, you may say, "Simmer down," "There's no point in getting angry," or "Be objective." In other words, you may try to get the person to "feel better," which usually means, feel in a way that *you* are more comfortable handling. This technique is not usually effective.

In the process of attempting to get the person to feel differently, we often cut off one possible way of allowing her or him to deal with the emotion—by talking it out. Proven methods for dealing with emotions are at the center of the *Three T's Emotional Expression Method*—tears, talk, and toil.

Encouraging someone to express his or her emotions through *tears* (or laughter, which is an emotional parallel to tears—have you ever laughed so hard you cried or encountered someone at a funeral getting a laughing jag?) is a constructive interpersonal device.[22]

Encouraging someone to express his or her emotions through *talk*—with you acting as a good listener, not an advice giver, counselor, or consoler—is another effective tool.

Toil, in the form of physical effort, is yet another way of allowing yourself or another person to cope with pent-up emotion. A game of tennis or volleyball, a long walk, or jogging are all constructive emotional releases. When combined with talking or relieving the pressure through laughter or crying, you have a formula for healthy emotional release.

Ironically, not only do many people discourage the experiencing of "bad" feelings, they try to protect against the backlash of feeling "too good." When someone is happy, do you say, "Better watch out, something is likely to go wrong," or "Don't go overboard," or "Keep it in perspective"? Discouraging others from feeling as they do tells a great deal about the discourager. It often indicates the discourager is uncomfortable, unsure what to do, and how to react.

There are cultural implications regarding the three T's. For some cultures, all three would be discouraged rather than encouraged. For example, in many Asian cultures, showing tears is a sign of weakness, and cultures that stress meditation and contemplation perceive that talking only clouds true feelings. They often believe that speaking is a negative act.[23] And, for those who follow the Hindu tradition, activity keeps a person from discovering reality and truth. Hence, they urge their members to avoid engaging in activity, but, instead, to sit quietly and meditate.

Communication Competency Checkup

The goal of this Communication Competency Checkup is to guide you in putting your skills and knowledge about the self and others to use and to help you summarize the material in this chapter.

© 1979 Redbook Magazine and Jerry Marcus

"This is nothing. When I was your age the snow was so deep it came up to my chin!"

1.   Analyze the cartoon from the perspective of someone who finds it funny by applying the notions of selective perception, selective organization, and selective interpretation. Then do the same analysis for someone who does not find the cartoon funny. How could the same cartoon get two different reactions?

2.   What elements of this cartoon did you selectively perceive, organize, and interpret? For example, did you selectively interpret the relationship between the two characters as that of father and child? Did you perceive the two characters as having particular traits (for example, did you see the taller one as "stupid" and the shorter one as "amazed")?

3. How do your perceptions of the cartoon reflect who you are?

4. What could the taller of the two cartoon characters do to increase his perceptual accuracy?

5. What emotions are the cartoon characters likely feeling?

6. Why might it be hard for the shorter cartoon character to express his feelings to the taller one? If he fails to express how he feels, how would you classify his emotional reaction to the taller man?

7. What advice could you give the shorter cartoon character to help him express how he feels to the taller one?

8. How do your answers to the questions posed in this Communication Competency Checkup reflect your culture?

NOTES

1. For a discussion of implicit personality theory, see Seymour Rosenberg and Andrea Sedlak, "Structural Representations of Implicit Personality Theory," in *Advances in Experimental Social Psychology,* vol. 6, ed. Leonard Berkowitz (New York: Academic Press, 1972), 235–39.

2. The original research that considered how traits interact to form total impressions, and the importance of central traits in the process, was conducted by Solomon Asch, in "Forming Impressions of Personality," *Journal of Abnormal and Social Psychology* 41(1946): 258–90.

3. Peter A. Andersen, "Cognitive Schemata in Personal Relationships," in *Individuals in Relationships,* ed. Steve Duck (Newbury Park, CA: Sage, 1993); T. N. Bradbury and F. D. Finchman, "Attributions in Marriage: Review and Critique," *Psychological Bulletin* 107 (1990): 3–33; Harold H. Kelley, "The Process of Causal Attribution," *American Psychologist* 28 (1973): 107–28; Valerie Manusov, "An Application of Attribution Principles to Nonverbal Behavior in Romantic Dyads," *Communication Monographs* 57 (1990): 104–18; Alan J. Sillars, "Attributions and Communication in Roommate Conflicts," *Communication Monographs* 47 (1980): 180–200.

4. Valerie Manusov, "It Depends on Your Perspective: Effects of Stance and Beliefs about Intent on Person Perception," *Western Journal of Communication* 57 (1993): 27–41.

5. Robert Rosenthal, *Experimenter Effects in Behavioral Research* (New York: Irvington, 1976).

Also see Mark E. Snyder, "Self-Fulfilling Social Stereotypes," *Psychology Today* 16 (July 1982): 60–68.

6. Benjamin J. Broome, "Building Shared Meaning: Implications of a Relational Approach for Teaching Intercultural Communication," *Communication Education* 40 (1991): 235–39.

7. T. Adler, "Even Babies Empathize, Scientists Find, but Why?" *APA [American Psychological Association] Monitor* 21 (June 1990): 9.

8. The notion that empathy is a *skill* that can be taught and developed is only one perspective of empathy. For a detailed discussion of empathy, particularly in intercultural encounters, see Benjamin J. Broome, "Building Shared Meaning."

9. S. M. Pfeiffer and P. P. Wong, "Multidimensional Jealousy," *Journal of Social and Personal Relationships* 6 (1989): 181–96.

10. Carol A. Sterns and Peter Sterns, *Anger: The Struggle for Emotional Control in America's History* (Chicago: Univ. of Chicago Press, 1986).

11. Min-Sun Kim, "A Comparative Analysis of Nonverbal Expression as Portrayed by Korean and American Print-Media Advertising," *Howard Journal of Communication* 3 (1992): 321. Also see Larry A. Samovar and Richard Porter, *Communication between Cultures,* 2nd ed. (Belmont, CA: Wadsworth, 1995).

12. Hu Wenzhong and Cornelius L. Grove, *Encountering the Chinese* (Yarmouth, ME: Intercultural Press, 1991), 116.

13. Carol Tavris and C. Wade, *The Longest War:*

Sex Differences in Perspective, 2nd ed. (San Diego: Harcourt Brace Jovanovich, 1984).

14. Ellen Bersheid, "Emotion and Interpersonal Communication," in *Interpersonal Processes: New Directions in Communication Research,* ed. Michael E. Roloff and Gerald R. Miller (Beverly Hills, CA: Sage, 1987); John W. Bowers, Sandra M. Metts, and W. T. Duncanson, "Emotion and Interpersonal Communication," in *Handbook of Interpersonal Communication,* ed. Mark L. Knapp and Gerald R. Miller (Beverly Hills, CA: Sage, 1985); Julia T. Wood, *Gendered Lives: Communication, Gender, and Culture* (Belmont, CA: Wadsworth, 1994).

15. J. Hall, "Gender Effects in Decoding Nonverbal Cues," *Psychological Bulletin* 85 (1978): 845–57.

16. S. E. Snodgrass, "Women's Intuition: The Effect of Subordinate Role on Interpersonal Sensitivity," *Journal of Personality and Social Psychology* 49 (1985): 146–55.

17. A summary of the emotion-ailment link is available in Jane E. Brody, "Emotions Found to Influence Nearly Every Human Ailment," *New York Times* (May 24, 1983): C1, C8. Also see S. Chollar, "Hidden Emotions, High Cholesterol," *Psychology Today,* 23 (September 1989): 24; and "Why Men Don't Cry," *Science Digest* 92 (June 1984): 24.

18. Valerian J. Derlega, Sandra Metts, Sandra Petronio, and S. T. Margulis, *Self-Disclosure* (Newbury Park, CA: Sage, 1993); V. G. Downs, "Grandparents and Grandchildren: The Relationship between Self-Disclosure and Solidarity in an Intergenerational Relationship," *Communication Research Reports* 5 (1988): 173–79; Lawrence B. Rosenfeld and Gary I. Bowen, "Marital Disclosure and Marital Intimacy: Direct-Effect Versus Interaction-Effect Models," *Western Journal of Speech Communication* 55 (1991): 69–84.

19. Joyce L. Hocker and William W. Wilmot, *Interpersonal Conflict,* 3rd ed. (Dubuque, IA: Wm. C. Brown, 1991).

20. Carol Tavris, *Anger: The Misunderstood Emotion* (New York: Simon and Schuster, 1983).

21. C. R. Bush, J. P. Bush, and J. Jennings, "Effects of Jealousy Threats on Relationship Perceptions and Emotions," *Journal of Social and Personal Relationships* 5 (1988): 285–303.

22. S. Chollar, "Why Men Don't Cry."

23. George A. Borden, *Cultural Orientation: An Approach to Understanding Intercultural Communication* (Englewood Cliffs, NJ: Prentice-Hall, 1991), 35.

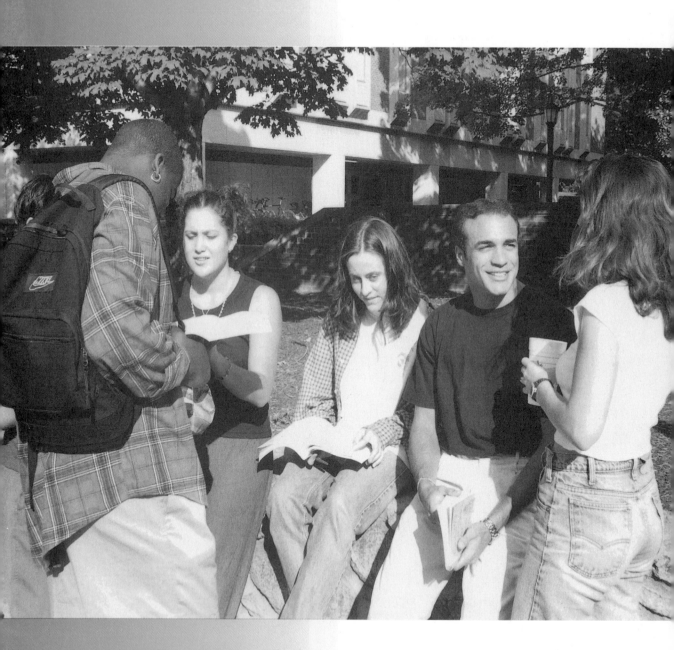

COMMUNICATION COMPETENCIES

This chapter examines listening. Specifically, the objective of this chapter is for you to learn to:

- Identify your own listening patterns.
- Define listening and summarize the four stages of the listening process.
- Describe the three levels of listening.
- Explain the importance of listening as part of the communication process.
- List some of the barriers to good listening.
- Apply several techniques for improving your listening skills, including methods for focusing your attention, organizing material, and providing feedback.
- Identify your listening response styles.
- Describe the process of listening to help.

KEY WORDS

The key words in this chapter are:

listening
hearing
active listening
egospeaking
selective listening
insulated listening
pseudolistening
red flag
green flag
external distractions
internal distractions
paraphrasing
chunking
ordering
reordering

In Center Harbor, Maine, local legend recalls the day when Walter Cronkite [at that time, television's leading news anchorman] steered his boat into port. The avid sailor, as it's told, was amused to see in the distance a small crowd of people on shore waving their arms to greet him. He could barely make out their excited shouts of "Hello Walter . . . Hello Walter." As his boat sailed closer, the crowd grew larger, still yelling "Hello Walter . . . Hello Walter." Pleased at the reception, Cronkite tipped his white captain's hat, waved back, even took a bow. But before reaching dockside, Cronkite's boat abruptly jammed aground. The crowd stood silent. The veteran news anchor suddenly realized what they'd been shouting: "Low water . . . low water." [1]

Like Cronkite, do you hear what you want to hear, or do you hear the words actually spoken? There appears to be enough research evidence to indicate that if you are typical, you are probably guilty of tuning out, yielding to distractions, becoming overly emotional, faking attention, or even dozing with your eyes open—all when you're supposedly listening.

The average North American spends 50 to 80 percent of her or his day listening but actively hears only half of what is said, understands only a quarter of that, and remembers even less. Our attention span rarely lasts more than 45 seconds at any one time. Most people use only 25 percent of their innate ability to listen. [2]

Listening, like so many communication variables, is influenced by culture. Some cultures, many in Asia, "are biased in favor of lengthy silences." [3] For these cultures, the amount of time spent talking and listening is far less than in cultures that value conversation. People in Japan and other Asian cultures, for example, are more likely to spend less time talking on the job than do North Americans. You only need to think of the Asian saying, "By your mouth you shall perish," to see that the emphasis is not on interaction, but on being still.

Not all cultures have the same attention span. In Buddhism, for instance, there is a concept called being "mindful." This means giving whatever you are doing your *complete* and *full* attention. It involves training the mind to focus on the moment, to keep it, as Buddha wrote, from thrashing around like a fish placed on the shore. [4] If your cultural orientation is to being alert, being in the present, you will certainly be able to listen more effectively than someone who is thinking about the past or the future while someone else is talking.

How well do you listen based on your cultural needs? How well do you take information gathered through your sense of hearing and give it meaning?

WHAT IS LISTENING?

Listening is the active process of receiving, attending to, and assigning meaning to sounds, and of remembering. It is active because it involves taking information from speakers, processing it, giving meaning to it, and, when appropriate, encouraging the continuation of communication by giving appropriate feedback. The process of listening usually proceeds through four stages: sensing, understanding, evaluating, and responding.

The first stage is *sensing.* Through your senses you become aware of a message. For example, someone speaks, you hear the sounds, and, in some cases, you see actions that clarify or enhance the sounds.

The second stage is *understanding.* If the sounds are familiar, you interpret them and understanding takes place. If a person says "D-E-S-K" and if you understand standard American English, you combine the letters into the word *desk,* and you picture a piece of furniture at which a person sits while doing certain types of work. You comprehend the intent of the sounds as they combine. If someone points at a desk and says the word, you have a further clue to the intended message.

The third stage is *evaluation.* After you understand the message, you may go through a stage in which you appraise it. If a speaker says, "Let's sit down at the desk and talk," you may evaluate the message ("This is a good suggestion" or "This is a bad suggestion") and decide how you are going to respond ("I think I'll agree" or "I think I'll refuse").

The fourth stage is *responding.* In this stage, you do something with the message. For example, you may sit down at the desk, indicating that you understood the message and chose to evaluate the invitation positively. Or you may say, "I don't want to sit down and talk right now," showing that you understood the message but do not want to accept the invitation. Even ignoring the message is a response, although an ambiguous one. It leaves the speaker wondering whether the message was received, whether it was understood, or whether the lack of response should be taken as an insult.

Listening is the most important of our communication skills. There is no other skill that could make you as well informed and desirable as a companion. Listening is the key skill for becoming a good communicator, an effective counselor, and a skilled leader.[5] Despite its great value, listening is probably the most underrated of the sensory skills. If you are typical, you probably received less than half a year of formal listening training in all of your elementary and secondary schooling.[6] Compare that short time to the usual six to eight years devoted to formal reading instruction, twelve years to writing, and one year to speaking. In contrast to the 50 to 80 percent of time spent listening, most North Americans spend only about 9 percent of their time writing, 16 percent reading, and 35 percent speaking. For your most used skill, listening, you received the least training. Little emphasis is placed on listening training in schools because people sometimes assume that normal hearing equals good listening. In fact, hearing and listening are not the same. **Hearing** is merely the biological act of receiving sounds, while listening is a much more active process.

Listening is a learned skill. The effectiveness of your listening often depends on what is going on in your mind as well as what is going on around you. You must learn to participate both mentally and physically in the communicative transaction. You must learn to listen in different ways at different times. You have to realize that listening productively and effectively just doesn't happen—it takes work. You cannot suddenly turn on your listening any more than you can say, "I'm going to run ten miles today even though I've never exercised a muscle." You must develop your listening skills

I think the one lesson I have learned is that there is no substitute for paying attention.
DIANE SAWYER

through training—and people who have listening training become more effective listeners.[7] In addition, many of the people you will be spending time with are going to be coming from backgrounds and cultures that are different from yours. There will be occasions in which you meet people who do not speak the same native language as you. As they speak languages different from your native language, your listening skills will be challenged.

THE REASONS FOR LISTENING

Listening is an important communication skill because it has so many uses. You listen for comprehension, appreciation, identification, evaluation, to help others, to build and maintain relationships, and to gain self-understanding.

Listening for *comprehension* involves grasping the meaning of the sounds you hear. Through comprehension you acquire information, ideas, and others' viewpoints. Comprehension is required in the classroom, at work, at home, and in social settings. By comprehending the messages you receive, you gain new ideas, learn new skills, test ideas, and expand your perspective.

You listen *appreciatively* to music, to the sounds of nature, and to the actor's voice. Appreciative listening differs from comprehensive listening because your purpose is not to gain information, per se, but to relax or to feel a particular way, such as peaceful, stimulated, or excited.

A third reason you listen is for *identification.* A doctor listens to the sound of a patient's heart to detect abnormality. A mechanic concentrates on the sounds of an engine to determine whether the car is running smoothly. You listen to the pitch of someone's voice to discern tension or relaxation. The sound of wind, the roll of thunder, and the crash of waves all supply useful information about the probable severity of an oncoming storm. In identification you use the sound to identify something—the sound reveals the "something" to you.

You *evaluate* what is being said by carefully analyzing whether the ideas are acceptable to you, meet your expectations, and are logical. You evaluate the messages of commercials, salespeople, friends, and family members. In a work environment, whether you are an employer or an employee, you constantly evaluate and are evaluated.

One of the most overlooked and underrated uses of listening is to *build and maintain relationships.* Unless communicators listen actively to what another person is saying, they miss what is happening in the other person's life, how he or she is growing and learning. In the end, without an understanding based on shared listening, the relationship stagnates.[8]

Listening also is useful for *helping others.* Listening that includes empathy—the ability to experience the world as others do[9]—lets the other person know that she or he is not alone. Helping professionals, such as doctors, nurses, clergy, and social workers can offer advice and assistance, but understanding friends and family can offer reassurance, concern, and comfort. The ability to comfort others is an important communica-

tion skill.[10] The easiest way to think of your role as an empathic listener is to picture yourself as a mirror. As someone explains her or his concerns, stressors, or conflicts you reflect what you are hearing by restating the ideas in your own words. Usually, the person who seeks an empathic listener needs reflection, not advice. Listening this way can reduce tensions, help solve problems, encourage cooperation, and promote open communication.

The sixth reason for listening is *self-understanding*. Listening to others' observations about you can lead to self-understanding and personal growth. Similarly, listening to yourself talk about who you are provides important data for self-analysis. Just by listening to yourself talk, you may discover that you feel more strongly about a topic than you had realized. You may become more intense than you would have predicted, or you may bring up arguments that you didn't realize were important to you.

INVESTIGATING YOUR LISTENING PATTERNS

Each of us follows a general pattern while listening, a pattern best recognized by looking at the behaviors that *detract* from listening effectively and efficiently. Knowledge

Checkup 4.1 provides you with the opportunity to investigate your perception of your personal listening patterns.

Knowledge Checkup 4.1

PAYING ATTENTION? TAKE THIS LISTENING SELF-EVALUATION TEST AND SEE[11]

How often do you find yourself engaging in the following listening patterns? Use this scale to indicate your response to each item.

Write **1** if you engage in the behavior almost always (91–100 percent) of the time.

Write **2** if you engage in the behavior usually (71–90 percent) of the time.

Write **3** if you engage in the behavior sometimes (31–70 percent) of the time.

Write **4** if you engage in the behavior seldom (11–30 percent) of the time.

Write **5** if you engage in the behavior almost never (0–10 percent) of the time.

_____ 1. When someone has just told me a dramatic or humorous story about herself or himself, I say, "That's nothing. Let me tell you what happened to me."

_____ 2. I let a lack of organization get in the way of my listening.

_____ 3. I interrupt if I have something I want to say.

_____ 4. When someone is telling me a story or making a point about something, as soon as I realize what he or she is driving at I let my mind wander until it's my turn to talk since I know what is going to be said.

_____ 5. I fail to repeat what is said before I react.

_____ 6. I give little verbal or nonverbal feedback to the other person.

_____ 7. I pay attention only to the words and ignore the tone and pitch being used.

_____ 8. I let emotionally charged words make me angry.

_____ 9. In a brief social conversation I use the other person's name rarely.

_____ 10. If I consider the subject boring, I stop paying attention.

_____ 11. I criticize the other person's delivery or mannerisms.

_____ 12. I do not take notes during lectures and phone calls.

_____ 13. I let distractions interfere with my concentration.

_____ 14. When someone is explaining something technical or complicated, I act as if I am following what she or he says, even if I am not, so I won't look or sound stupid.

_____ 15. I do not recognize when I am too upset or tired to listen.

_____ 16. I try to give advice when someone is telling me his or her problems.

_____ 17. I slump in my chair when listening in class.

This quiz is based on the skills you need to be a good listener. Add the numbers you assigned to the seventeen items. This is your total Listening Self-Evaluation score. The average score is 61. Is yours higher or lower? By itself, your total score is less important than your responses to the individual items. Items on which you rated yourself 1, 2, or 3 indicate areas in which you need to improve.

Bear in mind that people are often unaware of their true listening behaviors and your answers may not reflect how you really behave. You can check your answers by having someone with whom you interact regularly fill out the form reflecting on your behavior—not his or her own.

Based on this general knowledge about listening and your role as a listener, it is important that you understand some specific principles to guide your study of listening.

1. *Poor listening can be remedied.* Sharpening your listening skills requires patience and practice. Once you have learned the skills, you can put into practice what you need to become a skilled listener.

2. *There is no single "best" listening strategy.* Good listeners know how to decipher what various speakers mean in varying situations, and different situations require different listening strategies. Some communicators don't organize their ideas well; others do. Some realize that they must repeat their main ideas to ensure understanding; others ramble on without systematic repetition. Some people give you time to think about what they've said; others move rapidly ahead. Some choose simple and clear words; others use language that confuses and confounds. Regardless of the other person's strengths and weaknesses, it is the listener's responsibility to adapt and to understand.

3. *Good listening depends on finding some personal benefit in the speaker's words.* Because listening is hard work, you need to find some reason for paying attention.

4. *When you listen, you must actively participate in the communication process.* You have a responsibility to interpret what's said, assess its value, decide how to use it, and respond accordingly.

5. *Listening is a problem-solving task.* You must constantly be alert to the question, "What does this person mean?"

6. *You need to monitor the way you listen.* Not all situations require the same concentration of energy. Listening to a soap opera on television does not require the same level of concentration as listening to a teacher's lecture.

7. *You need to learn to listen for thinking cues.*[12] It is important to recognize that you should use the pauses found in a speaker's natural speaking pattern to process what is being said. This means you should process the message as it is being said—use the pauses to think about the message rather than waiting for the next point.

Use the fact that most speakers use *redundancy,* repeating their ideas over again, in the same or different words, to help you listen. Realize that if you miss something once it may well be repeated later in the interaction. Stay alert to the redundancy when it is presented.

You can use the *rapid predict-then-confirm strategy* to help you listen effectively. As you listen, predict what is coming up in a sentence and then wait to see if it occurs. Most of the time, your predictions will be correct. You may guess the exact words, but you should be able to identify and predict the general idea. Thus, you will be hearing prediction and confirmation based on recurring themes of the message, as well as the overall points and arguments. Be careful that you do not merely confirm your predictions by only listening to parts of the other person's message.

THE EFFECT OF GLOBAL AND LINEAR LEARNING STYLES ON LISTENING

Not all listeners process information in the same way. Part of this is due to the way the human brain works. The brain is divided into two connected hemispheres, and each hemisphere has special abilities. Though we use both sides, research shows that in many people there is a dominance of one side of the brain over the other.[13]

The left hemisphere of the brain is responsible for rational, logical, sequential, linear and abstract thinking. Left-brain dominated people, who are often referred to as *linear thinkers,* tend to listen and learn best from specific, sequentially presented information, and logic-based arguments. They tend to concentrate on the words being used and often ignore the impact of nonverbal nuances as they affect a message. For example, linear thinkers often misconstrue sarcasm and subtle humor.

On the other hand, those who are right-brain dominant, referred to as *global think-ers,* tend to listen and learn best from visual or pictographical input rather than from written instructions. They tend to gain the most from interaction rather than lecturing, and they are inclined to learn best from exploration and trying things out through experience and discovery. Global learners like to know what is generally going on rather than specifically how something is done.

Understanding there is a difference in the way people listen and obtain information allows a communicator to develop her or his messages in different ways, depending on the listener. For example, if you know the listener is left-brain dominant, then it is necessary for you to be sequentially organized, to be specific, to use logical arguments, and to tell specifically how something works or the definite outcomes that have been discovered. Conversely, a global listener requires an overall preview, examples, and word pictures. Don't be surprised, in interacting with a right-brain dominant person, if there are numerous interruptions for the purpose of asking questions, and much jumping to conclusions before you are finished with your explanation. And if you don't know the other person's brain dominance, use a varied approach to increase the likelihood of understanding.

Knowledge Checkup 4.2 will help you determine if you have a right- or left-brain dominance.

> After two days, a person will remember no more than 25% of a message.

Knowledge Checkup 4.2

LEFT/RIGHT, LINEAR/GLOBAL BRAIN DOMINANCE[14]

Answer all of the questions quickly and do not stop to analyze them. When there is no clear preference, choose the one that most closely represents your attitudes or behavior.

1. I usually have a place for everything, a system for doing things, and an ability to organize information and materials.
   a. _____ Yes
   b. _____ No

2. In thinking about the activities of my day, my typical "style" is:
   a. _____ I make a list of all the things I need to do, people to see.
   b. _____ I just let it happen.

3. Concerning hunches:
   a. _____ I would not rely on hunches to help me make important decisions.
   b. _____ I frequently have strong ones and follow them.

4. I think of daydreaming as:
   a. _____ a waste of time.
   b. _____ a viable tool for planning my future.

5. In a problem-solving situation, I:
   a. _____ think about the problem, write down all alternatives, arrange them according to priorities, and then pick the best.
   b. _____ wait to see if the situation will right itself.

6. In school I prefer:
   a. _____ geometry.
   b. _____ algebra.

7. When I read a play or a novel, I
   a. _____ picture the characters and locations as if they were in a movie or television.
   b. _____ read the words for understanding and clarity.

8. When I want to remember directions, a name, or a news item, I:
   a. _____ visualize the information.
   b. _____ write notes.

9. In sports or performing in public, I often perform better than my training and natural abilities warrant.
   a. _____ Yes
   b. _____ No

10. I learn athletics and dancing better by:
    a. _____ imitating, getting the feel of the music or game.
    b. _____ learning the sequence and repeating the steps mentally.

SCORING AND INTERPRETATION

Give yourself one point for each "b" answer on questions 1–5 and one point for each "a" answer on questions 6–10: _____ This total is your score. To assess your degree of left or right brain preference, locate your final score on this continuum:

LEFT 1 2 3 4 5 6 7 8 9 10 RIGHT

The lower the score, the more left-brained tendency you have. People with scores of 1 and 2 are typically highly linear.

The higher the score, the more right-brained tendency you have. People with scores of 9 and 10 are typically highly global.

Bear in mind that neither hemisphere preference is superior to the other. If you are extremely left or right dominant, it is possible to develop some of the traits associated with the other hemisphere.

Besides brain-dominance, culture can affect listening and learning abilities.[15] The learning style of Native American Navajos, for example, has four components: observe, think, understand or feel, act. This approach is in contrast to the Anglo process of act, observe or think or clarify, understand. Anglos tend to learn from trial and error, examining components in relationship to the whole. Native American Navajos spend much more time watching and listening and less time talking.

THE LEVELS OF LISTENING

Different situations require different listening strategies—for example, some speakers pack more content into what they say and so require greater concentration from the

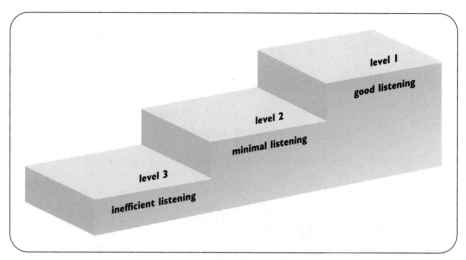

FIGURE 4.1 Three Levels of Listening

listener than those who speak in more "user-friendly" ways—however, every situation requires effective and efficient listening. There are three levels of listening, each representing a different degree of effectiveness (Figure 4.1). At the third level is inefficient listening, at the second level is minimal listening, and at the first level is good listening. An investigation of the weakest to the best levels should allow you to understand what you must do to improve your listening.

Level 3 Listening

Level 3 listening is characterized by listening now and then. You tune in and tune out, aware of the presence of others but mainly absorbed in your own thoughts.

You may be more interested in what you want to say than in what the other person is saying, listening only for pauses that will let you take control of the conversation. You probably sit passively and offer little feedback to the speaker. Perhaps you think about unrelated matters and make little effort to perceive the message. In short, you are not paying attention to the speaker. Level 3 listening can produce misunderstandings, hurt feelings, confused instructions, loss of important information, embarrassment, and frustration.

Level 2 Listening

In Level 2 listening, you hear words and sounds but do not actively try to grasp anything beyond surface meanings. Typical of this level is tuning out after you think you have enough information to guess the speaker's intent. As a result, you may grasp the basic meaning of the message, but miss the emotion and feeling and thus fail to comprehend the full content.

Level 2 listeners often seem emotionally detached from a conversation. Misunderstandings may occur because the listener often misses how the meaning of what is said is modified by the way in which it is said.

Level 1 Listening

Level 1 listening is **active listening.** You listen for main and supporting ideas, acknowledge and respond, give appropriate feedback, and pay attention to the speaker's total communication. In other words, a Level 1 listener is concerned about the content, the intent, and the feelings of the sender's message.

BARRIERS TO EFFECTIVE LISTENING

To become a good listener, you must be aware of the barriers that may interfere with the accurate reception of a message.[16] The first step, however, is to recognize your personal signals that indicate you are not listening. Knowledge Checkup 4.3 will help you answer the question "How can I tell if I'm not listening?"

Knowledge Checkup 4.3

YOUR NONLISTENING SIGNALS

Which of the following are your signals that you aren't listening to the other person? Check all those that apply.

_____   1. I daydream.

_____   2. I slouch down in the chair, if I am seated.

_____   3. I glance at my watch, the ceiling, or the floor.

_____   4. I play with some object, such as glasses, paper clip, or pencil.

_____   5. I stare into space.

_____   6. I drum my fingers on my arm or on a solid surface.

_____   7. I cross my legs and bounce my foot.

_____   8. I turn slightly away from the other person.

_____   9. I yawn, sigh, or show other signs of boredom.

_____   10. I don't look directly at the speaker.

Add any nonlistening acts you participate in while attempting to listen:

NONLISTENING CUES

You undoubtedly checked several items on the list. If you are aware of the behaviors that indicate you aren't listening, you can stop them and refocus your attention on the other person. For example, if you observe yourself yawning and realize you have quit listening because you're bored, stop yawning, focus on what the speaker is saying, and ask yourself, "Why is this material important to me?" Even if you don't find the material interesting, there may be important reasons for listening, such as to prepare for an upcoming test or to avoid appearing rude.

There are many reasons why you may not listen effectively, including overloading, poor listening habits, responding to emotionally loaded words, failing to receive the whole message, and allowing external and internal distractions get in the way. By being aware of these problems you increase the chances that you can avoid them and listen effectively.

Overloading

You may not be engaging in good listening if you feel overloaded, that is, you feel as if you couldn't possibly listen anymore because you already have too much information to retain. You are capable of grasping and retaining only a limited number of ideas at any given moment. The human brain works like a computer in that it receives information, stores it, and then responds when the proper stimulus has activated the retrieval process.[17] Similar to a computer, the human brain can in effect overload and "blow a circuit." Receiving too much information at one time, being upset by certain messages, and feeling out of control because of the situation or the participants can cause poor listening. Sometimes you may need to tell the sender that you just can't listen any longer, or you may need to leave the receiving environment. Other times you may have no choice but to continue listening, even though it's difficult to concentrate.

Feeling overloaded can be avoided in several ways. As explained later in this chapter, learning how to focus your attention and organize material, besides improving your listening skills in general, can be particularly useful for overcoming feelings of overload.

Poor Listening Habits

There are several poor listening habits that you may have developed over the years. Ask yourself:

Do you look for things to argue with or use as an excuse to justify not listening?

Do you like to grab center stage for yourself by interrupting?

Do you listen only to those points with which you agree or to those topics in which you are personally interested?

Do you avoid points with which you disagree or topics in which you are not interested?

Do you fail to listen long enough to get the whole message and therefore often make mistakes or jump to incorrect conclusions?

Do you imitate good listening by nodding, maintaining eye contact, and in other ways looking like you're listening?

Each of these questions relates to a poor listening habit. The first, *internally arguing with the speaker,* occurs when you doubt the value of listening or start arguing with a speaker, either of which may happen if a speaker's ideas seem illogical or if the information does not seem valid. For example, you may react negatively when you hear the word *always* and know there are exceptions, or when you realize that no evidence supports a conclusion, or when the speaker states that "everyone knows" but doesn't specify who "everyone" is. Nonetheless, to stop listening, or to listen without paying close attention, may not be the best response. Keeping an open mind and withholding final judgment will enable you to gather new information, some of which may be useful. There is always time to reject what a speaker has to say after you listen.

The second question concerns **egospeaking,** jumping into a communicative transaction because you have something you want to say or because you feel what you have to say is more important or more interesting than what the other person is saying. Egospeaking not only stops you from receiving the whole message, it irritates others because it is disrespectful. In addition, the moment you decide (consciously or unconsciously) to interrupt, you stop listening.

Once you realize what egospeaking is, you should be able to control it. Several physical clues will help you detect when you are about to egospeak. When most people start to interrupt, they literally jump into the conversation by raising their bodies, leaning forward, and moving their arms and hands upward, often pointing with a finger. If you catch yourself making such motions while someone else is talking, you are probably about to egospeak. Another way to detect that you are egospeaking is to listen to yourself. If you tend to enter conversations with such phrases as "That's interesting, but . . . ," or "Uh-huh, but what happened to me was . . . ," or if people ask, "What does that have to do with what we're talking about?"—you are probably egospeaking. Egospeaking becomes a problem if it is a typical feature of your communication because, if you egospeak often, you are probably not getting as much out of listening as you could.

The third question relates to **selective listening,** and the fourth relates to the flip side of this problem, **insulated listening.** People who listen selectively respond only to the points with which they agree and pay attention only when the topic is one in which they are personally interested. On the other hand, people with the habit of insulated listening do the opposite: They turn off anything with which they disagree and avoid any topic that may be "unpleasant," "uninteresting," or "too controversial." To counter both selective listening and insulated listening, keep in mind that "listening" does not equal "agreeing." You can listen to points with which you disagree and still disagree with them. You do not have to stop listening. Similarly, you can listen to topics in which you are not especially interested and choose to remain uninterested—listening to a topic does not mean you must be interested in it. You can choose to listen to a topic in which you are not personally interested for a variety of reasons, such as being polite or learning about the subject because people you talk with on occasion are interested in it.

The fifth question relates to *failing to receive the whole message.* Have you ever filled out an application form and found that on the line that said "Name" you wrote your first and last names in sequence before you saw that the directions said, "Print last name first"? This is an example of not allowing yourself to receive the whole message. You also may do this when you listen.

Read the following statement:

> Jack and Jill went up the
> the hill to catch a pile of water.

Now go back. Did you read the double word *the?* Did you read *fetch* or *catch?* Did you read *pail* or *pile?* Because you are probably familiar with the nursery rhyme "Jack and Jill," you may not have needed more than the first three words to know what followed. If you knew the rhyme but caught all the deviations, you are probably alert to the importance of paying attention to an entire message. If not, you need to practice receiving entire messages before jumping to conclusions.

The last question in the poor listening habits list refers to the habit called **pseudolistening.** Pseudolisteners act as if they're listening when they aren't. Most of us received good training in pseudolistening in school. No matter how dull the lecture, we knew we would get in trouble if we weren't "listening," so we nodded our heads at the right moments, made facial expressions that indicated interest and concern, and made sure we maintained steady eye contact. The teachers smiled back at us and praised our performance, often not realizing we were not really listening. For many people the teacher's positive reinforcement was powerful and the habit of pseudolistening stuck.

Responding to Emotionally Loaded Words

How do you feel when someone says to you:[18]

> "What you should have done was . . ."
> "You have to . . ."
> "Only someone stupid like you would . . ."
> "If you had done it my way . . ."
> "See, I told you that would happen!"
> "You do this all the time [sigh]."
> "You always . . ."
> "Are you going to be on time for a change?"

A judgmental word or phrase—called a **red flag**—evokes strong emotions and interferes with your willingness and ability to listen. If, for example, you have strong feelings against abortion and your communication partner mentions that she is in favor of abortion, you may immediately turn off the rest of her message.

Red flags also include people who provoke strong negative reactions. For example, merely seeing someone with whom you're having an ongoing argument may be enough to trigger thoughts that interfere with your ability to listen. Your mind may concentrate on the last argument, how to approach the person, or how to escape with dignity.

Often our strong negative reactions to other people grow out of our stereotypes toward their ethnic or cultural background. We see the color of their skin, hairstyle, or attire and react. These cultural red flags are as harmful as any you might use. They keep you from focusing on the content of the message.

Similarly, some topics may arouse negative emotions regardless of how they are discussed. For example, your feelings against the death penalty may be so strong that any mention of the topic—even by someone who agrees with you—interferes with your ability to listen.

In contrast, **green flag** words are words and phrases that stir up positive feelings, and they too may interfere with listening. If you are an avid sun worshipper and the person you are conversing with says that he has recently been in Hawaii, your mind might switch to a scene in which you are sunning yourself on a beach covered with palm trees. Green flags for college students may include spring break, a canceled exam, and graduation.

Green flags also include people who trigger strong positive emotions that interfere with your ability to listen. For example, meeting an old friend whom you haven't seen in years may cause such strong positive feelings that you fail to listen when she tells you she has only a few minutes to talk. Similarly, some topics may arouse positive emotions. For instance, your positive feelings toward parenthood may be so strong that you fail to listen to your acquaintance's reasons for deciding not to have children.

Both red and green flags lead you to stop actively participating in the listening act. Being aware of your red and green flags is the first step in combating their interference. Knowledge Checkup 4.4 provides the opportunity to think about your red and green flags. By being aware of them you can begin to avoid their effects on you.

> Most of us listen through a screen of prejudices . . . whether religious or spiritual, psychological or scientific. And with these for a screen, we listen. Therefore, we listen really to our own noise, to our own sound, not to what is being said.
> KRISHNAMURTI

Knowledge Checkup 4.4

SENDING UP YOUR RED AND GREEN FLAGS[19]

Part I

Following are some words and phrases that may be emotionally charged. Take a moment to check the ones that are red flags for you.

_____ You should	_____ What a waste
_____ You must	_____ You're always doing that
_____ Slow poke	_____ You're supposed to
_____ It's for your own good	_____ You're so stupid

_____ You have to   _____ You don't listen

_____ You're a failure   _____ You never get things done on time

Add any personal red flags not listed:

Part II

Identify red and green flags in each of the following categories. For each category, list five words or phrases that trigger you to react very positively or negatively.

Topic	Red Flag	Green Flag
Activities		
People		
Issues (topics)		

Once you are aware of some of your red and green flags, you can make a conscious effort to stop yourself from daydreaming or becoming irritated. You won't always be successful, but you can make progress.

External Distractions

Listeners may have problems receiving a message if there are **external distractions**—people, objects, or events in the environment that divert attention. Have you ever had difficulty receiving a message when a lot of people were talking, when machinery, such as a dishwasher, was running, or when the television set was on? External distractions are not limited to environmental noise. You may be distracted by a speaker's clothing, dialect, pronunciation, or poor grammar—or by the general setting. One reason teachers avoid holding classes outdoors is that the many external distractions—people walking by, the weather, and so on—interfere with good listening.

External distractions are usually obvious and, once pointed out, easy to eliminate. A change of location may be enough to reduce noise or remove distractions and recognizing that pronunciation and poor grammar are not good enough reasons to stop listening usually eliminates them as problems.

Internal Distractions

In comparison to external distractions, **internal distractions,** attention diverters that occur within you, are more difficult to recognize and often are more difficult to eliminate. A study of what students think about during a lecture found that only 20 percent actually pay attention to the message, and only 12 percent concentrate fully. The others are thinking erotic thoughts, reminiscing, and worrying.[20] Hunger pangs, having the flu, and an itch on your left leg are all internal distractions.

One typical product of internal distractions is daydreaming. Daydreaming, being lost in your own thoughts, is another common barrier to effective listening. When you daydream you may still be hearing sounds, but instead of focusing on what is being said you are floating in mental space—thinking of what you'll make for dinner, an upcoming test, your weekend plans, or anything else that, at that moment, strikes you as more interesting than the speaker's message.

To stop daydreaming you need to recognize you are doing it, identify what set you off, and in the future try to avoid the action or situation that stimulated it. For example, were you slumping in your chair? Were you looking out the window? Did a green or a red flag send your thoughts flying? Keeping in mind that the speaker's message is important for you may help you avoid daydreaming.

MAKING LISTENING WORK FOR YOU

Several techniques can help you avoid or overcome barriers to effective listening. By learning to be prepared to listen, to focus your attention, to organize what you hear, to receive the whole message, to paraphrase the speaker's message, and to provide the speaker with feedback, you can take an active role in the communication process and, as a result, become a more skilled listener.

BEING PREPARED TO LISTEN

There is an old saying that the time to repair the roof is when the sun is shining. The same advice holds true with regards to listening—the time to think about listening is *before* your communication partner sends his or her message. There are three ways you can prepare for a communication encounter before it begins.

First, learn all you can about the subject, the speaker, and the situation. This knowledge will help you understand and appraise what the speaker might say. For example, if you know that someone with whom you're going to talk is an active member of a religious group that is against birth control, if you are familiar with the topic and the various issues it raises, and if you know that the communication situation is a class discussion on human sexuality, you can make predictions about how this topic might be discussed. Making predictions helps prepare you—so long as you are open-minded and realize that your predictions may not be accurate.

Second, you can eliminate as many distractions as possible that might call your attention away from your communication partner. Distractions, as already considered, can be external and internal. Regarding external distractions, for example, outside noise may be reduced by shutting a door, phone calls may be eliminated by diverting them to an answering machine, and interruptions may be stopped by posting a "Do Not Disturb" sign on your door. Many internal distractions also may be eliminated; for example, having something to eat may reduce the possibility of your mind wandering to thoughts

For Better or For Worse®

by Lynn Johnston

of dinner and sitting in a comfortable seat may keep you from thinking about your sore back.

Third, it is helpful if you have a specific purpose in mind as you approach the communication encounter. Ask yourself what you and the other person hope to gain from talking. Although your purpose will differ from person to person and situation to situation, it is important to find some reason to listen. Of course it is possible to listen without having a specific reason for doing so, but having an objective makes listening an easier task. That is to say, you become motivated to listen. Ask yourself this simple question about human nature: Do I learn more when I am interested or bored? The answer is obvious. Regardless what prompts you to listen—whether the goal is a pragmatic one, such as listening to a customer to make sure you get an order correct, or a social one, such as listening to another person because she deserves your attention—if you have a purpose for listening you are less likely to be distracted.

FOCUSING ATTENTION

To be a good listener, you must know how to focus attention on the speaker. This focusing skill helps in two ways: It allows you to pick up nonverbal cues, and it shows the sender that you are paying attention.

People who wear glasses often say that they can't hear as well without their glasses. Although this may strike you as odd, it is probably true because without their glasses some receivers may miss a speaker's facial expressions, gestures, and body positions. As a result, they may miss much of the total message. By facing a speaker and watching carefully as she talks, you will catch both obvious and subtle cues about her intentions and emotions. Noting such factors as her breathing patterns, facial expressions, leg and arm positions, finger movements, and physical distance will help you to interpret her message.

There are four techniques you can use to help you focus your attention: paraphrasing, taking notes, repeating, and staying alert physically.

Paraphrasing

Listening with the intent of **paraphrasing,** restating the speaker's message in your own words, forces you to focus on the message being presented. Indeed, one of the most effective ways of checking whether you have received a message is to repeat it back. Restating not only gives you a chance to check the ideas you have received, but also informs the other person that you are listening. Given how rare good listening is, paraphrasing to demonstrate your attentiveness can be a great compliment. In addition, if you force yourself to paraphrase, you will find you must listen to the entire message without interrupting.

Paraphrasing is an excellent device to use in a telephone conversation. Repeating the name and number of a caller who is leaving a message makes you focus on important details and note them accurately. Restating the details of an order, the directions for how to get someplace, or what a caller wants saves time in the long run by eliminating unnecessary mistakes.

Skilled paraphrasers repeat only the speaker's general idea and not the entire message—they *paraphrase,* not *parrotphrase.* Also, in addition to paraphrasing the general idea, skilled paraphrasers also reflect what they perceive are the speaker's feelings. When done well, paraphrasing is the best way to demonstrate that you are focusing on the speaker and listening thoughtfully.

To signal your communication partner that you are going to paraphrase what he or she said, use a "paraphrase starter." Paraphrase starters include, "It sounds as if you . . . ," "You seem to be saying . . . ," "It appears to me that you believe . . . ," "What I perceive is . . . ," "What I heard you say was . . . ," and "So you believe that . . . ." Using a paraphrase starter invites your communication partner to listen to you and provide feedback concerning how successful you are at receiving the whole message.

The skill of paraphrasing is extremely important when you are interacting with people who may not speak the same native language as you. Being able to reword their thoughts enables both people to check the accuracy of the message. To develop your skill as a paraphraser, you might begin by reflecting on various responses to a particular message and assessing which is the best paraphrase. Skill Development 4.1 presents three messages, each with four responses. Which are the most accurate and effective paraphrases?

Skill Development 4.1

RECOGNIZING EFFECTIVE PARAPHRASING[21]

Select the effective paraphrase of the sender's message.

1. *Speaker:* "Sometimes I think I'd like to drop out of school, but then I start to feel like a quitter."
    a. "Maybe it would be helpful to take a break and then you can always come back."

    b. "You're so close to finishing. Can't you just keep with it a little bit longer?"

    c. "It sounds like you have doubts about finishing school but that you don't like to think of yourself as a person who would quit something you started."

    d. "What do you think the consequences will be if you drop out?"

2. *Speaker:* "I really don't want to go to a party where I don't know anyone. I'll just sit by myself all night."

    a. "You're apprehensive about going someplace where you don't know anyone because you'll be alone."

    b. "It would really be good for you to put yourself in that kind of a situation."

    c. "I can really relate to what you're saying. I also feel awkward when I go to strange places."

    d. "Maybe you could just go for half an hour and then you can always leave if you're not having a good time."

3. *Speaker:* "I get really nervous when I talk with people I respect and who I fear might not respect me."

    a. "I've really found it useful to prepare my remarks in advance. Then I'm not nearly as nervous."

    b. "You really shouldn't feel nervous with people you respect because in many ways you are just as good as they are."

    c. "You feel uncomfortable when you talk with people who you think may not regard you in a positive way."

    d. "Why do you think you get so nervous about people you respect?"

Answers

In the first situation, responses a and b offer advice, not a paraphrase, and response d poses a question that is not relevant since the speaker already indicates the consequence, "feel like a quitter." The only response that offers an effective paraphrase is c.

In the second situation, responses b and d offer advice, and response c expresses empathy, which may be helpful but, in this case, the feelings may not be accurately reflected (the speaker does not indicate feeling "awkward"). The only response that offers an effective paraphrase is a.

In the third situation, response a offers advice, response b tells the speaker that feeling nervous is foolish (so implies that she or he is stupid), and response d poses a question that the speaker already answered, people "might not respect me." The effective paraphrase is c.

Taking Notes

Some people find that taking notes improves their listening because it requires them to concentrate on what the speaker is saying. Since an average sender speaks 150 words per minute (about half the number of words on a typed, double-spaced page) and an average receiver can grasp meaning at rates as high as 500 words per minute, listeners should have time to jot down a speaker's ideas.[22]

To make your notes most useful, concentrate on the main ideas and supporting evidence. Write down only what is necessary to remember the most important information, use key words, and avoid writing complete sentences or every word the speaker says. By putting the ideas in your own words, you can check your understanding and immediately review the speaker's message. Note taking is a skill that must be practiced. It should be an automatic part of your listening routine in class, while talking on the phone, and when you feel you can't concentrate on or remember a spoken message without some reinforcement.

Repeating

Another way to focus your attention and increase your comprehension is by repeating. For example, when a person is introduced to you, focus your attention on the name and immediately repeat it by saying something like, "It's nice to meet you, Marcia." Call the person by name several times during your conversation. Then, when departing, repeat the name again. The more you repeat the name and look at the person, the stronger your memory is likely to be.

Staying Alert Physically

Most people don't realize how much their bodies reflect whether they're focusing on what is being said. For example, when you're interested in what another person is saying, you lean forward and align your body with the speaker's body; when you're enthusiastic about an idea, your posture straightens; when you're disturbed by what is being said, your body tenses.

Good listeners recognize that sometimes they must change body position in order to focus more intently. Think of your body as an auto engine. If you drive a gearshift car, you know that at certain times you need to upshift or downshift. You need more engine power to get up a hill and less to cruise comfortably along a level highway. Similarly, in listening, you must upshift or downshift your body when it needs a change in power. Level 3 listening doesn't take very much effort; much like easy driving, third gear will do. Level 2 listening takes more power, and Level 1 requires great concentration and physical involvement. Sitting or standing upright with your eyes on the speaker are your most powerful listening positions. They force you to focus all your attention on the speaker and the immediate situation.

Right now, while you are reading this book, sit up straight, center all your attention on the words you are reading, ignore any outside sounds, and underline the key words on this page. You will find that your power of concentration increases immediately because you have, in effect, shifted into first gear. Stay in this position as long as necessary to grasp the material you are reading. Once you have identified the general trend, shift out of first gear. (It helps to know that in writing and speaking, the writer or speaker usually makes a statement and then clarifies by defining terms and giving examples. You may need first gear for the statement, second gear for the definition, and, if you understand what is being said, third gear for the examples.) Shift back to first when a new idea is presented. When you are not in first gear you can relax your body, but you should still stay alert (Level 2 listening, second gear).

Because active listening is hard work, it is tiring to maintain maximum alertness. Certain activities, such as appreciative listening, usually require only third gear. In contrast, listening for comprehension, as in class lectures, usually requires frequent shifting from gear to gear. Such shifts do not take place automatically. You must psychologically and physically shift gears for yourself during the act of listening.

ORGANIZING MATERIAL

You can help yourself remember what is said by using the organizing techniques of chunking, ordering, and reordering. (These techniques may be useful for listening to class lectures or technical information, but may not be practical in an ongoing conversation.)

Chunking

Chunking is the grouping together of bits of information that share a particular relationship. This allows you to condense information for easier recall. For example, while discussing a story in an American literature class, you could group the terms that describe each character so that later you remember each person's physical and emotional description rather than random details. Also, in conversation, as you and a friend talk about people you know in common, you can remember the names your friend tells you by placing the people in categories such as "major," "hometown," or "groups to which they belong."

Ordering

Ordering is the arranging of bits of information into a systematic sequence. Thus, in chemistry class you can more easily remember a process by organizing it into a step-by-step progression. For example, first, get the equipment for the experiment; second, get the necessary chemicals; third, study the lab manual to determine the order in which the chemicals are mixed; fourth, mix the chemicals. Similarly, in planning a trip with a friend you can organize your ideas by each day of the trip.

Reordering

Reordering is the changing of an existing system of organizing information so that a new or different sequence is developed. Reordering is useful when you have difficulty remembering material in the sequence in which it is presented. For example, rather than remembering the causes of World War I by dates, you might remember them according to the causes in each country going from west to east (England, France, Germany, and Austria-Hungary).

Skill Development 4.2 will give you some practice in chunking, ordering, and reordering.

Skill Development 4.2

CHUNKING, ORDERING, AND REORDERING

1. Chunk these: Wheaties, Bananas, Peaches, Cheerios, Frosted Flakes, Pineapple, Shredded Wheat, Strawberries.

2. Chunk these: hammer, saw, screws, wood, bricks, chisel, screw driver, nails, plasterboard.

3. Order these: Christmas, Easter, Valentine's Day, Independence Day, Halloween, Labor Day.

4. Order these: France, Russia, Germany, England, Poland, India, Japan.

5. Reorder your answer for exercise 4.

6. Order these cities: Atlanta, Georgia; Baltimore, Maryland; Cleveland, Ohio; Dallas, Texas; Ft. Lauderdale, Florida; San Francisco, California.

Possible Answers

1. *Fruits* that are commonly put on cereals (bananas, peaches, pineapple, and strawberries) and *cereals* (Wheaties, Cheerios, Frosted Flakes, and Shredded Wheat).

2. The list contains *tools* used in construction (hammer, saw, chisel, and screw driver) and *materials* used in construction (screws, wood, bricks, nails, and plasterboard).

3. The sequence Valentine's Day, Easter, Independence Day, Labor Day, Halloween, and Christmas, orders the holidays from earliest to latest in the year.

4. and 5. The sequence England, France, Germany, India, Japan, Poland, Russia, orders the countries alphabetically. Other methods for ordering them include spatial—going from west to east (England, France, Germany, Poland, Russia, India, Japan), or east to west, and from the country with the largest population total to the smallest, and vice versa.

6. Among the many possibilities would be to chunk the cities by north to south location, by east to west location, by alphabetical or reverse alphabetical order.

PROVIDING FEEDBACK

As a listener, you can provide feedback to show attention to or interest in the subject, to stop speakers from using unfamiliar vocabulary, to discourage them from digressing and speaking in circles, to alert them to the need for examples, to make them focus on the issue, to signal the need for specifics, to show empathy, and to suggest that thoughts need to be organized more comprehensively. Regardless of the reason for your feedback, it should not be ambiguous. It is not much help to your communication partner if she or he must stop and take the time needed to decipher what emotion your facial expression is trying to convey.

The focus of Skill Development 4.3 is on methods you could use to provide feedback that attests to your listening. It calls for indicating nonverbal listening cues, such as raising your eyebrows in thought, verbal listening cues, such as asking a relevant question, and combined nonverbal and verbal listening cues, such as slapping your friend on the back and saying, "Congratulations!"

Skill Development 4.3

PROVIDING FEEDBACK TO INDICATE YOU ARE LISTENING

For each situation list several ways in which you could let others know you are listening to them. Be specific; for example, if you would ask a question as a verbal cue, indicate what the question is you would ask. As an example, answers are provided for the first situation.

Situation 1: Your friend just told you that she is going to Europe for the summer. You . . .

1. Nonverbal cues: raise my eyebrows; open my mouth wide
2. Verbal cues: say "Wow!"; ask, "What countries in Europe do you plan to visit?"
3. Nonverbal and verbal cues combined: nod and say "That's great."

Situation 2: Your best friend just told you that his brother was hurt in an auto accident. You . . .

1. Nonverbal cues:
2. Verbal cues:
3. Nonverbal and verbal cues combined:

Situation 3: Your psychology professor calls you into her office and tells you that she would like you to be her research assistant next year. You . . .

1. Nonverbal cues:
2. Verbal cues:
3. Nonverbal and verbal cues combined:

Situation 4: Your communication professor is giving a lecture on rhetorical theory and you don't understand the relevance of distinguishing *hearing* and *listening*. You . . .

1. Nonverbal cues:
2. Verbal cues:
3. Nonverbal and verbal cues combined:

Situation 5: A classmate tells you, "We went to the party and everyone was doing all kinds of stuff." You don't understand what "stuff" means. You . . .

1. Nonverbal cues:
2. Verbal cues:
3. Nonverbal and verbal cues combined:

LISTENING RESPONSE STYLES

There are four distinct response styles, each with advantages and disadvantages, and each useful in particular situations. How do you typically respond to others' statements and actions? Knowledge Checkup 4.5 will help you assess your usual listening response style. Discussion of each style, including its advantages and disadvantages, follows the knowledge checkup.

Knowledge Checkup 4.5
ASSESSING YOUR LISTENING RESPONSES[23]

Circle the letter that best describes your first response to the person in each situation. The goal is to tell how you would actually respond, not what the right response would be or how you would like to respond. Each is a school-related example. Put yourself into the situation, whether or not you have actually had the experience.

1. "I think I'm doing all right, but I don't know where I stand in the course. I'm not sure what my teacher expects of me, and she doesn't tell me how I'm doing. I'm trying my best, but I wish I knew where I stood."
    a. "Has your teacher ever given you any indication of what she thinks of your work?"
    b. "If I were you, I'd discuss it with her."

    c. "Perhaps others are also in the same position, so you shouldn't let it bother you."

    d. "It seems that not knowing if you're satisfying your teacher's requirements leaves you feeling unsure. You'd like to know just what she expects from you."

2. "The policy in the Chemistry Department is supposed to be to hire lab assistants from people in the advanced chem classes. And now I find that this person from a beginning class is getting hired. I had my eye on that job; I've been working hard for it. I know I could be a terrific assistant if I had a chance."

    a. "You shouldn't complain—they probably hired the best person to be an assistant."

    b. "Getting ahead is very important to you, even if it means hard work, and you feel cheated that someone else got the job as lab assistant."

    c. "What else besides being a lab assistant can you do to show them you're really capable?"

    d. "You should take some more chemistry classes to help you advance."

3. "I'm really tired of this. I'm taking more classes than anyone I know, and then on the same day three of my teachers tell me that there's another assignment due on top of what's already due. I've got so many people asking me to do things that I just can't keep up, and it bothers me. I like my teachers, and my classes are interesting, but I could use a vacation."

    a. "With so many teachers asking you to do extra assignments, it's difficult for you to accomplish all of it, and the pressure gets you down."

    b. "Are all these requests from your teachers required work?"

    c. "You seem to have too much work. Why don't you talk it over with your teachers?"

    d. "You're probably overworked because you're not organized."

4. "My teacher tells the class that he would appreciate getting term projects as soon as possible to help him with grading. So I work like mad to get it completed and on his desk early. What's my reward for helping him out? Nothing! No thanks, no nothing. In fact, I think my project will sit on his desk until all the projects are handed in."

    a. "How often do teachers do this to you?"

    b. "You ought to tell him how you feel."

    c. "You feel like he's taking advantage of you and that you're being treated unfairly."

    d. "You shouldn't get so angry."

5. "He used to be one of the guys until he was made the team's coach. Now, it's like he's not my friend anymore. I don't mind being told about my mistakes, but he doesn't have to do it in front of the rest of the team. Whenever I get the chance, he's going to get his!"

    a. "To be told about your mistakes in front of the rest of the team is embarrassing, especially by a person you once considered a friend."

    b. "If you didn't make so many mistakes, the coach would not have to tell you about them."

c. "Why don't you talk it over with a few other people on the team and then go talk to him about this situation?"

d. "How often does he criticize you in front of the others?"

Listed below are the possible responses for each of the five situations. If you circled answer a in situation number 1, circle 1a below (in the "information seeking response" category). If you circled answer b, circle 1b below (in the "recommendation response" category). Do this for your five responses.

Active response:	1d, 2b, 3a, 4c, 5a
Recommendation response:	1b, 2d, 3c, 4b, 5c
Information seeking response:	1a, 2c, 3b, 4a, 5d
Critical response:	1c, 2a, 3d, 4d, 5b

Underline the category (or categories) in which you have the most circled answers. This (or these) is your general listening response style.

Each of the responses in Knowledge Checkup 4.5 is an example of a different response style. The four response styles are active, recommendation, information seeking, and critical.

ACTIVE RESPONSE STYLE

If your general response style is active, you are probably nonjudgmental as you listen. Active listeners tend to focus on the essential themes and feelings that are being expressed and at the same time try to build mutual understanding. Active listeners also demonstrate a good grasp of paraphrasing because their feedback reflects both the content and the feelings of the speaker.[24]

The primary advantages for your communication partner of this response style are support and concern. With your support and concern, she or he can feel safe to explore whatever is on her or his mind, whether to clarify thoughts, feelings, or ideas. The primary advantage of active listening for you is that you come to know and understand another person in more depth than is usual in most relationships. Also, you feel the pleasure that comes from helping someone.

Although active listening has several important advantages, it has some drawbacks that need to be considered. First, to listen actively you must put aside your own prejudices and concerns—something that is quite difficult. Second, active listening requires time, and you may not have the time to spare. Third, active listening requires a great deal of skill. Focusing your attention exclusively on the other person, recognizing the main themes in the messages you receive, insightfully detecting the emotions being expressed, and communicating your understanding clearly and supportively are difficult tasks requiring a great deal of proficiency. And fourth, given the skill and time required to listen actively, it is apparent that this response style demands a great deal of energy to perform well.

RECOMMENDATION RESPONSE STYLE

If your general listening response style is to make recommendations, you are probably an advice offerer who tells the speaker what to do and what not to do. You attempt to solve the problem or to do the thinking for the talker. This is one of the most common reactions to another's problem.[25] North American men, in particular, often hear other's talk about a problem as a request for a solution, while North American women hear talk about a problem as a request to talk about the problem.[26]

The primary advantage of this response style to your communication partner is that if you are correct, your partner has a useful solution to a problem. You, of course, get to feel good about yourself—after all, you're smart and you're helpful.

Unfortunately, although a popular response, it may not be the most helpful. What may be a useful recommendation for you may not work for your communication partner. Also, by providing your own solution, instead of having your partner generate his or her own, you make it possible for your partner to avoid responsibility for the decision. And if your recommendation fails to work, you may lose a friend!

Before you make a recommendation, be as sure as possible that it is correct, that your communication partner is seeking your recommendation, and that you won't be blamed if the recommendation doesn't work. People may *seem* to want advice, but what they usually need is to talk about how they feel and what they think.

INFORMATION SEEKING RESPONSE STYLE

If your general listening response style is to ask for additional information, you probably want to clarify your understanding before you react. Questions can relate to the content of what someone says—for example, if your roommate asks you to "keep the place cleaner," you could ask, "what does 'cleaner' really mean?"—or the feelings communicated—for example, "how do you feel about the room not being as clean as you would like?" Questions often are useful for getting others to think about their problems, to see them more clearly, and to understand better how they feel about them—your roommate may not be sure what "cleaner" means until you talk about it, and may not realize how annoyed he or she feels about your not picking up your clothes and putting them in the laundry bag until the feelings are expressed verbally.

An information seeking response style is usually positive, but if you overuse it your communication partner may feel grilled or that you aren't dealing specifically with the problem and how she or he feels. As a result, your delay may be perceived as disinterest or lack of involvement.

For a response style to be effective, avoid seeking information just to satisfy your own curiosity. The other person might be confused about your purpose (e.g., a question such as "Did you grow up in a house that was 'super' clean?" may be of interest to you,

It takes two to speak the truth—one to speak and another to hear.
HENRY DAVID THOREAU

but not relevant to the conversation at hand). Also, your partner may become angry (e.g., "What does it matter how clean my home was?").

In addition to not asking questions just to satisfy your curiosity, don't ask questions that are disguised criticisms. Questions that look like traps are not helpful and may even make matters worse—your partner still has a problem, and now, added to that, you both have a damaged relationship. "Don't you think it's a little compulsive to want to clean the room more than once a week?" is not really a question; it is a critical statement in disguise.

It is important to remember that people from some cultures generally will not answer your request for additional information. In fact, they probably will think you rude for probing. For example, in the Japanese and Chinese cultures, as a way of saving face people often will say *yes* even when they mean *no*. And in many Latin cultures, where social harmony is important, people will often supply you with the response they think you want to hear rather than the "real" one.

CRITICAL RESPONSE STYLE

If your general response style is to criticize, you show a tendency to judge, approve, or disapprove of the messages you receive. Instead of focusing on content and emotion, you are probably listening for information that may be used to evaluate the speaker.

Negative judgments that are purely critical—"You were wrong to call him," and "You asked for it!"—are rarely helpful, although there is a slight chance that the person criticized may be motivated to consider changing (e.g., she may decide to stop calling him). Less critical responses may be taken as constructive criticism, as responses meant to help and not necessarily to hurt. Like purely critical responses, however, less critical responses are prone to get a defensive reaction. Your communication partner may feel attacked, and the usual (although not most helpful) response is for the person to attack back.

A critical response works best when your partner asks for your evaluation. Invited criticism is more likely to be listened to than uninvited criticism. Also, your critical response should be genuinely constructive and not designed as a put-down. Too often the phrase "I'm only telling you this for your own good" is not true.

LISTENING TO HELP

It is common for friends to call on each other to provide help in the form of listening. When stress builds, problems arise, and conflicts seem overwhelming, most of us seek out a friend to talk to—not so much to have the friend solve the problem for us, but simply to listen, provide support, and give us the chance to talk through and explore what is on our minds. Listening to help requires using all of the response styles. Generally perceived as most effective is the appropriate use of an active listening response style—which includes being nonjudgmental, providing feedback that reflects both the

content and the feelings of the speaker, and building mutual understanding. Also helpful is the appropriate use of an information seeking response style—which includes posing sincere questions in a supportive and noncritical way. You also may use a recommendation response style—which includes knowing when *not* to make a recommendation and understanding the potential benefits and harms of a recommendation from the other person's perspective. The least effective response style is probably the critical one, unless the evaluation is invited.

If you already are or plan to become a helping professional, working in psychology, social services, teaching, speech therapy, law, or medicine, you must possess good listening skills. Listening to help requires that you understand the basic helping process as illustrated in Figure 4.2.

The first step in listening to help is *involving* yourself in your communication partner's life. This requires acting as a mirror to reflect his or her problems or needs. Involving is the widest part of the funnel because the information you and your partner share is broad: You usually discuss a great many things as you get to understand more about your partner and the particular problem that served as the impetus for your getting together to talk.

After involving yourself in your communication partner's life, the second step is to help your partner *explore* the problem. This is often accomplished by listening carefully and posing feedback questions that stimulate your partner to talk and think about the problem. Paraphrasing is an especially productive way to probe a speaker for more information. In addition, your feedback should describe rather than evaluate, be specific rather than general, and take into account the other person's needs. Avoid trite

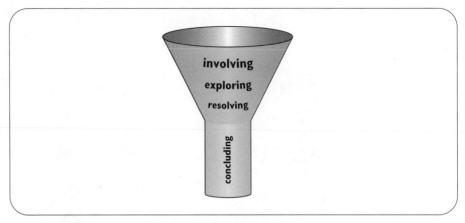

FIGURE 4.2   The Helping Process

statements ("That's too bad," "This too shall pass," and "We all go through that"); rather, invite the person to tell more ("Would you like to talk about that?" "Tell me about it," and "I'd be glad to listen"). This part of the funnel is narrower because you and your partner have narrowed the scope of what you talk about.

After involving and exploring, the goal of the third step is *resolving* the problem either through personal insight or a series of experiences that provide useful skills, such as how to communicate assertively. The funnel narrows still further as you and your communication partner focus specifically on alternatives to resolve the problem.

In the *concluding* step, the goal is for you, the listener, to summarize the involving, the exploring, and resolving steps, and indicate possible future actions. The stem of the funnel represents the culmination of your work, the final product of your listening to help.

Keep in mind that only if the troubled person asks for advice and you are trained to help people achieve behavioral change should you get involved beyond reflecting. People who try to play "Dear Abby" without the appropriate training, no matter how good their intentions, may do more harm than good. Also remember that to carry out the process, the person who listens to help should keep these questions in mind: What is the real problem (why is the person asking for help)? What is the person feeling (about himself or herself, the problem, the listener, and the process of getting help)? How can you be helpful (what can you realistically do)?

Hearing may be natural, but effective listening is not. It requires work: You need to evaluate your listening strengths and weaknesses; you need to recognize the barriers that interfere with your ability to be a good listener; and you need to develop the skills necessary to overcome those barriers. In addition, if you want to help others, you need to develop a large repertoire of listening response styles. Given the immense amount of time you spend listening, the work is well worth the effort.

Communication Competency Checkup

The goal of this communication competency checkup is to guide you in putting your skills and knowledge about listening to use and to help you summarize the material in this chapter.

FUNKY WINKERBEAN © 1988 North America Syndicate, Inc. Reprinted with special permission of North America Syndicate.

The teacher seems to be indicating that Funky is not displaying good listening skills in class.

1. In the classroom, which reasons for listening should be motivating Funky?

2. Based on Funky's response, what listening level is he displaying?

3. Which barriers to effective listening seem to be keeping Funky from being an effective listener, both in the classroom and now while talking to the teacher?

4. What specific techniques could Funky use to improve his listening skills and therefore maintain attention throughout the class and in the type of interpersonal conversation illustrated here?

5. Name one of Funky's red flags.

6. Consider this situation: In the teachers' lounge an instructor was discussing a class she recently taught. She said, "I was really afraid that the way I presented the material would confuse the students." What would a fellow teacher with an active response style say? What would a person with a recommending response style say? What would a person with an information seeking response style say? What would a person with a critical response style say? How would the teacher probably react to each colleague's response?

NOTES

1. Don Oldenburg, "Sometimes People Only Hear What They Really Want to Hear," *Washington Post,* as reprinted in *Cleveland Plain Dealer,* March 18, 1987, G1, using materials developed by Robert Montgomery in *Listening Made Easy* (New York, AMACOM, 1984).

2. Oldenburg, "Sometimes People Only Hear What They Really Want to Hear."

3. Satoshi Ishii and Tom Bruneau, "Silence and Silences in Cross-Cultural Perspective: Japan and the United States," in *Intercultural Communication: A Reader,* 7th ed., ed. Larry A. Samovar and Richard E. Porter (Belmont, CA: Wadsworth, 1991), 314.

4. Larry A. Samovar and Richard E. Porter, *Communication between Cultures* (Belmont, CA: Wadsworth, 1991), 125.

5. Beverly D. Sypher, Robert N. Bostrom, and Joy Hart Siebert, "Listening Communication Abilities and Success at Work," *Journal of Business Communication* 2 (1989): 293–303.

6. For a discussion of several studies concerning how time communicating is divided, see Andrew D. Wolvin and Carolyn Gwynn Coakley, *Listening,* 5th ed. (Dubuque, IA: Wm. C. Brown, 1995), 7–9.

7. Judi Brownell, "Perceptions of Effective Listeners: A Management Study," *Journal of Business Communication* 27 (1990): 401–15.

8. P. J. Kaufmann, *Sensible Listening: The Key to Responsive Interaction,* 2nd ed. (Dubuque, IA: Kendall/Hunt, 1993).

9. Benjamin Broome, "Building Shared Meaning: Implications of a Relational Approach to Empathy for Teaching Intercultural Communication," *Communication Education* 40 (1991): 235–49; Tom Bruneau, "Empathy and Listening: A Conceptual Review and Theoretical Directions," *Journal of the International Listening Association* 3 (1989): 1–20; James B. Weaver III and Michelle D. Kirtley, "Listening Styles and Empathy," *Southern Communication Journal* 60 (1995): 131–40.

10. Brant R. Burleson, "Comforting Messages: Their Significance and Effects," in *Communicating Strategically: Strategies in Interpersonal Communication,* ed. John A. Daly and John M. Wiemann (Hillsdale, NJ: Lawrence Erlbaum, 1991).

11. Adapted from Dr. Virginia Katz, University of Minnesota–Duluth, as cited in Oldenburg, "Sometimes People Only Hear What They Really Want to Hear"; and Lyman Steil, *Your Listening Profile* (New York: Sperry Corporation, 1980), 6.

12. Based on D. Aronson, "Stimulus Factors and Listening Strategies in Auditory Memory: A Theoretical Analysis," *Cognitive Psychology* 6 (1974): 108–32, as cited in Blaine Goss, "Listening as Information Processing," *Communication Quarterly* 30 (Fall 1982): 306.

13. Jerre Levy, "Right Brain, Left Brain: Fact and Fiction," *Psychology Today* (May 1985), 38–44. Also see Sally P. Springer and George Deutsch, *Left Brain, Right Brain* (San Francisco: Freeman, 1981); Michael S. Gazzaniga, "The Social Brain: It's a Case of the Left Brain Not Knowing What the Right Brain is Doing, and Therein Lies Our Capacity for Belief," *Psychology Today* (November 1985), 29–38; Betty Edwards, *Drawing on the Right Side of the Brain* (New York: Jeremy P. Tarcher/Perigee Books, 1989); and Kathleen Doheny, "When Left- and Right-Brainers Clash," *Cleveland Plain Dealer* (March 19, 1995), Living Section.

14. Adapted from an instrument developed by Paul Torrance and Bernice McCarthy, 1979. The complete instrument can be obtained from Excel, Inc., P. O. Box 6, Fox River Grove, Illinois.

15. Deborah Atwater, "Issues Facing Minorities in Speech Communication Education: Moving from the Melting Pot to a Tossed Salad," in *Proceedings from the Future of Speech Communication Education, Speech Communication Association Flagstaff Conference Report* (Annandale, VA: Speech Communication Association, 1989), 41.

16. Steven Golan, "A Factor Analysis of Barriers to Effective Listening," *Journal of Business Communication* 27 (1990): 25–36.

17. For a discussion of the cybernetic process, see Norbert Wiener, *The Human Use of Human Beings* (New York: Anchor Books, 1950).

18. Adapted from Madelyn Burley-Allen, *Listening: The Forgotten Skill* (New York: John Wiley and Sons, 1982), 44.

19. Adapted from a handout by George Tuttle and John Murdock, "Approaches to Teaching" at the Speech Communication Association Convention, Anaheim, CA, November 11, 1981, plus additional material from Burley-Allen, *Listening,* 42.

20. Cited by Ronald Adler, Lawrence Rosenfeld, and Neil Towne, *Interplay: The Process of Speech Communication,* 4th ed. (New York: Harcourt Brace Jovanovich, 1989), 182.

21. Based on a handout by an unidentified author entitled, "Listening," at the Speech Communication Association meeting, San Francisco, 1989.

22. Gerald M. Goldhaber, "Listener Comprehension of Compressed Speech as a Function of the Academic Grade Level of Subjects," *Journal of*

Communication 20 (1970): 167–73; David B. Orr, "Time-Compressed Speech—A Perspective," *Journal of Communication* 18 (1968): 288–92.

23. Adapted from Burley-Allen, *Listening,* 85–89.

24. For an extended discussion of active listening and response styles, see William E. Arnold, *Crisis Communication* (Scottsdale, AZ: Gorsuch Scarisbrick Publishers, 1980). For a discussion of monologic and dialogic listening, see Michael Beatty, *The Romantic Dialogue: Communication in Dating and Marriage* (Englewood, CO: Morton, 1986), Chapter 9.

25. C. I. Notarius and L. H. Herrick, "Listener Response Strategies to a Distressed Other," *Journal of Social and Personal Relationships* 5 (1988): 97–108.

26. Deborah Tannen, *You Just Don't Understand: Women and Men in Conversation* (New York: William Morrow, 1990).

CHAPTER 5

NONVERBAL COMMUNICATION

COMMUNICATION COMPETENCIES

This chapter examines nonverbal communication. Specifically, the objective of this chapter is for you to learn to:

- Describe the nonverbal behaviors important in assessing strangers.
- Summarize the role of culture in nonverbal communication.
- Recognize the stereotypes associated with physical appearance, including body type, physical attraction, clothing, and jewelry.
- Interpret and control facial movements and eye behavior.
- Assess the effects of physical and psychological contexts on the interpretation of nonverbal cues.
- Describe the importance and uses of touch.
- Use vocal cues to express emotions and regulate social interactions.
- Describe the types and uses of body movements, and learn to mirror body movements of others to increase their perceptions of similarity to you.
- Recognize and assess the effects of different time perspectives on interpersonal interaction.
- Recognize nonverbal messages that indicate deception.
- Use nonverbal behaviors to affect how you feel.

KEY WORDS

The key words in this chapter are:

nonverbal
    communication
ectomorphic body type
mesomorphic body type
endomorphic body type
conversational turn
    taking
territoriality
territorial invasion
territorial violation
territorial contamination
personal space
intimate distance
personal distance
social distance
public distance
paralanguage
vocalics
nonfluencies
emblems
illustrators
regulators
affect displays
adapters

Think back to the last time you walked into a room filled with strangers, such as a class or a party. How did you decide to whom you would speak? What clues did you look for and how did you interpret them? Before a word was spoken, a great deal of information was exchanged. Which actions and characteristics did you focus upon?

Rank the following items with respect to their importance to you in determining whether you approach someone or not. Rank the most important characteristic 1 and the least important 9.

_____ Body shape, whether she or he is fat or thin, muscular or flabby, short or tall.

_____ The clothing the person is wearing, whether it is clean or dirty, in or out of style.

_____ Jewelry, such as a wedding band or college ring.

_____ Eye contact, whether the other person looks at you and how long eye contact is sustained.

_____ Facial expression, whether the person is smiling or frowning, looking bored or puzzled.

_____ Distance, the space between you and the other person, such as how close you can get before the other person backs up or breaks eye contact.

_____ Voice, whether the person's voice sounds nasal, throaty, or resonant.

_____ Body movements, such as the person's gestures and stance.

_____ Touch, whether the person touches you, or how she or he responds to your touch.

These clues suggest the many forms of nonverbal communication. Before you ever learned about words and their association to particular meanings, you already were sensitive to the variety of nonverbal information you received. You recognized familiar faces, voices, smells, smiles, and frowns long before you knew the words *good* and *mine*. **Nonverbal communication**—the actions and attributes of people *other than words* and aspects of the environment that convey meaning—was the first form of communication you learned and used.

How you use nonverbal symbols and the meaning you give those symbols are skills you learned as part of your cultural experiences. For example, based on cultural tradition, people from Thailand do not touch in public, while in Russia and France men and women openly embrace.[1] The Japanese feel uncomfortable when their partner uses too much eye contact. The Arabs, on the other hand, engage in a great deal of direct gazing.[2] In the Mexican culture conversation is highly valued, yet for Buddhists, a peaceful mind and wisdom come during moments of silence.[3] These examples, and thousands of others, demonstrate that we have *learned* our use of much of our nonverbal communication.

Nonverbal reactions also can be innate, automatic, based on biological traits with which we are born. Closing your eyes and ducking your head when you hear a loud sound, when someone attempts to slap you, or when a pebble hits your windshield while you are driving are reflexive reactions. When you are feeling insecure, the sweating of your hands or the tightening of your stomach muscles are reflexive reactions. The fact that we are born with some of our nonverbal tendencies is clearly illustrated by the fact that "even people who are blind move their hands when they talk, although they've never seen anyone do it."[4]

On the other hand, some of our nonverbal behaviors are learned in much the same way we gain spoken language. By observing and imitating people around us as we grow, we learn not only to speak but to behave as our role models do and, so, we reflect those patterns. Every culture has its own body language. As anthropologists Edward and Mildred Hall indicate, "The important thing to remember is that culture is very persistent. In this country, we've noted the existence of culture patterns that determine [physical] distance between people in the third and fourth generations of some families, despite their prolonged contact with people of very different cultural heritages."[5] These cultural patterns are readily identifiable. Italians, for example, are noted for using their hands to a great extent when they speak and exert extensive vocal ranges when excited. In contrast, the British are noted for controlling their gestures and outward display of emotions.

FUNCTIONS AND CHARACTERISTICS OF NONVERBAL COMMUNICATION

Nonverbal communication has several functions, including its role in forming first impressions and its variety of possible relationships with verbal communication. In addition, nonverbal communication has several characteristics that give it its flexibility and uniqueness as a mode of communication.

FUNCTIONS OF NONVERBAL COMMUNICATION[6]

You base first impressions almost entirely upon nonverbal information, such as body shape, clothing, jewelry, eye contact, and facial expressions. The importance of nonverbal behavior, however, does not stop with first impressions. Rather, nonverbal communication is always an important part of the total communication process, which includes both verbal and nonverbal messages.

Sometimes nonverbal communication works in conjunction with verbal communication. You may use nonverbal communication to *complement* your words, as when you point south while saying, "They went down the hall that way." A complementing nonverbal message conveys the same meaning as the verbal message and, therefore, completes or supplements the verbal message. Holding your hands about eight inches apart as you say, "The fish was about eight inches long," would be a complementary verbal and nonverbal message.

You also may use nonverbal communication to *accent* your words, as when you pause before making a point in order to emphasize the thought's importance, or pound your fist on the table during an argument to add impact to your words.

Nonverbal messages also may be used to *regulate* both verbal and nonverbal communication. For example, signaling a waiter to come to your table is an attempt to regulate his actions. Similarly, if the waiter responds by holding up his pointing finger, he is regulating your waiting time. Also, putting your pointing finger to your lips to signal a noisy child to be quiet is an attempt to regulate her volume.

Besides working in conjunction with spoken words, nonverbal communication can *substitute* for spoken words. For example, nodding your head yes instead of verbally stating agreement, or holding up two fingers in response to the question "How many scoops of ice cream do you want?" are both examples of substituting nonverbal for verbal messages.

Nonverbal communication can *contradict* your spoken words. For example, glancing away from your friend as you hesitantly say, "I like that sweater," provides the listener with a contradictory message: positive words and evasive eye movement.

CHARACTERISTICS OF NONVERBAL COMMUNICATION

In addition to complementing, accenting, regulating, substituting, and contradicting verbal behavior, nonverbal communication has several identifiable characteristics that highlight its usefulness.

Emotions and feelings are more accurately and easily communicated nonverbally than with words. While words are best for conveying ideas, nonverbal communication is best for conveying feelings and emotions. For example, explaining the definition of communication to a friend may be quite easy with words. Consider the problems you would have if you were limited to nonverbal messages. Similarly, the emotions felt at a funeral of a loved one are communicated more concisely and effectively by crying or stifling your emotions than are attempts to put those emotions into words. This difference between verbal and nonverbal messages may stem from the fact that verbal messages need to be learned and most nonverbal messages are innate.

When considering how people express emotions and feelings nonverbally, you need to keep in mind the role of societal influence. For example, in many cultures outward signs of emotion are accepted as natural. People from the Middle East are generally expressive and animated. For the Japanese, however, external signs are often considered a mark of rudeness and an invasion of privacy.[7] Think a moment about what the implications are of the English expression, "Keep a stiff upper lip."

Nonverbal behaviors are not easily controlled consciously. Because nonverbal behaviors are for the most part performed without thought, they are relatively free of distortion or deception, especially in comparison to the more easily controlled verbal messages. For example, a warm face, stammering speech, or clenching a jaw are all involuntary reactions when a person is nervous or embarrassed. The behavior is automatic, an unconscious reflex.

When verbal and nonverbal communication conflict, the nonverbal messages are characteristically the more accurate reflection of feelings. Because nonverbal behaviors are often below our level of awareness and are not easily controlled, most individuals regard them as the more accurate indicator of a speaker's feelings. Because of the ease with which verbal communication can be manipulated, the presumption is that if someone is intent on covering up or lying, he or she can select the appropriate words more easily than faking nonverbal behaviors. No amount of verbal protesting and stating, "I'm not embarrassed," can cover up looking away from the other person and shifting your weight from foot to foot.

Nonverbal communication is more effective than verbal communication for expressing messages in a less confrontive manner. If you think something you might say is likely to elicit rebuke or embarrassment, you run less risk of these reactions if you avoid using words. For example, if you want to know whether your date likes you and are unwilling to ask directly, gently taking hold of the other person's hand and gauging the response (pulling away or allowing the hand-holding) may provide you with the information you need. The nonverbal behavior, in this instance, is less invasive—both you and the other person can opt out of the situation without a confrontation.

Nonverbal behaviors indicate how you should interpret the verbal messages you receive. Consider the difference between someone saying, "I think I understand your directions to Mario's Restaurant," in a confident tone of voice and someone saying the same thing in a hesitant tone, accompanied by head-scratching and raised eyebrows. In the first situation you might feel pleased with your ability to give directions; in the second one you probably should consider how to restate your message to make it clearer. The key to interpreting the content of verbal messages is the interpretation of their nonverbal underpinnings. In other words, do the cues such as tone of voice, facial expression, and stance, complement or contradict the words?

There are cultures that rely heavily on verbal language and others that put more stock in nonverbal messages. Anthropological studies show that cultures can be classified and placed on a continuum according to the emphasis they put on words versus nonverbal messages as tools for carrying meaning.[8] At one end of the continuum are the German, French, Scandinavian, North American, and English societies that believe verbal messages are extremely important. The Japanese, Chinese, and Koreans, on the other hand, believe that most meaning is found in the context in which people communicate. People know what is being felt without having to talk. The Korean language actually contains the word *nunchi,* which literally means "being able to communicate through the eyes."[9]

The functions and characteristics of nonverbal communication are displayed in a variety of ways. People communicate nonverbally through physical appearance, face and eyes, context of communication, touch, voice, body movements, and time.

PHYSICAL APPEARANCE

Your physical appearance includes everything that's visible to others, from the top of your head to the bottom of your feet, including your body shape and the clothing you wear. How much importance do you place on your own physical appearance? How much importance do you place on the physical appearance of others?

BODY SHAPE

If you are like most people, one of the first pieces of data you use to size up another person is body shape: whether the person is **ectomorphic**—thin and frail-looking; **mesomorphic**—muscular and well-proportioned; or **endomorphic**—fat and round.[10] Each body shape encourages different stereotypes. Thin people may be perceived as tense, serious, and cool; overweight people are often thought of as sluggish, sociable, and kind; and muscular people are often considered confident, energetic, and assertive. Although the relationship between these adjectives and body type is not well supported, the point is that others may ascribe these characteristics to people based on the shape of their body, and then respond to them based on their ascriptions. For example, people 55 years old and older are more attracted to ectomorphs and mesomorphs physically, socially, and as work partners, than they are to people with endomorphic body types.[11]

In addition to body shape, the consequences of being tall or short are well documented. Tall people have a distinct advantage over their shorter peers. For example, men 6 feet 2 inches and taller receive starting salaries about 12 percent higher than those under 6 feet; short actors often get the "short end of the stick" by being cast as buffoons, arch villains, or "small tough guys." Many jobs, from flight attendant to police officer, have traditionally required a certain minimum height.

Problems even extend to health. Researchers have found that men 5 feet 7 inches and shorter in North America are 70 percent more prone to heart attacks than men 6 feet and taller. This may be due to the stress felt by shorter men in a society where being tall is valued.

BODY IMAGE

How you feel about your appearance has greater influence on your interactions with other people than how you actually look. If you are uncomfortable with your appearance, you are likely to avoid interaction with others or at least assume that you deserve negative reactions. Teenagers suffering from acne may confine themselves to the house on weekends or assume that dating is out of the question, just as adults who put on a few pounds may skip a social event, wanting to lose weight before appearing "in public." How do you feel about the various parts of your body, as well as your overall appearance? Knowledge Checkup 5.1 will help you learn how you perceive your own appearance.

Knowledge Checkup 5.1

APPEARANCE SATISFACTION

How satisfied are you with the way each of your body parts looks?

If you are extremely satisfied, mark **7.**

If you are satisfied, mark **6.**

If you are slightly satisfied, mark **5.**

If you are neither satisfied nor unsatisfied, mark **4.**

If you are slightly unsatisfied, mark **3.**

If you are unsatisfied, mark **2.**

If you are extremely unsatisfied, mark **1.**

_____ hair	_____ eyes	_____ nose
_____ mouth	_____ back	_____ chest/breasts
_____ stomach	_____ hips	_____ sex organs
_____ teeth	_____ chin	_____ cheeks
_____ arms	_____ elbows	_____ forearms
_____ wrists	_____ hands	_____ fingers
_____ thighs	_____ knees	_____ calves
_____ buttocks	_____ height	_____ weight

_____ overall facial attractiveness

_____ overall body appearance

How does your feeling about a particular body part affect how you behave? How is your self-esteem affected by your physical appearance?

In general, the more physically attractive you perceive yourself to be, the more positive your self-concept is. This attitude explains why physically attractive people tend to be more independent and more resistant to pressure to conform than are less attractive people. Attractive females, for example, are generally more confident, and attractive males are generally more assertive and less critical than their less attractive peers.[12]

Also, if others perceive you as physically attractive, they are more likely to evaluate you positively. Attractive people are thought to be kinder, stronger, sexier, more interesting, poised, modest, sociable, and outgoing than unattractive people. Physically attractive people are given more help, receive more awards, and perceived as more credible (and are, therefore, more persuasive) than their physically unattractive counterparts.[13] Perceptions of physical attractiveness, however, are not based solely on physical characteristics. A recent investigation found that women rate a man as more physically attractive if he solicits his female partner's opinions, is sensitive to how she sees things, is altruistic, and, in general, is agreeable.[14]

On the other hand, attractiveness may not always be an asset. Research reveals that a businesswoman perceived as attractive may suffer unpleasant and unfair consequences from the perception. Because of her appearance, others may consider her unintelligent, self-centered, and fickle. Others may assume that she gained her power through her appearance rather than her ability. Being perceived as attractive also may make a businesswoman the target of coworkers' jealousy, gossip, and sexual harassment.[15] Some individuals, both men and women, are subject to PQS—*prom queen syndrome.* Individuals who are extremely attractive are often perceived to be unreachable, untouchable, and undatable by others because it is believed that the overly attractive person is "all dated up," "wouldn't go out with an ordinary someone like me," or "is so attractive that I'd be uncomfortable with everyone paying attention to them." In reality, those with PQS are often undated and lonely because of those misconceptions.

It is easy to imagine the influence of culture on attractiveness and the judgment of beauty. In North America, for example, we tend to value the appearance of slender women, but in many other cultures the definition of what is attractive calls forth a series of different images.[16] In Eastern Europe, for example, women who are heavyset often are deemed more attractive than lean and thin females. In fact, being skinny is associated with physical weakness. And in the Japanese culture diminutive females are deemed the most attractive.[17]

CLOTHING AND OTHER ARTIFACTS

Most of us assume that people wear clothes for protection and modesty, but that isn't always the case. For example, according to the observations of Darwin, the natives of Tierra del Fuego never wore clothes, in spite of severe weather conditions; modesty in some cultures—particularly those that are not westernized—has no relation to wearing, or not wearing, clothes.[18]

If protection and modesty are not the only reasons for wearing clothes, there must be other important reasons why people wrap themselves in cloth, leaves, bark, or skins. These reasons include communication. People take note of what you wear—just as you observe what they wear—to assess your current economic and social levels; your social, economic, and educational background; your level of success, social position, and sophistication; your value system, trustworthiness, and moral character. For example, a person who is wearing a uniform identified with a particular charity (e.g., the Salvation Army) can collect more donations than someone without the uniform, probably because the person is perceived as being trustworthy.[19]

Although it may not be fair—or wise—to judge people by their clothes and accessories, these judgments are a fact of life. And there is some evidence that your clothing preferences do, indeed, say something about your personality. To what extent do you enjoy being "in style"? Do you like to wear tight or skimpy clothes? Are you more interested in style or comfort? Knowledge Checkup 5.2 provides you with the opportunity to assess your clothing preferences.

Knowledge Checkup 5.2

CLOTHING PREFERENCES[20]

Indicate the extent to which each of the following statements accurately or inaccurately reflects your clothing preferences. Use this scale:

If the statement is very accurate, write **5.**

If the statement is fairly accurate, write **4.**

If the statement is neither accurate nor inaccurate, write **3.**

If the statement is fairly inaccurate, write **2.**

If the statement is very inaccurate, write **1.**

_____ 1. I like close-fitting clothes.

_____ 2. I usually dress according to the weather rather than for fashion.

_____ 3. When buying clothes, I am more interested in practicality than attractiveness.

_____ 4. I see nothing wrong with wearing clothes that reveal a lot of skin.

_____ 5. The people whom I know always notice what I wear.

_____ 6. It is very important to be in style.

_____ 7. There is nothing like a new article of clothing to improve my morale.

_____ 8. I buy clothes for comfort rather than appearance.

_____ 9. If I had more money I would spend it on clothes.

_____ 10. I like clothes with bold designs.

Scoring

Add responses to 5, 6, 7, 9 ("clothing consciousness") _____

Add responses to 1, 4, 10 ("exhibitionism") _____

Add responses to 2, 3, 8 ("practicality") _____

Clothing Consciousness

Males (scores from 16 to 20): generally conforming; believe that people can be easily manipulated and that clothing is a means to manipulate others; deferential to authority, custom, and tradition; (4–8): generally aggressive, independent, and outgoing; dependable.

Females (16–20): generally inhibited, loyal, anxious, kind, sympathetic, and conforming; (4–8): forceful, dominant, clear-thinking; independent.

Exhibitionism

Males (12–15): aggressive, confident, unsympathetic; moody; often impulsive; (3–6): nondisclosive; believe others are easily manipulated.

Females (12–15): radical; high moral self-concept; generally detached in relationships; (3–6): timid; sincere; accepting of others; patient.

Practicality

Males (12–15): generally inhibited; not leadership-oriented; cautious; (3–6): success-oriented; forceful; mature; serious.

Females (12–15): clever; enthusiastic; guarded; confident; outgoing; not leadership-oriented; (3–6): self-centered and independent.

What you wear matters more in some situations than in others and matters more to some people than to others. Your friends probably allow you more latitude in style and color than does your employer, and your choice of clothing for an informal party may be less consequential than your choice of clothing for a business luncheon.

What you wear in a business setting is important; what you wear to a job interview is crucial. An interviewer's first impression of you at an interview comes from what you wear.[21] If that initial impression is unfavorable, your opportunities may be immediately closed off. Dressing too differently from your interviewer may result in a poor evaluation, as may dressing in anything but conservative garb, which, for men, includes dark suits and solid white shirts with "power" ties of red or yellow; and, for women, a dark or medium-toned skirted suit, white or pastel blouses, closed-toed pumps, and modest jewelry. Whether or not you are comfortable with your appearance, you can control—at least to some extent—how the interviewer perceives you by choosing your clothes carefully.

Clothing—how much, how little, and what kind—reflects an individual's culture. For Filipinos, "values relating to status and authority are at the root of the Filipino's need to dress correctly."[22] The Spanish also link appearance to one's status.[23] In the Arab world, robes and veils are part of the attire for many women and are expressions of the cultural value of modesty. There are, of course, individuals in those cultures who choose not to wear "traditional" garb. Some Arabic women, for example, stress their independence by wearing Western-style clothing and no veil.

Certain accessories communicate specific messages. Wedding bands, college rings, and religious symbols all convey particular and relatively unambiguous messages. Jewelry also may be used to communicate social status and economic level, such as a Timex (low) versus a Rolex watch (high). A college student with a book bag slung over the shoulder conveys an image of normalcy, while that same person toting a leather briefcase most probably would be seen as different, atypical.

You react to what you wear just as others do: You may find that putting on your jogging outfit gets you ready, both physically and mentally, to run; wearing your favorite dress-up outfit helps get you in the mood for a sophisticated party. Your mood affects what you choose to wear, and what you choose to wear in turn affects your mood. Dress how you *want* to feel and, sure enough, you just might feel that way!

FACE AND EYES

Except in circumstances when you're trying to deceive someone, you communicate more about your emotions with your face—especially your eyes—than with any other part of your body.[24] You also depend more on other people's facial cues than on any other nonverbal behavior to ensure successful interactions. Facial cues may communicate five dimensions of meaning:

1. The extent to which communication is experienced as pleasant or unpleasant, good or bad (Does this person find interacting with you a pleasant experience?)

2. The level of interest in the communication (Is this person interested in you or what you're saying?)

3. The intensity of involvement in the communication (Is this person involved in your interaction?)

4. The spontaneity of the response (Is this person controlling his or her facial expressions or behaving naturally?)

5. The extent to which communication is understood (Does this person understand what you're saying?)

> The face is the mirror of the mind, and eyes without speaking confess the secrets of the heart.
> ST. JEROME

Looking at others' faces has early roots. Early in life you learned to search out the faces that meant warmth and security; soon after your birth, you recognized and were attracted to the faces of those who cared for you. Later you learned that this part of the body communicated even more useful information. Now you spend a lot of time looking at faces because faces identify people more than any other aspect of the body. Even young children, when they're asked to draw themselves, typically produce a large head with eyes, nose, mouth, and ears attached to a small body with little more than stick arms and legs. The head is what is important: It is what you speak to and what speaks back to you.

Because the face can be so revealing, you probably use a number of adaptive facial techniques to communicate a desired message. You may *qualify* your expressions by adding a second facial expression to change the impact of the first one. For example, after looking angry and yelling, "I can't stand it any longer!" you might look sad or confused in order to communicate, "I'm hurt and sad, as well as angry, and I want to talk about this."

You may *modulate* your facial expressions to communicate feelings stronger or weaker than the ones you're actually experiencing. For instance, to make the statement "I'm really upset with you" more intense, you could squint your eyes to show that you really mean what you're saying.

You may *falsify* your facial expression by showing an emotion when none is felt (you may have no particular feeling about your friend's new coat, but to maintain your friendship you look excited); evidencing little or no facial expression when you experience a particular feeling (you may feel angry about your friend's lateness, but keep your expression neutral to avoid an argument); or covering a true emotion by displaying a false one (you may express pleasant surprise when your parents unexpectedly show up to cover your real feeling of dismay).

People throughout the world use facial expressions to display emotion and express intimacy. People have learned, usually subconsciously, specific cultural norms regarding the amount and variety of facial expressions to reveal. For example, in many

BIG GEORGE   **By Virgil Partch**

*"I think you'd better cool it, Randy. Your father
is giving you one of his meaningful glances."*

Mediterranean societies, signs of grief, sadness, and even joy are, by our standards, greatly exaggerated. Crying at a North American funeral may be typical of that culture, just as grief wailing may be typical in a Mediterranean country. The Chinese and Japanese, on the other hand, do not readily show signs of emotion. Even the expression "save face" is a reminder that the face can reveal and/or conceal feelings.[25] Besides national cultural differences in the use of the face, there are, in our own society, gender differences. For example, compared to men, women use more expression and are more expressive. They smile more, are more apt to return a smile when someone smiles at them, and are more attracted to others who smile.[26]

Although overall facial expressions are important, the eyes hold perhaps the greatest fascination. Everyday expressions confirm the emphasis on sense of sight: You don't say "I feel/smell/hear/taste what you mean," or "I'll feel/smell/hear/taste you later," but "I *see* what you mean" and "I'll *see* you later." Old friends, of course, are a "sight for sore *eyes.*" The evil eye, a glance that can inflict harm, must, of course, always be guarded against! Looks can kill—at least figuratively!

Perhaps the most reliable measure of interest is pupil size. Findings from studies focused on pupil size confirm that pupils enlarge when you're interested in a subject and contract when you're uninterested. By noticing others' pupil size—certainly not something they can easily control—you can often gauge their level of interest.[27]

You also use your eyes to regulate the flow of conversation. Typically, a speaker looks away from the other person, glances back now and then to check for feedback, and then establishes full eye contact to indicate when it's time for **conversational turn taking,** indicating that it's the other person's turn to talk.

Facial cues can communicate the emotion you're experiencing, but your eyes indicate its intensity. For example, your face may communicate interest and happiness, but the intensity of that expression comes from your eyes. Think for a moment about all the messages we send with our eyes. We have all heard some of these words to describe a person's eyes: direct, sensual, expressive, blank, intelligent, penetrating, sad, cheerful, worldly, hard, trusting, suspicious. Our interpersonal relationships are affected by our establishing eye contact, avoiding eye contact, looking down, shifting our eyes, squinting, staring straight ahead, and even closing our eyes.

Culture modifies how much eye contact people engage in and who is the recipient of the contact. In most Western societies our communication partner is expected to look us in the eye, with a 3– to 10–second duration being most comfortable. Think about how you react when someone looks away while you're talking to him or her, or doesn't look at you at all. Arabs look directly in the eyes for long periods of time, while Asian cultures teach their children to focus their eyes on their superior's Adam's apple or tie knot.[28] People raised in rural Mexico will lower their eyes as a sign of respect. Certain groups of Native Americans also feel uncomfortable with unbroken eye behavior. So strong is that orientation that Navajos tell a folktale about a "terrible monster called He-Who-Kills-With-His-Eyes." The legend teaches the Navajo child that "a stare is literally an evil eye and implies a sexual and aggressive assault."[29]

Communication between black and white Americans is yet another area where cultural differences show. When speaking, African Americans tend to employ much more continuous eye contact than do whites. However, the opposite is true when blacks are listeners.[30]

In our society, gender also affects eye contact usage. Women tend to look more at their communication partner than men do, look at one another more, hold eye contact longer, and appear to value eye contact more than men.[31]

Paying attention to the facial expressions and eye behavior of others can increase your sensitivity to the communicative function of the face. Skill Development 5.1 should help you increase your skill by presenting you with four photographs of different facial expressions to analyze.

INCREASING YOUR SKILL AT INTERPRETING FACIAL EXPRESSIONS

1. What emotions are being communicated by the facial expressions in each picture?

2. What levels of interest and involvement are communicated facially by each person in each picture?

3. In each picture, what intensity of emotion is revealed by the facial expressions?

4. What nonverbal information did you use to answer questions 1 through 3?

5. Did anything besides facial expressions help you answer the questions?

6. Can you locate any cultural information in these pictures?

CONTEXT OF INTERACTION

Because meaning is contextual, nonverbal behaviors have little meaning outside the situation in which they occur. For example, nonverbal behaviors that communicate sorrow—slumped body, hand pressed against forehead, downward glance, sighs—also can communicate overwhelming happiness. You are more likely to interpret the behavior as sorrow if the physical context is a hospital and more likely to interpret it as happiness if the context is a game show and the person's score indicates she just won $10,000. Some context is needed to interpret the behavior correctly. In what ways did you use the physical context indicated in the photographs in Skill Development 5.1 to interpret the facial expressions?

Two contexts are important: physical and psychological. The *physical context* is composed of objects and their arrangement in the environment. It may include architecture, furniture, room color, and temperature. The *psychological context* includes a person's thoughts and feelings toward aspects of the physical context. For example, a student may feel that the seat she occupies in a classroom is "her seat."

PHYSICAL CONTEXT

Close your eyes. Now, describe the exact setting where you are sitting (e.g., if you are in a room—what are the colors of the walls and floor, what is the texture of the ceiling, what is the color of the clothing of the person closest to you; if you are outside— what color is the nearest building to you, what is the nearest physical object, what color is it?).

If you are typical, you probably couldn't accurately describe all of the details of the things and people around you. Most of us are unaware of much of the environment, yet it has a great effect on us. It even has a profound effect on infants. In a study with six-month-olds, it was found that when the setting in which the infants learned to move a mobile was changed, their ability to perform the task decreased. The researchers' argued that when a person learns a task, the setting in which the task is learned is part of the learning process; therefore, changing the setting reduces the extent to which the person's memory is jogged.[32] This conclusion may support an argument for taking tests in the same room in which you learn the material!

A physical context may be analyzed along a number of dimensions. For example, a physical context may be assessed according to its degree of *formality* (most business offices usually are formal), *comfort* (family rooms are very warm and comfortable), *privacy* (bathrooms are supposed to be private), *familiarity*—how ordinary or unusual it is (modern office buildings are traditionally strikingly unusual), and *closeness*—how close it encourages you to be with others (family rooms are supposed to be arranged so that people can feel close).

To create a desired effect (formal or informal, comfortable or uncomfortable, private or public, familiar or unfamiliar, close or distant), you may adjust a room's color, temperature, and furnishings. For example, red is perceived as hot and full of vitality, whereas pale blue and green are cool and calm. Brown is unhappy, purple can be depressed or dignified and gives off the most energy of the shades of a color wheel. White is neutral, which may account for its widespread use in a variety of shades and settings.[33]

Color and temperature interact. For example, a white room seems cooler than a red room when the temperature is identical. If your goal is comfort, keep in mind that perceptions of attractiveness decrease as temperature and humidity increase. Cool temperatures are better for working and warm ones for relaxing, although *cooler* and *warmer* are relative terms.

Next to raising or lowering the thermostat, the easiest way to change the environment is with furnishings and lighting. Rooms with indirect lighting, comfortable furniture, and carpeting and drapes are perceived as attractive, and they increase feelings of happiness and energy. Rooms with direct lighting, few sound-absorbing furnishings, and uncomfortable furniture cause occupants to feel tired and bored.[34] Chairs, for example, can greatly influence others' responses to a room. High-backed chairs covered with expensive cloth are more formal than low-backed ones in corduroy; soft, cushioned chairs are generally more comfortable than ones without cushions; several chairs indicate that a room is not private, that it is open to more than one person at a time; grouping chairs close together, facing each other or in a circle, encourages interaction.

Skill Development 5.2 will help you compare two environments. Specifically, you will describe those aspects of each setting on which you base your perceptions of formality, comfort, and so on, and discuss the differences in the use to which each setting is suited.

Skill Development 5.2
ASSESSING TWO ENVIRONMENTS

Analyze the following two settings with regard to their formality, comfort, privacy, familiarity, and closeness: a fast-food restaurant and a library reading room (or area) with which you are familiar. Indicate which part of the environment—color, temperature, furnishings, or lighting—you used as the basis for your assessment. For example, if you describe the fast-food restaurant as uncomfortable, specify why. Is it the uncushioned chairs, the bright lighting, the lack of soundproofing, the colors?

		Fast-Food Restaurant	Library Reading Room
1.	Formality	_____	_____
2.	Comfort	_____	_____
3.	Privacy	_____	_____
4.	Familiarity	_____	_____
5.	Closeness	_____	_____

Given your analyses of each environment, compare them with respect to the purpose of each. Does each environment communicate its purpose clearly? What changes would you make to each environment to make its purpose clearer and to increase the probability that it will be used "appropriately"?

Just as restaurants and libraries "tell us" what their purpose is by their formality, comfort, privacy, and so on, how you choose to decorate your office, room, or home communicates a great deal about who you are. For example, viewing slides of upper-middle-class homes, students accurately inferred the personality of the owners.

Decorating schemes gave important clues to the owners' intellectualism, politeness, maturity, optimism, tenseness, family orientation, reservedness, and adventurousness. The exterior of the homes gave clues to the owners' artistic interests, graciousness, privacy, and quietness.[35]

Another aspect of the physical environment is climate—typically ignored since no one can do much about it. Researchers in biometeorology have found that temperature, humidity, and atmospheric pressure all affect how we feel and, therefore, how we interact with others. For example, when barometric pressure falls (when the sky turns cloudy and it usually rains or snows), our bodies retain water, adding as much as an inch to our waistlines. The retained water may be a cause for increased irritability, not because of the extra inch, but because the water increases pressure on the brain. The good news is that high-pressure days (bright and clear) have the opposite effect. This effect could explain, in part, why people seem cheerier and more talkative when the weather is nice, but sadder and quieter when the weather is rainy or cloudy, especially for several days in a row.

PSYCHOLOGICAL CONTEXT

Psychological context may be divided into territoriality and personal space.

Territoriality is a feeling of ownership toward some fixed area. It may not be strictly logical to lay claim to certain areas of your environment, but you do it anyway. You feel that the room you sleep in is *your* room and the roses you tend are *your* roses. Because you feel that pieces of your environment belong to you, you act protective toward them, feel personally insulted if someone makes an unkind remark about them, and become sad or irate if something happens to them.

To lay claim to a piece of territory requires that you mark it with your ownership. You may leave an "occupied" sign on an airplane seat, drape your coat over the back of a chair in a restaurant, or spread your books on a desk in the library to indicate that the place is yours and that you will be returning to claim it—so others keep off! You may also formally mark your territory with your name or some representative symbol, such as a club's emblem or your initials. "This room belongs to _____" is a popular sign for those who want to emphasize that trespassing will not be tolerated.

You also may mark the boundaries of your territory. For example, a fence may separate your property from your neighbor's; painted lines separate your parking space from the next one; and a closed door clearly separates your room from the rest of the residence.

In a business setting, territory shows status. For example, the boss usually has a private office and the privilege of entering subordinates' work areas without knocking first. Similarly, the people with the most power and prestige most often get the largest and best-located offices.

Even the manner in which we organize our seating is swayed by culture. North Americans, when in group situations, usually talk to the people seated or standing in front of them instead of those beside them. Thus, seating arrangements are often face-to-face. The Chinese, on the other hand, often experience uneasiness when they are face-to-face and hence prefer side-by-side arrangements. People from cultures that value

conversation (such as the French, Mexicans, and Italians) often feel uncomfortable in North American homes when they go to sit down and find that the furniture is pointed toward the television set and not other people.

Problems arise if there is **territorial invasion** (someone tries to take over your territory and throw you out, as often happens when siblings fight over space in a shared bedroom); **territorial violation** (when someone uses your territory without your permission, such as your roommate borrowing your clothes); or **territorial contamination** (when someone makes your territory "impure," such as when an overnight guest sleeps in your bed).

Your reaction to an invasion, violation, or contamination can take several forms. You may decide to withdraw—a fight may not be worth your effort, or it may be all too clear you would lose. You might mark your boundaries more clearly, in hopes that the other person will withdraw and others recognize the territory as yours. Or, you might choose to fight—if the territory is important to you, you might respond to an intruder with threats and, in the end, violence.

How you respond depends on *who* enters and uses your territory (a friend is less threatening than a stranger), *why* she or he enters or uses it (for instance, a "mistake" is less significant than a "planned attack"), *what* territory is entered or used (you may care more about your bedroom than your seat in class), and *how* it is entered or used (an invasion is more threatening than a violation). How do you defend your territory? How do the "who," "why," "what," and "how" determine your response? Knowledge Checkup 5.3 will help you recognize your definition of and responses to someone using your territory.

Knowledge Checkup 5.3

ANALYZING YOUR TERRITORIAL DEFENSE

Answer the first three questions for the two situations, then, answer question 4.

Situation 1. You and a friend are eating pizza at a local restaurant when, all of a sudden, your friend reaches across the table, picks up your slice of pizza, and takes a bite.

Situation 2. You go to the library, gather some books and journals you need to read, and walk to your favorite and often-used desk in a remote, quiet corner. You discover a stranger sitting at "your" desk.

1. Is this an invasion, violation, or contamination? How do the "who," your assumptions about "why," your feelings about "what," and your perceptions of "how" affect your definition of your friend's behavior?

2. How would you react? Would you withdraw, remark your boundary, or fight? How does your analysis of the situation—as given in your answer to the first question—relate to your response?

3. Explain your responses to the two questions with reference to who you are, including your cultural background. Develop an explanation for someone with a different background, who responds differently to the incident.

4. What do your responses to the two incidents reveal about your feelings of territoriality?

Unlike territory, which remains fixed, your personal space goes where you go. **Personal space** is an invisible bubble of space around you—a body buffer zone. It is larger in front than in the back, and varies in overall size depending on where you are and with whom you're interacting. Your personal space probably contracts when you're with friends—you let friends get closer to you than strangers before you begin to feel uncomfortable.

In your next conversation with an acquaintance, try an experiment. As you talk, slowly, subtly, move closer to the other person and watch what happens. Most likely, the person will back away, countering each of your movements forward with a movement backward, without consciously being aware of what is happening.

As the experiment demonstrates, you hardly notice your personal space until someone violates it. Crowded elevators and theaters are uncomfortable partly because your space requirements are not met. When strangers touch you, they breach your space bubble and may leave you feeling exposed and vulnerable. Such violations may trigger a variety of nonverbal defensive reactions: You may shift your body away from the intruder, cut off eye contact to gain distance (a popular technique in elevators), or show nervous reactions, such as tightening your jaw, making downward or sideways glances, stroking your face, or tapping your fingers.

You protect your personal space because it serves several important purposes. Most importantly, it buffers you from others who might pose a threat. It also gives you room to breathe, move about, and act as you choose, free from crowding. It satisfies your psychological need to be separate from other people. Finally, given that distance communicates intimacy—closer is more intimate than farther—personal space allows you to regulate your intimacy.

Personal space requirements vary with age, gender, and personality, among other things. For example, as people get older their space requirements tend to increase; interacting females generally require less space than interacting males; introverts and people with low self-esteem usually require more than the average space between themselves and others.

Our response to any physical context not only reflects individual perceptions but deep-rooted cultural characteristics. For example, people from societies that emphasize privacy and the individual over the group (such as in England, North America, and Australia) demand more space than do those from communal cultures (such as in Latin America and the Mediterranean).[36] The need for large amounts of personal space also is part of the cultural experience of the people of Scotland and Sweden, for whom it reflects privacy, something desired in those cultures. And in Germany, private space is held sacred.[37] You can well imagine the potential for discomfort when a member of a culture that requires a great deal of space is confronted with members of a society that stand or sit close together.

Perhaps the most important overall determinant of spatial distancing is the relationship between the participants, including both the activity in which they are engaged (for instance, some sports require close contact) and their feelings for each other.

Personal space can be broken down into four zones:

1. **Intimate distance,** from touching to 18 inches, is reserved for intimate activities, including passing secrets, making love, and having confidential conversations.
2. **Personal distance,** from 18 inches to 4 feet, is used for discussing personal subjects.
3. **Social distance,** from 4 to 12 feet, requires a louder voice than intimate or personal distance and is thus used for more impersonal conversations, such as business transactions.

4.   **Public distance,** 12 feet and beyond, is usually used for group meetings and for hailing people. Distances farther than 25 feet limit communication to shouts and broad nonverbal gestures.[38]

Increasing your sensitivity to your own and others' personal space requirements, as well as knowing the norms and expectations for using the space in your environment, increase your ability to communicate skillfully. Recognizing how people use space and react to violations of space should help you to respond quickly and appropriately when problems of perceived inappropriate behavior arise. How do people use space in a setting such as a bookstore, supermarket, or department store? Knowledge Checkup 5.4 provides you with the opportunity to apply the information on personal space in an analysis of a common setting.

Knowledge Checkup 5.4

ANALYZING THE USE OF SPACE IN A COMMON SETTING

This activity requires you to observe how people use space in a particular setting and to note reactions to violations of spatial expectations.

Assignment: Select a supermarket, department store, college bookstore, or some other common setting in which people shop for things and then pay for them through a checkout line. Observe the interaction distances that seem usual between clerks and customers, between customers as they shop, and between customers in the checkout line.

1.   What are the average distances between the people you observed?

2.   How do people respond when one person comes too close to another or when one person touches another? How do people react to these violations of their space? How could they avoid violating each other's personal space?

3.   Think back to a foreign film or a film that contains interaction between North Americans and people of another culture, as well as people from the same culture. Or try to observe people who are from a culture other than your own. Describe their use of spatial distance during conversations.

TOUCH

Touch is the most relevant sense at the beginning of your life—it is how you first orient yourself to the world. By the time you learn to speak, however, sight and sound predominate and touch becomes less important. Nonetheless, the need for touch remains, although opportunities for touching and being touched decrease. The elderly may be the most touch-deprived members of Western society and, therefore, the loneliest.

Your skin is a sensitive receiver of communication: Pats, pinches, strokes, slaps, punches, shakes, and kisses all convey meaning. Touches may signal a particular relationship. Some are *professional-functional* ones, as when a doctor performs a physical examination. *Social* touches, such as handshakes, fulfill norms associated with greeting, acknowledgment, and parting. *Friendship* touches, such as shoulder-patting and hugging, convey the message that "We're friends," "I like you," or "I appreciate you." *Intimate* touches, such as kisses, can communicate love, while sexually arousing touches can increase the physical and emotional pleasures of lovemaking.

The messages that touch communicates depend on how, where, and by whom you're touched.[39] Slight variations in touch can communicate great differences of emotion. A person may touch your shoulder lightly to say "Listen to me," apply slight pressure to say "Seriously consider what I say," or squeeze forcefully to communicate "You'd better do as I tell you!"

The same type of touch on different parts of your body communicates different messages. A slap across your face may evoke fear or anger, while a slap on the back may cause happiness. Similarly, lightly stroking your hand may communicate concern, while the same touch on your head may communicate affection.

In addition to receiving messages, your skin also sends them. Polygraphs, for example, operate on the assumption that changes in your internal state are reflected in changes in your skin, and that these changes can be measured to determine whether you're telling the truth or lying.

The importance of touch for children has been well documented.[40] In general, the more caring (not abusive) touching an infant receives, the higher the probability that he or she will become a well-adjusted child, adolescent, and adult. Lack of touching during infancy has been implicated in health problems (such as allergies and eczema), academic problems (such as learning disabilities and low scores on intelligence tests), and decreased capacity for mature, sensitive tactile communication in adulthood (such as problems with showing affection by hugging). Feelings of trust and liking for others, on the other hand, have been linked to positive early tactile experiences. Parents who avoid touching their children or touch them only on certain "neutral" body parts often communicate that some parts are "better" than others, some are "more important" than others, and some parts are "bad." The action may result in an adult being alienated from all or certain parts of her or his body.

Most people, except those who have been abused, raped, or brought up in low- or no-touch families, associate touching with positive messages. Handshakes, probably the most common type of touch, connect people and help begin interactions on a note of shared status. Many cultures and co-cultures worldwide use touch to express affectionate greetings; for example, Americans kiss, Eskimos rub noses, and Burmese press their mouths and noses to another's cheek and inhale deeply.[41] For Muslims, greetings are exchanged by men holding each others' shoulders while hugging. (Not all cultures, of course, use touch as a form of greeting. For example, in cultures such as Japanese and Chinese, a bow instead of a touch is used as a form of greeting.)

Regardless of many of the positive messages associated with touch, many individuals avoid touching and being touched. Knowledge Checkup 5.5 provides you with an opportunity to assess your touch avoidance.

Knowledge Checkup 5.5

ASSESSING YOUR TOUCH AVOIDANCE[42]

Read the following statements concerning touch and indicate the extent to which you agree with each statement.

If you strongly agree, mark the statement **1.**

If you agree, mark the statement **2.**

If you are undecided, mark the statement **3.**

If you disagree, mark the statement **4.**

If you strongly disagree, mark the statement **5.**

_____ 1. I often put my arms around friends of the same sex.

_____ 2. I like it when members of the opposite sex touch me.

_____ 3. I like to touch friends of the same sex as I am.

_____ 4. I find it enjoyable when my companion of the opposite sex and I embrace.

_____ 5. Touching a friend of the same sex does not make me uncomfortable.

_____ 6. Intimate touching with members of the opposite sex is pleasurable.

Scoring

Add your responses to items 1, 3 and 5. This is your same-sex touch avoidance score. _____

Add your responses to items 2, 4 and 6. This is your opposite-sex touch avoidance score. _____

Add the two sums together to obtain your total touch avoidance score. _____

Same-sex and opposite-sex scores of 14 and 15, and a total score of 27 and above, indicate a high propensity to avoid touch. Same-sex and opposite-sex scores of 3 and 4, and a total score of 9 and below, indicate a high propensity to touch. Same-sex and opposite-sex scores between 5 and 13, and a total score between 10 and 26, indicate neither a high nor low propensity to touch.

Touch avoidance relates to several other communication behaviors. For example, the more a person avoids touch, the more likely it is that she or he will avoid verbal communication. In addition, touch avoidance is related to self-disclosure: People who disclose little tend to touch little, and those who are willing to self-disclose tend to touch a great deal. Also, men and women differ in their touch avoidance—men are more likely to be same-sex touch avoiders, while women are more likely to be opposite-sex touch avoiders.[43]

Avoiding touching is often associated with a negative attitude. We communicate dislike, disrespect, and refusal by not touching. Because we normally close a deal with a handshake, refusing to shake hands equates to refusing to complete a deal.

USES OF TOUCH

Touch is most useful for communicating intimacy, involvement, warmth, reassurance, and comfort. Touch has proven therapeutic power that nurses and other health care professionals employ to help their patients emotionally as well as physically. The therapeutic benefits of touch may derive in part from the effect that touch has on a recipient's willingness to talk. Because touch implies reassurance and caring, it encourages self-disclosure.

Touch helps to persuade people. For example, a study showed that a request for the return of a quarter left in a phone booth met with greater success when the new booth occupant was touched on the arm than when not touched. Similarly, requests to sign a petition received almost twice as many positive reactions when touch was involved— even when it was "accidental," as when fingers touched when a piece of paper was passed.[44]

Touch is also useful for communicating power relationships. In general, the person who initiates the touch is perceived as more powerful, more dominant, and of higher status than the one who is touched. In interviews, for example, while an initial greeting handshake is mutual and customary, the handshake that ends the interview is the prerogative of the interviewer, the person with more power in the situation. The interviewer may or may not offer to shake hands, but the lower status interviewee may be perceived as "pushy" if he or she makes the offer.

EXPECTATIONS FOR TOUCH

As is the case with most interpersonal variables, our cultural background determines expectations about touch.[45] Most of these variations relate to a culture's attitude toward *collectivism* (whether the culture is collective, in which the individual is subjugated to the group, or individualistic, in which the individual is stressed as important), *emotional restraint* (whether the culture encourages or discourages the expression of emotion), and *status distinctions* (whether they are rigid or flexible). For example, Canadians of English descent, Germans, Chinese, Scandinavians, and the English all have cultures that tend to discourage touching, especially for the upper classes.[46] ("Touching fellow workers and associates is not common in Japan. Patting someone on the back or putting a friendly arm around them is not done."[47]) These cultures also tend to be individualistic, discourage emotional expression, and have rigid status distinctions. On the other hand, Latin Americans, Israelis, Greeks, and Eastern Europeans are raised in cultures that tend to encourage touching. These cultures, in contrast to the first group, tend to be collective, encourage emotional expression, and have flexible status distinctions. North American culture falls between these two extremes. Although North American culture can be classified as nontouch, it is less extremely so than the Chinese or German cultures.

Regardless of cultural background, touch is expected in some situations and not in others. For example, you are more likely to touch others when giving them information or advice, asking a favor, expressing worry, or sharing an intimacy. You also are prone to touch a communication partner if you or the person is excited. You are less likely to touch another person when you are asking for information or advice, giving an order, agreeing to do something, or participating in a casual conversation. Casual, friendly settings, such as parties, are apt to encourage more touch than are formal work settings; private settings are more conducive to touching than public places.

Whether your expectations about touch are violated depends on several considerations. Where is the touch? How long does it last? How much pressure or intensity is used? What is your relationship with the person touching you? What are the circumstances—for example, are other people watching? What is your cultural background?

Reactions to being touched in the wrong place or by someone you don't like can range from politely ignoring the gesture to starting a fight.[48] If someone offers a limp handshake, you probably won't respond visibly, although you may form a particular impression of the person; if someone punches you in the arm, however, you are likely to respond, whether with a punch of your own, a verbal attack, or a smile.

Being sensitive to responses to touch can help improve your relationships. You can use touch to increase your persuasiveness, appear powerful, and communicate warmth, intimacy, and comfort—but only if your touch doesn't violate the other person's expectations.

Knowledge Checkup 5.6 calls for an analysis of your responses to being touched by acquaintances and close friends, as well as the touch you engage in with family and friends. Think carefully as you do the checkup—people tend to overestimate how often they are touched.[49]

Knowledge Checkup 5.6

ANALYZING YOUR TOUCH BEHAVIOR[50]

1. How often do people in your immediate family touch each other?
       very frequently   frequently   seldom   never

2. Pick two people with whom you interact regularly, a close friend and an acquaintance from work or school.
   a. How often do you and your close friend touch each other?
       very frequently   frequently   seldom   never
   b. How often do you and the acquaintance touch each other?
       very frequently   frequently   seldom   never

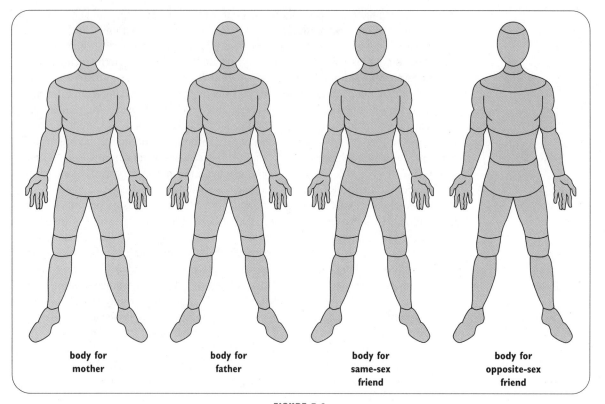

body for
mother

body for
father

body for
same-sex
friend

body for
opposite-sex
friend

FIGURE 5.1

c. What parts of the body are you most likely to touch when you touch your mother? Father? Same-sex friend? Opposite-sex friend? (Place a check mark on those parts of the body in Figure 5.1.)

d. On what parts of your body are each of these people likely to touch? (Place an X on those parts of the body in Figure 5.1.)

3. The numbers on Figure 5.2 identify various parts of the human body. (Note that the figure and identifying numbers and letters on the left represent the *front* of the body, and the figure on the right represents the *back* of the body.) Using those numbers, answer the following questions. Use as many numbers as are applicable.

a. What part of the body (front and back) are you most likely to touch?
   your closest same-sex friend
   your closest opposite-sex friend
   a stranger of the same sex
   a stranger of the opposite sex

b. What parts of your body are each of these people likely to touch?
   your closest same-sex friend
   your closest opposite-sex friend

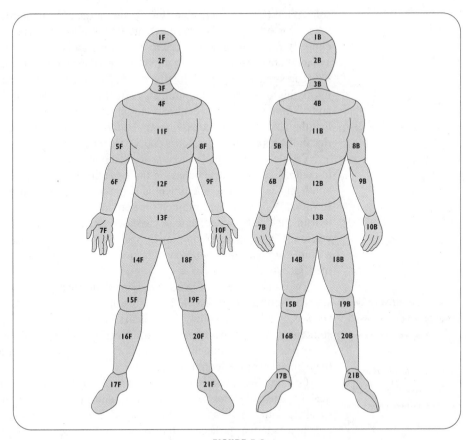

FIGURE 5.2

    c. What parts of the body do you feel should never be touched by another person other than yourself?

4. Write a two- or three-sentence statement about your touch behavior based on your responses to questions 1-3.

VOICE

Independent of the words you speak, your voice communicates a great deal about you. All by itself, your voice offers strong clues to your age, emotional state, education, home region, and status. **Paralanguage** or **vocalics**—variations in loudness (loud or soft), pitch (low or high), rate (fast or slow), quality (the particular resonance of your voice, for example, flat, breathy, nasal, throaty, or tense), articulation (slurred or clipped), duration (time it takes to emit a particular sound), and pronunciation (what syllables are stressed)—give your vocal cues their unique character. For example, when we express anger, we speak loudly, quickly, and with wide variations in pitch (although mostly high). When we communicate affection, we speak softly, slowly, in a low pitch, and with vibrancy. The vocal expression of joy is similar to the one for anger except that the voice is not quite so blaring. Sadness is expressed much as affection is except that in the expression of sadness pauses are irregular.

People's stereotyped reactions to different voice qualities indicate the importance of controlling your vocal behavior. For example, breathiness in males is associated with youth and an artistic temperament, and in females with prettiness, petiteness, and shallowness. Wide variations in pitch for both males and females are associated with being dynamic and extroverted, and an increased rate for both connotes animation and extroversion.[51] Of course, stereotyping by voice has its pitfalls: basing your mental picture of a blind date on a telephone conversation may lead to surprises when the two of you meet face to face.

Two other aspects of vocal behavior that affect perceptions are nonfluencies and silence. **Nonfluencies**—vocal behaviors that interrupt or disturb the flow of messages, such as "uh," "you know," and "stuff like that," unnecessary repetition of words, stuttering, incomplete sentences, and corrections—are usually associated with low credibility and lack of confidence. Keep nonfluencies to a minimum, even try to eliminate them, to appear more competent.

> In human intercourse the tragedy begins, not when there is misunderstanding about words, but when silence is not understood.
> HENRY DAVID THOREAU

Culture affects vocalics. For example, Arabs tend to speak loudly and with a great deal of gusto and enthusiasm. To them, loudness designates strength and sincerity, while speaking softly implies frailty. Similarly, Germans conduct their business with a "commanding tone that projects authority and self-confidence."[52] The Thai and Philippine societies, on the other hand, use so little volume it almost sounds as if they are whispering. For them, a soft voice reflects good manners.[53] When interacting with North Americans, people from the "quiet" societies often believe the loud volume means the American is angry, rude, or upset.

There are even paralanguage gender differences in North American society, most of which make sense when you consider general physical differences (which tend to make most women's pitch higher than most men's pitch) and differences in socialization. Women, socialized to be polite and deferential, tend to speak softly and use a lot of inflection, whereas men, socialized to be assertive and reserved, tend to speak loudly, with a lower pitch, and little inflection (except in emotional extremes such as anger or withdrawal).[54]

Differences in co-cultures in North American society also are evident. For example, African Americans tend to be more emotional, intense, dynamic, and enthusiastic in their use of voice than do white Americans.[55]

Silence—not speaking or making nonverbal vocal sounds, such as "um," when you are interacting with another person—is highly varied in meaning. Silence may communicate anger, attentive listening, grief, depression, respect, awe, or the message "leave me alone." Silence, when not understood, can strain interpersonal communication.

Many cultures feel comfortable with the absence of noise and talk and are not compelled to fill every moment with words like most North and South American people feel obliged to do. There are numerous Asian sayings that reflect this cultural bias toward quietness, such as, "Out of the mouth comes evil," "What is real is, and when it becomes spoken it is unreal," and "A flower does not speak."[56]

Even members of co-cultures living in the United States differ in their use of silence. Many Native Americans, for example, believe that silence is a sign of a remarkable person. From silence, it is believed, one derives "the cornerstone of character, the virtues of self control, patience, and dignity."[57]

How effective are you in conveying different emotions with your voice? Skill Development 5.3 provides you with an opportunity to practice using your voice to express emotions effectively. It also will help you test how effective you actually are in conveying different emotions vocally.

Skill Development 5.3

EXPRESSING YOUR EMOTIONS EFFECTIVELY

Read the following three sentences in different ways to communicate five emotions: anger, bewilderment, fear, happiness, and sadness. After you practice each several times, tape record your last attempts (do not record them in alphabetical order; rather, order them randomly).

What's happening? I thought we were going to get something to eat before the movie. Have our plans changed?

1. Are you satisfied that you were able to create five different meanings as you read the sentences? Which emotion was hardest to communicate? Which was easiest?

2. What variations in paralanguage did you make in each case to create the desired effect?

Play your five tape recorded readings of the sentences for four people, two of whom know how you typically use your voice to communicate different emotions, and two of whom are less familiar with your vocal expressiveness. Tell them you will play a tape in which you read the same sentences five different ways to communicate five different emotions (tell them the emotions in alphabetical order: anger, bewilderment, fear, happiness, and sadness). Ask them to determine which emotion is expressed in each reading.

1. Which emotions were correctly identified? Which were incorrectly identified? Which got a mixture of correct and incorrect identifications? Were there

any consistencies in incorrect identifications (e.g., were fear and sadness confused)?

2. Were the people familiar with how you usually use your voice better at identifying your emotions?

3. How successful are you at communicating your emotions by modulating your voice? How can you improve your vocal expressiveness?

Vocal cues play a significant role in communication aside from conveying emotions: They *regulate* and *structure* interactions, much as eye contact does. For example, if someone tries to interrupt when you are speaking, you can maintain your role as speaker in two ways. You can either fill your pauses with meaningless vocalizations such as "uh, well" or "but, uh," or you can alter your pitch and volume to signal "Don't interrupt me now!" The other person will rarely take over the speaking role if you use either of these techniques.

If, on the other hand, you want to stop speaking and let the other person begin, you can employ several techniques. You can use ascending pitch and volume, as if you were asking a question, and pause afterward. Alternatively, you can use falling pitch and volume and stretch out your final words. Of course, just keeping quiet is a sure signal that you're through, but your signal may go unnoticed for an embarrassingly long time if the other person is only half-listening. Listeners give priority to cues other than silence because silence can be ambiguous: It can mean a variety of things including "I'm through" or "I'm thinking."

Sometimes when you are listening you want to say something, but the speaker is unwilling to relinquish control. After trying the usual nonverbal methods for communicating your desire to speak—raising your hand, moving forward and gesturing, raising your eyebrows, opening your mouth—you may be forced to use a vocal stutter-start. A *stutter-start* is the pronunciation of a word with a repetition of the first sound, such as "m-m-m-m-maybe," or the use of an elongated nonfluency, such as "uhhhhhh." You may, of course, interrupt directly and begin speaking, but then the other person is likely to interrupt you in return to maintain the speaking role.

Another way to regulate a conversation is to encourage the other person to continue speaking. In addition to the nonvocal behaviors that communicate "I'm listening, please go on," such as head nods, sustained eye contact, and appropriate facial expressions, you may use encouraging vocalizations such as "uh-huh," "hmmmmm," "ahhhhh," and "ohhhhh."

One of the best ways to increase your proficiency in using vocal cues to regulate your conversations and to be sensitive to others' vocal attempts at control is to listen in on conversations and note how the communicators modulate their voices to manage the flow of talk. Knowledge Checkup 5.7 provides you with the opportunity to "listen in" on a conversation between a student and instructor and to get some practice recognizing how communicators regulate their conversations vocally.

Knowledge Checkup 5.7

USING VOCAL CUES TO REGULATE CONVERSATIONS

Read the dialogue and note the vocal cues used to regulate the conversation in these ways: (1) to maintain the role as speaker, (2) to get the other person to speak, (3) to take over as speaker, and (4) to get the other person to continue speaking. The conversation, between a student in a communication class and the instructor, takes place after class in the instructor's office.

Student:	I . . . well . . . had a little trouble understanding today's lecture on the voice. I . . .
Instructor:	What specifically did you have trouble with?
Student:	*(Leans forward and points at the instructor as if to speak.)*
Instructor:	*(Raising the pitch of his voice and speaking quickly.)* If you would ask questions in class, maybe you wouldn't have this problem.
Student:	B-b-b-but, I have trouble asking questions in front of the other students.
Instructor:	I used to have the same problem when I was a student. *(Leans back in chair, looks at student for several moments.)*
Student:	Gee, I would never have guessed that.
Instructor:	*(Lowering his pitch and speaking slowly.)* As I was saying, I used to have that problem until I realized that if I didn't understand something, and didn't ask, I would never get the information I needed.
Student:	I think I see what you mean.
Instructor:	Hmmmmmm.
Student:	But sometimes it's just hard for me.
Instructor:	*(Pitch rising as he speaks.)* But, you have to do it. *(Pause.)*
Student:	I guess you're right.
Instructor:	Uh-huh.
Student:	*(Pitch lowering, rate decreasing, and final two words stretched.)* I'm just going to have to do it.
Instructor:	If you give it a try, I'll work with you on it.

Your analysis of the dialogue may have revealed:

Student:	I . . . well . . . (**vocalized pause used to maintain his role as speaker**) had a little trouble understanding today's lecture on the voice. I . . .
Instructor:	(**interrupts to take over as speaker**) What specifically did you have trouble with?

Student:	*(Leans forward and points at the instructor as if to speak.)* (**attempt to take over as speaker**)
Instructor:	*(Raising the pitch of his voice and speaking quickly.)* (**rising intonation to maintain his role as speaker**) If you would ask questions in class, maybe you wouldn't have this problem.
Student:	B-b-b-but (**stutter-start to take over as speaker**), I have trouble asking questions in front of the other students.
Instructor:	I used to have the same problem when I was a student. *(Leans back in chair, looks at student for several moments.)* (**silence to get other person to speak**)
Student:	Gee, I would never have guessed that. (**relinquishes speaker role**)
Instructor:	*(Lowering his pitch as he speaks slowly.)* (**falling intonation to maintain his role as speaker**) As I was saying, I used to have that problem until I realized that if I didn't understand something, and didn't ask, I would never get the information I needed.
Student:	I think I see what you mean. (**relinquishes role**)
Instructor:	Hmmmmmm. (**vocal encourager to get other person to continue speaking**)
Student:	But sometimes it's just hard for me. (**relinquishes role**)
Instructor:	*(Pitch rising as he speaks.)* (**rising intonation to maintain his role as speaker**) But, you have to do it. *(Pause.)* (**silence to get the other person to speak**)
Student:	I guess you're right. (**relinquishes role**)
Instructor:	Uh-huh. (**vocal encourager to get other person to continue speaking**)
Student:	*(Pitch lowering, rate decreasing, and final two words stretched.)* (**falling intonation and stretching final words to get the other person to speak**) I'm just going to have to do it.
Instructor:	If you give it a try, I'll work with you on it. (**Finality**)

BODY MOVEMENTS

Body movements are motions such as gestures; head, arm, finger, leg, and toe movements; and changes in posture or trunk position. Some self-help books on nonverbal behavior suggest easy and clear interpretations of body movements. Merely by focusing on body movement, the writers contend, you can successfully understand and manipulate other people. Wrong! Although body movements provide a wealth of information, interpreting the information is not that simple. For example, according to some authors of popular books, crossing your arms on your chest, crossing your legs, and pointing your index finger are all supposed to signal defensiveness. Rubbing your eyes, touching your nose, and glancing sideways are all supposed to communicate suspicion. Rubbing your hand through your hair or taking short breaths is supposed to indicate frustration.

Although any of these examples may be true at particular times and in particular circumstances, they are generalizations. It is hard to interpret body movements without paying careful attention to the specific situation, including your relationship with the other person and the cultural context in which you're interacting. The same gestures may mean different things in different cultures. For example, what North Americans recognize as the "A-OK" gesture (making a circle with one's thumb and index finger), meaning "everything is fine," is a vulgar sexual threat in the Mediterranean area and a sign for money in Japan and Korea.[58]

Not only the gesture, but the size, intensity, and frequency of our actions can take on communicative importance. Italians, Middle Easterners, and South Americans are noted as being animated when they interact. On the other hand, many North Americans, Northern Europeans, and Asians equate vigorous action with a lack of manners and restraint.

TYPES OF BODY MOVEMENTS

Body movements fall into five categories: emblems, illustrators, regulators, affect displays, and adapters.[59]

Emblems are movements that have direct verbal translations in a given culture, such as the thumbs-up gesture, the "come here" signal, and the waves that mean hello and good-bye in North America.

Illustrators—which, like emblems, are used intentionally—add to or support what is said, as when you hold your hands different distances from the ground to indicate the relative heights of two friends or point to your car when talking about it.

Regulators, also used intentionally, influence who talks, when, and for how long. For example, moving close when greeting another person may initiate a conversation; moving backwards toward a door may signal the end of an interaction.

Less awareness and intentionality characterize affect displays and adapters. **Affect displays,** body movements that express emotions, are most commonly associated with the face—in fact, fear, anger, surprise, disgust, sadness, and happiness are six facial expressions that can be identified across all cultures. Other body movements also may express emotions. Foot-tapping, fidgeting, covering your mouth while speaking, and shifting your weight from foot to foot may indicate nervousness or boredom, depending on the context.

Adapters, which are seldom intentional, are body movements performed by habit. Your use of adapters often satisfies some physical need: You itch, so you scratch; your hair needs grooming, so you pat it; something is caught between two teeth, so you use

a fingernail to dislodge it. Interestingly, these adaptive behaviors satisfy not only your physical needs, but also your psychological needs. For example, stroking your chin calms you down, perhaps by distracting you from a stressful situation. Therefore, adapters may indicate psychological states. For instance, scratching when there is no itch often indicates nervousness, and stroking your hair may be your way of calming yourself.

USES OF BODY MOVEMENTS

Body movements also may be categorized according to their uses. One use of body movements is to communicate a degree of pleasure or displeasure, liking or disliking. For example, you may lean forward, face the other person directly, and assume a position that mirrors the other person's position to communicate liking. You may communicate dislike by reversing these behaviors, as well as by crossing your arms in front of you and tensing your body. In general, movement toward something with an open body position (such as open arms) indicates liking, and movement away from something with a closed body position (such as crossed arms) indicates disliking.

Body movements also may communicate a level of interest or arousal. Closing your eyes momentarily may mean simply that you're tired, or it may mean there is a lack of interest.

Finally, body movements may be used to communicate feelings of dominance or submissiveness, powerfulness or powerlessness. Dynamic gestures and erect posture indicate feelings of power or dominance, whereas slow, hesitant gestures and a slumped posture indicate feelings of powerlessness or submission.

Gestures are movements made by a particular part of your body, such as your hands. Your hands provide some of your most expressive gestures: You wave hello and good-bye, suggest that someone is mixed-up by moving your index finger in a circle while pointing to the side of your head, and suggest that you're thinking by rubbing your chin. Gestures also can communicate emotions. For instance, you drum your fingers to indicate impatience or boredom, or hit a table to emphasize that you really are angry.

What gestures would you expect to accompany these sentences?

Me? What did I do?
Take it! I give up!
You can trust me on this one.
Whew! That was a tough job!

Clearly, gestures can communicate very specific pieces of information.

Postures, movements that involve your whole body, are useful for communicating general attitudes. For example, the angle at which you turn your body toward another person may reveal your desire to include or exclude her or him. Turning your back on someone is typically interpreted as rejection, whereas standing face-to-face is seen as acceptance.

As has been seen throughout this chapter, the influence of one's culture can also be seen in the messages people associate with posture. In the United States, where being casual is highly valued by many, people often slouch when they stand or slump when they sit. In cultures that value formality, such as in Germany, Japan, and Sweden, a slouching posture is considered a sign of rudeness and poor manners.

Whether or not you mirror another's body movements may indicate your liking or perceptions of similarity. Films of group therapy sessions, when slowed down and viewed carefully, often reveal an intricate dance: People mirror the behaviors of individuals they like or want to encourage to like them and exhibit opposite body movements to individuals they dislike or reject. The changes in posture are subtle and rarely consciously performed. You may notice similar behavior in the way a seated group of people cross their legs. One change can set off a chain reaction—those who have positive feelings for the person who moved shift to a similar position, while the others quickly move to an opposite position.

Because mirroring nonverbal behaviors communicates liking and similarity, it may be useful for influencing others' feelings toward you. How does someone whose behavior you mirror respond to you? How do these responses differ from someone whose behavior you do not mirror? Skill Development 5.4 provides you with the opportunity to practice mirroring and to compare what happens when you mirror and don't mirror another person's body movements and other nonverbal behaviors.

Skill Development 5.4

INCREASING PERCEPTIONS OF SIMILARITY

Interact with a person who does not know you well (and thus does not know your usual body movements) and mirror that person's movements. Use similar gestures, posture, eye contact, facial expressions, touch patterns, and vocal characteristics. Do not mirror the person in a way that draws attention to your behavior. Be subtle.

How does the person whose nonverbal behavior you're mirroring respond to you? Note any reactions so that you can answer the following questions (plus any additional questions related to other aspects of the person's behavior that are important). What is this person's eye contact with you? How long does the person speak with you? How hard is it to encourage the person to speak? How close does the person sit or stand from you? How often does the person smile? At what angle is the person's body turned toward you? How often does the person touch you? In general, does it seem that this person likes you and feels comfortable with you?

Repeat the activity with another person, only this time use dissimilar gestures, posture, and so on. Again, do not act in such an obvious way that you draw attention to your behavior. Be subtle.

How does the person whose nonverbal behavior you're not mirroring respond to you? Note any reactions and answer the same questions you answered for the person whose behavior you mirrored. In general, does it seem that this person dislikes you and feels uncomfortable with you?

How do the reactions differ in the two situations? What does this imply about how mirroring behavior can be used as a persuasive device?

TIME

The Greek poet Euripides once wrote that "Time is a babbler, and speaks even when not a question is put." What he was telling us is that our use of time communicates. Although we can't hold or see time, many people respond to it as if it had control over their lives. Because time is such a personal phenomenon, we perceive and treat it in a manner that expresses part of our character.

Cultures, like people, present clues about their temperament by the way they conceive time. In North America, for example, we hear phrases such as, "He who hesitates is lost" and "A stitch in time saves nine." In contrast, in Chinese culture there is a Confucian proverb that states, "Think three times before you act." In which culture would you expect to meet many people who speak quickly and do things in a rush? And in which culture would you expect to meet many people who do things slowly and, it might seem, with great thought?

Most of the differences in cultural variations toward time can be seen in *punctuality,* the degree to which people are prompt, and the *pace of life,* the speed with which usual tasks are performed.

Differences in punctuality among people are apparent, a point to which any party host can attest. Guests from the "same" North American culture can be expected to arrive anywhere from "on time" (at the designated time or within fifteen minutes) to a "fashionable" hour or more late. If the guests are members of different cultures, the variation may be even greater. And if the event is a dinner party, where in the United States it is considered impolite to arrive too late (after all, the food is prepared and ready to be served), it is important to plan accordingly if the guest list is international. "In Britain it is correct to be 5–15 minutes late for an invitation to dinner. An Italian might arrive 2 hours late, an Ethiopian later, and a Japanese not at all—he had accepted only to prevent his host from losing face."[60]

How late is "late" for a business appointment? "In Britain and North America one may be 5 minutes late for a business appointment, but not 15 minutes and certainly not 30 minutes late, which is perfectly normal in Arab countries."[61]

Different responses to time also can be seen when we compare the Latin American culture with that of the German. In the Latin American culture, one is expected to arrive late to an appointment as a sign of respect. This same tardiness for the Germans would be perceived as rudeness. For the Germans, "promptness is taken for granted—in fact, it's almost an obsession."[62]

In addition to punctuality, interpersonal and intercultural differences in the use of time can be discovered by examining the pace at which individuals carry out certain acts. Most people in the United States seem to be in a hurry—there is always one more thing to do. From fast-food restaurants to microwave ovens, by either chance or design, the most occupied lane in the United States seems to be the "fast lane."

While it is generally true that people in the United States do things quickly—especially in comparison to many other cultures—variations can be detected throughout the country. A measure of the pace of life in different cities may be obtained from an examination of four common activities: the walking speed of pedestrians over a 60-foot path during working hours, how long it takes bank clerks to provide change for two $20 bills, how quickly postal clerks talk while explaining the differences among several ways to mail a package, and the proportion of people wearing watches during business hours.[63] Results of observations indicate that the fastest walking speed can be found in Springfield, Massachusetts, and Boston, Massachusetts, while the slowest is in Fresno, California, and Memphis, Tennessee. The fastest bank transactions are in Chattanooga, Tennessee, and Rochester, New York, and the slowest are in Los Angeles and San Francisco. The fastest talking postal clerks are in Columbus, Ohio, and Atlanta, Georgia, and the slowest are in Sacramento and Los Angeles. And the most watches are on the wrists of people in New York and Detroit, and the least may be found on wrists in Memphis, Tennessee, and East Lansing, Michigan. Overall, the fastest pace of life can be found in Boston, New York City, and Buffalo, New York, and the slowest can be found in several cities in California, with Los Angeles at the top of the list.

As great as the variations may be across the United States, cultures in other countries react to time even more differently and, therefore, conduct their daily lives at very different paces. The Japanese and Chinese cultures, for example, treat time in ways that often cause problems when people from either of these cultures come in contact with North Americans. A comparison between how the Japanese and Americans perceive the negotiation process indicates that

> when negotiating with the Japanese, Americans like to get right down to business. They were socialized to believe that "time is money." They can accept about 15 minutes of "small talk" about the weather, the trip, and baseball, but more than that becomes unreasonable. The Japanese, on the other hand, want to get to know their business counterparts. They feel that the best way to do this is to have long conversations with Americans about a wide variety of topics. The Japanese are comfortable with hours and hours, and even days of conversation.[64]

Knowing that people and cultures react differently to time can make you a more competent communicator in that you will be able to adapt and adjust your own reactions to time to meet the needs of your communication partners.

NONVERBAL CLUES TO DECEPTION

Lies come in a variety of packages. You may intentionally present information known to be false, or you may misdirect others by exaggerating, concealing the full truth, or simply reporting something in a neutral way regardless how you actually feel. Lying may not always work, but the truth of the matter is that lie detection is not easy. Although some people are more sensitive than others to nonverbal clues to deception—for example, young people and women are more accurate at detecting lying than men[65]—overall, none of us is very successful, not even law officers trained at catching liars.[66]

A variety of studies point to certain nonverbal behaviors that may suggest that someone is telling a lie. For example, some of the more reliable clues to deception, in North American society, are vocal: Liars tend to hesitate and pause, speak rapidly, and "sound nervous" (change paralanguage frequently). Several gestures, including shrugging, a lot of self-touching, and frequent hand movement, should alert you. Also, liars tend to look away from you much of the time, avoid your gaze after brief eye contact, and experience pupil dilation. In contrast, facial gestures are too easily controlled to offer many useful clues to lying. Unfortunately, if you suspect someone is trying to

Lying is done with words, but also with silence.
ADRIENNE RICH

deceive you, your suspicion increases the probability that you will perceive the person as dishonest; however, your suspicion does not increase your accuracy of deception detection.[67]

When stakes are high and lying must continue for a long time, liars often become extremely nervous. They tend to make very little eye contact, shift their eyes, move their feet, fidget, shift their weight, twitch, and make nervous facial gestures, such as licking their lips. Careful observation will reveal that the pupils of their eyes dilate at the moment they tell their lie.

You cannot, however, identify a liar on the basis of a single behavior; only when telltale behaviors appear in clusters should you begin to suspect that a speaker is not telling the truth. Because most of the behaviors that indicate lying can also indicate nervousness, be careful not to assume that nervousness equals lying. (How calm would you be if you were falsely accused of cheating on a final exam? As you explained your side of the story, would you behave as if you were nervous?)

The most important indication that someone may be lying has less to do with behaviors and more to do with *pattern violations*.[68] The more you know someone the more you can tell if he or she is lying[69]—what you notice is that the person is behaving differently from what you have come to expect. Your expectations are violated, and this violation is what sets in motion your suspicions.

Be cautious! Whenever you accuse a communication partner of lying you run the risk of being wrong and, whether right or wrong, damaging your relationship. Think twice before making an accusation, and ask yourself two questions. Why do I think this person is lying? This will help you determine exactly what your evidence is, whether single behaviors, clusters of behaviors, or pattern violations. Is it worth detecting a lie? The payoff for detecting the lie may not be worth it.

Nonverbal communication, which helps you transmit feelings and emotions, regulates your interaction with others, and works together with verbal communication to create messages, has many aspects. Physical appearance, facial gestures, eye behavior, touch, vocal characteristics, body movement, time, and the physical and psychological contexts within which each of these takes place all contribute to nonverbal communication. Although nonverbal communication often operates at a low level of awareness, understanding its role in communication and developing skills in this area of human interaction are crucial to your development as a competent communicator.

Communication Competency Checkup

The goal of this communication competency checkup is to guide you in putting your skills and knowledge about nonverbal communication to use and to help you summarize the material in this chapter.

Drawing by Koren; © 1988 The New Yorker Magazine, Inc.

"You are about to experience something rare in your life, Stan—rejection."

1. Based on the nonverbal information in the cartoon, what do you know about each of the three human characters—for example, their age, gender, emotional state, social status, and how they're interacting?

2. Is the woman's nonverbal behavior complementing or contradicting her verbal behavior? Explain your answer with reference to the touch behavior, the eye contact, and the posture you observe, as well as the tone of voice you presume the woman is using.

3. Describe the situation with respect to the couple's spatial relationship.

4. How could the woman communicate her verbal message using only nonverbal behaviors?

5. Pretend you are the woman and read the cartoon caption as if you were calm. Read it as if you were worried about what might happen if the man got angry. Read it as if you had noticed the man with the dog listening in. Read it as if this were the third time you needed to repeat the statement to the man with whom you are holding hands. How do the readings differ in loudness, pitch, rate, voice quality, articulation, and pronunciation?

6. If the man had been smiling before the woman spoke, what might have been his reason for smiling? If he was smiling after she spoke, how would you interpret this?

NOTES

1. Larry A. Samovar and Richard E. Porter, *Communication between Cultures* (Belmont, CA: Wadsworth, 1991), 202.

2. Samovar and Porter, *Communication between Cultures,* 198–99.

3. Larry A. Samovar and Richard E. Porter, *Communication between Cultures,* 2nd ed. (Belmont, CA: Wadsworth, 1995), 180.

4. Norbert Freedman, *You Have to Move to Think* (Brooklyn, NY: Clinical Behavioral Research Unit at Downstate Medical Center), n.d.

5. Edward T. Hall and Mildred Hall, "The Sounds of Silence," *Playboy* (June 18, 1971), 148. Also see Edward T. Hall, *Beyond Culture* (New York: Doubleday, 1992).

6. Mark L. Knapp and Judith A. Hall, *Nonverbal Communication in Human Interaction,* 3rd ed. (Fort Worth, TX: Holt, Rinehart and Winston, 1992), 17–25.

7. Dale G. Leathers, *Successful Nonverbal Communication: Principles and Applications,* 2nd ed. (New York: Macmillan, 1992), 355–56.

8. Edward T. Hall, *Beyond Culture* (New York: Anchor Books, 1976).

9. Samovar and Porter, *Communication between Cultures,* 199.

10. For a discussion on body types see J. Corey Butler, Richard M. Ryckman, Bill Thornton, and Rachel L. Bouchard, "Assessment of the Full Content of Physique Stereotypes with a Free-Response Format," *Journal of Social Psychology* 122 (1993): 147–62; Juan B. Cortes and Florence M. Gatti, "Physique and Propensity," *Psychology Today* 4 (May 1970): 42–44, 82–84; Richard M. Ryckman, Michael A. Robbins, Bill Thornton, and Linda M. Kaczor, "Public Self-Consciousness and Physique Stereotyping," *Personality and Social Psychology Bulletin* 17 (1991): 400–05; W. H. Sheldon, *The Varieties of Temperament* (New York: Hafner, 1942).

11. Enid J. Portnoy, "The Impact of Body Type on Perceptions of Attractiveness by Older Individuals," *Communication Reports* 6 (1993): 101–08.

12. Virginia P. Richmond, James C. McCroskey, and Steven K. Payne, *Nonverbal Behavior in Interpersonal Relations* (Englewood Cliffs, NJ: Prentice-Hall, 1987).

13. For summaries of the research on the role of physical attractiveness in human interaction, see Dale Leathers, *Successful Nonverbal Communication: Principles and Applications,* 2nd ed., 140–144; Loretta A. Malandro and Larry L. Barker,

Nonverbal Communication (Reading, MA: Addison-Wesley, 1983).

14. Bruce Bower, "Nice Guys Look Better in Women's Eyes," *Science News* (March 18, 1995): 165.

15. Nancy Baker, *The Beauty Trap* (New York: F. Watts, 1984). For a summary of research, see N. Wolf, *The Beauty Myth* (New York: William Morrow, 1991); "When Beauty Can Be Beastly," *Chicago Tribune,* 21 October 1985, sec. 4, 22.

16. Loretta A. Malandro, Larry Barker, and Deborah Ann Barker, *Nonverbal Communication* (New York: Random House, 1989), 28–29.

17. Samovar and Porter, *Communication between Cultures,* 2nd ed., 188.

18. Charles Darwin, *The Expression of Emotions in Man and Animals* (Chicago: University of Chicago Press, 1965; originally published, 1872).

19. Samuel G. Lawrence and Mike Watson, "Getting Others to Help: The Effectiveness of Professional Uniforms in Charitable Fund Raising," *Journal of Applied Communication Research* 19 (1991): 170–85.

20. Based on a questionnaire developed by Lawrence B. Rosenfeld and Timothy G. Plax. For the complete questionnaire, see Lawrence B. Rosenfeld and Timothy G. Plax, "Clothing as Communication," *Journal of Communication* 27 (1977): 23–31.

21. For information on clothing to wear to interviews, see John T. Molloy, *Dress for Success* (New York: Warner Books, 1975); John T. Molloy, *The Woman's Dress for Success Book* (Chicago: Follett, 1977); Lawrence B. Rosenfeld, "Beauty and Business: Looking Good Pays Off." *New Mexico Business Journal* (April 1979): 22–26.

22. Theodore Gockenour, *Considering Filipinos* (Yarmouth, ME: Intercultural Press, 1990), 59.

23. William V. Ruch, *International Handbook of Corporate Communication* (Jefferson, NC: McFarland Press, 1989), 166–67.

24. Knapp and Hall, *Nonverbal Communication,* 1992.

25. Judee K. Burgoon, David B. Buller, and W. Gill Woodall, *Nonverbal Communication: The Unspoken Dialogue* (New York: Harper & Row, 1989), 192–95.

26. Judy C. Pearson, Lynn H. Turner, and William Todd-Mancillas, *Gender and Communication,* 2nd ed. (Dubuque, IA: Wm. C. Brown, 1991), 139.

27. For a discussion of pupilometrics, see E. H. Hess, A. L. Seltzer, and J. M. Shlien, "Pupil

Response of Hetero- and Homosexual Males to Pictures of Men and Women: A Pilot Study," *Journal of Abnormal Psychology* 70 (1965): 165–68; and E. H. Hess and J. M. Polt, "Pupil Size as Related to Interest Value of Visual Stimuli," *Science* 132 (1960): 349–50.

28. Helmut Morsbach, "Aspects of Nonverbal Communication in Japan," in *Intercultural Communication: A Reader,* 3rd ed., ed. Larry A. Samovar and Richard E. Porter (Belmont, CA: Wadsworth, 1982), 308.

29. "Understanding Culture: Don't Stare at a Navajo," *Psychology Today* (June 1974): 107.

30. Marianne LaFrance and Clara Mayo, *Moving Bodies: Nonverbal Communication in Social Relationships* (Monterey, CA: Brooks/Cole, 1978), 188.

31. Barbara Westbrook Eakins and R. Gene Eakins, *Sex Differences in Human Communication* (Boston: Houghton Mifflin, 1978), 150–52. Also see Julia T. Wood, *Gendered Lives: Communication, Gender, and Culture* (Belmont, CA: Wadsworth, 1994).

32. Bruce Bower, "Infant Memory Shows the Power of Place," *Science News* (April 18, 1992): 244–45.

33. Burgoon, Buller, and Woodall, *Nonverbal Communication,* 130.

34. Maslow and Mintz compared reactions to photographs of faces made in a "beautiful" room (one with windows, attractive draperies, and indirect lighting), an "average" room (a professor's office), and an "ugly" room (a storage area with a single overhead light bulb). See Abraham H. Maslow and N. L. Mintz, "Effects of Aesthetic Surroundings: I. Initial Effects of Three Aesthetic Conditions upon Perceiving 'Energy' and 'Well-Being' in Faces," *Journal of Psychology* 41 (1956): 247–54; and N. L. Mintz, "Effects of Aesthetic Surroundings: II. Prolonged and Repeated Experience in a 'Beautiful' and 'Ugly' Room," *Journal of Psychology* 41 (1956): 459–66.

35. Edward Sadalla, "Identity and Symbolism in Housing," *Environment and Behavior* 19 (1987): 569–87.

36. Carol Dolphin Zinner, "Beyond Hall: Variables in the Use of Space," *Howard Journal of Communication* 1 (Spring 1988): 32.

37. Edward T. Hall and Mildred Reed Hall, *Understanding Cultural Differences: Germans, French, and Americans* (Yarmouth, ME: Intercultural Press, 1990), 38.

38. Edward T. Hall, *The Hidden Dimension* (Garden City, NY: Doubleday, 1966).

39. Stanley E. Jones, *The Right Touch: Understanding and Using the Language of Physical Contact* (Cresskill, NJ: Hampton Press, 1994).

40. R. Heslin and T. Alper, "Touch: The Bonding Gesture," in *Nonverbal Interaction,* ed. John M. Wiemann and Randall P. Harrison (Beverly Hills, CA: Sage, 1983), 47–75; Ashley Montagu, *Touching: The Human Significance of the Skin,* 3rd ed. (New York: Harper & Row, 1986).

41. For a discussion of this and other affectionate greetings, see Peter Farb, *Word Play* (New York: Alfred A. Knopf, 1974).

42. This instrument is adapted from the eighteen-item questionnaire developed by Andersen and Leibowitz. For the complete instrument, see Peter A. Andersen and K. Leibowitz, "The Development and Nature of Touch Avoidance," *Environmental Psychology and Nonverbal Behavior* 3 (1978): 89–106.

43. Joseph A. DeVito, *The Nonverbal Communication Workbook* (Prospect Heights, IL: Waveland Press, 1989), 140.

44. Chris R. Kleinke, "Compliance to Requests Made by Gazing and Touching Experimenters in Field Settings," *Journal of Experimental Social Psychology* 13 (1977): 218–23; Frank N. Willis and Helen K. Hamm, "The Use of Interpersonal Touch in Securing Compliance," *Journal of Nonverbal Behavior* 5 (1980): 49–55. For a comparison of the use of touch versus the use of voice as means to influence others, see Martin S. Remland and Tricia S. Jones, "The Influence of Vocal Intensity and Touch on Compliance Gaining," *Journal of Social Psychology* 134 (1994): 89–97.

45. Judee Burgoon and Joseph B. Walther, "Nonverbal Expectancies and the Evaluative Consequences of Violations," *Human Communication Research* 17 (1990): 232–65.

46. Samovar and Porter, *Communication between Cultures,* 2nd ed., 197.

47. Diana Rowland, *Japanese Business Etiquette* (New York: Warner, 1985), 53.

48. Burgoon and Walther, "Nonverbal Expectancies."

49. Stanley E. Jones, "Problems of Validity in Questionnaire Studies of Nonverbal Behavior: Jourard's Tactile Body-Accessibility Scale," *Southern Communication Journal* 56 (1991): 83–95.

50. A modification of DeVito, *The Nonverbal Communication Workbook,* 142.

51. David W. Addington, "The Relationship of Selected Vocal Characteristics to Personality Perception," *Speech Monographs* 35 (1968): 492–503; David W. Addington, "The Effect of Vocal Variations

on Ratings of Source Credibility," *Speech Monographs* 38 (1971): 242–47.

52. Ruch, *International Handbook of Corporate Communication,* 191.

53. Samovar and Porter, *Communication between Cultures,* 206.

54. Deborah Tannen, *You Just Don't Understand: Women and Men in Conversation* (New York: William Morrow, 1990); Pearson, Turner, and Todd-Mancillas, *Gender and Communication,* 139; Wood, *Gendered Lives,* 164–65.

55. Michael L. Hecht, Mary Jane Collier, and Sidney A. Ribeau, *African American Communication: Ethnic Identity and Cultural Interpretation* (Newbury Park, CA: Sage, 1993), 113.

56. Samovar and Porter, *Communication between Cultures,* 225.

57. Richard L. Johannesen. "The Functions of Silence: A Plea for Communication Research," *Western Speech* 38 (1974): 27.

58. Robert G. Harper, Arthur N. Wiens, and Joseph D. Matarazzo, *Nonverbal Communication: The State of the Art* (New York: John Wiley, 1978), 64.

59. Paul Ekman and Wallace V. Friesen. "The Repertoire of Nonverbal Behavior: Categories, Origins, Usage, and Codings," *Semiotica* 1 (1969): 49–98.

60. Michael Argyle, "Inter-Cultural Communication," in *Cultures in Contact: Studies in Cross-Cultural Interaction,* ed. Stephen Bochner (New York: Pergamon Press, 1982), 35.

61. Argyle, "Inter-Cultural Communication," 35.

62. Hall and Hall, *Understanding Cultural Differences,* 35.

63. Robert V. Levine, "The Pace of Life," *American Scientist* (September-October, 1990): 450–59.

64. Richard Brislin, *Understand Culture's Influence on Behavior* (Fort Worth, TX: Harcourt Brace Jovanovich, 1993), 211.

65. Devorah A. Lieberman, Thomas G. Rigo, and Robert F. Campain, "Age-Related Differences in Nonverbal Decoding Ability," *Communication Quarterly* 36 (1988): 290–97; Steven A. McCormack and Malcolm R. Parks, "What Women Know That Men Don't: Sex Differences in Determining the Truth Behind Deceptive Messages," *Journal of Social and Personal Relationships* 7 (1990): 107–18.

66. Bella M. DePaulo, "Spotting Lies: Can Humans Learn to Do Better?" *Current Directions in Psychological Science* 3.3 (1994): 83–86.

67. For an excellent summary of the literature concerning deception, see Pamela Kalbfleisch, "Deceit, Distrust and the Social Milieu: Application of Perception Research in a Troubled World." *Journal of Applied Communication Research* 20 (1992): 308–34; Gerald R. Miller and James B. Stiff, *Deceptive Communication* (Newbury Park, CA: Sage, 1993).

68. Charles F. Bond, Adnan Omar, Urvashi Pitre, and Brian R. Lashley, "Fishy-Looking Liars: Deception Judgment from Expectancy Violation," *Journal of Personality and Social Psychology* 63 (1992): 969–77.

69. Thomas H. Feeley, Marck A. deTurck, and Melissa J. Young, *Baseline Familiarity in Lie Detection,* paper presented at the International Communication Association convention, Albuquerque, NM, May 1995.

CHAPTER 6

VERBAL COMMUNICATION

COMMUNICATION COMPETENCIES

This chapter examines verbal communication. Specifically, the objective of the chapter is for you to learn to:

- Understand the relationship between language and meaning.
- Distinguish between abstract and concrete language, denotative and connotative meaning, and private and shared language.
- Recognize differences in the goals and strategies of feminine and masculine language use.
- Identify and overcome barriers to verbal interaction caused by language problems.
- Improve your use of language to ensure clear communication.
- Recognize and avoid sexist and racist language.
- Recognize and appreciate intercultural differences in the use of verbal language.

KEY WORDS

The key words in this chapter are:

verbal language
syntactic rules
semantic rules
pragmatic rules
denotation
connotation
semantic differential
private language
shared language
tag questions
polarization
indiscrimination
facts
inferences
fact-inference confusion
allness
static evaluation
bypassing
relative words
euphemisms
clichés
emotive words
nonemotive words
distorted language
qualifiers
oxymoron
sexist language
racist language

Lisa and Eric just attended a college production of the musical *West Side Story*. As you listen in on their conversation, keep the following question in mind: Do their language differences reflect differences in what each values and who they are?

Lisa: Well, what did you think of the show?

Eric: I thought the guy playing Tony had a great voice, but it overshadowed Maria's singing. The chorus had some blending problems, and the orchestra drowned the singers out during the solos.

Lisa: I thought the conflict between the two gangs developed a real sense of the growing conflict between different groups in our society.

Eric: Did you notice that during the entire production the guy playing Baby John was singing flat?

Lisa: This production had a lot of the same qualities as *Romeo and Juliet* since it dealt with the same social and cultural issues. I thought it was wonderful.

Eric: A musical production can't be good if the singers and the orchestra aren't right! I think they needed more time rehearsing.

Lisa: Oh well, everybody has to have some opinion, even if it isn't right!

Eric and Lisa appear to be talking *at* each other and not *with* each other. The barriers to interpersonal communication that they are experiencing—and ways to overcome those barriers—are part of the subject matter of this chapter.

THE IMPORTANCE OF VERBAL COMMUNICATION

Before you went to school you accomplished the most complex feat you will ever accomplish: You mastered the basics of **verbal language,** the ability to communicate using the words and grammatical system of a particular society. You discovered how to use the words in the way people around you use them. You learned to create sentences that fit the rules for how sentences should be created in your culture's language. You learned to say "put the pen on the table" and not "the pen on the table put." You learned to use words to mean what others in your culture generally mean—you said "dog" and not "bird" when you pointed at a four-legged, furry animal that barked.

If you were fairly typical, by age four you had learned enough basic vocabulary to survive for the rest of your life.[1] You learned meanings for words like *love, good,* and *right* that are too subtle for dictionaries to explain fully. You learned rules for combining words that are so complex that researchers and philosophers have yet to spell them out in a comprehensible way. Did you ever stop to think about how you are able to put together sentences that you have never heard before and understand statements that are new to you? You knew how to use language to satisfy your need to understand the

world, to express yourself, and to form relationships—all by the age of four, all without the aid of formal schooling!

What is so engrossing about the way in which we learn to talk is that while so much of the learning process is universal, there is also a great deal of it that is culture-specific. Language represents the experiences within a geographic or cultural community. Through social interaction our culture teaches us both the symbol (be it a sound or written marks) and what that symbol stands for. We hear the sound symbol *dog,* and we have a cultural picture in our heads of what the symbol means. Members of different cultures will usually have different sounds and marks, and they also may have different pictures in their heads for what the symbols mean. *Dog* in some parts of the world, such as Hong Kong, China, and Korea, is considered food—quite a different word picture than is used in North American culture. What pictures do you think form in heads throughout the world for words such as *freedom, affirmative action,* and *God*? Obviously, these terms, and many others, have different connotations. Cultures differ and so do the words they use and the meanings they give to words.

Language is a powerful and useful tool. You use it to organize information you gather; to relate to people and events you experience; to regulate your own behavior, as when you talk to yourself while choosing a course of action; and to regulate the behavior of others, as when you try to persuade your friends to see one movie instead of another. Consider what it would be like to lose your ability to communicate verbally. How would you make sense of new information if you couldn't use words to place the information into categories? How would you keep track of where you should be if you couldn't use words to remind yourself? How would you interact with others? Life would be difficult, frustrating, and probably not as productive as it could be—for you as well as for those you encounter.

Language is your primary tool for survival. Understanding obstacles to its use and developing ways to overcome them can help you communicate more effectively. But there is still another reason for studying verbal communication: *Your language reflects who you are and how you perceive yourself.*[2] What differences do you presume between Lisa and Eric based on their conversation? Do they "see" the same things?

Your language both reflects and affects what you perceive. It was argued more than sixty years ago that we are prisoners of our language, that what we experience is largely due to the language habits of our community. The Sapir-Whorf hypothesis states that the language we use guides how we see and interpret the environment and helps shape our ideas (exactly how much it guides us is part of an ongoing debate among linguists); also, a people's language serves as a key to understanding their culture.[3] To understand a person's verbal communication is to understand how that person sees the world, how that person thinks—the reality in which that person's culture lives.[4]

Many examples support the Sapir-Whorf hypothesis. For one, Eskimos have no single word for snow but a great many discrete words for different kinds of snow.[5] The Masai of Africa have seventeen terms for cattle. Arabic has over 6,000 words relating to what most Americans call a camel. And Americans have a wide vocabulary for distinguishing types and models of cars. This reflects the importance of snow for Eskimos, cattle for the Masai, camels for Arabs, and cars for Americans. The point isn't that Americans cannot see the distinctions in snow that Eskimos see, but that they do not see them because such subtleties about snow aren't important to them. The vocabulary you use reflects your interests and concerns, the way you look at the world, and the distinctions among objects, people, and events that are important to you.

Grammar, too, serves as evidence for the Sapir-Whorf hypothesis. How you think about something is reflected in and affected by the grammar you use. In English, for example, you would say, "the white wine" (the specific, white, comes first, and the general, wine, follows), while in French you would say, "le vin blanc" (the general, wine, comes first, and the specific, white, follows).[6] As with differences in vocabulary, differences in grammar do not necessarily reflect inabilities to think differently, but rather preferences for what is important to a particular language community.

We can observe an extension of the Sapir-Whorf hypothesis by looking at the language patterns of some of the many co-cultures in the United States. These groups have evolved an *argot*—a special vocabulary that mirrors their experiences, experiences that are often different than those of the mainstream culture. An understanding of these unique vocabulary systems is important because you might hear private words and phrases that sound foreign or alien to you. Second, these specialized vocabularies, as noted by the Sapir-Whorf hypothesis, can offer insight into the experiences of these co-cultures.

Street gangs have acquired a rich vocabulary that reflects their experiences. "Claim" or "turf" is an area that each gang maintains as belonging to them. Again, these are "logical" words to describe the idea or action: "claim," a marking off of territory, "turf," a piece of territory. "Signs" are hand signals used to communicate to other gang members. Based on the bridge between the argot and the implied meaning, what do you think gangs mean by "homeboy," "buster," and "claimer"? A "homeboy" is a member of the same gang, a "buster" is someone who doesn't stand up for the gang, and a "claimer" is someone who wants to be a member of the gang but has not yet proven himself or herself.

Members of the male gay co-culture, because they may live two lives (one among the dominant culture and one among members of their own co-culture), have developed a rather extensive argot. A fellow gay is often referred to as "a member of the family." In this case, "family" means the brotherhood of homosexual men. A bisexual may be labeled as "AC/DC," much like electrical alternating and direct ("straight") current. In asking whether a fellow gay has come out to society the question is asked, "Have you told your story?" Even "coming out" signifies no longer hiding the person's sexual preference. And, in asking whether a vacation resort has a gay clientele, the question may be couched as, "Is it festive?"[7]

The argot of African Americans mirrors their environment, perceptions, and values. "Feel draft" expresses some African Americans' feelings of racism in white people. A person who attempts to emulate or to please white people is frequently referred to as a "Tom" or an "Oreo." "Tom" refers to the subservient slave, Uncle Tom, in *Uncle Tom's Cabin,* and "Oreo" refers to the cookie—dark on the outside and white on the inside. "The man," referring to anyone who has power, harks back to slavery days when "the man" or "master" had all the power.[8]

There are many co-cultures in any society that have extensive argot, each of which is composed of a vast number of words. Argots also are regional, for example, African Americans in Los Angeles might well have different terms than the African Americans in San Diego, even though the two cities are only 120 miles apart. Finally, argots are subject to change. A term that is used one month may be discarded the next. In fact, because most co-cultures feel alienated from the dominant culture, they are constantly changing their argot.

Many studies have linked ethnic identification with ethnic language use. For example, Mexican Americans who were strong ethnic identifiers were found to be frequent users of Spanish language media,[9] and in a study of Welsh speaking individuals living in England, language maintenance was found to be a function of ethnic identification.[10]

Today there are over 6,000 languages spoken on the planet, but within the next 100 years most will be gone, and it is estimated that the entire population of Earth will speak between 250 and 600 languages. This may facilitate communication between groups of people, but it also means the loss of aspects of the cultural identity of the people whose language disappears.[11]

CHARACTERISTICS OF LANGUAGE

Before examining the relationship between language and meaning, barriers to effective language use, and ways to use language effectively, it pays to look at some features that characterize all languages. An understanding of these characteristics provides the background for grasping why verbal language is simultaneously a useful tool and one difficult to master.

First, verbal language is *symbolic.* Words have no meaning in themselves, but are assigned meaning by people. If you don't believe this, try eating the next line.

PIZZA

If words were not symbols but things, you could eat the word *pizza* and drink the word *Pepsi.* Unfortunately, if you eat part of this page, all you'll feel is nauseous. There is nothing pizza-like about the word *pizza,* and nothing liquid-like about the word *Pepsi.* If there were a logical connection between a symbol and what it symbolized, wouldn't it seem silly for the word *big* to have fewer letters than the word *small*? Why would *ten, diez,* and *dix* all mean the same thing (and why is it that none of the three has ten letters)?

Ten, diez, and *dix* all have the same meaning, although they are different symbols. And the word *dog* is a single symbol that can be used to refer to a large variety of four-legged animals that bark. Different symbols can relate to the same thing, just as different things can have the same symbol.

Although the connection between a word and what it symbolizes is arbitrary, people often act as if words had some inherent meaning. There is a story that illustrates this problem: A professor placed a "cookie" on each desk in his class. After his students came into the room, saw the cookies, ate them, and thanked him, he told them the cookies were made from dog biscuits. Many students got sick! The reality of the good cookie was overshadowed by the two symbols *dog* and *biscuits.* The students confused the words for the reality.[12]

If the connection between a symbol and the object, idea, or event that it refers to were simple, communicating would be rather easy. Every time you said the word *car* it would mean the same thing to you as it meant to the person with whom you were talking. But because the relationship between a word and what it symbolizes is arbitrary, meanings are in the people who use the words, not in the words themselves. No meaning is inherent in any symbol. People attach a specific, personal meaning to every word they use. For example, for you, the word *car* may mean a 1996 Toyota Camry, even though the same word could refer to many different automobiles. For someone else, car might mean a different specific automobile, such as the one she owns, or all autos of a particular make, such as Ford. And if the person is from a nonmotorized culture, the word *car* might be a funny-sounding word without meaning.

Just because meanings are in people, not in words, does not imply that communication is impossible. You daily talk to people; you are reading this book right now. How is this possible? Even though each of us has his or her own dictionary, people with a common language also *share* a dictionary. This common dictionary is what makes it possible to communicate. You can speak to others and read this book because of societally shared meanings.

Language is *dynamic.* In addition to shared meanings and individual meanings, new words with new meanings and old words with new meanings constantly are created. For example, the *New American Heritage Dictionary of the English Language* has about 16,000 new entries.[13] Some of these are new words created by newspapers and trade magazines (e.g., political managers are referred to as "handlers," and "input" refers to entering information into a computer). Others evolved through the everyday speech of people (e.g., "igg" meaning "to ignore," "suss" meaning "to discover," and "diss" meaning "to show disrespect"); others came about through necessity—the need to label new inventions and identify newly evolved attitudes (e.g., "telephone tag" evolved following the proliferation of answering machines; "mini-van" describes a cross between a car and a truck; and "pro-choice" and "pro-life" describe attitudes toward abortion).

Another characteristic of verbal language is that it is *rule-governed.* Three different kinds of rules guide the use of verbal language: syntactic, semantic, and pragmatic. Rules that govern how words can be arranged are called **syntactic rules.** For example, syntactic rules that guide English dictate the syntax, "Did you wash the car?," whereas syntactic rules that guide German would have the sentence read, "Did you the car wash?"

Semantic rules govern the relationship between words and the meaning assigned them. Unless you agree with your friend that "food" is for eating and "cars" are for driving, you are going to have a hard time negotiating where to eat and how to get there! Although there is general agreement in a language community regarding what a particular symbol symbolizes—otherwise it would be impossible to communicate with each other—specific meaning is often ambiguous. Your meaning for the word *dog* may be a collie with distinct markings, whereas your communication partner may think about a mixed-breed dog he had as a pet.

Pragmatic rules, which concern how verbal language is actually used, help reduce ambiguity. Pragmatic rules guide your interpretation of messages by drawing attention to the relationship you have with the sender and the context in which the messages are sent. "How are you?" has the same meaning from a semantic perspective regardless of who says it. However, if the words are spoken by an acquaintance in passing (meaning: "Hello"), a friend who knows you haven't been feeling well (meaning: "I'm worried about you"), or a doctor (meaning: "How can I help you?"), the meaning changes. Similarly, if your doctor asks, "How are you?" in her office (meaning: "Why are you here?") or on the golf course (meaning: "Hello"), the meaning also changes.

LANGUAGE AND MEANING

The specific meaning you attribute to a symbol—which reflects something about who you are and your culture—differs according to how concrete or abstract the symbol is, its denotations and connotations, and whether the language is private or shared.

ABSTRACT AND CONCRETE SYMBOLS

Symbols differ in the degree to which what they refer to is concrete or abstract. Concrete symbols are highly specific and refer to one thing. Abstract symbols, on the other hand, are general and may refer to many things. For example, consider a baseball team named the Baltimore Orioles by its owner. The name Baltimore Orioles is a concrete symbol

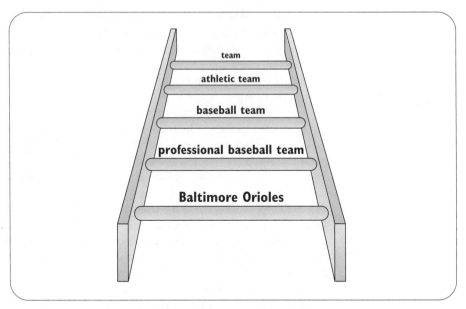

FIGURE 6.1   Ladder of Abstraction

because it refers to one particular team—a reality that can be verified. As we move from this concrete symbol to more abstract ones, we move from the reality of the particular baseball team to more general concepts. A useful model of this movement from concrete to abstract is the *ladder of abstraction,* with its first rung the most concrete and its final rung the most abstract symbol. A progression for Baltimore Orioles from most concrete to most abstract, from the first rung to the last rung on the ladder of abstraction, is illustrated in Figure 6.1.

The symbol that stands for the particular object—the name that refers to the particular object, "Baltimore Orioles"—is the most concrete level of language possible. It appears on Rung 1. A description of the physical characteristics of the object is also concrete, but not as concrete as the symbol for the particular object, so it appears on Rung 2. "Professional baseball team" may seem fairly concrete, but it is still a broad category that encompasses a variety of teams. "Baseball team" is more abstract because this category expands to semi-professional, amateur, collegiate, high school, and peewee teams. "Athletic team" is still more abstract because this term may refer to teams that play any sport, such as baseball, football, or soccer. The category "team" is the most abstract term when contrasted with the label "Baltimore Orioles" because it includes all groups of people who designate themselves or are designated as a team, including work, social, and sport teams. Thus, it occupies the highest rung on the ladder of abstraction.

The more abstract a symbol is, the greater the probability that different people attach different meanings to it. A person who tells his friend, "It's important to have many friends," may run into trouble with the friend's interpretations of *many* and *friends*

Words, like eyeglasses, blur everything that they do not make clearer.
JOSEPH JOUBERT

because both words are abstract. *Many* could mean three to some people and twenty to others, and *friend* could mean anything from a passing acquaintance to an intimate confidante. The speaker may have something particular in mind, but so will the friend, and the differences between them may be great.

People's tendency to assign different meanings to the same symbol is only one problem with abstract language. People also use the same abstract word to mean different things on different occasions. You might use the abstract word *love* to refer to one set of feelings when talking about the person with whom you are romantically involved and another set when talking about a good friend. A problem could arise if a listener is unaware that *love,* is being used to refer to two different feelings, one, deep emotional commitment (referring to your romantic partner) and the other, friendship (referring to your friend). One way to resolve this problem is to use less abstract symbols, such as "when I am with you I get the feeling I never want to leave" versus "I like it when we're together."

As you move up the ladder of abstraction, more and more meanings may be attributed to the symbols you use. But to communicate clearly, both you and the person with whom you're communicating must have similar notions of what your symbols refer to. Thus, the less abstract your language is, the higher the probability that you and the other person will agree on meaning. Telling the doctor, "I don't feel well," is not as useful as giving a detailed, concrete description of where, when, and for how long you have had pain.

It is a useful skill to be able to move up and down the ladder of abstraction—to make your messages more or less concrete depending upon your communication goals. For example, you may want to be purposely vague when you tell someone "Let's get together" because you don't know whether you really want to get together and you cannot think of a more creative way to say good-bye. On the other hand, you may have specific intentions for getting together, in which case "Let's meet tomorrow for lunch at 12:30 in front of Elmo's Restaurant" is a less abstract and more appropriate message. Skill Development 6.1 will help you construct two ladders of abstraction, one for an object, and one for the message "I'm going out."

Skill Development 6.1

CONSTRUCTING A LADDER OF ABSTRACTION

Ladder 1: Select the specific name of your favorite food, car, movie, or campus organization and place it on the bottom rung of the ladder of abstraction. Complete each step of the ladder with one or more words until you are at the most abstract level.

_____ most abstract level

_____

_____

_____

_____

_____ most concrete level

Ladder 2: With "I'm going out" on the most abstract level, fill in the remaining rungs until you are at the most concrete level. Indicate here to whom you're saying "I'm going out," for example, your roommate or your mother: _____. As you move from rung to rung, explain your possible motivation for the particular message you choose.

                                                                       Explanation

"I'm going out" _____ most abstract level

_____

_____

_____

_____

_____ most concrete level

1. What happens to meaning as you move up the ladder of abstraction? What happens when you move down the ladder?

2. How can the ladder of abstraction help you communicate more effectively?

DENOTATION AND CONNOTATION

The meaning of a symbol is affected not only by its level of abstraction but also by its denotations and connotations. **Denotation** refers to the usual associations that members of a particular language community have for a symbol. **Connotation** refers to the associations for a symbol that are more personal and may not be shared by every member of the language community. For example, a denotation for "home" may be shelter, while connotations could include warmth, pleasant retreat, place back in the city, or where my folks live.

Denotations

An examination of any dictionary will confirm that most words have several denotations. The most commonly used 500 words in English have approximately 14,000 definitions. Of course, the more denotations a word has, the more ambiguous it is.

    The word *team,* used earlier in the ladder of abstraction, has several denotations in addition to "an athletic group." It refers to a clique, assemblage, association, band or collection of people, crew, and an organization. Individuals unfamiliar with English may be unaware of any given word's multiple denotations. Assuming that only one denotation exists, a word may be used incorrectly in varying contexts. For example, a denotation for "got" is "obtained." A new English speaker who knew this denotative connection could say, "I obtained up this morning at 7 A.M." The speaker failed to recognize that not all denotations are equal and interchangeable.

Connotations

The connotations of a word refer to the attitudes or feelings people have for the word or what it symbolizes. What are your connotations for the word "car"? Is it something good or bad? Fast or slow? A plaything or a workhorse? Necessary or frivolous? If you have had good experiences with cars—no accidents and few repairs—you are likely to have positive associations with the symbol. Problems with cars in the past are likely to give rise to negative connotations. There can be as many connotations as there are people who use the word, whereas the number of denotations is limited.

The following words refer to the same thing, but their connotations may be different. What is your reaction to each word? What are your connotations?

fired

released

axed

dehired

let go

deselected

canned

involuntarily separated

The connotations you have for a word are more likely to determine your response than the denotations, probably because you learned the connotative meanings for many words before you learned their denotations. For example, in your family you may have learned that unpaid bills are an annoyance before you ever understood what unpaid bills were. The process of reacting first and learning the denotation second is a hard habit to break.

Because connotations are more subtle and varied than denotations, new English speakers have a great deal of difficulty mastering this aspect of language. Words such as *love, hate,* and *democracy* have a great number of connotations. For example, you may "love chocolate," "love your mate," "love your mother," "love going to the movies," and "love the way your car drives." The word *love* is the same, but the connotations are seemingly different. Grasping the subtlety of these differences requires familiarity with a culture that takes time to develop.

One device used for measuring connotative meaning—the attitudes and feelings you have toward a concept or term—is called the **semantic differential,** a tool that measures a person's reactions to an object or concept by marking spaces between a pair of adjectives, one positive and one negative, with each space representing an attitude position.[14] For example, rate the concept *my high school education* on the following scales by circling the number that best reflects your feelings. The endpoints 1 and 7 are defined by the adjectives. The numbers between them represent less extreme positions. For example, on the first scale, 1 is bad, 2 is somewhat bad, 3 is slightly bad, 4 is neither good nor bad, 5 is slightly good, 6 is somewhat good, and 7 is good.

bad	1 2 3 4 5 6 7	good
not satisfying	1 2 3 4 5 6 7	satisfying
boring	1 2 3 4 5 6 7	exciting
tense	1 2 3 4 5 6 7	relaxed

You can get a sense of whether your connotations for the concept *my high school education* are positive or negative simply by adding your responses to the four scales and comparing your sum with the highest score possible, 28, and the lowest score possible, 4. If your sum is close to 28, your connotations are positive. On the other hand, if your score is close to 4, your connotations are negative.

PRIVATE AND SHARED LANGUAGE

Private language refers to language whose meanings are agreed upon by one segment of a larger language community; **shared language** refers to language whose meanings are agreed upon by all members of the language community. Private language may consist of both specialized words and specialized meanings for common words. For example, "RAM" (random-access memory) and "memory cache" may not mean much to people unfamiliar with computers; "ollies" may defy definition by anyone who doesn't ride a skateboard; "vertebral subluxation" may confuse those outside the chiropractic profession; and, although you have probably suffered from cephalalgia, only your doctor would call a headache by this name. Also, as people develop a more intimate relationship they typically develop a more private language.[15]

Specialized words are often called *jargon*. They have two purposes. First, they serve as shorthand for those familiar with them. The third cervical vertebra can be shortened to the specialized symbol "C3" to save chiropractors time when talking to each other and to patients familiar with their vocabulary. Specialized words also help identify those who use them as members of the same group. With the right vocabulary, you can sound like a lawyer, doctor, teacher, mechanic, or plumber because each profession has its own language. Who would say the following sentence? (And what does it mean?)

That the sense of smell used by these cattle was established because of the marked audible variation in inhalation intensity as the animals grazed.

The sentence, which means "We knew the cattle used their sense of smell while grazing because we heard them sniffing," is from the book *Ethology of Free Ranging*

Domestic Animals. The sentence won an Obscure Prose in Scientific Literature Award from the *Veterinary Record.* The meaning of each word is clear, but the joint meaning of the words would make sense only to someone specializing in cattle care.

In addition to using specialized words, specialized language may use common words in special ways. What meanings would you assign to the following words and phrases in classified advertisements to sell houses?

Owner will sacrifice.

Must sell.

Cozy, intimate.

Secluded.

The first two probably mean "for sale," the third may mean "very small," and the fourth probably means "very far from the nearest city." Although the common meanings of these words are clear, their specialized meanings in this context may not be so obvious.

The problems associated with private and shared languages are magnified when the communicators, because of cultural and translation differences, use language to share ideas and feelings. Try to imagine how difficult it would be for someone who spoke English as a second language to determine the real meaning for argots and idioms.[16] If you were just learning to speak English, and you translated one word at a time, what would you make of these sentences?

"She has a buzz on."

"Do you want to go window shopping?"

"It's raining cats and dogs."

"It's just a ballpark figure."

"Couch potato."

"Don't jump down my throat."

"He started life with two strikes against him."

"We should stop hitting our heads against a brick wall."

To be an effective communicator you should be aware of the language proficiency of your communication partner. If he or she speaks the commonly spoken language as a second language or comes from a culture different from your own, you should define your words or try to use words that are easy to understand.

Communication is also a problem when you talk with people who, because of particular interests or group affiliations, have developed a specialized language. For example, people who bet on race horses with some regularity have their own vocabulary. If someone told you, "The bug boy was riding the chalk horse who hung in the lane and was also rank," would you understand what he was talking about? Would you know that a "bug boy" is an apprentice jockey, a "chalk horse" the horse that is the favorite to win, "hung in the lane" an indication the horse went wide and slowed down, and "rank" a charge that the horse was not running in a straight line but sideways and misbehaving? The language reflects the experiences of people who are members of a particular group. Being aware of group membership—sociological information—can help you understand, or at least appreciate, specialized languages.

Shared language—words that have similar meanings for those who are communicating—is the basis for effective communication. Problems occur when language is too abstract, when connotations differ widely, or when language is private and you happen to be the outsider. Under these circumstances, the meanings attributed to the words and phrases could be different enough to render communication ineffective.

FEMININE AND MASCULINE LANGUAGE[17]

In many ways, women and men differ in their assumptions about what constitute appropriate communication goals, as well as what strategies are useful for achieving those goals.[18] Although not all men communicate in stereotypical "masculine ways," and not all women communicate in stereotypical "feminine ways," there are enough differences between women and men to distinguish them *in general*.

COMMUNICATION GOALS

The differences in women's and men's goals for communicating are given expression and reinforcement in the games each play as children. The rules for communicating in boys' games stress their using communication to assert themselves and their ideas, to get something specific accomplished, to attract an audience, and to compete for attention. In contrast, the rules for communicating in girls' games stress their using communication to cooperate, to include others and not exclude them, and to listen and respond to others sensitively.

From children's play to adult behavior, women tend to have as their primary communication goal to establish and maintain relationships with others. Communication is a way to make connections, provide support, and achieve closeness and understanding. Men have as their primary goal to accomplish some task, exert control, increase their status, and maintain their independence. Communication is a way to prove oneself, to demonstrate that one has knowledge and skills.

Men, in general, value talking with their male friends because of the playfulness and camaraderie of those talks, and the practical value that conversation with male friends has—whether how to fix the car, compute taxes, or take care of the lawn. Conversation is something they *like*. Women, in general, value talking with their female friends because of their shared empathy and the resulting feeling of "being understood." Conversation is something they *need*. "Like" versus "need" results in more women calling women "just to chat" than men calling men.[19]

CHARACTERISTICS OF WOMEN'S AND MEN'S TALK

Although there is overlap in the topics about which men and women speak—for example, both, in general, talk about work, movies, and television with opposite-sex friends, and personal appearance, sex, and dating with their same-sex friends—there are also many differences. For example, women spend more time discussing relationship problems, family matters, weight, food, clothing, and men. Men spend more time talking about music, current events, sports, business, and other men. These differences could pose a problem when men and women talk: each thinks the other's choice of topic is "trivial."[20]

Five features distinguish women's speech, all of which help women achieve their communication goals.[21] First, women tend to respond to what they hear with sharing similar experiences of their own, allowing the conversation to grow as stories are woven together, rather than building on each other in a tit-for-tat, "you tell your story and I'll tell mine," fashion. Second, women pay close attention to the feelings and perceptions expressed by their communication partner so that they can offer support—"You must have felt terrible"—and probe for more information about what was perceived and felt—"What else happened? How did you feel?" Third, to help maintain their relationships by keeping up on what is happening in their communication partner's life, women tend to ask questions and in other ways invite their partner to talk about his or her experiences, such as "How was work today?" Fourth, to encourage their communication partner to talk, women tend to respond directly to what their partner says, asking

for details and using both verbal—"That's interesting"—and nonverbal—head nods—encouragement. Finally, to keep their conversation open and inclusive, women tend to use tentative language, such as qualifiers ("It may be possible that . . .") and **tag questions,** questions added onto the end of statements, such as "That dinner was terrific, don't you think?" Tentative language encourages the communication partner to enter into the conversation.

In contrast to women's speech, men's speech has several distinguishing features that help them achieve their different communication goals.[22] To assert their status and value, men tend to be task-oriented, avoid discussing feelings, and dominate conversations, often by introducing (and therefore controlling) the topic of conversation. Also, compared with women, men's talk tends to be more dynamic, direct, and assertive—language that may separate communicators and help them maintain their independence. For example, men are more likely to interrupt and challenge their communication partners.[23] Finally, although men and women talk about themselves the same amount, men tend to be less intimate in their disclosures, choosing, instead, to reveal things about themselves that are more superficial than what women are likely to reveal.

He doesn't push her to talk as a way of respecting her independence; *she* wants comfort and connection and sees his lack of responsiveness as his being uncaring.

She tells him about a problem as a way of talking about the problem; *he* sees it as an opportunity to offer a solution; *she* interprets his wanting to offer a solution as dismissive of how she feels.

He sees sympathy as condescending; *she* interprets his lack of sympathy as his being unresponsive.

She listens to his story and then tells a similar one of her own as a way of building a connection; *he* sees her story-telling as an attempt to usurp control of the conversation.

She includes a lot of details in her conversation as a way to allow him to be more involved in what she is saying and to enhance their talking; *he* wants her to get to the point because what is important is the point, not the conversation.

She wants to talk about their relationship because talking about it keeps it working well; *he* doesn't want to talk about it unless there is a problem to solve.[24]

In many ways, communication between the sexes is a "cross-cultural" experience.

Despite the many differences *between* genders there is much variety *within* genders.[25] For example, whether a person has a cooperative or competitive orientation is more important than gender for predicting how the person will interact.[26] Indeed, an individual's gender may be less predictive of her or his communication style than feelings of power in a given situation. For example, in gay and lesbian relationships—where one would predict that gender differences in communication would be reflected perfectly—differences in communication have more to do with power differences in the relationship (e.g., who is earning more money) than the couple's gender.[27]

BARRIERS TO SUCCESSFUL COMMUNICATION: OUR IMPERFECT LANGUAGE

In addition to communication problems associated with cultural and gender differences, there are also barriers to successful communication that are inherent in language.[28] Language is a tool created by people and, like any tool, it has limitations. Among the most common barriers to successful communication are polarization, indiscrimination, fact-inference confusion, allness, static evaluation, and bypassing.

POLARIZATION

Polarization is the tendency to describe people, ideas, and events in either-or terms. When you use polarized language, an idea is either ridiculous or wonderful, a new acquaintance is either friendly or aloof, and a movie is either the best you've seen or the worst. The problem stems not simply from your wanting to make events seem more dramatic, but from the English language. The English language tends to consist of well-defined extremes and few words to describe the points in between. How long do you need to write the opposite of each of the following words?

cold

tall

relaxed

illegal

guilty

You probably needed only a few seconds to come up with the five opposites: hot, short, tense, legal, and innocent. But now see how long it takes you to come up with the midpoint for each pair.

If you were able to identify true midpoints at all, it probably took you much longer than it did to think of opposites. And you may have noticed that some of your midpoints, which may be one word or whole phrases, are not specific to a particular pair of opposites. Average, OK, usual, normal, and neither-nor constructions (neither hot nor cold, neither short nor tall) are cited as typical midpoints for most pairs. What was your midpoint for legal and illegal, and guilty and innocent? A midpoint exists or we wouldn't need courts.

A problem with many word pairs is that there is no real midpoint to refer to. For example, if you're not happy, you're sad—and any response that falls between the two extremes is usually interpreted as sad. If, in response to your question "How are you?" someone said "OK," "average," "usual," or "neither terrific nor terrible," you would probably think he or she was not doing well.

Although there are instances when either-or language is appropriate—either you are reading this book or you're not, either you had lunch yesterday or you didn't—such language still denies that there are degrees of virtually everything. You might be reading this book but not concentrating, which is different from reading intently, just as an apple and a cup of coffee for lunch is different from a three-course meal. There are degrees of reading and degrees of eating lunch.

The tendency of our language to polarize can have dramatic results. For example, if you call yourself a healthy person and you get ill (which is not an unusual occurrence for healthy people), you may begin to call yourself unhealthy because our language lacks a midpoint between the two. Such a change in labels could affect your behavior. For instance, you might avoid skiing because you fear that going out in cold weather will make you sick.

To avoid the problems of polarization, be aware that the world comes in shades between the colorful extremes of our language. People and events are rarely one thing or another. Be aware that reality is often the middle ground, somewhere between the dramas of the polarized extremes. By increasing your vocabulary to include midpoints, you can avoid limiting yourself to polarized opposites.

INDISCRIMINATION

No two people, ideas, events, or processes are identical. However, to deal with the world as if everything were unique would be an overwhelming task. Our language helps us to categorize things that are similar by providing general nouns, such as *house* (when no

A good catchword can obscure analysis for fifty years.
WENDELL L. WILLKIE

two houses are the same) and *cat* (when no two cats are the same). Difficulties arise when we focus only on the similarities between things, because then we lose or ignore the differences. The problem is one of **indiscrimination,** the failure to see things as unique and individual.

Stereotypes, oversimplified images of things or people, whether related to gender, age, race, or some other feature, are examples of the process of indiscrimination. Stereotypes are based on similarities, whether positive or negative, and once an individual is placed in a general category, all the presumed similarities are attributed to him or her. Stereotypes are quick ways to organize information about people. If stereotypes are incorrect, the qualities that make the person unique are lost. For example, a seventy-five-year-old person may have nothing in common with other seventy-five-year-olds except for age. The category "senior citizen," however, includes a host of presumed similarities among the people so labeled, such as inflexibility and loss of memory.

Another problem with indiscrimination is that once a person, idea, or event is categorized, the tendency is to keep her/him/it pigeonholed. New information may be ignored or denied to keep the classification intact. The goal is to keep life simple, neat, and well organized, even though life is often complex, messy, and chaotic.

The process of indiscrimination is one reason why first impressions are so important to relationships. We use the first pieces of information we receive to categorize the other person—for example, by race, height, weight. Then we use subsequent information to fill out the categories rather than to change them. Our first impression thus tends to stick.

To avoid the problem of indiscrimination, be aware that no two people, ideas, objects, events, or processes are identical, even if they share the same category—or are called by the same name—because of some similarities. Keep in mind that differences are as important as similarities, and that there is always more to know about everything. Avoid hardening of the categories.

Focusing on similarities may be appropriate when differences are not particularly relevant (only a baker may care about the 100 varieties of flour available in a new supermarket). However, to avoid stereotyping and oversimplifying people, ideas, objects, events, or processes that are better understood as complex, an important skill to develop is recognizing and communicating differences. Skill Development 6.2 provides you with the opportunity to learn how to avoid the problem of indiscrimination.

Skill Development 6.2

COMMUNICATING DIFFERENCES

1. List five characteristics that individuals who share the title *teacher* have in common.

2. List five characteristics that differentiate one *teacher* from another.

3. Using your responses to questions 1 and 2, describe two *teachers* you know.

4. What is useful about nouns such as *teacher*?

5. What problems occur when nouns such as *teacher* are used?

FACT-INFERENCE CONFUSION

Facts are statements based on observations; they relate directly to what you see, hear, touch, taste, or smell.[29] **Inferences** are conclusions that are suggested by observations but not based on them. For example, the statement "Amir is six feet tall" can be verified by measuring Amir's height in stocking feet: It is a fact. The statement "Amir is handsome," however, is an inference. Several facts may be put together and the conclusion drawn that Amir is handsome, but there can be no direct observation of the conclusion that he is "handsome."

Fact-inference confusion, the tendency to respond to something as if it were observed when, in reality, it is merely a conclusion, occurs because English makes no grammatical distinction between facts and inferences. The two statements, "Amir is six feet tall" and "Amir is handsome," are grammatical equivalents. The tendency, then, is to interpret inferences as facts, so that "Amir is handsome" has the same truth value as "Amir is six feet tall."

Problems occur when you state inferences as if they are facts, because while you and others may agree on the truth of facts, there is no guarantee of agreement on the truth of inferences. You may state an inference as a fact and expect others to treat it as such, but you may run into misunderstandings if you fail to recognize that the inference is really a subjective opinion. For example, "Amir is handsome" may seem like a fact to you, given that Amir is six feet tall and has brown eyes and black hair, and that these are your criteria for handsomeness. However, someone else, while agreeing with the facts of Amir's physical traits (six feet tall, brown eyes, black hair), may consider blue eyes and blond hair the necessary criteria for handsomeness. Thus, for this person, Amir is not handsome.

How good are you at distinguishing facts from inferences? If the grammar of your native language does not make such a distinction, like English, the odds are that you are not too good at making the differentiation. Given the potential problems that can arise, Knowledge Checkup 6.1 will provide you with some experience distinguishing facts from inferences.

Knowledge Checkup 6.1

DISTINGUISHING FACTS FROM INFERENCES[30]

Read the following story, assuming that all the information is accurate and true. Then, for each statement, indicate T (true), F (false), or ? (don't know).

A certain West Coast university scientist chartered a ship for exploration purposes. When a large white bird was sighted, the scientist asked permission to kill it. He stated that white albatrosses are usually found only off the coast of Australia. He wanted the bird as a specimen for the university museum. The crew protested against the killing of the bird, calling the scientist's attention to the old sea superstition that bad luck followed the killing of a white albatross. Nevertheless, the captain granted permission to kill the bird and the bird was killed. These mishaps happened after the bird was killed: The net cables fouled up three times, a rib was broken when Jackie Larson, a scientific aide, fell down a hatch ladder, and the scientist became seasick for the first time in his life.

1. The scientist had never been seasick before.   T F ?
2. The purpose of the voyage was primarily pleasure and sight-seeing.   T F ?
3. The scientist asked the captain for permission to kill the bird.   T F ?
4. Jackie Larson broke his rib.   T F ?
5. The white albatross was sighted near Australia.   T F ?

Key

1. T—The story specifies that "The scientist became seasick for the first time in his life."
2. F—The story specifies that "A . . . scientist chartered a ship for exploration purposes."
3. ?—We do not know whom the scientist asked.
4. ?—We do not know if Jackie Larson broke a rib or if it was the ship's rib. In addition, we don't know if Jackie Larson is a male or a female.
5. ?—We do not know where the ship was when the sighting was made.

Statements 3, 4, and 5 are inferences because they are not based on observations, but only suggested by them. Statements 1 and 2 are facts because they are based on observation.

Be aware that factual statements can be made only after an observation and are limited to what is observed, whereas inferences can be made anytime and go beyond what is observed. Also, although facts have a high degree of certainty, inferences vary in their probability—some being highly probable and others being highly improbable. Recognize facts and inferences for what they are and avoid confusing them. When confronted with an inference, ask yourself, "What is the probability that this inference is true?" An inference should spark questions and a search for the facts, if any, that support it.

ALLNESS

Allness is the assumption that when you say something, you've said all there is on the subject. The much-told story about six blind men and an elephant is an excellent illustration of this concept. Never having felt an elephant before, each blind man examines a small part and, based on the little information gathered, attempts to describe the entire beast. The first blind man touches the elephant's side and describes it as a wall; the second touches the tusk and describes it as a spear; the third touches the trunk and likens the elephant to a snake; the fourth touches the knee and describes the elephant as a tree; the fifth touches the ear and says the elephant is like a fan; and the sixth touches the tail and likens the elephant to a rope. Each is right and each is wrong.

The point to the story is that we are all similar to the blind men when it comes to describing anything in the world. We see only a small part of something and, based on insufficient information, assume we can describe all of it. Whether it's another person, an idea, or an event, we know very little in comparison to what can be known. What you say about something is what you choose to say at the moment, or all you know about it at the moment, and not all there is to know. Our language, however, does not reflect this.

Be aware that whatever you or someone else says about something, there is more that can be said. Keep an open mind and realize that our finite language is being used to describe infinitely complex things.

STATIC EVALUATION

Everything in the world is continuously changing, continuously in process, but our language tends to remain static. The result is called **static evaluation,** the inability of our language to account for constant change. When you meet a person for the second time you act as if she or he is the same person, but in reality that person has changed, just as you have changed. Since the first meeting each of you has gotten older and has had experiences that have changed you. Although changes may be minor, they exist. Our language rarely takes these changes into account. Statements are fixed in time, whether past, present, or future, even when the subject of the statement changes.

Each student's Permanent Record in education is testimony to the problem of static evaluation. If a student is evaluated negatively by one teacher, subsequent teachers who read the evaluation may take it for the current reality. The former teacher's point of view becomes imposed on new situations and the student has an uphill battle to persuade others that he or she has changed. To confront this problem, some schools now restrict teachers from reading Permanent Record folders before a student completes the class, except for medical information.

Be aware that everything that is said applies to a particular time. A new perspective, or at least a healthy skepticism of the old perspective, is necessary to keep up with changes. When you communicate, let others know the time frame for what you're saying and ask others for their time frames. Skill Development 6.3 will help you eliminate static evaluation from your communication by presenting two static messages for you to revise.

Skill Development 6.3

ELIMINATING STATIC EVALUATION

Combating the problem of static evaluation requires dating your communication—specifying the time frame for a particular message. Rewrite the two statements to eliminate their static evaluations, making up the details that you need. For example, "Shana is a great athlete" could be recast as "Shana is the only student ever to graduate from Brush High School who was awarded ten athletic letters and chosen to five all-conference teams."

1. Nico is a faithful friend.
2. Roxanne likes to run.

What are the advantages of avoiding static evaluation? What problems are raised by recasting your messages to eliminate their static evaluation?

BYPASSING

At one time or another, you've probably told someone how to locate a particular address only to find out later that your directions didn't work, that the person was unable to find the right street (e.g., your definition of "go a little way" means a quarter of a mile to you but only 100 feet to your listener). You thought you were clear, and you probably were—for you. Most people speak until their message is perfectly clear to themselves, which does not mean that it is clear to the other person! Those speakers are likely to be bypassing. **Bypassing** occurs when you assume incorrectly that your meaning for your words is the same as another person's. However, as you learned earlier, different people assign different meanings to the same words because meanings are in people, not in words.

To avoid the problem of bypassing, don't assume that your meaning is shared merely because the other person nods encouragingly and seems to understand. Ask questions when you are unsure whether your meaning and another's are the same.

USING LANGUAGE EFFECTIVELY

Barriers to successful communication may begin with the limitations inherent in our language, but they do not end there. The way we use language—the words we select and the way we put them together—poses more problems. Among the most common communication problems are the use of unclear language and the use of language that

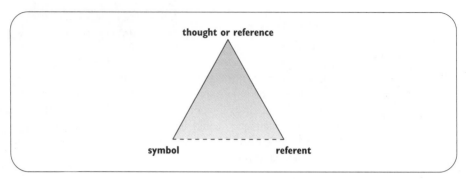

FIGURE 6.2 **Ogden and Richard's Triangle of Meaning**

creates negative impressions. If you are aware of the problems you face when selecting words to communicate, you increase your chances of communicating effectively.

It is also important to remember that one of the hallmarks of a competent communicator is adaptability. This means being able to adapt your language to both the setting and the people with whom you are communicating. Part of that adaptation involves knowing what to and what not to do. The recommendations that follow should help you tailor your language to meet the unique demands of each communication encounter.

UNCLEAR LANGUAGE

Given the arbitrary relationship between symbols and their referents, different words may refer to essentially the same thing. The "Triangle of Meaning,"[31] Figure 6.2, displays the relationship of a thought or reference, a symbol (word), and a referent (what the word refers to). The dotted line between the symbol and referent indicates an indirect relationship between a word and what it is supposed to represent.

For example, the thought "carbonated water with flavoring" relates to the word "soda" and to the object (a flavored carbonated drink). The word "soda," however, bears no direct relationship to the physical object. If it did, you could drink the letters S-O-D-A. In addition, the carbonated drink also can be referred to by the symbols, "pop," "Coke," "fizz," and "drink." Because of this arbitrary relationship between a word and a thing, meaning may be unclear. A glance at *Roget's International Thesaurus* proves that every idea can be expressed in many different ways. Each way, however, presents a slightly different slant, much like our earlier list of synonyms for the word *fired.* The most widespread examples of unclear language include relative words, euphemisms, clichés, emotive words, distortions, qualifiers, and oxymorons.

> Words are, of course, the most powerful drug used by mankind.
> RUDYARD KIPLING

Relative Words

Relative words gain their meaning by comparison and clarification. Unless the point of comparison is specified, relative words lack clarity. For example, consider the following questions: Is your car fast? Are you smart? Are you tall? Is your school a good one? It's

impossible to define *fast, smart, tall,* and *good* without knowing the basis for comparison: Fast compared to a new Jaguar? Smart compared to Albert Einstein? Tall compared to professional basketball player Michael Jordan? Good compared to Harvard? A competent communicator is specific with respects to the comparison, for example, "My car is fast. It goes from 0 to 60 in 10 seconds."

Whenever you evaluate something without indicating your criteria, the meaning for your words is likely to differ from another person's meaning. An easy class for you may not be easy for someone else, and a good restaurant for you may not please your friends. To what other classes are you comparing the class? What is your basis for comparison? Is it the amount of homework? How lively the class meetings are? How strict the grading is? With what other restaurants are you comparing the restaurant? What is your basis for comparison? Is it the prices? The way the food is prepared? The amount served?

Euphemisms

Euphemisms, inoffensive words or phrases substituted for possibly offensive language, abound in the English language. Think of the effects of these words and their substitutions:

"downsizing" for "firing personnel"

"underclass" for "poor people"

"stout" or "chubby" for "fat"

"solid waste" or "refuse" for "garbage"

"offensive move" for "attack"

"preowned automobile" for "used car"

The goal of a euphemism is to soften the blow of what you have to say. Unfortunately, softening often leads to an unwanted side effect: lack of clarity.

How can you tell a friend his sweater is ugly? Telling him outright may be too blunt, but what happens when you use the words "unique," "interesting," or "makes a fashion statement"? And how do you respond to a friend who asks how you like her new furniture when you hate it? Do you call it "original"? How about "tasteful"? Or do you change the subject?

The Pentagon has created several memorable euphemisms. For example, "combat" is "violence processing" and "civilian casualties" are "collateral damage." Educational institutions have their own fair share of euphemisms. For example, the term "remedial English" has been replaced with "developmental English," the "remedial reading room" has become "the skill-development center," and "pay raises" have become "salary adjustments."

Although politeness and attempts to help people feel better about themselves are laudable, when a euphemism distorts meaning, it needs to be replaced with more accurate, more direct language. If you use "I" language to assume responsibility for your opinions, you can say what is on your mind without resorting to unclear language. For example, you may tell the friend whose sweater you find ugly, "I like sweaters that are less colorful." Such a statement lets him know that you don't like the sweater and why, and that the opinion is yours.

Clichés

Clichés are trite expressions that convey a common or popular thought. They lack originality and impact because of overuse. When what are now clichés first began being used, they had particular meanings based on what they were actually describing. In time, the original meaning disappeared and only the sentiment was left. For example, "put to the acid test" dates back to a time when gold was in wide circulation and users questioned whether they had the genuine ore. Nitric acid was applied, and if the sample was false, the acid decomposed it. Do you know the original meaning of the phrase "have an ax to grind"? According to one story, a man approached a young metal apprentice and persuaded him, by flattery, to sharpen his ax. The boy sharpened the ax but received no thanks. From that point on, whenever the boy saw someone flattering someone else, he wondered whether the flatterer had an ax to grind, that is, some hidden purpose in mind.

Although the meaning of a particular cliché may be clear to the person using it, others may not understand its point. Try to imagine what it would be like to discover the meanings of "can of worms," "behind the eight ball," "high on the hog," "dime a dozen," and "play it by ear" if you were not born and raised in the United States. The meaning of your clichés may be clear to you, but how would a person learning English as a second language interpret them?

Clichés not only hamper clarity, they can lower the credibility of the person who uses them because they lack originality and are so common. How creative and original is the communicator who relies on clichés such as "the bottom line," "state of the art," "networking," "cutting edge," "meaningful dialogue," "the straight and narrow path," "talk is cheap," and, last but not least, "last but not least"?

To avoid the possibility of lowering your credibility, avoid using clichés. And to avoid possible misunderstandings when speaking with people whose background is different from your own, avoid clichés altogether or clarify them.

Emotive Words

Emotive words seem to be descriptive but actually communicate an attitude toward something or someone. Depending on your likes or dislikes, you select the words that communicate your attitude. Clarity is sacrificed when the word is used as a description rather than an expression of a point of view. For example, a 1956 Chevrolet may be called a "car" (neutral attitude), a "jalopy" (negative attitude), or a "classic" (positive attitude). Notice that the description "1956 Chevrolet" is **nonemotive,** that is, it does not communicate an attitude toward the object.

Someone who saves money may be called "thrifty" (positive) or a "tightwad" (negative). A small house may be called "cozy" (positive) or "claustrophobic" (negative). Such emotive words seem to describe something, but what they describe is less important than the speaker's attitude.

The shared meanings of emotional words are often so powerful that people may use them to alter the reality of what is being discussed. Reflect for a moment on the emotional language used as part of the abortion controversy. One side talks of the "unborn child" while the other states "undeveloped fetus." If you think of the images created by these words you have two very different pictures of the same concept.

Emotional words are most destructive in human communication when they are directed at people with the intent of belittling them. What images are called forth by phrases such as "health nuts," "welfare chiselers," "do-gooders," "fat bureaucrats," "male chauvinist pigs," and "religious fanatics"? Are these words accomplishing any real purpose other than to arouse emotions?

Listen for emotive and nonemotive words and separate them from what the speaker is describing. The clearest meaning occurs when what is described and how the speaker feels about it are both known.

Distortions

Communication is least clear when language is used to distort meaning. Attempts to exaggerate or to minimize the value, importance, or worth of something usually involve **distorted language.**

Advertisers use phrases such as "gives you more" without explaining more of what. They tell you "you can be sure" without mentioning what you can be sure of. They describe drinks as "the real thing" and cigarettes as having "real taste" without defining the word *real*. And they describe products as "new" and "improved" without explaining what's new or how they're improved.

Qualifiers

Qualifiers, words that clarify or limit the meaning of an idea, may be used to make a claim more accurate, but questions remain about the meaning. For example, a dish washing product may leave dishes virtually spotless, but what does a "virtually spotless" dish look like? Other qualifiers that may distort meaning include "up to" ("up to ten days' relief"), "as much as" ("as much as a full day's supply"), "like" ("feels like real wood"), "fights" ("fights cavities"), and "helps" ("helps prevent tooth decay"). The hope is that the qualifier will be forgotten and the residual message, the information you remember, will be that the dishes will be spotless, relief will last ten days, the supply will last a full day, the product is real wood, the toothpaste stops cavities, and the toothpaste prevents tooth decay. Do not ignore exaggerations or qualifiers when assessing the meaning of messages you receive; also, try to avoid using distortions in your own messages.

Oxymorons

Oxymorons are self-contradictory phrases. For example, how can someone be "cruel to be kind" and how can something be "almost unique"? Have you ever heard a book hailed an "instant classic," a trip described as a "working vacation," a milk substitute called a "nondairy creamer," a person described as being "vaguely aware," and a guess at your car's repair cost called an "exact estimate"? Each phrase contains two words that contradict each other, resulting in a lack of clarity. Oxymorons confuse rather than clarify, so rather than assume what a speaker means, ask questions. Substitute more precise language for oxymorons in your own language. For example, "cream substitute" is more precise than "nondairy creamer."

In order to modify your own use of relative words, euphemisms, qualifiers, clichés, emotive words, distortions, and oxymorons, it is necessary to be able to recognize them when they occur. Knowledge Checkup 6.2 provides you with the opportunity to check your ability to detect the various types of unclear language.

Knowledge Checkup 6.2

RECOGNIZING UNCLEAR LANGUAGE

Read the following paragraph from a hypothetical teacher evaluation. Identify the uses of relative words, euphemisms, qualifiers, clichés, emotive words, distortions, and oxymorons.

> *I am very pleased to evaluate the instructor who is being considered for a full-time position. It is my opinion that his approach to teaching is quite interesting. Although some might claim that he has an ax to grind in the classroom, I find his teaching style clean as a whistle. His lectures are spontaneously planned, giving them a quality that is virtually unmatchable. The acid test of whether he should be hired is that he is a grade-A teacher.*

The unclear language you should have spotted is:

> *I am very pleased to evaluate the instructor who is being considered for a full-time position. It is my opinion that his approach to teaching is quite interesting* **(relative term—interesting compared to what?)**. *Although some might claim that he has an ax to grind* **(cliché)** *in the classroom, I find his teaching style clean as a whistle* **(cliché)**. *His lectures are spontaneously planned* **(oxymoron—how can a lecture be both spontaneous and planned?)**, *giving them a quality that is virtually unmatchable* **(distortion—what is a "virtually unmatchable" quality?)**. *The acid test* **(cliché)** *of whether he should be hired is that he is a grade-A* **(emotive word)** *teacher.*

How well did you do? Do you think you could catch instances of unclear language in fast-moving conversations? Listen for your own uses of unclear language and substitute clearer words and phrases.

Sexist Language

In recent years, there has been an increasing awareness of the sexist nature of some of our everyday language. Much of this language is perceived as belittling others because of their gender. A communicator who is sensitive to the feelings of others avoids words and phrases that might be viewed as demeaning or offensive (unless, of course, the goal is to arouse negative feelings).

Sexist language expresses stereotyped sexual attitudes or a sense that one gender is superior to another. Traditionally, English has been a sexist language. For example, words used to describe males—independent, logical, aggressive, confident, strong—often have positive connotations, whereas those used to describe females—dependent, emotional, gullible, timid, weak—often have negative connotations. Men and women are too often viewed as opposites.[32] Contrast these different stereotypical descriptions of the same behavior in men and women:[33]

> He's curious; she's nosy.
>
> He's a bachelor; she's a spinster.
>
> He's suffering a mid-life crisis; she's menopausal.
>
> He's firm; she's stubborn.
>
> He's ambitious; she's clawing.
>
> He's versatile; she's scattered.
>
> He's concerned; she's anxious.

By contrast, a nonsexist language either makes no reference to gender or does not imply superiority of one gender over another. For example, references to people in general include women and men, so the word *mankind* is inappropriate. Words such as *humanity, people,* and *humankind* are both more accurate and nonsexist.

Nonsexist Communication

You can eliminate sexist language in three ways. The first calls for circumventing the problem by eliminating gender-specific terms or substituting neutral terms. For example, using the plural *they* eliminates the necessity for *he, she, she and he,* or *he and she.* Eliminate derogatory terms, such as "chick," "hunk," "broad," "little woman," and "stud." When no gender reference is appropriate, substitute neutral terms to solve the sexism problem. For example, given that both men and women work for the postal system, substitute *letter carrier* for *mailman.* Of course, some terms refer to things that could not possibly have gender; make those terms gender-neutral. For example, a *man-hole* is a *sewer lid* and something *man-made* is *synthetic.*

The second method for eliminating sexism is to mark gender clearly—to heighten awareness of whether the reference is to a female or a male, if the gender is known. For example, rather than substitute "letter carrier" for "mailman," use the terms mailman and mailwoman to specify whether the letter carrier is a man or a woman. Other examples include:

Saleswoman and *salesman* (rather than *salesperson*)

Congresswoman and *congressman* (rather than *congressperson* or *member of congress*)

Chairman and *chairwoman* (rather than *chair* or *chairperson*)

Policeman and *policewoman* (rather than *police officer*)

Inherent in this second approach is the notion that there is nothing sacred about putting he before she. Use both orders interchangeably—*she and he, him and her,* and *hers and his.* Adding *she, her,* and *hers* after *he, him,* and *his,* without changing the order, continues to imply that males are the more important gender and should come first.

The third method for eliminating sexism is to increase your awareness of its occurrence. Becoming aware of sexism in your own language can serve as the stimulus for change. And becoming aware of sexism around you, such as in advertising and the media, can stimulate you to articulate your opposition to its presence.[34]

Skill Development 6.4 will help you avoid the use of sexist language by giving you practice in recognizing and eliminating the sexism in five messages.

Skill Development 6.4

ELIMINATING SEXIST LANGUAGE[35]

Rewrite the following sentences to make them gender-neutral.

1. The average student is worried about his grades.
2. Ask the student to hand in his work as soon as he is finished.
3. Writers become so involved in their work that they neglect their wives and children.
4. The class interviewed Chief Justice Rehnquist and Mrs. O'Connor.
5. I'll have my girl type the letter and get it out to you.

Rewritten, gender-neutral sentences:

1. "The average student is worried about grades" eliminates the *his* form altogether.
2. "Ask the students to hand in their work as soon as they are finished" uses the plural to eliminate the singular *he.*
3. "Writers become so involved in their work that they neglect their families" eliminates the assumption that writers are men. To use more of the language of the original, the word *spouses* could be used to substitute for *wives:* "Writers become so involved in their work that they neglect their spouses and children."

4. Either "The class interviewed Chief Justice Rehnquist and Justice O'Connor" or "The class interviewed Mr. Rehnquist and Ms. O'Connor" treats both the male and the female justices in a parallel manner.

5. "I'll have my secretary type the letter and get it out to you" eliminates the stereotyped image of secretaries as women and avoids language that is patronizing.

Racist Language

Racist language expresses stereotyped racial attitudes or feelings of superiority of one race over another. Whereas sexist language in the United States has traditionally divided the world into "superior" males and "inferior" females, racist language usually divides the world into "superior" and "inferior" racial groups. All the same sexist assertions about women have been made for so-called inferior racial groups. For example, _____ (fill in any group) are less intelligent and more emotional than _____ (fill in any group). As with the word *male,* connotations of the word *white* are positive—clean, pure, innocent, and bright—and connotations of the word *black* are negative—dirty, dark, decaying, and sinister, as are those for *yellow*—chicken, afraid, and sickly.

It is generally perceived as being callous and tasteless to use words such as "Hymie," "Kike," "Dago," "Wop," "Jap," "Spic," "Chink," "Chinaman," "Kraut," and "Pollack" when referring to people from different ethnic backgrounds. These types of words are a sign of verbal bigotry. It is also insensitive not to respect the wishes of members of a particular group who prefer words such as "Asian" for "Oriental," "Native American" for "Indian," and "African American" for "Negro."

Racist language reflects indiscrimination; that is, it fails to make important distinctions among people who may have only one characteristic in common. Members of a racial group may differ more from each other than they do from members of other racial groups. Remarks that encompass entire groups of people should be eliminated from your communication. Avoid abstractions and be concrete: Refer to your own experience and to the particular limitations of your own experience.

To communicate effectively, you must understand how meaning and language are connected, that is, what words symbolize and how the thoughts they stimulate relate to each other. You must also understand barriers to successful communication and gain appropriate skills to overcome those barriers. Language may have problems that reflect its imperfection, and you may not always put this imperfect tool to the best use, but effective verbal communication can be a reality. By combining your understanding and skill with your motivation, you can become a competent communicator.

Communication Competency Checkup

The goal of this Communication Competency Checkup is to guide you in putting your skills and knowledge about verbal communication to use, and to help you summarize the material in this chapter.

© Jefferson Communications, Inc., 1981. Distributed by C J N T N S.

Sometimes students and teachers do not communicate effectively. This student and this teacher have a problem: the teacher has presented a definition of *communication* that is meaningless to the student.

1. Describe, from the student's point of view, the relationship between the word *communication* and what it refers to (note the student's thought, "Huh?"). Do a second description from the teacher's point of view. Can you define the problem identified in this cartoon by comparing your two descriptions?

2. Analyze the teacher's language in terms of abstractness versus concreteness. What are the denotations and connotations of the teacher's words? Is the language private or shared?

3. Language is an imperfect tool and, as this teacher demonstrates, can be used imperfectly. What problems of verbal interaction does this cartoon highlight?

4. If the teacher hired you as a consultant to help prepare the lesson on communication, what advice would you offer? What does the teacher need to understand about language in terms of (a) the relationship between language and meaning, and (b) barriers to verbal interaction? What specific skills does the teacher need to develop in order to overcome barriers to verbal interaction?

5. If the teacher were male, what expectations would you have for how he might communicate with you as you consult with him? What differences would you expect if the teacher were female? How might your gender affect how you would communicate with the teacher as you work with her or him to create a student-sensitive, comprehensible lesson on communication?

NOTES

1. For excellent discussions of language learning see John L. Locke, "Phases in the Child's Development of Language," *American Scientist* 82 (September-October 1994): 436–45; Rita C. Naremore and Robert Hopper, *Children Learning Language: A Practical Introduction to Communication Development* (New York: Harper & Row, 1990); and Barbara Wood, *Children and Communication: Verbal and Nonverbal Language Development,* 2nd ed. (Englewood Cliffs, NJ: Prentice-Hall, 1981). For classical studies of language acquisition, both verbal and nonverbal, see Jerome S. Bruner, *Child's Talk: Learning to Use Language* (Oxford: Oxford University Press, 1983); Jean Piaget, *The Child's Conception of the World,* trans. Marjorie Wordon (New York: Harcourt Brace, 1928); and B. F. Skinner, *Verbal Behavior* (Englewood Cliffs, NJ: Prentice-Hall, 1957).

2. Anita Vangelisti, Mark Knapp, and John Daly, "Conversational Narcissism," *Communication Monographs* 57 (1990): 251–74; and Karen Foss and Belle Edson, "What's in a Name: Accounts of Married Women's Name Choices," *Western Journal of Speech Communication* 53 (1989): 356–73.

3. Benjamin L. Whorf, *Language, Thought and Reality,* ed. J. B. Carroll, (Cambridge, MA: Technology Press of Massachusetts Institute of Technology, 1956); Harry Joijer, "The Sapir-Whorf Hypothesis," in *Intercultural Communication: A Reader,* 7th ed., ed. Larry A. Samovar and Richard E. Porter (Belmont, CA: Wadsworth, 1994).

4. Stephen W. Littlejohn, *Theories of Human Communication,* 4th ed. (Belmont, CA: Wadsworth, 1992), 190–214.

5. For a discussion of whether Eskimo people really do have a large vocabulary for snow, see L. Martin and G. Pullum, *The Great Eskimo Vocabulary Hoax* (Chicago: University of Chicago Press, 1991).

6. For a discussion of the issues raised in this section, see Sarah Trenholm, "The Problem of Signification," in *Human Communication Theory* (Englewood Cliffs, NJ: Prentice-Hall, 1986), 68–96.

7. For a discussion of gay communication, see *Alternative Communications: Journal of the Caucus of Gay and Lesbian Concerns* (Annandale, VA: Speech Communication Association); James Chesebro, ed., *Gayspeak: Gay Male and Lesbian Communication* (New York: The Pilgrim Press, 1981); and R. Jeffrey Ringer, ed., *Queer Words, Queer Images* (New York: New York University Press, 1994).

8. For a discussion of Black English, see Naremore and Hopper, *Children Learning Language,* 67, 155, 157–58; Clarence Major, *A Dictionary of Afro-American Slang* (New York: International Publishers, 1971); W. Labov et al., *A Study of the Nonstandard English Used by Negro and Puerto Rican Speakers in New York City,* Final Report, U.S. Office of Education Cooperative Research Project No. 3288 (Washington, DC: U.S. Office of Education, 1968); as well as the work of Howard A. Mims, Speech and Hearing Department, Cleveland State University, Cleveland, Ohio.

9. Howard Giles and Patricia Johnson, "Ethnolinguistic Identity Theory: A Social Psychological Approach to Language Maintenance," *International Journal of the Sociology of Language,* 1987, No. 68: 69–99.

10. M. Y. Young and R. C. Gardner, "Modes of Acculturalization and Second Language Proficiency," *Canadian Journal of Behavioural Science* 22 (1990): 59–71; and M. S. Trueta, "Language and Identity in Catalonia," *International Journal of the Sociology of Language* 47 (1984): 91–104.

11. "Languishing Languages: Cultures at Risk," *Science News* (February 25, 1995): 117.

12. S. I. Hayakawa, *Language in Thought and Action,* 4th ed. (New York: Harcourt Brace, 1978).

13. Jim Wise, "Word Game" [Durham, NC] *Herald-Sun* (September 6, 1992): E-1, E-8.

14. Donald K. Darnell, "Semantic Differentiation," in *Methods of Research in Communication,* ed. Philip Emmert and William D. Brooks (Boston: Houghton Mifflin, 1970), pp. 181–96.

15. Robert Ball and Jonathan G. Healey, "Idiomatic Communication and Interpersonal Solidarity in Friends' Relational Cultures," *Human Communication Research* 18 (1992): 307–35.

16. Roger E. Axtell, *Do's and Taboos of Using English around the World* (New York: Wiley, 1995).

17. This section is based, in large part, on Wood's discussion of female-male language differences: Julia Wood, *Gendered Lives: Communication, Gender, and Culture* (Belmont, CA: Wadsworth, 1994), Chapter 5, especially pp. 137–48.

18. Karen Foss and Sonja Foss, *Women Speak: The Eloquence of Women's Lives* (Scottsdale, AZ: Gorsuch Scarisbrick, 1991); Sara Steen and Pepper Schwartz, "Communication, Gender, and Power: Homosexual Couples as a Case Study," in *Explaining Family Interactions,* ed. Mary Anne Fitzpatrick and Anita L. Vangelisti (Thousand Oaks, CA: Sage, 1995); Lea Stewart, Alan D. Stewart, Sheryl Friedley, and Pamela Cooper, *Communication between the Sexes: Sex Differences and Sex-Role Stereotypes*

(Scottsdale, AZ: Gorsuch Scarisbrick, 1990); and Deborah Tannen, *You Just Don't Understand: Women and Men in Conversation* (New York: William Morrow, 1990).

19. M. A. Sherman and A. Haas, "Man to Man, Woman to Woman," *Psychology Today* 17 (June 1984): 72–73.

20. Sherman and Haas, "Man to Man, Woman to Woman."

21. Wood, *Gendered Lives,* 141–43. Also see Cynthia L. Berryman and James R. Wilcox, "Attitudes toward Male and Female Speech: Experiments on the Effects of Sex-Typical Language," *Western Journal of Speech Communication* 44 (1980): 50–59; and Anthony Mulac, John M. Wiemann, Sally J. Widenmann, and Toni W. Gibson, "Male/Female Language Differences and Effects in Same-Sex and Mixed-Sex Dyads: The Gender-Linked Language Effect," *Communication Monographs* 55 (1988): 315–35.

22. Wood, *Gendered Lives,* 143–45.

23. Steen and Schwartz, "Communication, Gender, and Power," 322–24.

24. Wood, *Gendered Lives,* 145–48.

25. Steen and Schwartz, "Communication, Gender, and Power," 338–41; C. J. Zahn, "The Bases for Differing Evaluations of Male and Female Speech: Evidence from Ratings of Transcribed Conversation," *Communication Monographs* 56 (1989): 59–74.

26. B. Aubrey Fisher, "Differential Effects of Sexual Composition and Interactional Content on Interaction Patterns in Dyads," *Human Communication Research* 9 (1983): 225–38.

27. Steen and Schwartz, "Communication, Gender, and Power: Homosexual Couples as a Case Study."

28. N. Coupland, H. Giosychles, and J. M. Wiemann, *Miscommunication and Problematic Talk* (Newbury Park, CA: Sage, 1991).

29. Based on definitions included in Joseph A. DeVito, *The Communication Handbook: A Dictionary* (New York: Harper & Row, 1986).

30. This test is adapted from William V. Haney, *The Uncritical Inference Test* (San Francisco: International Society for General Semantics, 1969), 2.

31. C. K. Ogden and I. A. Richards, *The Meaning of Meaning* (New York: Harcourt Brace, 1923).

32. Barbara Bate, *Communication and the Sexes* (New York: Harper & Row, 1988); Judy C. Pearson, L. H. Turner, and William Todd-Mancillas, *Gender and Communication,* 3rd ed. (Dubuque, IA: Wm. C. Brown, 1991); Laurie P. Arliss and Deborah J. Borisoff, *Women and Men Communicating* (Fort Worth, TX: Harcourt Brace, 1993); Julia Wood, *Gendered Lives.*

33. For a discussion of male/female stereotypes and language usage, see Deborah Borisoff and Lisa Merril, *The Power to Communicate: Gender Differences as Barriers* (Prospect Heights, IL: Waveland Press, 1985); Julia Wood, *Gendered Lives.*

34. Lana F. Rakow, "Don't Hate Me Because I'm Beautiful," *Southern Communication Journal* 57 (1992): 132–42.

35. Adapted from *Guidelines for Nonsexist Use of Language in NCTE Publications,* rev. ed. (Urbana, IL: National Council of Teachers of English, 1985).

CHAPTER 7

STRESS AND COMMUNICATION ANXIETY

COMMUNICATION COMPETENCIES

This chapter examines stress and communication anxiety. Specifically, the objective of the chapter is for you to learn to:

- Distinguish stress from distress and eustress.
- Identify verbal and nonverbal behaviors that accompany distress and eustress.
- Describe the three stages of stress reactions.
- Recognize your personal sources of stress.
- Use both self-help stress management techniques and stress management techniques that require the assistance of other people.
- Identify the presence of personal communication anxiety.
- Define communication anxiety and identify its causes and effects.
- Assess the extent of your own communication anxiety and choose appropriate short-term or long-term methods of treatment.
- Utilize the Stress Management Model for buffering, controlling, and combating stress.

KEY WORDS

The key words in this chapter are:

stress
eustress
distress
stressor
alarm stage
adaptation or resistance
    stage
exhaustion stage
burnout
buffering stress
controlling stress
combating stress
self-defeating attitudes
time management
listening support
technical challenge
    support
technical appreciation
    support
emotional support
emotional challenge
    support
reality confirmation
    support
personal assistance
    support
communication anxiety
publicly anxious people
privately anxious people
systematic
    desensitization
positive visualization

It's 7:00 A.M. and a call from a friend jars you out of a restless sleep. He asks, "What's happening today?" It's Tuesday, which means three hours of classes and work after school. It also means finding out about the raise you were promised. And to top it off, you have a blind date at 8:00 P.M. with the cousin of a friend.

How do your respond? Do you pull the blanket over your head and go back to sleep? Do you laugh or cry? Do you stare at your face in the mirror and wonder how you're going to survive? Or do you take a deep breath, exhale, and feel yourself getting excited by what is clearly going to be a challenging day?

STRESS AND COMMUNICATION

Stress is your body's reaction to any event that pushes it out of what you consider to be normal; it is your body's preparation to respond to the unusual. The stress process is sequential (see Figure 7.1): (1) an event occurs, (2) you perceive it to have a particular effect on you, (3) the event is related to something you need or want, and (4) you determine how you feel about it.

For example, consider that Tuesday morning after a sleepless night. Although you have several potential sources of stress, including classes, work, and the possibility of a raise, let's focus on the blind date. The blind date is your *event.* You *perceive* the date as making you nervous. You *want* to have a successful date so you can please your friend who set you up, begin a new relationship that might become an important one for you, and, perhaps, even relax. How do you *feel* about the date? If you have confidence in your ability to communicate with strangers and have been successful on previous first dates, you may feel terrific and not even use the word *stress* to define the situation. On the other hand, if you're like most people, even if you feel confident about your ability to communicate in this situation and have had more successes than failures on first dates, you may feel anxious and use the word *stressed* to describe yourself.

The blind date evoked a reaction. If you were confident, then your reaction was actually **eustress,** or stress perceived as positive. If you were anxious about the date, it was **distress,** stress perceived as negative. The word *stress* can be misleading because it does not indicate whether your feelings are positive or negative. Your body responds in the same way regardless of how you feel. As you knock on your date's door, perhaps a knot forms in your stomach, whether you perceive the situation negatively or positively.

When written in Chinese the word crisis is composed of two characters. One represents danger and the other represents opportunity.
JOHN F. KENNEDY

There is nothing in any event that in and of itself makes it a **stressor,** a source of stress. What makes it a stressor are your perceptions. As a result, every event and situation is a potential stressor.

VERBAL AND NONVERBAL REACTIONS THAT REFLECT FEELING STRESSED

Individuals who feel distress or eustress display a variety of predictable verbal behaviors. For example, when people feel their needs are being thwarted—as in conflict

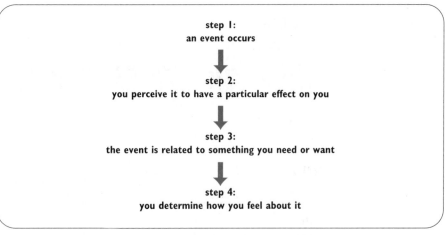

step 1:
an event occurs

↓

step 2:
you perceive it to have a particular effect on you

↓

step 3:
the event is related to something you need or want

↓

step 4:
you determine how you feel about it

FIGURE 7.1 **Four-Step Stress Sequence**

situations—they tend to attack the other person rather than to discuss the underlying issues. If asked for clarification or additional explanation, they tend to repeat exactly what was said the first time. And they often swear for emphasis. Consider the following conversation in which Robert is distressed:

Jon: Where are you going tonight?

Robert: I told you I have a blind date with Dale's cousin.

Jon: I thought we were going to get some dinner together.

Robert: I already told you! I have a date with Dale's cousin!!

Jon: Okay, I was just asking!

Robert: I have a date and I'm tired and I have a quiz tomorrow and who knows what Dale's cousin is like! I have a date! I have a date! I have a date! Now get the _____ off my back!

People who feel stress may appear self-engrossed because they lead the conversation to their own areas of expertise or interest. If they can't direct the topic of conversation, they often remain quiet. Or they may grow impatient and use a variety of interjections, such as "yes, yes, uh-huh, yes," to encourage the other person to hurry. For example, on the day of a blind date, that topic may consume all of your thoughts. Because you are anxious, talking with your friend becomes an either-or proposition: Either you talk about the date—and you use impatient interjections to get your friend to hurry up and get to the topic you wish to discuss—or you don't talk at all. Knowledge Checkup 7.1 provides you with the opportunity to assess your verbal communication reactions to stressors.

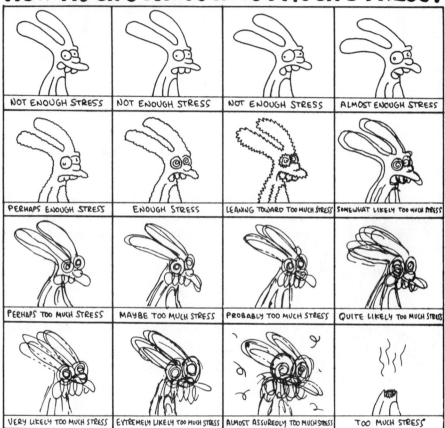

Knowledge Checkup 7.1

SELF-ASSESSMENT OF YOUR STRESS REACTIONS

Check each behavior that you personally experience when you feel pressured.

_____ verbally attack people

_____ repeat the same words over and over without variation

_____ talk obsessively about the source of stress

_____ make errors in grammar and pronunciation

_____ encourage others to speak quickly

_____ experience lack of quick recall, resulting in pauses

_____ talk only if you can talk about the source of stress

_____ others:

Although there are a relatively small number of verbal reactions that indicate a person may feel stressed, there are a large number of nonverbal responses to stressors. Knowledge Checkup 7.2 gives you the opportunity to identify your nonverbal stress signs.

Knowledge Checkup 7.2

YOUR NONVERBAL SIGNS OF STRESS

Put a check mark next to as many of these nonverbal signs of stress as you experience.

_____ gritting teeth

_____ sweating palms

_____ tightened stomach muscles

_____ chewing on pencils

_____ hair twirling or twisting

_____ shifting position in a chair

_____ moving, walking, and eating rapidly

_____ finger drumming

_____ fist clenching

_____ jaw clenching

_____ head scratching

_____ nail biting

_____ leg bouncing

_____ using facial expressions such as repeatedly wetting the lips, clearing the throat, and wrinkling the forehead

_____ using eye movements such as rapid blinking, squinting, and looking away

_____ pacing

_____ shifting weight

_____ wiggling

_____ eating too much or not at all

_____ drinking or smoking more than usual

_____ hands trembling

_____ sleeping too much or too little

_____ withdrawal—avoiding interaction

_____ using a sarcastic or nasty tone

_____ engaging in vocal explosiveness—accenting key words when there is no reason to do so

_____ speeding up at the ends of sentences

_____ using higher voice pitch than normal

_____ overarticulating—enunciating words so clearly and precisely that it draws attention

_____ others:

Was it difficult or easy for you to identify your verbal and nonverbal reactions to feeling stressed? Your responses to stress are probably well patterned, and, with a little thought, you were probably able to identify them. How obvious is it to you that you have a particular and identifiable set of verbal and nonverbal reactions to stress? It may be useful to have someone who is familiar with how you typically behave look over the list of verbal and nonverbal reactions to stress and identify those that characterize your behavior.

STAGES OF STRESS REACTIONS

Reactions to stress occur in three stages: alarm, adaptation or resistance, and exhaustion. By being aware of your reactions, you can begin to identify those situations that you consider stressful.

The Alarm Stage

In the **alarm stage** your body's systems are alerted to a potential threat. The primary physiological reaction is the production of adrenaline. This reaction causes your muscles to tense and get ready for action, your heart rate to increase, and your senses to become more acute. For example, when you see someone with whom you've had an argument, you may find yourself tightly clenching your jaw, feeling your heart pounding, and becoming aware that your palms are sweating. All of these reactions—which include a heightened awareness of yourself, the other person, and your surroundings—prepare you to meet the person.

The Adaptation or Resistance Stage

The second phase in reacting to stress is **adaptation** or **resistance.** You may adapt to a situation by accepting it and adjusting your behavior to meet its demands, or you may resist by denying or ignoring it. When you saw the other person walking your way you could have adapted by accepting that the meeting would happen, whether you liked it or not, and thinking about what to say, or you could have resisted by turning in another direction and walking away—essentially refusing to meet.

The Exhaustion Stage

The last stage is the **exhaustion stage.** After surviving a stressful situation, you feel physically and mentally drained. All you may want to do is rest or escape. After confronting someone with whom you're having a conflict you may feel a strong desire to sleep or avoid working any more that day.

Prolonged fatigue without signs of relief can lead to **burnout**—physical, emotional, and mental exhaustion. Physical exhaustion, characterized by feeling tired and weak, may lead to such things as increased illness, higher incidence of accidents, frequent headaches, and nausea. Emotional exhaustion, typified by feelings of helplessness, depression, and entrapment, may lead to continual crying, inappropriate laughter, and loss of emotional control. And, mental exhaustion, distinguished by negative attitudes toward yourself, your work, and life in general, may lead to work dissatisfaction, feelings of inferiority, and a damaged self-concept.[1]

RECOGNIZING YOUR STRESSORS

You don't have to look far to recognize your stressors. Although college is supposed to be one of the most enjoyable times of life, this is hardly the case for students who find themselves facing the tremendous pressures of learning, relational development, adjusting to new and conflicting ideas, holding down a job, caring for children, and the myriad of other possible stressors. The suicide rate is higher among college students than among nonstudents of the same age group, and many students drop out of school because they cannot cope with the strain. For students who do not drop out, the counseling center serves an important function: Between 5 and 10 percent of the college population seeks professional psychological help.[2] In the adult non-school population, people vary in their causes of stress. Women tend to feel more role conflict (home versus work) and men report more work-related stress.[3]

All people, regardless of their cultural background, suffer from some degree of stress. However, what situations and events are perceived as stressors are greatly influenced by culture. For example, in a culture that places a great deal of value on competition, such as in the United States, finishing last in a tennis tournament might stress someone. In a culture that places more value on human relationships than competition, such as some groups of Native Americans, losing would not generate a stressful reaction. Instead, stress might be produced if someone in the family brought shame to all members of the family by engaging in aggressive behavior. In cultures such as in the United States, people grow up with cultural expectations that life should be easy and filled with happiness. When life does not meet these expectations, North Americans often feel stressed. However, in many cultures—such as in India, Greece, and Mexico—people are raised to believe that life is difficult, and would, therefore, not be as upset when faced with tragedies and disappointments.

Culture not only influences what is perceived as a stressor, but it also determines a person's response to stress. In the United States, as in many Mediterranean cultures, people are taught to express their anger and frustration orally and physically, and they are even encouraged to tell others when they feel stressed. While North Americans use expressions such as "Get it off your chest," in many Asian cultures people are taught to conceal their feelings and not to engage in behaviors that express outward emotions.[4]

There are even cultural differences in how stress is handled. In the United States people often are encouraged to seek the help of others when they feel stressed. Whether through talking to a psychologist or one's best friend, stress is shared. However, in the Buddhist tradition, people are taught to meditate or engage in reflective activities if they are under stress.

To deal with stress, you must first recognize your sources of stress. Knowledge Checkup 7.3 will help you analyze those aspects of your life that are likely to trigger stress reactions.

Knowledge Checkup 7.3
YOUR STRESS ANALYSIS

Answer the following questions. Each time you answer yes, give examples.

1. What are your current life goals? Do any of your important goals conflict with each other? (*Sample:* Yes, I want to work full-time so I can be financially independent, but I also want to be a full-time student who makes the Dean's List each semester.)

2. What are your important values? Do your values conflict with those of people who are important to you?

3. Are there times when you can't get all your work done? Are there times when you are bored because there is not enough work to do?

4. Do you avoid saying no?

5. Do you give other people more importance in your life than you give yourself?

6. Are there certain people and/or events in your life that you perceive as stressors?

7. Do you feel it is necessary to alter your emotions to make them socially acceptable?

8. Do you eat foods that you consider unhealthful?

9. Do you find it difficult to get away from people or events that you perceive as stressors?

10. Do you get angry or depressed when you do not come in first in competitive activities?

11. Are any of your family relationships distressing?

12. Do you avoid taking the time to do nice things for yourself?

RESPONDING TO YOUR STRESSORS: SELF-HELP TECHNIQUES

Don't be disturbed if you answered yes to many or all of the questions in Knowledge Checkup 7.3. It only means that you are typical of those who were socialized in the North American culture and that, like any other typical person, you need to take action to buffer, control, and combat your stress.

You use the technique of **buffering stress** when you anticipate a stressor and develop a plan that helps you deal with the situation before you experience distress. For example, because you anticipate that a group meeting in one course may possibly be scheduled right after one already planned in another course, you begin preparing now for the meeting already planned and save study time to prepare for the unscheduled meeting later.

Controlling stress takes place when the stress you feel is not strong enough to require combat, but you take action to ensure that it doesn't increase. This situation could occur when you determine, after several semesters of experience, how many close relationships you can participate in at one time without feeling overburdened. By getting close to no more than the predetermined number of people, you effectively control your stress.

You use the technique of **combating stress** when the stress becomes distress and you need to reduce or eliminate the negative feelings through self-help techniques or techniques requiring others. Among the self-help techniques you may use to buffer, control, and combat stress on your own are attitude changes, time management, exercise, and meditation. Techniques requiring others include self-help groups and professional help.

Attitude Changes

Most people in the United States regard perfection, speed, pleasing others, winning, and strength as highly desirable. Although no one could possibly live up to the North American ideal, to be less than perfect is to be considered flawed and undesirable. To be less than quick at doing everything is to appear insecure. Not to want to please others is to be self-centered. Not to win all the time is to be a loser. And not to be physically and emotionally strong is to be impotent and impaired.

Attitudes that include having to be perfect, fast, other-centered, winning, and strong all the time are **self-defeating.** Self-defeating attitudes increase the probability that you will perceive people and events as threatening and, therefore, increase your feelings of distress. Increased feelings of distress mean increased use of your verbal and nonverbal communication indicators of stress, such as biting your nails, shifting your weight from foot to foot, or speaking nonfluently. Self-defeating attitudes also increase the likelihood that your communication will reveal your low self-esteem. For example, you may avoid communicating with others, criticize yourself a great deal, or speak hesitantly for fear of being wrong.

The most common anxiety-producing myths in our society are those that insist we must be perfect, quick, pleasing, winning, and strong. How susceptible are you to the stresses produced by these myths? What steps can you take to overcome your stressors?

Perfection   Questions 1, 7, and 10 in Knowledge Checkup 7.3 indicate whether you think it is necessary and important to be perfect. Though striving to do your very best is not in and of itself negative, it may become a stressor if you believe that anything less than perfection in everything you do means that you are a wretched person.

Because no one is perfect, it is important to recognize that the possibility of achieving perfection is indeed a myth. Acknowledging the myth for what it is can aid you in catching the potential stressor before it becomes distressful. For example, in question 1 you might have indicated that one of your goals is to work full-time to be financially independent. Do you want to do this because being financially independent will make you the "perfect" spouse or the "perfect" daughter or son? The other goal is to make the Dean's List every semester. Do you think that being on the Dean's List will make you the "perfect" student? Neither one of these goals is in and of itself wrong. But problems arise when you attempt to achieve either or both of them in order to perceive yourself as perfect.

The stress associated with always striving for perfection may become self-defeating as energy gets drained in unproductive worry. In place of telling yourself that you have to be perfect, tell yourself that being imperfect does not mean being inefficient, ineffective, inadequate, defective, or corrupt. All people make mistakes and you are entitled to your share, no matter what you have been told. That does not mean you can goof off! The next time you hear your internal voice say, "Be perfect," respond with, "I can be myself," "I can make mistakes," "I can be human," and, possibly most difficult of all, "I can accept failure."

> I am five-years-old. I am the best little boy in the world, told so day after day. The worst thing I have done to date is to consider—just to consider—ripping off the mattress tag that says DO NOT REMOVE THIS TAG Under Penalty of Law.
> JOHN REID, *THE BEST LITTLE BOY IN THE WORLD*

Speed   Question 3 indicates whether you subscribe to the "hurry-up" myth. Do you feel you should always be doing something? Do you feel that you lack the time to do everything you ought to do? When your internal voice says, "Hurry up," "Stop wasting time," "You're not going to make it," or "You'll never get it done," respond with, "I can take the time I need," "I deserve some time just to do nothing," "I'll get it done, but at a pace that's comfortable," and "I'll examine the time available and come up with a plan to accomplish the project within the schedule."

Pleasing Others   One of the most pervasive myths is that it is crucial to please others. In an attempt to please others, people often become nonassertive or passive—willing to let others have their way and let their own needs and wants go unfulfilled. By being passive you deny yourself the opportunity to express your wants, needs, and thoughts. Therefore, you increase your level of frustration and become distressed.

Questions 2, 4, 5, 6, 7, 9, and 11 in Knowledge Checkup 7.3 all relate to pleasing others. Often this myth becomes so important that you consider yourself selfish, inconsiderate, rude, and aloof if you put yourself first. It is natural for young children to want to please their parents, and because they are rewarded for complying, such behavior is reinforced. The attitude based on pleasing behavior thus becomes a way of life—a way of life that may make a person strive for goals that are emotionally and physically destructive.

Your internal voice tells you to express your emotions in line with societal expectations. The messages might be, "Don't be impulsive," "Control yourself," "Act like a grown-up," and "A proper lady doesn't get angry, she cries." To cope, you may respond, "I can express how I feel so long as I don't hurt someone else," "Anyone can get angry and anyone can cry, it has nothing to do with gender," "I have the right to show my feelings and not fear them as weaknesses," or "I can own my feelings."

Perhaps question 4 best summarizes this myth: Are you someone who can't say no? Before discussing this misconception, answer the following questions:

> Do you believe other people can make you feel bad or good by what they say or do?
>
> Do you believe you can make other people feel bad or good by what you say or do?

If you believe other people can make you feel bad or good by what they say or do, and/or you can make other people feel bad or good by what you say or do, you are incorrect. You may believe that by saying "the right thing" or doing "the right thing" you can make other people happy. In fact, you can't make anyone feel anything; only the other person can make himself or herself feel a particular way. Likewise, no one can make you feel anything; only you can choose how to feel. Your behavior may *invite* another person to feel a particular way—for example, giving someone a single rose may invite the person to feel lovingly toward you—but it is up to the other person to decide whether to accept the invitation. In addition to evoking feelings of love, giving someone a single rose may elicit feelings of anger (for example, if the person thinks the rose is part of a scheme to manipulate him or her), hurt (if a dozen roses were expected), amusement (if the rose is seen as part of an obvious "I'm sorry" ploy), disbelief (if the rose is thought to be too expensive a gift)—any variety of feelings. The other person will *choose* how she or he will feel.

If your internal voice tells you, "Others can make you feel good or bad by what they say or do," substitute, "Wrong! Others may invite me to feel a particular way, but how I feel is my choice." Similarly, when you think you can make others feel a particular way, substitute the word *invite* for *make* and you will be a step closer to eliminating the myth that it is necessary to please others.

Winning   How important is it to you to be a winner? What will you do to win? How do you feel when you don't win? These are some of the issues implied in question 10. In North America, where there is an emphasis on individualism, people have the attitude that "Winning isn't everything; it's the *only* thing." If you are one of those people, your internal voice screams continuously, "Win, win, win," and "Second place is no place." To silence the voice, respond with, "I only have to do my best, winning isn't everything," "Not everything is a contest that must be won or lost." It is important to remember that if you believe winning is crucial you may encounter difficulties when interacting with people from cultures that stress collectivism, such as in Mexico, Japan, and China. Many people from collective cultures do not have the competitive voice driving them to be individual winners at any cost.[5]

Physical and Emotional Strength Question 8 in Knowledge Checkup 7.3 relates to the myth of being physically and emotionally strong. The United States is in the midst of a "health" phase. It doesn't take much for a North American to feel guilty about his or her physical appearance. Gaining a pound, eating two scoops of ice cream instead of one (or better yet, none), not being a jogger or an aerobics enthusiast—any of these can set off a health-conscious internal voice: "You didn't exercise today," "Nobody loves a fat person," "Why do you think they call it *junk* food?" Although certain foods are indeed better for your health than others, it is often the guilt associated with eating poorly and not exercising that is the major stressor, not the junk food or lack of exercise. Respond to the internal voice with messages such as, "Though I should be exercising now, I have to finish my work." (Do not lie to yourself! Lying to yourself doubles the anxiety: the original guilt plus the added guilt.)

Overcoming self-defeating attitudes associated with having to be perfect, quick, pleasing, winning, and strong requires training. The appropriate responses to the internal messages driving your behavior do not come automatically for many people. Skill Development 7.1 presents three situations that require a coping response to offset the self-defeating internal voice's messages.

Skill Development 7.1

DEVELOPING COPING RESPONSES TO SELF-DEFEATING ATTITUDES

Here are a series of experiences you could have. Assume you have the experience. Make a coping response to counterbalance your internal voice in each situation.

1. Your term paper is due next week. You have completed the research, but have not written the paper. A friend has an extra ticket for a concert and wants you to attend—the look on your friend's face indicates how important it is for you to go. You really need time to finish the paper. Your internal voice says, "It's really important to please one's friends—after all, that's what friends do."
   Your coping response is:

2. A family member calls to say that your pet, whom you've had since you were six years old, has been hit by a car and will probably die. Your companion says, "Hey, it's only an animal." Your coping response to your internal message to hold back tears is:

3. Your instructor hands back your English theme. You worked hard on it and had it checked by the writing lab tutor, who told you it was excellent. To your surprise and disappointment, when the instructor hands back your paper you're told, "Weak paper. Did you read the assignment?" You've always been told to "respect your elders" and that "teachers are always right," so your first inclination is to leave the class and say nothing.

Your coping response is:

Time Management

Very few people have unlimited time. If you are typical, you are under pressure to fill your precious hours with work, school, relationships, and other responsibilities. As a result, you are often caught in a web of conflicting demands that require you to use **time management**—a method for setting priorities for the use of your time and then deciding what to do when and for how long. By managing your time effectively, you reduce the stress in your life and, therefore, reduce the number of verbal and nonverbal indicators that you are feeling stressed.

If you have a habit of procrastinating or often feel time-stressed, the first step to developing a time management plan is to keep a daily log.[6] You need to discover how you spend your time—what you do and approximately how long each activity takes—before you can begin to organize your responsibilities. How long are you sleeping each night? How much time does eating really take? When do you study and for how long? How often and for how long do you exercise? You accomplish a hundred separate activities each day, and you need to know what they are and how long they take before you can make a time management plan. If your days follow a fairly regular routine, you may have to keep a daily log for a week or less before you can make a plan. If, however, your days do not follow a regular schedule, you may need to keep a daily log for more than a week to ensure getting all your activities catalogued.

Once the daily log is complete, decide whether you want to develop a general weekly schedule—which serves as a master schedule from which you can quickly develop specific daily schedules or "to do" lists—or a specific weekly schedule—which outlines specific activities and the time devoted to each for five weekdays or a full seven-day week. (Large monthly calendars may be kept, too, which allow for longer-term planning. These calendars, however, are very general, noting events such as semester breaks, tests, assignment due-dates, and regular appointments.) If you have little or no experience with time management, it may be better to begin with a general weekly schedule and use it to develop daily schedules or "to do" lists.

With a completed daily log and a decision made as to the type of plan desired (general or specific, daily or weekly, itemized or "to do"), the next step is to look at specific activities and prioritize them. Divide each activity noted on the log into three categories of importance: *must do,* priority A, *should do,* priority B, and *might do,* priority C. Priority A activities are those that you must do during a given day; these need to be planned first. For example, the paper due tomorrow needs to be typed today—there is no alternative. Priority B items are activities you should do, but there is no particular urgency. For example, you should call home because it has been several days since you spoke with your family, but whether you call today or tomorrow is not very important. Priority C activities are those things you would like to do if time allows. For example, if the paper is typed in one hour instead of the planned three, you have time to watch the video tape you rented. A danger in marking log activities with an A, B, or C is that the items you would like to do but are not things you must do, which should be labeled C, get a B or A with justifications such as, "It's important to go to the movies with friends because maintaining friendships is necessary for a healthy life." Although the sentiment is correct, the logic bears scrutiny. Be careful that you keep the A, B, and C lists honest.

Once you (1) know your activities and approximately how long each takes, (2) decide on the type of schedule desired, and (3) understand your priorities (keeping in mind you must do such things as eat and sleep, too), you can develop a schedule for managing your time. List A activities first, then B, then C activities, as time allows. Overestimate how long each activity will take to allow for some flexibility, and be sure to allow time for recreation! The object is to reduce stress by developing a schedule that eliminates having to think about what to do, keeps you from becoming lazy, controls breaks, and helps you prevent putting off unliked tasks until they prey on your mind and distract you constantly. The goal of time management is to buffer, control, or combat stress by avoiding overscheduling, underscheduling, conflicting schedules, and, most importantly, procrastination.

The Time Management Model presented in Skill Development 7.2 will help you develop a useful approach to budgeting your time by providing some experience in scheduling two weekdays.

Skill Development 7.2

TIME MANAGEMENT MODEL

Step 1: Keep a log of all the activities in which you participate tomorrow and the next day (or the next two weekdays). Do not omit anything, including sleeping, talking with friends, walking to and from activities (as part of the time the activity takes), eating, and so on.

Step 2: Once the log is completed, list all the activities in which you participated both days (these are activities that may have to be scheduled every day), and those that occurred only on one day (these may not have to be scheduled every day).

Step 3: Prioritize all your activities with an A (must do), B (should do), or C (might do). Be sure the approximate length of time needed for each activity is noted clearly.

Step 4: Using the form below, schedule your A activities first, B activities second, and C activities third. Slightly overestimate the time each activity requires to build some flexibility into the schedule. Don't be surprised if there is no time for C activities, and little for B activities.

Step 5: Follow the schedule and keep notes on what changes may have to be made when a full time management plan is developed.

Day One

ACTIVITY

6 A.M.	_____
7 A.M.	_____
8 A.M.	_____
9 A.M.	_____
10 A.M.	_____
11 A.M.	_____
12 P.M.	_____
1 P.M.	_____
2 P.M.	_____
3 P.M.	_____
4 P.M.	_____
5 P.M.	_____
6 P.M.	_____
7 P.M.	_____
8 P.M.	_____
9 P.M.	_____
10 P.M.	_____
11 P.M.	_____
12 A.M.	_____
1 A.M.	_____

Day Two

ACTIVITY

6 A.M.	_____
7 A.M.	_____
8 A.M.	_____

9 A.M. _____

10 A.M. _____

11 A.M. _____

12 P.M. _____

1 P.M. _____

2 P.M. _____

3 P.M. _____

4 P.M. _____

5 P.M. _____

6 P.M. _____

7 P.M. _____

8 P.M. _____

9 P.M. _____

10 P.M. _____

11 P.M. _____

12 A.M. _____

1 A.M. _____

Just setting a schedule and sticking to it may become frustrating, so it is important to create a reward system for fulfilling your goal. If your schedule gives you an hour to study, set aside the last ten minutes to do something you will enjoy. It may be taking a short walk, watching a little TV, getting some ice cream, shooting a couple of baskets, or phoning a friend. Do whatever you feel will reward you for "being good." This technique allows you to look forward to the pleasure that will come from doing what, in some instances, you'd prefer not to do. It also works on the principle of costs and rewards in that you are getting something you need or want in exchange for doing something that takes effort. Just be sure that after enjoying your reward, you return to your schedule and complete your tasks.

Once you have implemented your schedule (and you may need to develop several, for example, one for weekdays and one for the weekends), evaluate the results and either continue with the schedule or make the necessary adjustments. Warning: Once you become skilled at time management, you will find it hard to waste time or use procrastination as an excuse for not getting things done. Are you ready to let go of these stressors, or are they comfortable alibis for you?[7]

Exercise

You may have heard that exercise is an excellent way to protect yourself from the negative effects of stress.[8] Exercise serves three functions—none of which relates to the self-defeating attitude, "It is necessary to be strong."

First, exercise may help you to avoid stressors. Once you are aware of your verbal and nonverbal indicators of stress, you can act on them to ensure that a stressor doesn't become a distressor. If, for example, while typing a research paper, you realize that you can feel your body tightening, your palms starting to perspire, and that you are furiously pounding the keyboard, you can act on these messages—you are feeling stress. An exercise break, whether spent taking a short walk or tossing a ball, may relieve your initial stress reactions, refresh your energies, and enable you to get back to the task.

Second, exercise can help you escape from distress. Assume that you ignored your initial stress reactions and continued to work on the research paper. In a short time you will be experiencing distress: You are swearing at the instructor for assigning the paper, making typing mistakes, and finding it hard to sit still. Then, to make matters worse, your companion walks in with a smile and an energetic, "Hi, how's it going?" You can think of only two possible responses: kill or escape. Exercise is one way to escape constructively.

Third, being involved in an ongoing exercise program allows an individual who has gone through distress to recover more quickly than would the sedentary person. If, instead of exercising to escape, you were to scream at your friend for five minutes, your level of physical fitness would determine how quickly your body returned to an unstressed condition after the outburst. Physiological reactions to stress are similar to those experienced while exercising. In both there is an increased heart rate and muscle activity. If the body is well exercised, its ability to cope with changes and recover are increased. (An additional benefit of exercise, such as walking, is that it can give you the opportunity to have long, uninterrupted talks with friends—which also helps reduce your stress.)

To improve your physical fitness as a coping behavior, an exercise program is needed. You may think that you are already short on time, but it is possible to introduce exercise into your daily life without making any drastic changes in your routine. Simply walk up the stairs rather than take the elevator, park your car in the farthest lot rather than the closest, walk or bike to the store rather than drive, do isometric exercises while watching television or sitting in class, take an exercise class to fulfill part of your graduation requirements, or join a lunch time exercise program where you work. If you have more time, play tennis with friends, jog in good company, or exercise with supportive, caring people.

Meditation

Another self-help technique is meditation—not meditation from a spiritual point of view, although many religious traditions say spiritual meditation relieves stress, but rather meditation as a practical tool you can use on your own to lessen stress. Meditation

may help those who use it because it seems to block the stress mechanism that is related to different ailments.[9]

Meditation is a useful activity for several reasons. First, when you meditate you increase your level of concentration, and this facilitates problem solving. Second, meditation increases your ability to see what is going on around you, which helps you identify your sources of stress and the effects of your stress. Third, in addition to increasing your ability to see what is outside you, meditation increases your ability to see inside of yourself, to pay attention to the inside as well as the outside. Fourth, meditation is useful for coping with stress because it teaches you how to be quiet and to calm your mind. Fifth, meditation invites you to focus on the present, to look directly at your stress while, at the same time, relaxing and bringing your stress under control. Sixth, and finally, meditation can offer insight into yourself, which may provide the basis for understanding and coping with your stress. Meditation provides the opportunity to engage in "careful, non-judgmental self-observation."[10]

There are, perhaps, as many meditation and relaxation techniques as there are people who meditate. Two techniques proven to be successful in dealing with stress are: (1) repeating a word, sound, or phrase; and (2) paying attention to your breathing. When you experience stress, you might try one or both of these techniques for approximately twenty minutes.

Repeating a Word, Sound, or Phrase   Repeating a word, sound, or phrase is one of the oldest and most common of all meditation procedures. First, select a word, sound, or phrase with which you are comfortable. Once the selection is made, you should repeat it over and over. The selected word, sound, or phrase is often a reflection of one's religious or cultural background. A Christian might say the word *amen,* a Jew *shalom,* a traditional Buddhist or Hindu *om,* and an agnostic or atheist might feel comfortable repeating the word *one* or *peace.*

The basic idea behind this technique is that you try to control and still your mind by repeating your selected word, sound, or phrase. Our minds are always very busy, constantly thinking different thoughts; indeed, we tend to thrash around from idea to idea and thought to thought. Repeating the word, sound, or phrase over and over again, the mind eventually quiets down. It is hoped that when this happens you can begin to experience a sense of inner peace. This calming effect should help you feel less stressful at the same time it is assisting you in understanding the origins and consequences of your stress.

Paying Attention to Your Breathing   Paying attention to your breathing is a slightly more involved method of meditation than repeating a word, sound, or phrase, yet it, too, is thousands of years old. As you move through the steps of this technique, your goal is to relax, be calm, and pay attention to the moment.

First, find a comfortable place to sit.

Second, close your eyes to reduce distractions.

Third, bring your focus and awareness to your body. Begin with your feet and work upwards. Ask yourself how you feel. Are you comfortable? Tense? At ease?

Fourth, begin to pay attention to your breathing. Are you breathing too fast? Too slow? In an irregular fashion? Your breath both mirrors your mental state and can transform it.

Fifth, still paying close attention to your breathing, begin to notice each time you inhale and exhale. As you monitor your breath you should mentally say the words "rising, falling" with each inhale and exhale. Whenever your mind begins to wander, bring it back by once again mentally saying "rising, falling." Over a period of time, and with practice, you will find that this process becomes easier, more enjoyable, and an excellent means for coping with your stress.

> Meditation is not a means to an end. It is both the means and the end.
> KRISHNAMURTI

RESPONDING TO YOUR STRESSORS: SEEKING THE HELP OF OTHERS

It is often possible to work alone in buffering, controlling, and combating feelings of stress, but you may sometimes find it necessary to turn to others. When work, school, or relationship concerns overwhelm you, you may turn to friends and family for support. And when distress becomes extreme, you may find that outside sources of help are necessary. Almost everyone needs social support to respond to everyday stressors. There are seven types of social support—listening support, technical challenge support, technical appreciation support, emotional support, emotional challenge support, reality confirmation support, and personal assistance support—and in any given situation receiving one or a combination of them can be important.[11]

Most of us need and appreciate **listening support**—listening without offering advice, asking penetrating questions, or making judgments.[12] For example, after you've ended a long-term friendship, you may feel better if you can talk to someone who will reflect what you say and express concern and understanding, but will not judge you or tell you what to do. Truly good listeners are most helpful because they do not offer advice, tell the talker what to do or what not to do, try to solve the problem, or do the thinking for the talker ("Maybe you should call your friend"). Instead, they ask questions that encourage the other person to talk and think about the problem, but avoid pushing the talker to reach conclusions ("How do you feel about this relationship?"). And they avoid making critical comments that express approval or disapproval of the other person's comments or actions ("I think you're a fool to end such a great relationship").

When you're feeling stressed, you may actively seek out a good listener to test your thoughts.

Technical challenge support urges you to think about a task or an activity in new ways. This challenge, which motivates and stretches you, has as its goal to increase your creativity, excitement, and involvement.[13] Unlike listening support, which anyone can provide, this support needs to be provided by someone you see as an expert in the area of the task or activity; otherwise, you may dismiss what is said to you as unimportant. Although it may seem that being challenged might raise someone's level of stress, often the opposite is true. For example, in a study of hospice workers (hospice workers provide social services to people who are very ill and likely to die within a short period of time—an exceedingly stressful occupation), it was found that technical challenge support was the most effective type of support for reducing stress. This support helped focus the workers and encourage them to develop strategies for doing their jobs better. This, in turn, increased their feelings of being useful to their clients and in control of their work, which reduced their feelings of stress.[14] When you are having trouble writing a paper, you may benefit from a teacher's challenge to approach the paper a new way or to rethink some parts of what you have written. Getting yourself on a new and better track for writing the paper should help reduce your stress.

Unlike technical challenge support that helps you look at your work in a new way, **technical appreciation support** is the acknowledgment you need from another person when you have done a good job on something.[15] Like technical challenge support, technical appreciation, to be meaningful, must come from an expert, someone you respect and trust to be honest with you. For example, after you've worked hard on a paper about Jane Austen, the comment, "Good work," will be meaningful only if it comes from your instructor or some other expert in English literature. Friends or relatives who say the same thing may not have the same effect unless you perceive them as experts. Although you may appreciate a friend's or relative's comment, it is not technical appreciation but, rather, emotional support.

Emotional support is provided by people who tell you that they are on your side whether or not they agree with what you are doing.[16] The key to emotional support is that it comes from someone who cares more about you as a person than about a particular piece of your work, a problematic relationship, or even the bad mood you're in. Thus, a father can give emotional support to a daughter who has just failed a test by communicating his caring for her personally regardless of the test and regardless of his own feelings about the bad grade.

Emotional challenge support encourages you to evaluate your attitudes, values, and feelings.[17] This type of challenge can help you get out of an emotional rut, to assess whether your feelings are perhaps too strong (not doing well on a single research paper, or even in a single course, may not be as catastrophic as it seems at the time), or too weak (not caring about an upcoming test may be unrealistic), and may even help you determine why you feel the way you do (you may not care about the upcoming test because you see yourself as incapable of doing well). Like technical challenge support, this type of support may seem "unsupportive," but this is not the case. Expressed correctly, that is, sincerely, honestly, and with the goal of helping the other person, this support can prove very advantageous.

Reality confirmation support comes from people with whom you can check your perceptions of life and its complexities.[18] Such support can help you gain a perspective on your problems and aid you in developing reasonable courses of action. For example, students in the middle grades and high school often call each other the minute they arrive home and talk for hours about what just happened in school. Their goal is to verify that they see things similarly.

A seventh type of social support, different from the others in that instead of focusing primarily on providing information (as with technical challenge support, for example) or emotional support (as with technical appreciation support, for example), personal assistance support focuses on providing more tangible aid. **Personal assistance support** comes from people who provide you with services or help, such as running an errand or driving you somewhere.[19] This support could come in the form of your roommate returning a library book for you because you don't have time to do it yourself, typing your English paper because you have to study for a test, or taking you shopping because your car won't start.

To help you distinguish among the several types of social support and gain some practice in providing them, Skill Development 7.3 presents situations for you to respond to. The particular type of support you should offer in each situation is indicated, as well as an example.

Skill Development 7.3

PROVIDING SOCIAL SUPPORT

Read each situation and write one appropriate, supportive statement you could make. The type of support you should offer differs for each situation.

1. "I've been trying and trying, but I can't get the answer to this accounting problem."

   Listening support response (example):

   Sounds like you're having some trouble with this particular problem. What have you tried so far?

   Listening support response:

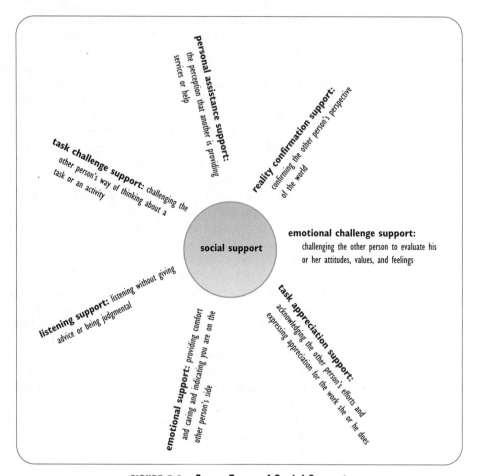

FIGURE 7.2   Seven Types of Social Support

2.   "This studying is driving me crazy! I have a test coming up, and I can't remember the names of the planets in order from the sun."
     Technical challenge support response (example):

> *What about trying a new way? Maybe you can take the first letter of each planet and use it in developing a sentence that you can memorize. Think of the sentence and you'll have the clues you need to list the planets in order.*

Technical challenge support response:

3.   "I got an A on my chemistry test—the first one in the course!"
     Technical appreciation support response (example):

> *That's great! As a chemistry major, I know how hard that first test is.*

Technical appreciation support response:

4. "After a year of dating, Dale told me it's all over between us."
Emotional support response (example):

   It must be upsetting to date someone for so long and then realize the relationship might be over.

   Emotional support response:

5. "I failed my first English paper! I'll never get a good grade in the class! My life is over!"
Emotional challenge support response (example):

   Sure, it's aggravating to fail anything, but you may want to take a second look at how you feel about this particular paper.

   Emotional challenge support response:

6. "I thought being a senior would be terrific, but with looking for a job and thinking about moving, well, to tell you the truth, I'm scared."
Reality confirmation support response (example):

   I see graduating the same way. Looking for a job is not only hard, but it makes it clear that we're moving on to another part of our lives—one where what's in store is unknown. I'll certainly miss being here!

   Reality confirmation support response:

7. "My cold is worse than yesterday; I'm going to have to stay in bed today. The problem is I have this paper to hand in!"
Personal assistance support response (example):

   I'll take the paper and make sure the professor gets it before class.

   Personal assistance support response:

The varieties of social support you need may be provided by different people with whom you interact. For example, student-athletes' social support networks consist predominantly of coaches and teammates, who mostly provide task challenge support, friends, who mostly provide listening support, and parents, who mostly provide task appreciation support.[20] Sometimes, however, you need to seek support from professionals or from groups specifically created to address certain problems.

Professional Help

Assistance in dealing with stress can be provided by professionals, such as social workers, counselors, and psychologists. Turning to these sources should be regarded as a sign of strength and willingness to take action, not as a sign of weakness. It takes courage to assume control of your life and not allow your past history or other people to control you.

Self-Help Groups

Self-help groups are a common form of support for people with identifiable stress-related problems. Chronic drinkers may attend meetings of Alcoholics Anonymous or Rational Recovery, overweight individuals may turn to Overeaters Anonymous, and divorced or widowed parents may join Parents without Partners. A wide range of self-help groups are available, including ones designed to deal with the stress related to traumatic events, such as rape, incest, and child abuse. In addition, religious groups, hobby groups, and study groups also provide you with support by enhancing opportunities for interpersonal relationships and giving you time off from your stressors.

COMMUNICATION ANXIETY

Before reading ahead, complete Knowledge Checkup 7.4, designed to assess your feelings of comfort and discomfort while communicating. The first part focuses on your communicating in general. The remaining parts focus on your feelings about communicating in specific settings.

Knowledge Checkup 7.4

COMMUNICATION APPREHENSION IN GENERALIZED CONTEXTS QUESTIONNAIRE[21]

Indicate the degree to which each of the following statements applies to you. Many statements are similar to other statements. Do not be concerned by this. Work quickly; record your first impression.

Circle **1** if you strongly agree.

Circle **2** if you agree.

Circle **3** if you are undecided.

Circle **4** if you disagree.

Circle **5** if you strongly disagree.

General

1 2 3 4 5	1. When communicating, I generally am calm and relaxed.
1 2 3 4 5	2. I find the prospect of speaking mildly pleasant.
1 2 3 4 5	3. In general, communication makes me uncomfortable.
1 2 3 4 5	4. I dislike using my body and voice expressively.
1 2 3 4 5	5. When communicating, I generally am tense and nervous.

Group Discussions

1 2 3 4 5	6. I am afraid to express myself in a group.
1 2 3 4 5	7. I dislike participating in group discussions.
1 2 3 4 5	8. I am tense and nervous while participating in group discussions.
1 2 3 4 5	9. Engaging in a group discussion with new people makes me tense and nervous.
1 2 3 4 5	10. I am calm and relaxed while participating in group discussions.

Meetings and Classes

1 2 3 4 5	11. I look forward to expressing my opinions at meetings and classes.
1 2 3 4 5	12. Generally, I am nervous when I have to participate in a meeting or class.
1 2 3 4 5	13. Usually I am calm and relaxed while participating in meetings and classes.

1 2 3 4 5   14. I am very calm and relaxed when I am called upon to express an opinion at a meeting or in a class.

1 2 3 4 5   15. Communicating in meetings or classes generally makes me uncomfortable.

Interpersonal Conversations

1 2 3 4 5   16. While participating in a conversation with a new acquaintance I feel very nervous.

1 2 3 4 5   17. Generally, I am very relaxed while talking with one other person.

1 2 3 4 5   18. Ordinarily, I am very calm and relaxed in conversations.

1 2 3 4 5   19. I am relaxed while conversing with people who hold positions of authority.

1 2 3 4 5   20. I am afraid to speak up in conversations.

SCORING

General

Total your scores for items 3, 4, 5. Score A _____

Total your scores for items 1, 2. Score B _____

(18 − Score A) + Score B = _____

Group Discussions

Total your scores for items 6, 7, 8, 9. Score C _____

Indicate your score for item 10. Score D _____

(24 − Score C) + Score D = _____

Meetings and Classes

Total your scores for items 12, 15. Score E _____

Total your scores for items 11, 13, 14. Score F _____

(12 − Score E) + Score F = _____

Interpersonal Conversations

Total your scores for items 16, 20. Score G _____

Total your scores for items 17, 18, 19. Score H _____

(12 − Score G) + Score H = _____

Save your scores. You'll learn how to interpret them as the chapter progresses.

A form of stress specifically related to communication is called **communication anxiety**—the fear of engaging in communication interactions. This term should not be applied to people who are merely quiet or choose to limit severely their participation in communication situations.

The messages that communicatively anxious people tell themselves are, "I lack the ability and confidence to share my true self with someone else," and, "I can't interact when I'd like to." Communication anxiety, sometimes called *shyness,* can be emotionally based and/or based on a lack of communication skills.

No matter which term is selected, once a person accepts the label, his or her attitudes and actions reflect the label. Often these people think that others don't take them seriously, so they are afraid to seek help and advice. As a result, they become increasingly isolated, nonassertive, and withdrawn.

It is estimated that between 80 and 93 percent of all people feel some communication anxiety and that 15 to 20 percent of all college students have high levels of communication anxiety.[22] Although most of the research on shyness has been conducted in the United States, the proportion of shy people found in other cultures that value talk is essentially the same as in the United States, such as in Mexico; however, it is lower in other cultures, such as in Puerto Rico and Israel. Variations within cultures also exist. For example, American Jews have a lower proportion of shy people than other groups of Americans, and although women and men in the United States are about equally shy, more men than women in Japan report being shy, and more women than men in Israel, Mexico, and Germany report being shy.[23]

COMMUNICATION ANXIETY AND YOU

Up until now the discussion of communication anxiety has centered on people in general. Let's examine your score on the first section of Knowledge Checkup 7.4 to see how you label yourself. As you consider the results, remember that this knowledge checkup is not an objective measure. Rather, it reflects your self-perceptions. According to a national sampling, a score of 14 or above in the General section of the questionnaire indicates that you perceive yourself as more apprehensive about communicating than the average person.[24]

Private and Public Communication Anxiety

Publicly anxious people are strongly hesitant about communicating with others and display their anxiety through such outward signs as avoiding eye contact, blushing, perspiring, and speaking in a quavering voice when forced to communicate in public settings. In contrast, **privately anxious people** mentally resist active communication, but will participate—often by forcing themselves. They seldom display the outward physical reactions of stress, such as fingernail biting, sweaty palms, or dry mouth, but still feel discomfort. Famous people who admit to being privately shy include Carol Burnett, Johnny Carson, and even one of America's most prominent interviewers, Barbara Walters.[25] Each has gained success by learning to cope with communication anxiety.

Situational Communication Anxiety

Another way to look at communication anxiety is to discern whether it is situational or general. Once again examine your scores for Knowledge Checkup 7.4. If you think of yourself as a communicatively anxious person but scored lower than 14 on the General section, you may have been surprised. There is a simple explanation: You may be anxious in some contexts but not in others. Look at your scores for the other segments of the questionnaire. If you received a score of over 16 for Group Discussion, or over 15 for Meetings and Classes, or over 13 for Interpersonal Conversations, you may have identified specifically where your anxiety lies. It is not uncommon for some people to display anxiety in only one context, whereas others display anxiety in several or all contexts.

CAUSES OF COMMUNICATION ANXIETY

There are several theories about what causes communication anxiety. Some researchers say it is caused by environmental variables, while some believe it is caused by genetic factors.[26]

Communication anxiety seems to be associated with being brought up in an authoritarian home, having attended authoritarian schools, and being the product of an authoritarian religion. These forces may have taught you to control what you say or emphasized the importance of being "seen but not heard." In addition, if your parents were communicatively anxious, there is a 70 percent chance that you are anxious because you are imitating their patterns.[27] Some evidence also exists that communication anxiety may be inherited. Research with twins raised in the same environment has revealed that identical twins, who are biologically the same, are much more likely than fraternal twins, who are biologically different, to have the same tendency to engage in or avoid social interaction.[28]

Worry is interest paid on trouble before it falls due.

W. R. INGE

Lack of communication skills often results from attending schools that don't teach students how to organize ideas or develop effective speaking and listening skills. Or it may stem from parents who limited their children's exposure to the question-answer process and thus prevented them from playing with language and developing the basic communication skills. As a result of their restricted early years, communicatively anxious people—both women and men—tend to fear rejection, criticism, and imperfection.

THE EFFECTS OF COMMUNICATION ANXIETY

Most people with communication anxiety believe that they suffer negative consequences, that they have given up control of themselves to someone else or to an unknown force, that they are puppets whose strings are being pulled by their master: fear.

There are some demonstrated effects of communication anxiety.[29] In classroom situations, communicatively anxious students volunteer rarely, if at all.[30] They often drop classes that require oral communication or miss class when oral participation is necessary. These patterns can affect learning and grades.[31] Some anxious students even fail to graduate with only one course to complete—a required course in speech communication.

People with communication anxiety often choose college majors that require few, if any, oral presentations, such as research or technical fields. And in the workplace, if they must participate orally—whether one-on-one, in a group, or in a public setting—they miss promotions and pay increases because they are handicapped by their fear.[32]

In interpersonal situations, people with communication anxiety talk very little about themselves and seem overly concerned that the other person understand and agree with them. They also are nonassertive, tending to yield to the other person and submitting themselves to the other's directions. Insofar as perceptions of communicatively anxious people are concerned, after interacting for only 15 minutes with strangers, communicatively anxious students are perceived as less attractive, trustworthy, and satisfied than students who are not communicatively anxious. These perceptions persist even when two communicatively anxious students interact—in other words, communicatively anxious people see each other as less attractive socially than people who are not communicatively anxious.[33]

Finally, although they have as much desire for social relationships as people who are not communicatively anxious, people who are afraid to communicate have half as many steady dates. Also, while those less communicatively anxious "play the field," their anxious colleagues tend to have a small number of exclusive relationships. The overall picture of the communicatively anxious person is generally one who has difficulty forming interpersonal relationships and who, therefore, works hard to maintain ones he or she can establish.

DEALING WITH COMMUNICATION ANXIETY

If your scores on Knowledge Checkup 7.4 indicated that you are anxious in one or more communication contexts, you may be wondering what you can do. First, be assured that communication anxiety is not an incurable illness. In most people the problem is either psychological and related to feelings of insecurity or low confidence, or it stems from a lack of communication skills. In any case, remedies are possible.

Second, recognize that you must identify your particular needs in order to select the appropriate course of action. The next time you feel communicatively anxious, ask yourself: *What aspects of this situation make me uncomfortable?* Do you feel prepared to deal with the situation? Are you afraid of failing? Also ask yourself, *What is happening to my body?* Are you feeling tense? Are you panicking? Do you have a mind block?

Knowing the factors that contribute to your communication anxiety and the extent of your reactions will help you assess the seriousness of your situation and plan an appropriate course of action. If your communication anxiety tends to be mild and infrequent, you can probably manage it by using short-term stress reducers. However, if you often feel communicatively anxious, if particular situations are always extremely stressful, and if you think of your anxiety as a serious handicap, you may want to seek a more permanent solution.

The success rate in teaching communicatively anxious people to cope with or alter their behavior is extremely high. But, like any attempt at changing personality or learning, the treatment or training is effective only if the person truly wants help and diligently applies himself or herself. Three options for changing are communication skills training, systematic desensitization, and positive visualization.[34]

Communication Skills Training

If you find you lack the skills necessary to participate in a conversation, give a speech, or ask questions, you may benefit from communication skills training.[35] Taking a basic communication course should help develop some fundamental skills. Enrolling in classes or workshops that teach techniques of assertiveness, public speaking, conversation, decision making, and group participation also should put you on the road to eliminating your anxiety. As you work through this book, for example, you are constantly required to test your newly found knowledge of communication techniques. If you have communication anxiety, as you start applying these skills in real-life situations you should find yourself feeling more and more confident.

In general, effective communication skills training requires several steps:[36]

1. Identify the specific skill in which you are deficient.
2. Define the skill specifically in terms of the behaviors involved—what you have to do to perform the skill.
3. Establish obtainable goals for acquiring the new skill. (If a skill requires complex behaviors, do not expect too much too soon. Make your goals reasonable ones.)
4. Observe a person who performs the skill well.

5. Understand what it is that you need to do to perform the skill, and be able to explain what you know to others.

6. Practice the new behaviors in a nonthreatening environment where someone you respect can observe you and make suggestions for improvement.

7. Practice the new behavior in the natural environment.

Unfortunately, if your communication anxiety is general or is very high, communication skills training alone is of limited usefulness. Systematic desensitization and visualization, added to the skills training, may be more beneficial.

Systematic Desensitization

If you tend to get extremely nervous when you think about communicating or actually try to communicate, you may benefit from **systematic desensitization**—a process in which you gain control over your anxiety by learning to recognize your stressors and use relaxation techniques to combat their effects.[37] In such a program, a competent professional (such as a psychologist, hypnotherapist, or trained communication practitioner) will:

1. Help you identify your stressors.

2. Teach you relaxation techniques.

3. Set up situations that are more and more anxiety-provoking (beginning, perhaps, with "You are talking to a friend on the phone" and ending with "You are getting ready to deliver a speech and you lose your notes").

4. Teach you how to apply the relaxation techniques when an anxiety-provoking situation occurs. The goal is for you to visualize yourself in an anxiety-provoking situation and to apply the relaxation technique to reduce your fear.

Systematic desensitization typically requires five to seven one-hour sessions. The technique is highly successful, with 80 to 90 percent of people receiving this treatment reporting a reduction in their communication anxiety.[38]

Positive Visualization

Many people are immobilized by their fear of a communication situation. In **positive visualization,** a person prepares for the anticipated unpleasant experience by picturing the situation being carried out successfully.[39] Once the individual develops this "mental film," he or she repeats it over and over before the event so that the expected outcome will be positive rather than negative. Positive visualization is, in effect, a constructive form of self-fulfilling prophecy. For example, if you fear meeting strangers, before your next introduction practice the following technique. Close your eyes and picture yourself being introduced, shaking hands, saying your name, listening to the other person's name, asking a question, hearing the answer, saying good-bye, and feeling pleased about the whole experience. Envision this sequence repeatedly. You may be amazed to find that because you are prepared and are expecting positive results, the event will be much to your liking and less stressful than if you had predicted failure.

Skill Development 7.4 provides an opportunity to practice positive visualization by describing a situation that is anxiety-arousing for most people, and then outlining a positive visualization scenario designed to reduce your anxiety.

Skill Development 7.4

PRACTICING POSITIVE VISUALIZATION

A friend of yours asked you to participate in a fund-raising drive for the American Cancer Society. You agreed to help because you think the drive is worthwhile. Later you realize you have other priorities and should have said no. You decide to back out, but the person is a good friend. You are anxious about confronting your friend. You think of what you are going to say and review it several times, until you feel comfortable with the language. The plea is prepared and you have rehearsed it.

To help you prepare further and to help yourself relax, you are going to use positive visualization. Do the following:

Close your eyes and visualize the friend.

Picture yourself walking to the friend's apartment, saying "hello," and explaining the fact that you are overcommitted and must back out of your prior acceptance to help.

Visualize yourself relaxed as you present your ideas.

See and hear the friend assenting to your reversal.

You are feeling positive about what you did and the outcome of your having acted assertively.

In the future, whenever you are preparing for what you perceive might be a stressful communicative situation, use a similar positive visualization exercise.

THE STRESS MANAGEMENT MODEL

To deal with stress effectively, it is often necessary to change old patterns and substitute new, more productive ones. Though each situation may require a new adaptation, the stress management model presented here should provide a starting point. It won't apply in every situation, particularly if a stressor appears suddenly and permits little time to react. But it should help you to deal with stressors that regularly disturb you and lead to teeth grinding, hand clenching, and similar reactions.

Stage 1: *Identify the distress:* What's wrong?

Stage 2: *Identify your goal or objective:* What would I like to be different?

Stage 3: *Attempt to alleviate the distress:* What have I done to get rid of the distress?

Stage 4: *Identify rewards from the status quo:* What do I gain from *not* alleviating the distress?

Stage 5: *Consider alternative strategies:* What techniques, such as communication skill training, can I realistically use to alleviate the distress?

Stage 6: *Develop an action plan:* What do I do and when do I do it?

Stage 7: *Perform a follow-up analysis:* Was my plan effective in buffering, controlling, or combating the distress?

Communication Competency Checkup

The goal of this Communication Competency Checkup is to guide you in putting your skills and knowledge about stress and communication anxiety to use and to help you summarize the material in this chapter. Les, the character in the cartoon, obviously perceives himself as having communication anxiety.

FUNKY WINKERBEAN
by Tom Batink

FUNKY WINKERBEAN © 1988 North America Syndicate, Inc. Reprinted with permission of North American Syndicate.

1. Name some common verbal and nonverbal behaviors that Les is likely to display because of the stress he feels.

2. What approaches could Les use to buffer, control, and combat his stress?

3. Define *communication anxiety* as it relates to Les.

4. Besides the negative outcomes he is stating, what are some additional problems caused by being communicatively anxious?

5. Name specific things Les could do to overcome his communication anxiety. What types of social support could help Les?

6. Is Les privately or publicly anxious? Explain your answer.

7. In which context(s) identified in Knowledge Checkup 7.4 is Les most communicatively anxious?

8. List the steps in the Stress Management Model and apply the model to Les's situation.

NOTES

1. For further discussion of burnout, see Ayala M. Pines, Elliot Aronson, and Ditsa Kafry, *Burnout* (New York: Free Press, 1981).

2. Beele A. Edson, "Communicating Intrapersonally about Stress: The Dynamics of Self," an unpublished paper presented at the Basic Course Conference, Western Speech Communication Association Convention, Tucson, Arizona, February 15, 1986.

3. R. J. Burke and E. R. Greenglass, "Sex Differences in Psychological Burnout in Teachers," *Psychological Reports* 65 (1989): 55–63; E. R. Greenglass and R. J. Burke, "Work and Family Precursors of Burnout in Teachers: Sex Differences," *Sex Roles* 18 (1988): 215–29.

4. Fred E. Jandt, *Intercultural Communication: An Introduction* (Thousand Oaks, CA: Sage, 1995), 192.

5. Larry A. Samovar and Richard E. Porter, *Communication between Cultures* (Belmont, CA: Wadsworth, 1991), 128.

6. Information on time management presented here is adapted, in part, from material made available to students by the Learning Assistance Program at Appalachian State University, Boone, North Carolina, during the 1995–1996 academic year.

7. Donald Tubesing, *Kicking Your Stress Habits* (Duluth, MN: Whole Person Associates, 1981).

8. Donald B. Adrell and Mark J. Tager, *Planning for Wellness: A Guidebook for Achieving Optimal Health* (Dubuque, IA: Kendall/Hunt, 1982); Covert Bailey, *Fit or Fat* (Boston: Houghton Mifflin, 1978).

9. Steven Peikin, *Gastro-Intestinal Health* (New York: HarperCollins, 1991), 98.

10. Jon Kabat-Zinn, *Full Catastrophe Living: Using the Wisdom of Your Body and Mind to Face Stress, Pain, and Illness* (New York: Bantam Doubleday Dell, 1990), 163.

11. For information on the various types of social support available and their benefits, see Terrance L. Albrecht, Mara B. Adelman, and associates, *Communicating Social Support* (Newbury Park, CA: Sage, 1987); D. C. Ganster and Bart Victor, "The Impact of Social Support on Mental and Physical Health," *British Journal of Medical Psychology* 61 (1988): 17–36; Jack M. Richman, Lawrence B. Rosenfeld, and Charles J. Hardy, "The Social Support Survey: An Initial Evaluation of a Clinical Measure and Practice Model of the Social Support Process," *Research on Social Work Practice,* 3 (1993): 288–311.

12. B. Gottlieb, *Social Support Strategies: Guidelines for Mental Health Practice* (Beverly Hills, CA: Sage, 1983).

13. B. Gottlieb, "The Development and Application of a Classification Scheme of Informal Helping Behaviors," *Canadian Journal of Behavioral Science,* 10.2 (1978): 105–15; E. Litwak and P. Messeri, "Organizational Theory, Social Supports and Mortality Rates: A Theoretical Convergence," *American Sociological Review,* 54 (1989): 49–66; I. G. Sarason, H. Levine, R. Basham and B. Sarason, "Concomitants of Social Support: The Social Support Questionnaire," *Journal of Personality and Social Psychology,* 44 (1983): 127–39.

14. Jack M. Richman and Lawrence B. Rosenfeld, "Stress Reduction for Hospice Workers: A Support Group Model," *Hospice Journal,* 3 (1987): 205–21.

15. G. Yukl and D. D. Van Fleet, "Cross-Cultural, Multimethod Research on Military Leader Effectiveness," *Organizational Behavior and Human Performance* 30 (1982): 87–108.

16. J. House, *Work Stress and Social Support* (Reading: MA: Addison-Wesley, 1981); S. Jayaratne and W. Chess, "The Effects of Emotional Support on Perceived Job Stress and Strain," *Journal of Applied Behavioral Science* 20 (1984): 141–53; H. O. F. Veiel, M. Crisand, H. Stroszeck-Somscher, and J. Herrie, "Social Support Networks of Chronically Strained Couples: Similarity and Overlap," *Journal of Social and Personal Relationships* 8 (1991): 279–92.

17. J. Plas, K. Hoover-Dempsey, and B. Wallston, "A Conceptualization of Professional Women's Interpersonal Fields: Social Support, Reference Groups, and Persons-to-Be-Reckoned-With," in *Social Support: Theory, Research and Applications,* ed. I. G. Sarason and B. R. Sarason (Boston: Martinus Nijhoff, 1985), 187–204.

18. C. Dunkel-Schetter and C. Wrothman, "Dilemmas of Social Support: Parallels between Victimization and Aging," in *Aging: Social Change,* ed. S. B. Kiesler, J. N. Morgan, and V. K. Oppenheimer, (New York: Academic Press, 1981), 349–81.

19. R. Caplan, S. Cobb, J. French, R. Harrison, and S. Pinneau, *Job Demands and Worker Health* (Ann Arbor, MI: Institute for Social Research, 1980); S. Cobb, "Social Support and Health through the Life Course," in *Aging from Birth to Death: Interdisciplinary Perspectives,* ed. M. W. Riley (Washington DC: American Association for the Advance-

ment of Science, 1979), 93–106; Veiel, Crisand, Stroszeck-Somscher, and Herrie, "Social Support Networks of Chronically Strained Couples"; B. Wellman, "From Social Support to Social Network," in *Social Support: Theory, Research and Applications,* 205–22.

20. Lawrence B. Rosenfeld, Jack M. Richman, and Charles J. Hardy, "An Examination of Social Support Networks among Athletes: Description and Relationship to Stress," *Sport Psychologist,* 3 (1989): 23–33.

21. Modification of an instrument developed by James McCroskey and presented in Virginia P. Richmond and James C. McCroskey, *Communication: Apprehension, Avoidance, and Effectiveness,* 4th ed. (Scottsdale, AZ: Gorsuch Scarisbrick, 1995), 133–35.

22. Philip Zimbardo, *Shyness: What It Is; What to Do About It* (Reading, MA: Addison-Wesley, 1977), 13–14.

23. Richmond and McCroskey, *Communication,* 26–27.

24. Richmond and McCroskey, *Communication,* 46, plus correspondence with James C. McCroskey.

25. Jules Asher, "Born to Be Shy?" *Psychology Today* (April 1987): 64.

26. Richmond and McCroskey, *Communication,* 29–32, 49–55, 63–65.

27. For a discussion of the research on causes of communication apprehension, see Gerald M. Phillips, *Help for Shy People* (Englewood Cliffs, NJ: Prentice-Hall, 1981), especially Chapters 3 and 4.

28. Richmond and McCroskey, *Communication,* 29–30.

29. John Daly and James McCroskey, eds., *Avoiding Communication: Shyness, Reticence, and Communication Apprehension* (Beverly Hills, CA: Sage, 1984), especially 125–43. In addition, for an extensive discussion, see Richmond and McCroskey, *Communication,* and Phillips, *Help for Shy People.*

30. James W. Chesebro, James C. McCloskey,

Deborah F. Atwater, Rene M. Bahrenfuss, Gordon Cawelti, James L. Gaudino, and Helene Hodges, "Communication Apprehension and Self-Perceived Communication Competence of At-Risk Students," *Communication Education* 41 (1992): 345–60.

31. For a discussion of the effects of communication apprehension on math, English, reading, and intelligence scores, as well as grades in general, see John Bourhis and Mike Allen, "Meta-Analysis of the Relationship between Communication Apprehension and Cognitive Performance," *Communication Education* 41 (1992): 68–76.

32. See Daly and McCroskey, *Avoiding Communication.*

33. Richmond and McCroskey, *Communication,* 58–59.

34. For a summary of techniques useful for dealing with communication anxiety, see Joe Ayres and Tim Hopf, *Coping with Speech Anxiety* (Norwood, NJ: Ablex, 1993); Richmond and McCroskey, *Communication;* and Phillips, *Help for Shy People.*

35. Gerald Phillips, "Rhetoritherapy: The Principles of Rhetoric in Training Shy People in Speech Effectiveness," in *Shyness: Perspective on Research and Treatment,* ed. W. H. Jones, J. M. Cheek, and S. R. Briggs (New York: Plenum Press, 1986), 357–74.

36. Richmond and McCroskey, *Communication,* 107.

37. Susan Glaser, "Oral Communication Apprehension and Avoidance: The Current Status of Treatment Research," *Communication Education* 30 (1981): 323–29; James McCroskey and Virginia Richmond, *The Quiet Ones: Communication Apprehension and Shyness* (Annandale, VA: Speech Communication Association, 1991).

38. Richmond and McCroskey, *Communication,* 100.

39. Joe Ayres and Theodore S. Hopf, "The Long-Term Effect of Visualization in the Classroom: A Brief Research Report," *Communication Education* 39 (1990): 75–78.

CHAPTER 8

INTERPERSONAL RELATIONSHIP PROCESSES

COMMUNICATION COMPETENCIES

This chapter examines interpersonal relationship processes. Specifically, the objective of the chapter is for you to learn to:

- Define the framework for a relationship, including personal and relational goals, the structure of the relationship, and the rules of the relationship.
- Distinguish relationship structures according to dominant/submissive and loving/hostile behaviors.
- Specify the rules for relationships.
- Identify the components of relationship commitment and assess your commitment in an important relationship.
- List the components of intimacy and distinguish an intimate experience from an intimate relationship.
- Identify the resources offered in relationships.
- Understand and adapt to cultural differences in the interpersonal setting.

KEY WORDS

The key words in this chapter are:

relationship
complementary
    relationship
symmetrical relationship
parallel relationship
rules
commitment
intimacy

Write four personal want ads for people to fill the following relationship vacancies in your life. Specify the characteristics you want in the other individual as well as the personal qualities you have to offer.

1. Advertise for a person with whom you wish to establish a work relationship.
2. Advertise for a person with whom you wish to establish a friendship.
3. Advertise for a person with whom you wish to establish a loving and caring relationship.
4. Select a culture other than your own that you know the most about. Write an advertisement seeking a relationship with a person from that culture.

How do your four advertisements differ from each other?

Do your descriptions relate to each relationship's goal, such as "to have fun," "to get a job done," or "to keep from being bored"? Do they refer to whether you are the superior person in the relationship, "the leader," or the subordinate one, "the follower"? Do some characterizing words focus on the amount of love and affection or hate and hostility you want in the particular relationship? Did you concern yourself with some of the rules that make each relationship unique, such as "to date each other exclusively," or "to have a 50-50 partnership in the business"? Did you use such words as *commitment* or *intimacy?*

What do the variety of types of relationships you have and the myriad ways you describe and distinguish them reveal about yourself?

RELATIONSHIP DIMENSIONS

When you say that you have a "relationship" with another person, what do you mean? On a formal note, the *Random House Dictionary of the English Language* defines a **relationship** as "a connection, association, or involvement . . . an emotional or other connection between people." Although you may have some intuitive sense of what an "emotional connection" is, what does "or other connection" refer to? Do you and a salesman with whom you never interacted before have a relationship when you hand him a candy bar you wish to purchase, he says, "Fifty cents, please," and you hand him the change and walk away after a quick "thank you" and "you're welcome"? Relationships are more than such a simple exchange, as the synonyms for *relationship—dependence, affinity, concern, alliance, affiliation, association,* and *tie*—indicate. Each of these words reveals the complexity of human connectedness.

To use the word *relationship,* three conditions must be satisfied: (1) you and the other person need to be aware of each other and take each other into account, (2) there needs to be some exchange of influence, and (3) there needs to be some agreement about what the nature of the relationship is—impersonal or personal, formal or informal— and what the appropriate behaviors are given the nature of the relationship.[1] Rituals, for example, do not constitute a relationship since the same transactions could take place with a machine—as they often do, given the abundance of computers and automated teller machines (ATMs). And interacting with a person with whom there is no agreement about what your relationship is or what behaviors should govern your interaction—which may occur when interacting with a stranger from a culture very different from your own—makes it impossible to have a relationship. Indeed, you may describe such an encounter this way: "His behavior was bizarre and unpredictable; it was impossible to have a relationship with him!"

Before examining the topic of relationships in detail, it is important to highlight three ideas that stem from the conditions that must exist in order to use the word *relationship*. First, all human interaction does not involve relationships. That is to say, relationships are not inevitable. Simply exchanging messages with another person, such as when you buy a pack of gum, does not automatically mean that you and the other person share a relationship. Relationships are far more complex and involve much more than an exchange of messages.

Second, no two relationships are alike. Although many of our relationships contain common characteristics, each one is unique. The reason for this uniqueness is obvious: Each relationship involves a different set of people. You communicate differently depending upon whether you are with your mother, father, brother, sister, lover, friend, boss, or fellow employee.

Third, all relationships change. Relationships, like all aspects of life, are constantly in a state of flux. It is our unwillingness to accept change that causes serious problems in many of our relationships.

Relationships come in a variety of forms, from the work-on-a-class-project type to the live-together-forever type. In most instances our relationships can be classified as (1) role relationships, (2) acquaintances, (3) friends, (4) good friends, and (5) intimate relationships. These five types of relationships are distinguishable by their communication—for example, we laugh more with intimate partners than acquaintances, speak more personally with good friends than friends—as well as their complexity.[2] That is to say, the components of a role relationship are less complex than those of an acquaintance relationship, which are less complex than those of friend relationship, and so on. An intimate partner relationship is the most complex relationship available to us, the one with the most perplexing goals, structure, and rules.

It's the friends that you can call up at 4 am that matter.
MARLENE DIETRICH

Role relationships are characterized by your interacting with others in light of the roles you and the other person both play. You may be an employee communicating with a boss, a customer talking with a salesperson, a student interacting with a professor, or a patient describing an ailment to a doctor. In each of these situations, behavior is dictated by your role. In most instances role relationships involve very little individuality (for example, enacting the role of "student" is usually limited to performing stereotyped "student behaviors") and seldom focus on personal, intimate information (unless the doctor asks for this information).

Acquaintances are people in your life, for either short or long periods of time, that share a common experience or context with you. You may know this person from work, school, religious group, sports team, or political club. Most of your communication with an acquaintance focuses on the common experience. For example, an acquaintance in a class is someone with whom you may discuss the tests, professor, assignments, and even

other students. Although you may talk about your opinions (such as what you think the professor does well) and attitudes (such as what you dislike about the term paper assignment), rarely will you talk about anything more personal.

Friends are much more than acquaintances—you know more about your friends, they know more about you, you feel more comfortable with them, and enjoy their company more and for longer periods of time. You get to share more personal information with friends than acquaintances and to talk about a larger range of topics. While the conversation with the class acquaintance may be limited to class concerns, there is no such automatic limitation on conversations with friends (the list of taboo and permitted topics is the result of often complex negotiations over time).

Good friends are much more than friends—you know more about your good friends than your friends, and, likewise, they know that much more about you. Typically, you are more open and honest with good friends than acquaintances or friends because you believe they are accepting of what you say and do. This mutual acceptance also encourages more spontaneous behavior, as well as more mutual dependency, than in the other relationships discussed so far.

Finally, people with whom you have an *intimate relationship* are much like good friends with a few significant additions. For one, intimate relationships have the most complex set of rules about what may or may not be discussed and what behaviors may or may not be tolerated. For example, a good friend may not care too much (or at all) whether you have other good friends, but your intimate partner may not take kindly to your having additional intimate partners. Similarly, while there is usually no problem discussing past good friends with a current good friend, discussing past intimate relationships may be taboo with your present intimate partner.

In addition to the emotional, intellectual, and spiritual intimacy available in good friend relationships, intimate relationships may include sexual intimacy. Do not confuse

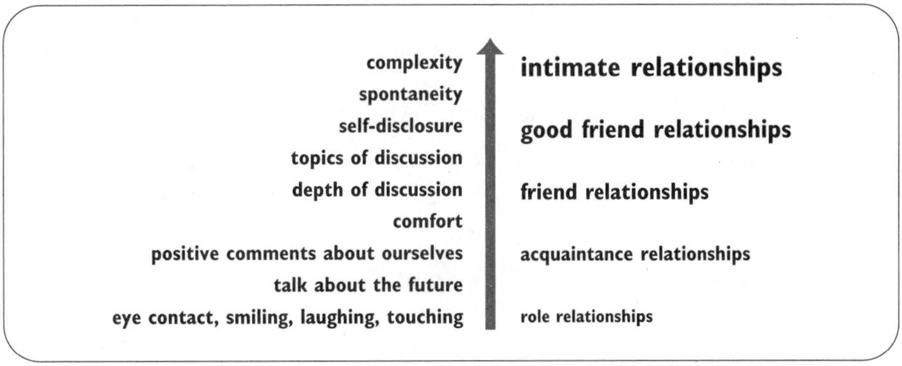

complexity   **intimate relationships**
spontaneity
self-disclosure   **good friend relationships**
topics of discussion
depth of discussion   **friend relationships**
comfort
positive comments about ourselves   **acquaintance relationships**
talk about the future
eye contact, smiling, laughing, touching   role relationships

FIGURE 8.1 Five Types of Relationships

an intimate relationship with a "one night stand." The hallmarks of an intimate partner relationship are greater commitment and longer duration than in any other type of relationship, neither of which are present in a brief encounter, no matter how intense.

Communication plays a key role in all five types of relationships. It is the messages you send others and the messages they send you that help establish, maintain, and change these relationships. Even your movement from one relationship level to another is influenced by communication. Changes in communication as you move from a role relationship to an intimate relationship include the following (see Figure 8.1): an increase in open and honest self-disclosure; a decrease in stress-related behaviors, such as leg bouncing, preening, and nail biting; an increase in feeling relaxed; an increase in spontaneous behavior; an increase in the number of positive comments you receive from the other person; an increase in talk about the immediate and future plans for the relationship; an increase in eye contact, smiling, laughing, and touching; and an increase in the number of different topics you talk about and the depth to which you discuss them.[3]

CULTURE AND RELATIONSHIPS

Culture plays a major role in our relationships. While there are many similarities in how relationships are perceived across cultures, there are also numerous differences. In Japan, for example, individuals interact most frequently with members of the same sex; there is limited interaction between opposite-sex individuals.[4] The Arab culture, for religious reasons, is another culture that fosters same-sex relationships and limits and clearly defines opposite-sex contact. In the Mexican culture there is a blending of different generations that is not nearly so prevalent in the more generation-segregated United States; hence, you find close relationships between people from different age groups. There are also cultures that keep intimate relationships to a minimum. There is a famous German saying that makes this point clearly: "A friend to everyone is a friend to no one.'' The opposite view may be found in many African cultures, where a large number of close relationships is encouraged. In the Maasai culture, for example, there is the belief that everyone is interconnected. Compare the German saying to the Maasai saying that "The child has no owner." This is a clear indication that everyone is linked to everyone else.[5]

THE FRAMEWORK FOR INTERACTION

Relationships are complex. To understand them means breaking them down into their component parts and looking at each part separately, even though you probably rarely sit down and consciously analyze them because relationships often seem to "just happen." For the sake of analysis, however, the components of a relationship are divided into two broad categories: those related to the framework for interaction and those related to the relationship's quality or outcomes.

Each of your relationships has goals, structure, and rules that form the context within which you and the other person interact. Your communication both reflects and determines these three dimensions for each of your relationships.

GOALS

Relationships form because of some *goal* or outcome that each person wishes to achieve. The goal may be to learn something about yourself, to learn something about the environment, to overcome loneliness, to change another's attitude or behavior, to complete a project, to kill time, to release tension, to be entertained, to help someone, or to become intimate with someone. There may be as many goals as there are individuals, cultures, and relationships.

The differences among the personal advertisements you wrote at the beginning of this chapter reflect the differences in your goals for each relationship.[6] Although the general goal for each—"a work relationship," "a friend relationship," or "a loving relationship"—is prescribed, you meet your specific needs and desires by seeking particular characteristics in a partner in a relationship. Knowledge Checkup 8.1 will help you look at your relationships with respect to the goals you have for them.

Knowledge Checkup 8.1
WHAT ARE YOUR RELATIONSHIP GOALS?

Part I

Reread the personal ads you wrote at the outset of this chapter. What were your *specific* goals for each type of relationship? List them.

Advertisement 1:

Advertisement 2:

Advertisement 3:

Advertisement 4:

Part II

Select three relationships in which you are currently involved: (a) an acquaintance relationship, (b) a friend relationship, and (c) a good friend relationship.

1. What are your goals for each relationship?

    (a)

    (b)

    (c)

2. How do you know these are your goals?

You probably found that your advertisements for love, friendship, and work relationships had different goals. On the other hand, you may have found some similarities. Assume, for example, that you seek a person with whom to share a loving relationship who is kind and considerate, a friend who jogs and likes unusual experiences, and a work partner who is responsible and has good research skills. Each set of characteristics reveals different relationship goals: to share a long-term intimate relationship, to provide companionship, and to complete some task efficiently.

Comparing the characteristics you listed in each of your ads with those listed by your classmates should help to clarify your goals for these types of relationships. An advertisement for a work partner that focuses exclusively on intelligence, experience, and a willingness to work hard reveals different goals from one seeking a partner who is easygoing and flexible. Someone advertising for a friend who is a good listener has a different goal from someone who seeks a person with whom to share weekends of mountain climbing. An advertisement for a partner in a loving relationship that lists quiet, warm, and considerate as desired characteristics displays different goals from an ad that seeks someone wild, exciting, and willing to take risks.

As you compare your other-culture advertisement with classmates you probably will be struck by the fact that not all cultures have the same goals for their relationships nor do they apply the same list of traits when seeking partners to fulfill those goals. In Indian and Arabic cultures, for example, the male generally would be interested in a subservient woman. In Scandinavia, on the other hand, many women would be repelled by a male who would want to control them.

Researchers pay more attention to close, personal, intimate relationships than to any other ones because intimacy offers great rewards and exacts great costs. Intimate relationships provide stimulation (an escape from loneliness and boredom) and an opportunity to share experiences (whether a beautiful sunset or a horrible test grade). Intimate relationships frequently present a nonthreatening arena in which to try out new ideas and behaviors and often increase enjoyment of certain activities (a party with close friends is usually more fun than one with strangers). Intimate relationships also provide the opportunity for self-disclosure, the self-revealing communication that strips away the front you present to others and displays the person you think you really are. Accompanying the rewards, however, are potentially great costs, the greatest of which is rejection by the other person.

Regardless of the particular goals you have for an intimate relationship, you should bear two things in mind. First, people rarely set out to form an intimate relationship in a rational and intellectual way. Their conscious aim often is something other than to begin an intimate relationship. People seldom enter a classroom with a specific plan for leaving with an intimate relationship, although many individuals have met in class and eventually lived together or gotten married.

Second, most relationships are not formed with the primary goal of achieving intimacy. Usually, relationships form as accompaniments to everyday activities. For instance, you like to jog, so you meet people who share the same interest; you may not think about extending the relationship beyond your noontime run. Or a class project may require you to work with another student; your only goal may be to fulfill the assignment.

Nonetheless, your specific goal may be to find someone with whom you can follow a path toward intimacy, a person with whom to share your innermost thoughts and feelings and, eventually, your love. If this is the case, your goal—to seek out and develop an intimate relationship—is predetermined and conscious, not a by-product of other relationships with different goals.

> We always believe our first love is our last, and our last love our first.
>
> GEORGE WHYTE-MELVILLE

How can you determine what the specific goals are for your many relationships? Skill Development 8.1 presents four questions that will help you determine your goals for any relationship. Practice using the four questions by applying them to one of your important relationships, perhaps one for which your goals are unclear to you.

Skill Development 8.1

ASCERTAINING YOUR RELATIONSHIP GOALS

Select an important relationship in which you are now involved (for example, a work relationship or a friendship), the goals for which may be unclear to you. Answer these questions regarding that relationship:

1. I am in this relationship in order to . . .
2. I stay in this relationship with this person because . . .
3. I want to continue in a relationship with this person until . . .
4. This relationship will end once . . .

What have you discovered about your goals for this relationship?

How do each of the four questions help you ascertain your relationship goals?

If you apply the four questions to more than one relationship, ask yourself: Which one of the four questions is, in general, most important (e.g., the question "in order to . . ." may be the most revealing, or the "will end once . . ." may give you the most information)? What does this tell you about your relationship goals?

STRUCTURE

Look back at your relationship ads. The characteristics you want in a partner often reflect how you expect to interact with her or him. For some people, the patterns of interaction in the work, friendship, and loving relationships might be similar, even if the goals are different. For example, you might want to be the person who controls what happens, whether the goal is to complete a project with a work partner or to see a movie with a friend. For other people, the patterns of interaction may differ for each relationship. For example, you may picture yourself the boss with your work partner, the equal of your friend, and the subservient member of your loving relationship.

A relationship is like a dance—two people move together in a coordinated display. The partners may glide about smoothly, anticipating each other's movements and responding with grace, or they may appear awkward and out of step. Relationships are distinguished by the *structure* of their communication—how their talk is organized and coordinated—much as dancers are distinguished by their choreography.

Two dimensions characterize the structure of a relationship: dominance/submission and love/hostility.[7] The dimension of dominance/submission describes how much control you and the other person have over each other, while the dimension of love/hostility reflects how much affection or love you give and receive. In Figure 8.2, dominance and submission are the endpoints of the vertical line through the circle, and hostility and love are the endpoints of the horizontal line. The two dimensions are independent of each other, that is, you can be both dominant and loving (stereotypical "parent" behavior), dominant and hostile ("exploitive manager" behavior), submissive and loving ("good little child" behavior), and submissive and hostile (stereotypical "downtrodden worker" behavior).

The behaviors indicated on the circle represent variations of the behaviors associated with dominance, submission, love, hostility, and their combinations, such as loving and dominant, hostile and submissive. The terms that describe behaviors along the inside edge of the circle (*pities, clings, bitter,* and *exploits*) are extreme or exaggerated behaviors, and those toward the center (*helps, respects, skeptical,* and *competes*) are moderate or less exaggerated behaviors. For example, the exaggerated form of love is compulsively loving, whereas the moderate form is affectionate.

Looking at how two individuals' bids for dominance/submission and love/hostility may combine in a particular relationship, three possible relationship structures may be seen: complementary, symmetrical, and parallel.[8]

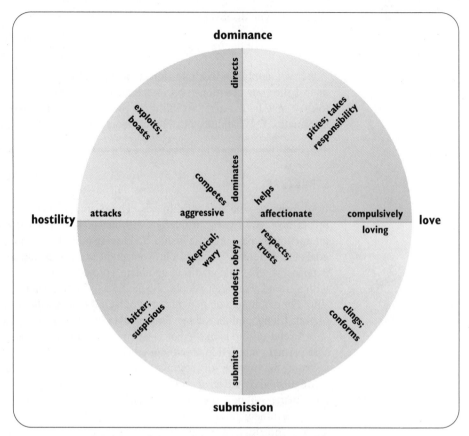

FIGURE 8.2 **Primary Components of Relationship Interaction**

In a **complementary relationship,** one partner's behavior complements or completes the other's—the behaviors seem to go together. The relationship is based on differences (for example, one partner may be dominant while the other is submissive) which, when they come together, form a stable relationship. Each partner has particular duties and obligations, whether one "brings home the bacon" while the other "keeps the home fires burning," or one cooks the meals while the other cleans up. The partners work better in combination than alone.

The relationship between dominant and submissive behaviors often is complementary. Dominance tends to provoke its opposite from the other person: subordinance. Submission tends to provoke its opposite: control.

Although the relationship between love and hostility is usually not complementary, such a relationship is possible. One partner may be loving and the other hostile—for example, when one partner, tiring of the relationship, picks fights and behaves in a hostile way, while the other, enjoying the relationship, remains loving. The more the

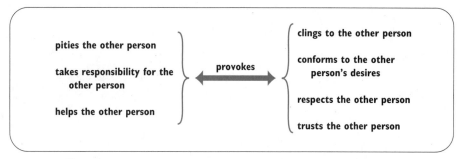

FIGURE 8.3   Loving-Dominant Behavior/Loving-Submissive Behavior

loving person is loving, the more the hostile person is hostile, and the more the hostile person is hostile, the more the loving person is loving. Typically, however, loving behaviors arouse a loving response and hostile behaviors arouse a hostile response in a relationship described as symmetrical.

A **symmetrical relationship,** unlike a complementary one, implies balance: The partners contribute equally to their relationship. While the partners in a complementary relationship create a whole from their two separate parts, partners in a symmetrical relationship maintain their individual identities. In the ideal symmetrical control relationship (for which there are few examples), power is equally distributed, independence is stressed, and both partners are either submissive or dominant.

Unlike dominant and submissive behaviors, which tend to provoke their opposites, loving behaviors tend to evoke love and hostile behaviors tend to evoke hostility. For example, when you tell someone "I love you," you probably expect a similar confession. An opposite or neutral response ("I don't love you!" or "Oh") is usually unexpected and unappreciated.

Combining a loving or hostile behavior with a dominant or submissive one, the tendency is to provoke the same feeling—love or hostility—and the opposite behavior—dominance or submission. Therefore, loving-dominant behaviors (as indicated in Figure 8.2), such as "pitying the other person," "taking responsibility for the other person," or "helping the other person," tend to provoke loving-submissive behaviors from the other person, such as "clinging" and "conforming," or "respecting" and "trusting"; in other words, the result is symmetrical feeling and complementary control behavior (see Figure 8.3). For example, a parent's loving-dominant message, "You poor child, here, let me help you with your math homework," is likely to get a loving-submissive message from the child, such as, "Please help me. I'd really appreciate it."

Likewise, loving-submissive behaviors, such as "clings" and "conforms," or "respects" and "trusts," tend to provoke loving-dominant behaviors, such as "pities" and "takes responsibility" or "helps" (see Figure 8.3). For example, the loving-submissive message, "I think it's terrific that you know how to use the new computer," is likely to evoke a loving-dominant message in return, "Let me show you how to use it. It's really not hard once you know what to do."

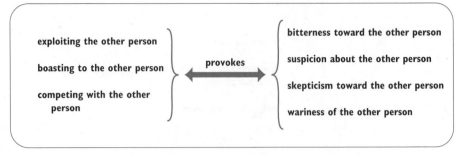

FIGURE 8.4 **Hostile-Dominant Behavior/Hostile-Submissive Behavior**

Hostile-dominant behaviors, such as "exploiting the other person" and "boasting to the other person" or "competing with the other person," tend to provoke hostile-submissive behaviors, such as "bitterness" and "suspicion," or "skepticism" and "wariness" (see Figure 8.4). For example, a manager's hostile-dominant message, "I've been on the job here twice the time you have, so do the job the way I say to do it," is likely to get an employee's hostile-submissive message in response, "Well, okay, but just because you've been here a long time doesn't make you a genius!"

In turn, hostile-submissive behaviors, such as "bitterness" and "suspicion" or "skepticism" and "wariness," tend to provoke hostile-dominant behaviors, such as "exploitation" and "boastfulness" or "competitiveness." For example, a child's hostile-submissive message, "Gee, I never get to do anything I want to do. How come?" is likely to get a parent's hostile-dominant message in return, such as, "I'm the parent and you'll do what I say!"

The third relational structure, **parallel relationship,** is not represented in Figure 8.2. It is a hybrid form in which complementary and symmetrical aspects are combined. Under some circumstances one partner may be dominant and the other submissive; other times, the partners may reverse roles; and occasionally, both partners may be dominant or both may be submissive. Similarly, the expression of feelings depends on the situation. In general, the parallel structure is the most flexible, allowing contributions to the relationship to vary from time to time and topic to topic.

What is the structure of one of your family relationships? What is the structure of one of your non-family relationships? Knowledge Checkup 8.2 will help you analyze the structure of these two relationships.

Knowledge Checkup 8.2

RELATIONAL STRUCTURE ANALYSIS

Select two relationships with specific people: one family, the other, non-family. Using Figure 8.2 as a guide, indicate the extent to which you and the other person are dominant, submissive, loving, and hostile. Use the ten-point scale to mark your responses.

Family Relationship

1	2	3	4	5	6	7	8	9	10
almost never									almost always

_____ 1. I am dominant.

_____ 2. The other person is dominant.

_____ 3. I am submissive.

_____ 4. The other person is submissive.

_____ 5. I am loving.

_____ 6. The other person is loving.

_____ 7. I am hostile.

_____ 8. The other person is hostile.

Non-Family Relationship

1	2	3	4	5	6	7	8	9	10
almost never									almost always

_____ 1. I am dominant.

_____ 2. The other person is dominant.

_____ 3. I am submissive.

_____ 4. The other person is submissive.

_____ 5. I am loving.

_____ 6. The other person is loving.

_____ 7. I am hostile.

_____ 8. The other person is hostile.

To determine whether you perceive each of your relationships as predominantly dominant-loving, dominant-hostile, submissive-loving, or submissive-hostile, plot your responses on Figures 8.6 and 8.7. (An example of plotted results for a father-son relationship is given in Figure 8.5.)

As you plot your responses to items 1, 3, 5, and 7 (your perceptions of yourself in each relationship), and to items 2, 4, 6, and 8 (your perceptions of your partner in each relationship) on Figures 8.6 and 8.7, consider these questions for each selected relationship:

1. Does your four-sided figure fall predominantly into any one of the four quadrants? What about your partner's?

2. How do the two four-sided figures compare? How do they describe the structure of your relationship?

3. What predictions could you make for each of your relationships given the two four-sided figures?

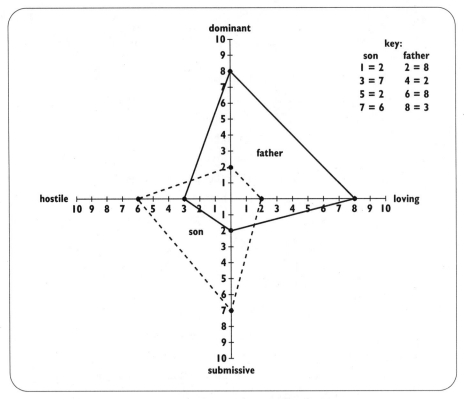

dominant

key:

	son		father
	1 = 2		2 = 8
	3 = 7		4 = 2
	5 = 2		6 = 8
	7 = 6		8 = 3

father

hostile

loving

son

submissive

FIGURE 8.5 **Father-Son Relational Structure Analysis**

Using the terms *complementary, symmetrical,* and *parallel,* describe each relationship.

Family relationship:

Non-family relationship:

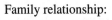

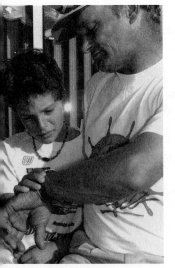

Figure 8.5 shows plots for one person's responses to items 1, 3, 5, and 7 for himself, and to items 2, 4, 6, and 8 for his perceptions of his father. The son's four scores for himself were plotted as follows: The response to item 1 was a 2, so a point was placed on the dominant line at number 2; the response to item 3 was a 7, so a point was placed on the submissive line at number 7; the response to item 5 was a 2, so a point was placed on the loving line at number 2; and the response to item 7 was a 6, so a point was placed on the hostile line at number 6. The four points were joined to form the four-sided figure. The son's four scores for his perceptions of his father were plotted as follows: The response to item 2 was an 8, so a point was placed on the dominant line at number 8; the response to item 4 was a 2, so a point was placed on the submissive

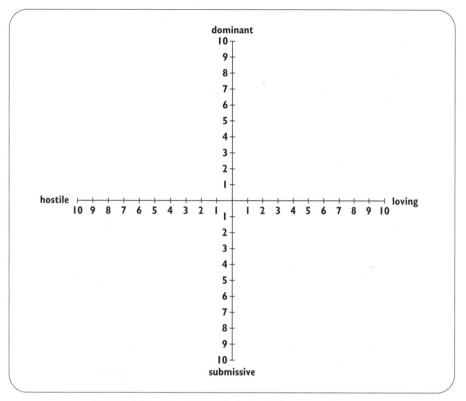

FIGURE 8.6   Your Family Relational Structure Analysis

line at number 2; the response to item 6 was an 8, so a point was placed on the loving line at number 8; and the response to item 8 was a 3, so a point was placed on the hostile line at number 3.

The son perceives himself as predominantly submissive and hostile (because the four-sided figure formed by his scores falls predominantly into the submissive-hostile quadrant) and his father as predominantly loving and dominant (because most of the four-sided figure formed by the scores for the father falls into the dominant-loving quadrant). Given the son's perception of their relationship as complementary for both control and affection, what predictions could you make for their relationship? (For example, do they fight with each other? If they fight, what do you think the underlying issue is that they fight about?)

Analyzing the structure of your relationships could help you discover why some are more satisfying than others. For example, the father-son relationship in Figure 8.5 is likely to be unsatisfactory from the son's perspective: The two probably fight often, the son probably harbors a great deal of quiet resentment, and when they fight the underlying issue is probably who's in control.

Although most people in North America prefer the parallel relationship structure, not every close relationship takes this form.[9] Do you insist on being dominant or

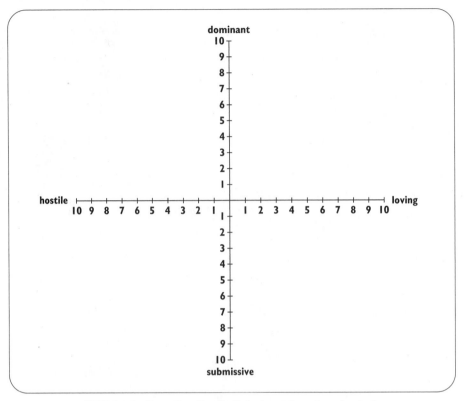

FIGURE 8.7   Your Non-Family Relational Structure Analysis

submissive but have a partner who seeks equality? Do you wonder whether your expressions of love will receive loving responses? Questions such as these should help you further analyze the structure of your relationships.

RULES

Look back once again at your relationship ads. What rules are implied for the relationships sought in your ads? For example, "Do your fair share" might be a rule that will guide your work relationship, and the rule "Stick up for the other person" might guide your friend relationship; in the first instance, you want someone who is hardworking; in the second, you seek someone loyal.

Rules, the regulations that govern actions in a relationship, are necessary for you to make predictions about another person's behavior. If you don't know the rules governing your interaction, you can't predict whether the person to whom you nod and say hello will, in return, ignore you, hit you, or start screaming. But because most people share the same rule for greeting behavior, you can predict a reciprocal response: A nod and hello will get you a nod and hello in return. Rules organize the world for you, add predictability, and reduce uncertainty.

Researchers who have conducted studies in various parts of the world uncovered a small number of rules that help structure relationships.[10] Like all rules, some may be more important than others in particular relationships and in particular societies, and some may even be broken. The five *relational rules* found are:

1. You should respect the other's privacy.
2. You should look the other person in the eye during conversations.
3. You should not divulge something that is said in confidence.
4. You should not criticize the other person publicly.
5. You should seek to repay debts, favors, or compliments, no matter how small.

Several specific *structure rules* that help structure particular relationships, such as loving, friendship, and work relationships, also turned up. Specific rules for friendships were:

1. You should stand up for the other person in her or his absence.
2. You should share news of success with her or him.
3. You should show emotional support.
4. You should trust and confide in each other.
5. You should volunteer your help in time of need.
6. You should strive to make the other person happy when you are with her or him.
7. You should not nag the other person.

To what extent do the relational and structural rules found in relationships around the world exist in your own relationships? Are there differences in how the rules apply to your good friend, friend, and acquaintance relationships? You may find that the relational rule "you should respect the other's privacy" is very important in your good friend, friend, and acquaintance relationships, but that "you should not criticize the other person publicly," while also important in all three relationships, is most important in your good friend relationship and only moderately important in your acquaintance relationship. Similarly, you may find that the structural rule "you should volunteer your help in time of need" is very important in all three relationships, but that "you should trust and confide in each other" is only important in your good friend relationship. What do the differences and similarities in how these rules apply to your different types of relationships reveal about your relationships as well as your relationship rules?

The differences and similarities you find among the three relationships in terms of their rules are determined, in part, by your cultural values. The twelve rules are influenced and modified by culture; therefore, others would not necessarily answer the same way. For example, the rule concerning privacy is a perfect illustration of how different cultures can respond differently to the same message. Some cultures don't even have a word or definition for the concept of "trespassing." In relationships in these societies,

To dream the person you would like your partner to be is to waste the person your partner is.

invasion of someone's personal territory is simply not a matter of consideration. People touch and get close to others with no thought of doing something that would make the other uncomfortable. Privacy is not valued. In cultures such as those of the Arabs, Greeks, and Mexicans, which have a strong group orientation, seclusion is not part of an individual's set of needs. There is a definite contrast when compared to customs found in the French, English, German, and North American cultures.[11] In the latter, privacy and personal space are valued. Think of what is being said by the proverb "A man's (or woman's) home is his (or her) castle" when compared to the Mexican proverb "Mi casa es su casa" ("My house is your house"). Also consider that many people living in the United States are from different cultures; when people from these different cultures form relationships, clashes are likely over such factors as territory, privacy, self-disclosure, and the expression of emotions.

A friendship may evolve into a love relationship. If it does, new rules arise, mostly concerned with self-disclosure and the expression of emotion. Should the love relationship culminate in marriage or a living-together commitment, the number of rules increases dramatically to virtually all forms of interaction, both with the partner and with people outside the relationship. Rules may develop about who can dance with whom at a party (relatives may be OK, but not people one dated in the past), who can have lunch with whom, and even who a person can talk with on the phone. The multitude of rules arises from an attempt to keep the interaction orderly, but the very number of rules points to the high probability of conflict and friction between spouses or relational partners.

Unique rules, as well as universal rules, govern interaction in a work relationship. Less concern is placed on intimacy, but more is placed on task-maintenance rules, such as "Both people should accept a fair share of the workload" and "Workers should cooperate."

Rules also exist for topics that should and should not be discussed.[12] For example, in both platonic and intimate relationships, talking about the current or future state of the relationship may be considered taboo because partners fear that such talk might destroy the relationship. Thus, for example, you might want to talk about making a lifelong commitment, but avoid the topic because you fear scaring away your partner.

To further complicate matters, how rules apply to particular situations may be unclear. For example, you may know, in general, rules about kissing once you are in a relationship that includes kissing, but be unaware about the rules governing the *first* kiss. When should it happen? Should it happen? How should you go about it? What should you say, if anything? How can you avoid looking like an idiot or the most desperate person in town?

You may not consciously apply the general rules, but you probably resort to them anyway because they create a structure that makes beginning interaction moderately predictable and not unpleasant. As a relationship grows, however, more rules need to be negotiated. Whether you and your partner sit down face-to-face and discuss existing rules or ones that need to be created, or whether you proceed in a less formal way, the task cannot be avoided. The more the relationship reflects your own and your partner's individual characteristics, the more specific the rules for your interaction must be.

What rules guide your relationships? Knowing what the rules are and understanding why they exist can help you make your interactions clearer. Knowledge Checkup 8.3 will help you uncover and analyze your relationship rules.

Knowledge Checkup 8.3

YOUR RELATIONSHIP RULES

Select two relationships: an important family relationship and an important non-family relationship. Answer each of the following questions.

1. What are three rules that you have for each person?
    Family member
    Non-family person

2. What are three of the other person's rules for you?
    Family member
    Non-family person

3. What are three shared rules that give the relationship excitement?
    Family member
    Non-family person

4. What are three shared rules that give the relationship stability?
    Family member
    Non-family person

5. What are three shared rules that give the relationship personal and mutual benefits?
    Family member
    Non-family person

6. Write two positive and two negative statements concerning how you feel about the rules. (Are some hard to follow? Are they negotiable?) Rewrite two rules to reflect the way you would like to change them.
    Family member
    Non-family person

7. How do you ensure that the other person follows the rules?
    Family member
    Non-family person

8. What does the other person do to make sure you follow the rules?
    Family member
    Non-family person

QUALITIES AND RESOURCES OF RELATIONSHIPS

Once you understand the goals, structure, and rules that establish the framework for a relationship, you can begin to consider the relationship's quality and the resources it provides. The advertisements you wrote at the outset of this chapter probably identify what you see as the desirable resources of each relationship, that is, what you want each relationship to provide. Do you picture the work relationship as giving you the chance to get a good grade, earn a promotion, or impress someone? Do you see the friendship as releasing you from boredom? Do you imagine that a loving relationship will supply security, respect, and intimacy? If you analyze your ads carefully, you'll find much useful information about how you personally define the desirable outcomes of your relationships.

You already have a sense of the characteristics that contribute to a relationship's quality, that is, its "goodness" or "badness." If asked, you could probably rank your relationships along a continuum from good to bad, from high quality to low. Similarly, you could probably also describe your relationships with respect to the resources or benefits they provide.

While goals, structure, and rules are "either-or" propositions (your relationship has one goal or another, one type of structure or another, and one set of rules or another), qualities and resources exist in terms of "more or less" (your relationship is more or less intimate, more or less affectionate).

Two qualities that are important for understanding any relationship are commitment and intimacy, and four important resources are affection, esteem, information, and services.

COMMITMENT

Commitment is a popular word to toss into magazine articles and sprinkle into conversations. It appears to imply a great deal about a relationship:

"She's afraid of committing herself to the relationship."

"He considers the expensive birthday present a commitment."

"If you're not committed to completing the project, why did you agree to do it in the first place?"

What is your level of commitment in a relationship with a good friend or intimate partner? Does it differ from your commitment in an important work relationship? Before we take a closer look at the notion of commitment, complete the self-analysis in Knowledge Checkup 8.4.

Knowledge Checkup 8.4

COMMITMENT PROBE[13]

Do the following exercise twice. First, think of a relationship you have with a good friend or intimate partner—whether you are dating, exclusively involved, or married—and with that relationship in mind, mark each statement (using the first column of blank spaces) according to how true it is for you. Then think of a person with whom you have an important work or school relationship and with that relationship in mind respond to the statements again (using the second column of blank spaces).

Mark **1** if the statement is definitely false.

Mark **2** if it is mostly false.

Mark **3** if it is neither true nor false.

Mark **4** if it is mostly true.

Mark **5** if it is definitely true.

_____ _____ 1. It is likely that my partner and I will be together six months from now.

_____ _____ 2. I am not attracted to other potential partners.

_____ _____ 3. A potential partner would have to be truly outstanding for me to pursue a new relationship.

_____ _____ 4. It is likely that this relationship will be permanent.

_____ _____ 5. My partner is likely to continue this relationship.

_____ _____ Total your five responses. This is your commitment score.

A relationship identified as "casual dating" has an average commitment score of 13, one identified as "exclusively involved" has an average score of 17, and a marriage relationship has an average score of 21. Where does your friendship or intimate relationship fit along this continuum?

Although the term *commitment* is often applied to relationships on a path toward intimacy (such as dating relationships), it is equally important in long-term work relationships, particularly partnerships. Scores below 16 indicate a weak or unstable work partnership, one likely to break up if an attractive offer comes along from outside the relationship. The higher the commitment score, the more stable the relationship and the higher the probability that it will continue. Where does your work or school relationship fit along this continuum?

Commitment, a pledge to the continuation of a relationship, has three aspects: your commitment, your perception of the other's commitment, and what it is you are committed to. In general, you link your commitment with the perceived commitment of the other person (consider your response to item 5 in Knowledge Checkup 8.4). If you think your partner is less committed than you, you are likely to decrease commitment; similarly, if you think the other person is more highly committed, you might increase your commitment. A relationship is unstable if the levels of commitment are unequal. For example, if you see your relationship as a long-term involvement to which you're highly

LEHMAN

FALLING IN LIKE

© 1993 Andrew Lehman. Distributed by Carmen Syndication.

committed, a problem may arise if your partner sees it as a casual pastime involving little commitment.

The phrase "commitment to a relationship" is vague, but you usually have a particular object in mind. For example, you may commit yourself to continuing the relationship even if you and your partner are separated by geographical distance, or you may commit yourself to increasing the intimacy of your relationship, or you may commit yourself to working together to increase business sales.

INTIMACY

Intimacy is an umbrella term that includes, among other things, emotional closeness and intellectual sharing.[14] Consider these questions with respect to one of your relationships:

1. How much do you know about each other?
2. To what degree are your life and the other person's life intertwined and interdependent?
3. Do you trust each other?

Each of these questions relates to one aspect of intimacy and underscores the difficulty of defining precisely what intimacy is. Essentially, **intimacy** is a quality of a relationship based on detailed knowledge and deep understanding of the other person. Trying to enumerate specific behaviors ("This relationship is an intimate one because . . .") results in a long list that contains seemingly trivial items.

Intimacy is an expectation you have for a relationship, an anticipation that you and your partner will come to know each other more and more deeply, more and more personally—that you will continue to share intimate experiences.

Intimacy and intimate experiences are not identical. Although any relationship may include an *intimate experience*—a "one-night stand" or a moment of important personal sharing, for example—it is only in intimate relationships that continued intimate experiences can be expected.

The first duty of love is to listen.
PAUL TILLICH

The intimacy of a relationship may be determined by examining three factors, each related to the three questions you answered at the beginning of this section. First, what are the breadth and depth of the information you and your partner know about each other? Breadth refers to the number of topics you discuss and depth pertains to how important and personal the information is. As breadth and depth increase, so does intimacy.

Both the breadth and depth of the information we share with our partners reflects our cultural background. In many cultures people are expected to know what someone else is thinking and feeling. Hence, in cultures such as the Japanese, expressions of intimacy are very different from those used in the United States.[15] There is often difficulty when someone from a "revealing" culture—such as North America where *self*-image, *self*-esteem, and *self*-awareness are important and the word *I* appears with great regularity—attempts to get highly personal with someone from a "nonrevealing" culture. The Chinese culture, for example, suspends thought of the self to the degree that there is no specific symbol for selfish. (Actually, the closest symbol for selfishness is two different symbols that mean "I" placed together.) Learning all you can about another person's openness, based on his or her cultural background, helps you decide how much information you should disclose and how much you should expect the other person to disclose without making your partner feel uncomfortable.

Second, in what ways are you and the other person's lives interdependent? As you and this person share and learn to depend on each other for services, support, and understanding, you become mutually dependent for the satisfaction of your needs, wants, and desires. Intimacy and interdependence, however, are not related in a simple way—as when one increases the other increases. Rather, the most intimate relationships are characterized by an interdependence that allows each person's maximum satisfaction but also has limits and flexibility so that one person doesn't feel overwhelmed or smothered by the other.

Third, how much do you trust the other person to accept you as you are, to avoid purposely hurting you, to keep your best interests and the best interests of your relationship in mind, to share with you, and to continue the relationship? Your answers determine the degree to which you allow yourself to be vulnerable to your partner. Without trust, the information you share will be mostly superficial. You might fear being exploited, so you keep yourself separate from the other person, perhaps reaching out occasionally to have an intimate experience, but avoiding the belief that intimate experiences characterize your relationship.

What is your level of intimacy in an important relationship with a family member? Does it differ from your commitment in an important non-family relationship? Knowledge Checkup 8.5 provides you with an opportunity to analyze the level of intimacy in two of your relationships.

Knowledge Checkup 8.5
INTIMACY PROBE

Do the following exercise twice. First, think of a relationship you have with a good friend or intimate partner—whether you are dating, exclusively involved, or married—and with that relationship in mind, mark each statement (using the first column of blank spaces) according to how strongly you agree or disagree with it. Then think of a person with whom you have an important work or school relationship and with that relationship in mind respond to the statements again (using the second column of blank spaces).

Mark **1** if you strongly disagree with the statement.

Mark **2** if you disagree with the statement.

Mark **3** if you neither disagree nor agree with the statement.

Mark **4** if you agree with the statement.

Mark **5** if you strongly agree with the statement.

_____ _____ 1. The other person and I have a great deal of information about each other.

_____ _____ 2. The other person and I are highly interdependent.

_____ _____ 3. The other person and I perform a great many services for each other.

_____ _____ 4. The other person and I support each other.

_____ _____ **5.** The other person and I understand each other.

_____ _____ **6.** The other person and I satisfy each other's needs and wants.

_____ _____ **7.** The other person and I accept each other as we are.

_____ _____ **8.** The other person and I avoid hurting each other.

_____ _____ Total your eight responses. This is your intimacy score.

Examine the total scores. A total score of 32 and above indicates a high degree of intimacy, while a score of 20 or below indicates a low degree of intimacy. High scores tend to indicate a relationship that is more fulfilling.

Examine each of the eight scores for each relationship. The higher a particular score, the higher is that aspect of intimacy in the relationship and, therefore, the greater the possibility that the individual item may be an integral part of the relationship.

The discussion so far of intimacy implies that men and women establish intimacy similarly. This is not the case.[16] Women and men, no matter what country they come from, represent two different cultures.[17] For example, in North American culture, women value personal talk, while men develop their intimacy by doing things together. A friend is someone you do things for, such as favors, and with, such as participate in sports or fix a car. For men, mutual liking and closeness, feelings of interdependence, and mutual appreciation are often an outgrowth of shared activities that do not depend on disclosure.

As you can imagine, differences in female and male means of establishing intimacy can be a source of problems in the formation of different-sex relationships. The "inexpressive" male shows his caring and desire for intimacy by fixing his friend's car and planning a camping trip; the "disclosive" female interprets his lack of expressiveness as avoiding closeness. This problem escalates when considering the meaning and timing of sex in a relationship. Many women think of sex as a way to *express* intimacy that is already developed, but for many men sex is a means to *create* intimacy.[18]

RESOURCES

Relationships, whether intimate or not, serve as sources for tangible benefits, such as money and gifts; intangible benefits, such as affection and emotional support; and service benefits, such as help with your gardening or getting you a book from the library. Important resources in a relationship include affection (expressing and receiving warmth, tenderness, and caring), esteem (obtaining confirmation of who you are in relation to others), services (having things done for you), and information (receiving needed information about yourself and the environment).[19]

Affection and esteem are more important resources in love and friendship relationships than they are in work relationships. By contrast, service and information resources are more important in work relationships than they are in love and friendship relationships. Although some resources may be more important than others in a particular relationship, most relationships have many resources.

What are the resources available to you in your important relationships? Do the resources tend to be the same from relationship to relationship, or do they differ? What do the resources you consider important in a relationship tell you about who you are and what kinds of relationships you desire?

A relationship's framework—its goals, structure, and rules—and its qualitative aspects—including commitment, intimacy, and resources—may be joined together within a larger context: time. Because relationships are continuously evolving, you can expect that your goals will change. A relationship's structure will change, stabilize, and change even more; some rules will be clarified, others will be abandoned, and new rules will emerge. Commitment will vary, as will what you and the other person commit yourselves to; intimacy will increase, stabilize, and continue to change. And new resources will be added, old resources may be discarded, and available resources will vary in importance.

How time affects a relationship depends on the relationship's unique characteristics. Changes are complex because alterations in one aspect of a relationship's framework, such as adding the rule "We date each other exclusively," or in one of its qualitative aspects, such as becoming more intimate, cause modifications in other dimensions of the relationship. For example, adding a rule about exclusivity will most likely cause changes in the relationship's goals (is marriage or a committed relationship a goal now?), structure (should decision making be more evenly shared now?), and what resources are important (are more services expected now?). Relationships are dynamic, continually adapting and developing, as they pass through time. A relationship is not a thing, but a process—an ever-changing process.

Communication Competency Checkup

The goal of this Communication Competency Checkup is to guide you in putting your skills and knowledge about interpersonal process to use and to help you summarize the material in this chapter.

The teacher and student are involved in a conflict. An analysis of their relationship—goals, structure, rules, commitment, intimacy, and resources—will help clarify some possible sources of their trouble.

1. What are several goals the teacher might have for this teacher-student relationship? What are several of the student's possible goals?

2. Describe the probable structure of their relationship in terms of dominance/ submission and love/hostility. Is the relationship complementary, symmetrical, or parallel?

3. List several rules that affect interaction between teachers and students. What new rules would you recommend for teacher-student relationships and what effects would they have on how teachers and students relate to each other?

4. How committed do the two people in the picture seem to their teacher-student relationship?

5. Does the relationship between teachers and students allow for the development of intimacy?

6. What common resources are available to teachers in their teacher-student relationships? What resources are available to students?

NOTES

1. Charles R. Berger, "Revisiting the Relationship Construct," *Personal Relationship Issues,* 1 (1993): 25–27.

2. A study of communication in children's friendships found that "Children talk friendships into existence. That is, they create a relationship from a happenstance by means of talk," 415. Also, changes in the friendship were signaled to the children by changes in their talk. See Julie Yingling, "Constituting Friendship in Talk and Metatalk," *Journal of Social and Personal Relationships* 11 (1994): 411–26.

3. Jesse G. Delia, "Some Tentative Thoughts Concerning the Study of Interpersonal Relationships and Their Development," *Western Journal of Speech Communication* 44 (1980): 97–103; Steve Duck, *Understanding Relationships* (New York: Guilford Press, 1991).

4. William B. Gudykunst, Stella Ting-Toomey, Sandra Sudweeks, and Lea P. Steward, *Building Bridges: Interpersonal Skills for a Changing World* (Boston: Houghton Mifflin, 1995), 358.

5. Lisa Skow and Larry A. Samovar, "Cultural Patterns of the Maasai," in Larry A. Samovar and Richard R. Porter (Eds.), *Intercultural Communication: A Reader,* 3rd ed. (Belmont, CA: Wadsworth, 1991), 93.

6. William W. Wilmot, *Dyadic Communication,* 3rd ed. (Reading, MA: Addison-Wesley, 1987).

7. L. S. Benjamin, "Structural Analysis of Social Behavior," *Psychological Review* 81 (1974): 372–425; Rolfe LaForge, "Interpersonal Check List (ICL)," in John E. Jones and J. William Pfeiffer (Eds.), 1977 *Annual Handbook for Group Facilitators* (La Jolla, CA: University Associates, 1977),

89–96; Timothy Leary, *Interpersonal Diagnosis of Personality* (New York: Ronald Press, 1957).

8. Looking at relationships in terms of complementary, symmetrical, and parallel structures was first developed by Gregory Bateson, *Naven* (Cambridge: Cambridge University Press, 1937), and then further explicated by Paul Watzlawick, Janet Beavin, and Don D. Jackson, *Pragmatics of Human Communication* (New York: Norton, 1967). For a more current description, see Wilmot, *Dyadic Communication.*

9. Mark Randall Harrington, *The Relationship between Psychological Sex-Type and Perceptions of Individuals in Complementary, Symmetrical, and Parallel Relationships,* thesis, University of North Carolina at Chapel Hill, 1984.

10. A summary of the series of investigations, including comparisons of the rules for different types of relationships in different parts of the world, is available in Michael Argyle and Monika Henderson, "The Rules of Relationships," in Steve Duck and Daniel Perlman (Eds.), *Understanding Personal Relationships* (Beverly Hills, CA: Sage, 1985), 63–84.

11. Carol Dolphin Zinner, "Beyond Hall: Variables in the Use of Personal Space," *Howard Journal of Communication* 1 (Spring 1988): 28–29.

12. A detailed analysis of taboo topics in relationships is available in Leslie A. Baxter and William Wilmot, "Taboo Topics in Close Relationships," *Journal of Social and Personal Relationships* 2 (1985): 253–69.

13. Adapted from Mary Lund, "The Development of Investment and Commitment Scales for Predicting Continuity of Personal Relationships,"

Journal of Social and Personal Relationships 2 (1985): 3–23.

14. Elaine Hatfield, "The Dangers of Intimacy," in Valerian J. Derlega (Ed.), *Communication, Intimacy, and Close Relationships* (Orlando, FL: Academic Press, 1984), 207–20.

15. Stella Ting-Toomey, "Intimacy Expressions in Three Cultures: France, Japan, and the United States," *International Journal of Intercultural Relations* 15 (1991): 31–35.

16. Julia T. Wood and C. C. Inman, "In a Different Mode: Masculine Styles of Communicating Closeness," *Journal of Applied Communication Research* 21 (1993): 279–95.

17. An extended discussion of male and female communication patterns is available in Deborah Tannen, *You Just Don't Understand: Women and Men in Conversation* (New York: William Morrow, 1990).

18. C. K. Reissman, *Divorce Talk: Women and Men Make Sense of Personal Relationships.* (New Brunswick, NJ: Rutgers University Press, 1990.)

19. Terrance L. Albrecht, Mara B. Adelman, and associates, *Communicating Social Support* (Newbury Park, CA: Sage, 1987); J. House, *Work Stress and Social Support* (Reading, MA: Addison-Wesley, 1981); Jack M. Richman, Lawrence B. Rosenfeld, and Charles J. Hardy, "The Social Support Survey: An Initial Evaluation of a Clinical Measure and Practice Model of the Social Support Process," *Research on Social Work Practice,* 3 (1993): 288–311; C. Streeter and C. Franklin, "Defining and Measuring Social Support: Guidelines for Social Work Practitioners," *Research on Social Work Practice* 2 (1992): 81–98.

CHAPTER 9

BEGINNING, MAINTAINING, AND ENDING INTERPERSONAL RELATIONSHIPS

COMMUNICATION COMPETENCIES

This chapter examines the role of communication in beginning, maintaining, and ending interpersonal relationships. Specifically, the objective of the chapter is for you to learn to:

- Describe the role of attraction in new relationships.
- Recognize several important objectives to be accomplished during the beginning phase of a relationship.
- Apply the five steps of relationship formation to a new relationship.
- Recognize the role of information sharing in the maintenance of a relationship.
- Apply two techniques—developing a supportive and confirming communication climate and self-disclosing—for maintaining and enhancing your relationships.
- Apply several methods for increasing relationship satisfaction.
- Describe the characteristics that distinguish relationship termination processes.
- Recognize the most common communication strategies for relationship termination.
- Recognize cultural variations in interpersonal relationships.

KEY WORDS

The key words in this chapter are:

approachability cues
free information
supportive behaviors
confirming behaviors
attacking behaviors
disconfirming behaviors
self-disclosure
Johari Window
affinity seeking
compliance gaining

Imagine yourself at a party. A stranger walks toward you. Imagine who this stranger is, including how she or he looks, talks, and acts. What does this stranger believe, value, like, and dislike?

Now, imagine meeting the stranger for the first time. What do you do? What do you say? Are you nervous about this first meeting or is this a person with whom you feel automatically at ease? What happens to the two of you?

You and the stranger find out that you will be working together on an important project. What do you plan to do to ensure that you have a good relationship? Do you presume that a good relationship will "just happen"?

RELATIONAL DEVELOPMENT: BEGINNING, MAINTAINING, AND ENDING RELATIONSHIPS

Establishing a new relationship—one that goes beyond an hour or two of superficial cocktail chatter—is difficult for most of us. Meeting strangers seems to bring out our deepest insecurities and our best-hidden, self-perceived flaws.

Although the romantic view of relationships is that they "just happen"—from the magical moment when two lovers swoon at first sight until the tragic end when circumstances pull them apart forever—relationships do not drop from the sky fully formed, a gift from some Relationship Fairy. Relational development—whether between lovers, friends, acquaintances, or coworkers—follows a predictable pattern. Relationships have a recognizable beginning, middle, and end, and the communication that takes place during each phase is highly complex.

Culture influences nearly every aspect of the communication process, including relational development. For example, in the Arab, Indian, Chinese, Japanese, and some African cultures, many people have their partners selected through arranged marriages—someone other than the partners, usually parents or a professional matchmaker, decides who will be matched—and in much of Mexico chaperones are very common. Beginning relationships these ways surely affects all three stages of relational development.

The discussion of relational development that follows reflects a very North American point of view and may, therefore, not accurately describe relational development for people in other cultures. For example, a man and woman who meet because their parents arranged it after negotiating marriage terms will experience a different relational development than a man and woman who meet at work and decide for themselves that they would like to get to know each other better. Please keep this limitation in mind as we learn about the stages of relational development.

BEGINNING A RELATIONSHIP

A relationship begins when you are attracted to someone and initiate interaction. The attraction may include sexual or romantic feelings, but these are not always involved. Being attracted to someone, however, does not automatically mean that you will initiate

From *Do You Hate Your Hips More Than Nuclear War?* published by Penguin Books, 1988.
Used with permission of Libby Reid.

interaction. Interaction is usually initiated when you want to learn something about the other person—background, values, interests, and personality—and when you want to create a favorable impression. Regardless of where it may end, the relationship process begins with attraction.

On any given day, you encounter many people with whom you can choose to form a relationship. Not everyone, of course, has an equal probability of being chosen: You are attracted to some people and not to others, just as some are attracted to you and some are not. Each of us carries a mental list of criteria for attraction. Knowledge Checkup 9.1 will help you identify the reasons you may be attracted to someone when your goal is a long-term intimate relationship.

Knowledge Checkup 9.1

DESIRED CHARACTERISTICS IN A LONG-TERM, INTIMATE PARTNER

Rank the following characteristics in the order of their importance to you in describing a person with whom you would form a long-term relationship. Rank the most important characteristic 1 and the least important 15.

_____ adaptability

_____ college graduate

_____ creativity

_____ desire for children

_____ exciting personality

_____ good earning capacity

_____ good health

_____ good heredity

_____ good housekeeper

_____ intelligence

_____ kindness and understanding

_____ physical attractiveness

_____ religious orientation

_____ cultural background

_____ similar interests

Attraction

Think of people to whom you are attracted and the traits they share. Do they seem to have similar physical characteristics? Do they live nearby? Do they do things for you without asking for too much in return? Do they have qualities you lack but which seem to fit well with your own? Are they similar to you? Do you have some personal motives for forming a relationship that are more important to you than who or what the other person is? Does being with them help you feel good about yourself? Do they remind you of members of your family? Your answers to these questions correspond to the seven bases of attraction: attractiveness, proximity, personal rewards, complementarity, similarity, personal motives, self-esteem enhancement, and attempting to overcome family-of-origin problems.

Attractiveness   *Attractiveness* is your impression of someone as appealing. Although it seems undemocratic to judge people by the way they look (similar to judging a book by its cover) the reality is that we do.[1] The more someone is considered physically attractive, the more she or he is seen as desirable, especially in the early stages of relational development.

You may have a personal list of desired attributes—what did your stranger at the party look like? But, no universal description exists of what people find attractive. Such a description varies from person to person and from time to time. For example, at one time plumpness was considered attractive; now the preference is thinness. Tall and slender, brown eyes, and a clear complexion might constitute attractiveness for many people, but not for all and certainly not for all time.

A paradox exists in evaluating attractiveness: Although people may agree that person A is more attractive than person B, they may disagree on *why* person A is more attractive. However, even in the absence of consensus on a definition of physical attractiveness, attractiveness matters in initial impressions.

BEAUTIFUL CHILD CONTEST, 1940
Registration Coupon

Please enter the name and photograph of my child in The News Beautiful Child Contest.

Child's name ALLAN HARVEY ROBBIN

Date of birth SEPT. 21, 1939   Boy or girl   BOY

Height   27 IN.   Weight 18½ LBS.

Color of hair BROWN   Color of eyes BROWN

Mother's maiden name   MILDRED SIMON

Father's name   MURRAY ROBBIN

Father's occupation   PHOTOGRAPHER

Home address 7292 KRIEG AVE.

City BRONX   State N.Y.

Signed   Mrs. Mildred Robbin

(signature of parent of guardian)

Sender's name   Mrs. M. Robbin

Sender's address 7292 KRIEG AVE. BRONX, N.Y.

Fasten this coupon to the photograph submitted. This coupon is printed for your convenience. You may write the information requested here or on any piece of paper. Send your photographs to Beautiful Child Contest, The News, 220 E. 42d St., New York, N. Y. Unless otherwise indicated, we will use the full name of the child in the event his or her photograph is published.

The role of culture in both evaluating attractiveness and in forming initial impressions is interesting. Our judgment of beauty, like most aspects of culture, is developed so early in life that we hardly recognize its hidden grip (infants as young as three and six months prefer pictures of faces rated attractive by adult judges[2]). Yet there are countless studies that tell us that beauty is as much in the eye of the culture as it is in that of the beholder. For example, though certain African tribes stretch their lips to make themselves attractive, extremely big lips are not a North American measurement of attractiveness. And on several occasions African Americans have protested U.S. beauty pageants because they felt blacks were being judged by white beauty standards.

However, beauty is not culture specific: Many of the attributes of attractiveness are shared around the world. Raters from a variety of cultural backgrounds shown pictures of people representing diverse cultural groups show strong agreement regarding who is attractive. Although you may not find someone from another culture particularly attractive given your own standards for beauty, you will agree with others that this person is, as a representative of that culture, most attractive.

A single dominant guideline for determining physical attractiveness seems to cut across cultures. Recent evidence points to the fact that "attractive," within any culture, means "average."[3] The attractive person has neither a big nose nor a small nose, neither very large eyes nor small eyes, is neither very tall nor very short, and so on. With this as the guiding principle, two modifications to the "average is beautiful" hypothesis have been researched. First, although the average face may be perceived as attractive, the most attractive face, both female and male, has larger eyes relative to face size, and shorter distances from mouth to chin and from nose to mouth.[4] Also, women with a low waist-to-hips ratio—that is, a small waist relative to large hips—are perceived as more attractive than women with less of an "hourglass figure."[5] The roots of these guidelines for attractiveness may be biological: The "average" woman represents her sex best, and, therefore, may be the best person with whom to have children, and a woman with a low waist-to-hip ratio tends to get pregnant more easily.[6]

How high did you rank physical attractiveness in Knowledge Checkup 9.1? A recent survey reveals that men rank the item third and women rank it sixth, which indicates that both groups give high importance to physical beauty.[7]

Often included as an aspect of attractiveness is demeanor, how the other person behaves during an encounter. Someone who follows the rules for interacting, who, for example, maintains eye contact and doesn't criticize, is more likely to be found attractive than someone who is less socially adept. Although in this instance, "attractive" may imply "comfortable" and "predictable," the perception is that the nice person is, indeed, more physically attractive. For example, a man who solicits his woman partner's opinion, shows sensitivity to her perspective, and is agreeable is perceived as more physically and sexually attractive than if he does not do these things. Similarly, men rate women who are agreeable as more attractive and desirable as a date than those who are not agreeable.[8] However, what characteristics of demeanor found to be attractive shift from culture to culture. For example, in many Asian cultures men would find women who are acquiescent, docile, and quiet far more attractive than women who are spirited, vivacious, and lively.[9]

In general, attractive people are assumed to be warmer, more sensitive, kinder, more modest, more sociable, and better husbands or wives than their unattractive peers.[10] The beauty prejudice even finds its way into schools. Physically attractive students are judged more favorably by teachers in several areas, including intelligence, academic potential, grades, friendliness, popularity, and outgoingness. They also are recommended more often for placement if seen as in need of special help, such as that provided by learning disability services. And the positive characteristics attributed to the attractive children affect perceptions of their parents; they are perceived as caring more about education.[11]

Do not be misled: Physical attractiveness has its burdens. In some instances, because of good looks, a person may be considered conceited or aloof. A phenomenon known as the "prom queen syndrome" indicates that because others fear they will be rejected if they approach an attractive person for a date, the good-looking person is not asked out.

Proximity Marrying the person next door doesn't happen just in old-fashioned Hollywood musicals, such as *Meet Me in St. Louis* with its love song, "The Boy Next Door." To be attracted to someone takes some interaction, and you are most likely to interact with people whom you encounter frequently. Whether meeting at the mailbox when you both fetch the mail or sitting next to each other in a class, the effect is the same: You get the opportunity to communicate. *Proximity,* how near you are to someone, is an important determinant of attraction.

Familiarity, although it may breed contempt, more often breeds liking. As the other person becomes more predictable, interaction likely increases. Increased interaction, in turn, leads to other bases of attraction. You may go on to discover interests, physical attributes, and personality traits that enhance attraction.

A lack of familiarity is one reason people often fail to develop relationships with others from different cultures. There is a low level of predictability when you are not familiar with the other person. How often are you attracted to someone you don't understand? You would indeed feel uncomfortable if your culture stressed action and activity and you found yourself in the company of someone who believed in a tranquil and calm approach to life. This difference in the pace at which people conduct personal and private matters is often a major barrier to interpersonal understanding.

Personal Rewards   According to an *economic model* of relationships, we are attracted to people with whom a relationship *costs* little yet provides many *rewards*. This calculation may seem self-serving, but it makes sense. Relationships have goals, and achieving goals entails costs. Costs may take many forms. You may have to do something for the other person in return for what he or she does for you; you may be expected to behave in a way that does not fit your self-image; or you may need to expend money, time, or emotional energy. Nevertheless, there is a reward: achieving your relationship's goal. The question is whether the rewards are sufficient to offset the costs.

The reward-cost balance is not assessed simply. The time and effort you invest in a relationship are not tangibly calculable, nor are the rewards you receive. Moreover, you may not even expect your rewards to correspond directly to your investment; depending on the relationship, you may be satisfied with less, or you may want more. Comparing costs and rewards of relationships is a psychological process, not an accounting procedure that leads to balanced books.[12]

If you think your rewards adequately offset your costs, you will usually perceive a relationship as attractive. If you think your rewards are inadequate, you will probably find the relationship too costly and consider it unattractive. Ultimately, however, you can determine the attractiveness of a relationship only after you assess the other relationships open to you. Can you form another relationship? Is the other, new, relationship likely to provide more rewards than the current one?

If you are in a relationship that seems, on the whole, unsatisfactory, ask yourself what benefits make the relationship attractive. If you stay in an unsatisfactory relationship, chances are that some reward makes the costs bearable. The reward may be hard to recognize at first, but it's there. Perhaps the reward is not being alone, or not having to change, or having someone to turn to in times of stress, or not having to seek out and develop another relationship.

Complementarity   *Complementarity* is the attraction of opposites. Although a common saying is that "opposites attract," complementarity in fact is rather limited—not simply to particular people, but to particular people in particular situations. For example, a dominant older sister may enjoy her younger brother's submissive behavior, but she may be annoyed by such behavior in her friends.

Complementarity is at work when you find it enjoyable to talk to someone whose job is completely different from yours or who doesn't agree with you on certain issues.

Taking pleasure in diversity can bring numerous rewards, one of which is discovering that the differences that have kept you away from people might be the very thing that could attract you to them. From learning about new foods to different ways of envisioning God, each culture has something to offer those of us who are willing to be open to new experiences.

But the excitement of exploring differences, although important in some relationships, interestingly enough is not as strong a source of attraction as its opposite, similarity. In general, attitude dissimilarity, especially when discovered during an initial encounter, may immediately spell doom for any possibility of a close relationship.[13]

Similarity   *Similarity* occurs when people have characteristics in common, whether these are age, looks, attitudes, opinions, values, beliefs, experiences, or ideas. This principle of attraction gets support from published research: Birds of a feather *do* flock together. You are most attracted to those you perceive as similar to yourself. For example, husbands and wives tend to be of similar age (especially in first marriages), education, race, religion, and ethnic background. Partners also tend to hold similar attitudes, opinions, and socioeconomic status. How important similarity is to a relationship depends on several things, including knowing such things as your own attitudes or opinions, knowing the other person's attitudes or opinions, determining how important similarity is for the particular relationship, and determining how important dissimilarity is.[14]

Now more than ever before the notion of similarity takes on new meaning as we approach people who often come from backgrounds that are quite different from our own. What is important to remember is that while cultures might be different in many areas, we still can find similarities among all cultures. A search for similarities will assist you in your efforts to become a competent communicator in interpersonal settings.

Review your ranking of the fifteen items in Knowledge Checkup 9.1 and study them in light of the similarity thesis. You may be surprised to find that you described someone whose characteristics are similar to your own and that you gave the highest rankings to those characteristics you find most important or attractive in yourself. If your ranking didn't follow this pattern, you may not consider similarity very important in judging attractiveness—at least with respect to the fifteen ranked items. Knowledge Checkup 9.2 provides the opportunity for you to compare your ranking with that of the general population.

Knowledge Checkup 9.2

COMPARING YOUR PREFERENCES WITH THE GENERAL POPULATION[15]

Listed are how the top thirteen characteristics in Knowledge Checkup 9.1 were ranked by the general population. The highest preference in a mate is ranked 1 and the lowest is ranked 13. For example, both males and females ranked "kindness and understanding" as the most important quality in a mate. List your rankings in the column headed "You."

Males	Females	You	
1	1	_____	kindness and understanding
2	2	_____	intelligence
3	6	_____	physical attractiveness
4	3	_____	exciting personality
5	4	_____	good health
6	5	_____	adaptability
7	7	_____	creativity
8	10	_____	desire for children
9	9	_____	college graduate
10	11	_____	good heredity
11	8	_____	good earning capacity
12	12	_____	good housekeeper
13	13	_____	religious orientation

Compare your rankings with those of the general population.

1. Are there any significant differences?
2. How might any differences affect your finding a mate?
3. How important is it to know what the other person finds attractive?
4. Are you willing to present a false image or lie to find a mate?

Personal Motives   Other people may attract you because of a variety of personal motives, motives that go beyond how the other person looks, how close she or he is, or perceived similarities and dissimilarities. Sometimes, the who, what, and where of the other person are less important than your personal motives for making initial contact.

There are at least six different personal motives for wanting to initiate conversation with another person.[16] First, you may talk to someone because of the *pleasure* often inherent in such contact—it may be fun, exciting, and stimulating for you. Second, you may initiate contact to *express concern*—to help someone, say thank you, or show encouragement. Third, you may feel the need to talk to someone to *reduce your loneliness,* reduce the burden of some problem, or simply to get reassurance that someone is there to listen to you. Fourth, it is common to use others as a *distraction,* to put off doing your work or to take a break from a difficult or boring task. Fifth, talking with someone may help you *relax,* feel less tense. And, sixth, you may initiate a conversation to *entice* someone to do something for you, whether to hold the door while you manage packages or direct you to the nearest restaurant.

Self-Esteem Enhancement   How important is it to you that the potential partner enhances your self-esteem? Have you ever thought what it would do to your self-esteem to be seen with this other person?[17] If you have ever felt pride being seen with someone, or if you ever felt embarrassed when someone you were with did something foolish and other people saw you together, you experienced what this source of attraction is all about. You may feel that being seen with the school's smartest person, or strongest person, or most handsome or beautiful person, reflects positively on you. This increases your self-esteem, and attraction for this person is high. On the other hand, if you feel that being seen with someone who acts foolishly or inappropriately or is known to be a "bad" person reflects negatively on you, you may experience a decrease in self-esteem. Attraction for this person is low.

Attempting to Overcome Family-of-Origin Problems   If you think about it, the six bases for attraction discussed so far would make it reasonable for you to be attracted to a very, very large number of people. After all, there are many people you may find attractive, live close to, have the potential to have a good cost-reward balance with, who may enhance your self-esteem, and so on. Why is it, then, that most people seem to have a very small number of people—maybe as few as two, three, or four—to whom they are truly attracted, as in "I could spend the rest of my life with this person"? The answer may be rooted in your early experiences with your family.

First, you are most familiar with the people with whom you grew up—perhaps your mother, father, brothers, and sisters—so you seek people who reflect their characteristics. These are the characteristics you know and with which you are most comfortable. Have you found that your boyfriend or girlfriend "fits in" very easily with your family? It's because he or she is like a member or members of your family!

Second, if there is some particular problem you had in your family, you may seek a person with whom to "solve" the problem. For example, if you feel you did not get enough love from your father (and this will probably be on a less-than-conscious level), you may seek out a person who has the characteristics of your father (the sex of the person is not relevant, only the characteristics), form a relationship with this person, and hope to get the love you feel you missed. Unfortunately, if the person to whom you are attracted does, indeed, have the characteristics of your father, the odds of getting what you want are no higher than they were when you lived at home. But this does not stop you—on a psychological level, at least—from trying.[18]

Which basis or bases of attraction best explain why you are attracted to certain people? Knowledge Checkup 9.3 provides you with the opportunity to explore this question.

Knowledge Checkup 9.3
YOUR BASES OF ATTRACTION

What are the bases of attraction in three of your current relationships? With three current friend or good friend relationships in mind, answer the following questions.

1. Do you find the other person physically attractive? If you do, why? Do you consider the other person attractive because of her or his demeanor? If you do, why?
   Person 1:
   Person 2:
   Person 3:

2. Before you became friends or good friends, was the other person someone with whom you were in contact often because of your close proximity? Explain the typical circumstance of your interaction.
   Person 1:
   Person 2:
   Person 3:

3. What are the costs and rewards associated with each relationship? What is the balance between the costs for staying in the relationship and the rewards you get from it? Do rewards exceed costs? Do costs exceed rewards? Or are the two about equal?
   Person 1:
   Person 2:
   Person 3:

4. In what ways are you and the other person different? Do you find these differences a source of attraction?
   Person 1:
   Person 2:
   Person 3:

5.   In what ways are you and the other person alike? Do you find these similarities a source of attraction?
Person 1:
Person 2:
Person 3:

6.   Do you have any personal motives for being with this person, such as to reduce your loneliness or distract you?
Person 1:
Person 2:
Person 3:

7.   Does being with this person enhance your self-esteem?
Person 1:
Person 2:
Person 3:

8.   In what ways is this person like a member or members of your family? Do you think there may be some problem with your family or a member of your family you are trying to resolve with this friend?
Person 1:
Person 2:
Person 3:

As you look over your answers to the eight questions for each friend or good friend, consider if one or a small number of the eight bases for attraction are more important than the others for predicting your attraction. What do your bases for attraction reveal to you about the relationships you have? What it is you may be seeking in your friend or good friend relationships?

Objectives

Once you identify someone with whom you hope to form a relationship, you may pursue two goals: (1) to initiate contact and gather enough information to decide whether to continue the relationship, and (2) to leave the other person with a favorable impression of yourself.

Initiating Contact and Gathering Information   Beginning a relationship is often anxiety-provoking. Regardless of your background and education, the odds are you received little or no training in forming relationships. Here are several steps you can take to improve your skills in this area.[19]

Step One: Look for Approachability Cues.   The first step in meeting new people is to look for **approachability cues,** indications that the other person is available for conversation. A person may be approachable when she or he smiles at you; is alone, relaxed, not busy,

in a place where talking with strangers is okay (such as the student union), or talking with some of your friends; maintains eye contact with you for a moment beyond what is usual (which is less than three seconds); has an open body position (arms and legs not crossed); displays a good mood (pleasant facial expression); says or waves hello; or (if you're looking for a prospective mate) has "an empty ring finger."

The approachability cues presented have a strong North American bias. There are, of course, cultural differences in the use of such factors as eye contact, facial expression, gestures, use of space, and vocal variety (e.g., volume and pitch variations). You might, therefore, find yourself using any of the approachability cues with someone who has a different meaning for the message you selected. People from Asian cultures, for example, don't smile frequently or have much eye contact with strangers. A person from one of those societies would, indeed, be put off by your impertinent and brash behavior if you smiled a great deal while talking to him or her, or if you used extensive eye contact.

Step Two: Initiate a Conversation. Once you decide to approach someone, the second step is to initiate a conversation. The "opening line" when initiating contact poses a special problem for most people. "What should I say first?" is a good question. One technique is to tell the person your reason for approaching. You may ask for information ("I'm new on campus. Can you tell me where the Student Union Building is located?"; "Do you have the time?"; "What's your major?"; "Seen any good movies lately?"); introduce yourself ("I'm Bill. I wanted to meet you since we'll be sitting next to each other in this class."); talk about something you have in common ("Did you understand one word of the professor's lecture?"; "Do you come here often?"); or offer a sincere compliment ("That's a great picture of Bach on your shirt!").

> The miracle is this—the more we share, the more we have.
> LEONARD NIMOY

When initiating a conversation with someone from a different culture, you should keep in mind that members of many cultures feel uncomfortable talking to strangers. A person from such a society, therefore, might not respond as favorably as a North American to your attempts at contact. While you may have the best of intentions, he or she may perceive your actions as aggressive and a sign of poor manners.

Step Three: Find Topics to Talk About. The third step, finding topics to talk about, quickly follows initiating the conversation. Perceived similarities often provide topics of conversation. For example, you may attend the same school or classes, enjoy the same types of food, sports, or movies, or come from the same town. Although perceived differences also may suggest topics of conversation, such talk tends to separate you from the other person rather than bring you closer together.

Recognize that not all cultures are interested in the same topics. What seems like normal conversation in your culture might not be of the least interest in another. In the Buddhist tradition, for example, people refrain from all gossip. In North America and England, gossip is a favorite pastime. If you were to employ this conversational technique with a Buddhist, he or she would most likely only respond out of politeness, not interest. Many Asians, after visiting the United States, often express a lack of understanding as to why Americans spend so much time talking about other people and have entire newspapers dedicated to the topic.

Step Four: Talk about a Variety of Topics. The fourth step builds on the third. To gather enough information to decide whether to pursue a relationship, you need information on a variety of topics. Even very limited relationships, such as many between employers and employees, require a range of background knowledge.

You can make transitions to new topics by noting what the other person says and using the information to guide you. Rarely are casual conversations so structured that everything communicated is immediately pertinent. More often, extra or **free information**—elaborations—are provided as well. Use this free information to find new topics of conversation. For example, if you ask someone whether he likes Mexican food and he responds, "Yes. I also like Italian food, French food, and hamburgers and fries. In fact, I like just about every kind of food," you have more information than you requested. You can then use this free information to extend the conversation to talk about food in general, diets, and even travel to foreign places.

Skill Development 9.1 will help you practice probing for information by considering how someone might probe you for information to form a relationship and, then, how you might probe someone else.

Skill Development 9.1

PROBING FOR INFORMATION

1. Write a question someone could ask you about something you know. (Example: "What do you like to do on vacations?")

2. List two follow-up questions the other person could ask you based on your answer. (Example: If you like to travel, follow-up questions could be, "Where have you been lately?" and "What's the nicest place you've ever visited?")

3. What two questions could you ask someone who tells you, "I'm planning on going into sales when I finish my education."

You can increase the probability of getting free information by asking questions that require detailed answers instead of ones that can be answered yes or no. A question-probe series, such as the one you developed for Skill Development 9.1, encourages the other person to offer additional pieces of information.

Other techniques for obtaining free information include giving compliments—direct ones, such as "That's a nice dog," or indirect ones, such as "How would you finish this report for the manager?" (which implies the other has knowledge you don't)—and telling something about yourself (which implies you trust the other person and which encourages the other person to speak about herself or himself).

Step Five: Share Plans for Future Interaction. The fifth step, sharing your plans for future interaction, completes the first phase of relationship development. If at the end of your first conversation you have enough information to conclude that another meeting is a good idea, communicate this to your partner. You may be indirect ("Are you planning to see the movie the professor recommended this weekend?") or direct ("I'd like you to come with me Saturday night to see the movie the professor recommended"). Being direct is more threatening than being indirect—for both of you; but, it is also more honest and likely to yield the information you need. Indirect statements or questions may be safer, but they are also less useful. Direct communications reveal what people are thinking, feeling, and wanting.

Creating a Favorable Impression Creating a favorable impression enhances the other person's attraction for you. Therefore, you should convey certain characteristics if you want to continue to interact: *cooperativeness, caring,* and *memorableness.* To be perceived as cooperative, you should follow conversational rules and behave according to the norms of the person with whom you're interacting. When you follow the rules, you make it easier for the other person to predict your behavior. Seeming cooperative will further reduce the tension that often accompanies initial interactions.

To be perceived as caring, you should solicit information about the other person and listen attentively. Such attention tells the other person, "I care about what you have to say. You're important to me."

As with many interpersonal situations, an awareness of cultural differences is important to keep in mind when attempting to be friendly. Many people from English, German, Asian, and Scandinavian cultures feel uncomfortable when others become too friendly and ask what they perceive to be personal questions. People from these cultures tend to be rather private and believe that only close friends should know about personal matters.

To be perceived as memorable, you should communicate your most dynamic and interesting self-image. You may communicate information that shows you have an uncommon family (for example, you are one of ten children), that you are adventurous (you participate in a dangerous sport), that you are creative (you write screenplays), that you are industrious (you hold down several jobs), or that you have had unique experiences (you had an accident ten minutes after getting your driving license—by running into a police car).

You need to remember that many cultures do not value individualism as much as they do collectivism. Being memorable to people from a Chinese culture, for example, is not based on what you have done as an individual, but what you have done as a group member.[20] In their thinking, helping your family or your company is far more important than helping yourself.

How can you communicate that you are cooperative, caring, and memorable? Skill Development 9.2 will help you practice creating a favorable impression.

Skill Development 9.2

CREATING A FAVORABLE IMPRESSION

To ensure that your relationship partner perceives you as cooperative, caring, and memorable, prepare several alternative means for communicating each impression.

Cooperative

List two conversational rules you can follow to communicate that you are cooperative. For example, you can provide the other person with opportunities to speak and you can maintain sustained eye contact with her or him.

1.

2.

Caring

List two ways you can communicate "I care" to the other person. For example, you can lean forward while listening and ask meaningful questions.

1.

2.

Memorable

List two facts about yourself that are memorable. For example, maybe you have a twin sister or brother, or perhaps you are finally able to return to school and finish the degree you started several years ago.

1.

2.

MAINTAINING A RELATIONSHIP

When you think you have enough information to decide whether to continue a relationship, the initial phase of relationship development is complete. Deciding to pursue a relationship requires that you examine your goals and quickly assess the probability of attaining them. Will this person be helpful on the term project? Will this person be a good friend? Will this person be the type of spouse you seek? Whatever your needs, if the response is a tentative yes, you move into the second phase of relationship development: maintaining the relationship.

Objectives

Objectives during the maintenance phase of relationship development include developing a framework for the relationship—goals, structure, and rules—and maximizing certain relational qualities—commitment, intimacy, and resources. Tentative explorations of who the other person is give way to a more intense examination. Among the decisions that need to be made are:

What are your personal goals?

What are your goals for the relationship?

What is the best balance between dominance and submission and between love and hostility?

What rules are important, and what new rules should be developed to meet the unique demands of your particular relationship?

How committed should you be?

How important is intimacy?

What resources are crucial to goal attainment and relational satisfaction?

How might the answers to all these questions change as the relationship develops?

You can't tackle all these questions in a totally rational way. You can't successfully make lists, check alternatives, assign weights to items, and develop equations. If people behaved this rationally, relationships wouldn't be so interesting or exciting. Rather, you should try to answer these questions spontaneously and unself-consciously. Attention to these issues prior to commitment could lead to more effective, long-lasting relationships.

Achieving Your Objectives

If you aim to answer many or all of the previous questions, you need information, and you will continue to need information throughout the life of your relationship. Information is the basis for relational decision making. Setting the stage for information sharing—making it appropriate to share, as well as encouraging sharing—requires that you use your communication skills to create a confirming, supportive communication climate. It also requires that you self-disclose (let the other person know who you are), use affinity-seeking strategies (strategies to get the other person to like you), and compliance-gaining tactics (tactics to get the other person to do what you want).

Supportiveness and Confirmation   Your willingness and desire to communicate openly and freely—as well as the degree to which you feel relaxed, comfortable, and cooperative—depend on the extent to which you feel valued.[21] **Supportive** and **confirming behaviors** communicate this message by indicating that you are acknowledged, understood, and accepted. **Attacking** and **disconfirming behaviors** communicate the opposite message and curtail effective communication. In an attacking and disconfirming environment, the aim is to protect yourself, not to share information.

Supportive language has several identifiable characteristics:[22]

1. Because it depends on "I" language, supportive language is descriptive and not evaluative. The emphasis switches from judging the other's behavior (attacking)—"You're too quiet"—to describing what you experience (supportive)—"When you don't talk I think you're angry."[23]

2. Because it focuses on immediate thoughts and feelings, supportive language is spontaneous and not manipulative. The emphasis switches from following a calculated plan (attacking)—"I think it would be best if we considered ending our relationship"—to communicating honestly in the here-and-now (supportive)—"I no longer want to be in a committed relationship."

3. Because it focuses on accepting the other person's feelings and putting yourself in the other person's place, supportive language is empathic and not indifferent. The emphasis switches from treating the other person in a neutral and detached way (attacking)—"I don't want to take sides in your fight with your partner"—to communicating your understanding and caring for how the other person feels (supportive)—"I can feel how angry you are with your partner."

4. Because it focuses on remaining open to new ideas, perspectives, and the possibility of change, supportive language is provisional and not certain. The emphasis switches from dogmatic declarations (attacking)—"We'll handle the problem this way"—to tentative conclusions (supportive)—"Let's try the idea

and see if it works." People who communicate their certainty also communicate their superiority, their being right or better.

Just as supportive behavior is best understood by contrasting it with its opposite, attacking behavior, confirming behavior is best understood by contrasting it with its opposite, disconfirming behavior—the "what not to do."[24] How do you feel in each of these situations?

Someone fails to acknowledge what you say either verbally or nonverbally.

Someone interrupts you in order to change the topic.

Someone responds to your comment with an irrelevant or tangential remark.

When you ask a simple question or make a simple statement, someone responds with an impersonal monologue, such as, "Why, when I was your age, I . . . ."

Someone's comments are so ambiguous that you can't determine their true meaning.

Someone's verbal and nonverbal behaviors contradict each other, such as when someone says, "I love you," with a giggle or a yawn.

Communicating that you value the other person entails more than simply avoiding these disconfirming behaviors, although that's an excellent start. You must also acknowledge the other person by communicating that you are physically and mentally available for the interaction. You can do so both nonverbally and verbally.

Nonverbal behaviors that communicate interest and attention include standing no more than a few feet from the other person, maintaining eye contact, making appropriate facial gestures, leaning toward and directly facing the other person, maintaining an open posture, and touching the other person. If you were actually to go out and employ these behaviors, you would probably find the other person speaking more, appearing more animated, and reciprocating your interest and attention.[25]

It is universal for people to want to believe that they are of value and possess some worth, yet the manner in which these feelings are communicated is determined by their culture. Hence, you need to be aware that the advice offered here is based primarily on North American norms. You must realize that prolonged eye contact, touching, being animated, and direct facing are often the messages that make members of some other cultures feel uneasy. If at all possible, know your partner and his or her cultural biases before you decide what is the best way to present yourself.

Verbal behaviors that acknowledge the other person communicate your understanding of what the other is both saying and feeling. Two useful techniques are paraphrasing—putting the other person's thoughts and feelings in your own words—and asking questions. For example:

Statement: "I think it's time to change the work schedule, to make some improvements. I'm not sure about who should take vacation time first, but I'm leaning toward my going in early June and your going in late June."

Paraphrase: "You think the old schedule had some problems, right? You sound unsure about what specific changes might help things."

Question: "What are the advantages of changing the schedule?" or "What is the problem you're trying to solve?"

Reflecting thoughts and feelings demonstrates that you're listening and opens the way to continued communication. If your paraphrase is incorrect or your question misses the other person's point, further communication can clarify what was said. If your paraphrase or question is on target, the other person is encouraged to continue talking. Paraphrasing and asking questions compliment the other person, conveying "You are important to me, so I'm listening to what you say and taking note of how you feel."

Skill Development 9.3 will help you practice communicating in a supportive and confirming way. Five situations are presented. In the first four, an attacking response is given, and you are asked to provide a supportive one. In the fifth situation, you are asked to provide a friend with a confirming response that reflects both the content and feelings of the friend's message.

Skill Development 9.3

GIVING SUPPORTIVE AND CONFIRMING RESPONSES

The first four items present a nonsupportive, defense-arousing reaction. Give an appropriate supportive response that could substitute for the defensive one.

1. Situation: You walk into your dorm room and see your roommate's clothes strewn all over.
   Evaluative: "You're a slob! Your clothes are all over the room!"
   Descriptive:

2. Situation: In the past your roommate has had to type well into the night to get assignments completed for the following day. This means the light stays on and you have trouble sleeping.
   Manipulative: "Don't you agree that it's a good idea to do your work assignments as soon after receiving them as possible?"
   Spontaneous:

3. Situation: Your friend tells you about a quarrel with a friend you have in common.
   Indifferent: "There are always two sides to any argument."
   Empathic:

4. Situation: Your friend tells you that the library doesn't seem to have sources needed to write an assigned paper.
   Certain: "You can fix that problem by learning how to use the on-line bibliographic references!"
   Provisional:

5. Situation: A friend of yours tells you, "I'm having a really hard time balancing classes and my work at the department store. I hope I don't mess up both!"
Disconfirming: "You think you have problems? I can't get a date for the party on Saturday!"
Confirming response (reflect both the content and feeling):

Self-Disclosure   **Self-disclosure**—intentionally letting the other person know who you are by honestly communicating self-revealing information—does much to develop and maintain a relationship.[26] It creates a pool of shared knowledge and, therefore, makes it possible to develop joint views, joint goals, and joint decisions. It also helps the partners in a relationship to help each other, keep up with each others' lives, and learn what the other person is thinking, doing, and feeling.[27]

Self-disclosure varies according to the type of relationship. In intimate relationships, there tends to be much self-disclosure that shows a great deal of breadth and depth—relational partners reveal a great many personal thoughts and feelings on a large number of topics. In contrast, in nonintimate relationships, self-disclosure often has little breadth and depth and accounts for only a small percentage of total communication—relational partners reveal little, speaking superficially on a few topics. Many relationships are characterized by self-disclosure that has little breadth yet great depth. Business partners, for example, may discuss their thoughts and feelings about their work setting in great and personal detail, but avoid discussions of non-work-related matters altogether.

No matter what its depth, breadth, and amount, self-disclosure fulfills several individual and relationship functions.[28] It can be used for:

> The art of pleasing consists in being pleased.
> WILLIAM HAZLITT

1. *catharsis,* to help you "get something off your chest";
2. *self-clarification,* to help you learn about your own ideas by talking them out with another person;
3. *reciprocity,* to encourage the other person to respond to your disclosures with disclosures of her or his own;
4. *relational maintenance,* to inform the other person of changes in your life;
5. *relationship enhancement,* to open up new areas for discussion and increase the depth of messages;
6. *impression formation,* to create a particular impression by disclosing selected information about yourself; and
7. *manipulation,* to get the other person to do what you want.

Disclosure used for manipulation seems to deny the basic notion of honesty, but there are times when you can be both honest and manipulative. For example, you might tell another person "I love you" because you honestly feel that way and also because you know you can then ask for particular favors.

How much are you willing to disclose to an acquaintance? How much are you willing to disclose to a good friend? How willing are you to receive feedback on your disclosures from these communication partners?

Disclosure involves both a willingness to talk and a willingness to listen to feedback. Knowledge Checkup 9.4 will help you assess the extent to which you are willing to disclose and to receive feedback about your disclosure. Select one person you consider an acquaintance and another you consider a good friend, and keep these people in mind as you respond to the knowledge checkup.

Knowledge Checkup 9.4

DISCLOSURE AND FEEDBACK IN TWO RELATIONSHIPS

This self-assessment is divided into two parts: willingness to disclose and willingness to listen to feedback. Before each item in the first part, place a number from 1 to 6 to indicate how much you are willing to reveal. A 1 indicates that you are willing to self-disclose nothing or almost nothing, and a 6 indicates that you are willing to reveal everything or almost everything. Use the values 2, 3, 4, and 5 to represent the points between these extremes.

1	2	3	4	5	6
I am willing to disclose nothing or almost nothing.					I am willing to disclose everything or almost everything.

For both Parts 1 and 2, use the first column to respond to the items with an acquaintance in mind (select one acquaintance and keep her or him in mind throughout the knowledge checkup), and the second column to respond to the items with a good friend in mind (select one good friend and keep her or him in mind throughout the knowledge checkup).

Part 1: Extent to which I am willing to self-disclose my

_____ _____ 1. goals

_____ _____ 2. strengths

_____ _____ 3. weaknesses

_____ _____ 4. positive feelings

_____ _____ 5. negative feelings

_____ _____ 6. values

_____ _____ 7. ideas

_____ _____ 8. beliefs

_____ _____ 9. fears and insecurities

_____ _____ 10. mistakes

_____ _____ Totals

Before each item in the second part, place a number from 1 to 6 to indicate how willing you are to receive feedback about your self-disclosure. A 1 indicates that you refuse or resist feedback, and a 6 indicates that you consistently encourage feedback. Use the values 2, 3, 4, and 5 to represent the points between these extremes.

1	2	3	4	5	6
I refuse or resist feedback.					I encourage feedback.

Part 2: Extent to which I am willing to receive feedback about my

_____ _____ **1.** goals

_____ _____ **2.** strengths

_____ _____ **3.** weaknesses

_____ _____ **4.** positive feelings

_____ _____ **5.** negative feelings

_____ _____ **6.** values

_____ _____ **7.** ideas

_____ _____ **8.** beliefs

_____ _____ **9.** fears and insecurities

_____ _____ **10.** mistakes

_____ _____ Totals

In general, total scores of 40 and above are considered high, while those below 40 are considered low. If you scored high on the first part and low on the second, you are probably more willing to disclose than you are to listen to feedback. If you scored low on the first part and high on the second, you are probably more willing to listen to what others have to say than you are to disclose things about yourself. If you scored low on both, you probably avoid self-disclosing and receiving feedback. And if you scored high on both, you are probably willing to disclose and receive feedback—a perfect candidate for a high-information-sharing relationship.

You can use your scores to create a **Johari Window,** a model that illustrates how your willingness to self-disclose and receive feedback operates in a relationship.[29] Imagine a box that contains everything there is to know about you, including your goals, strengths, weaknesses, positive and negative feelings, and so on (Figure 9.1).

The box may be divided into two parts: things you know about yourself and things you do not know about yourself (Figure 9.2).

The box also could be divided into two other parts: things others know about you and things others do not know about you (Figure 9.3).

FIGURE 9.1   Everything There Is to Know about You

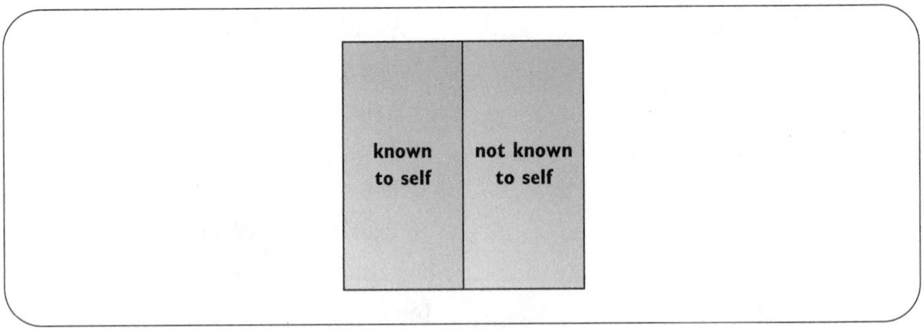

FIGURE 9.2   Everything about Yourself Known and Unknown to You

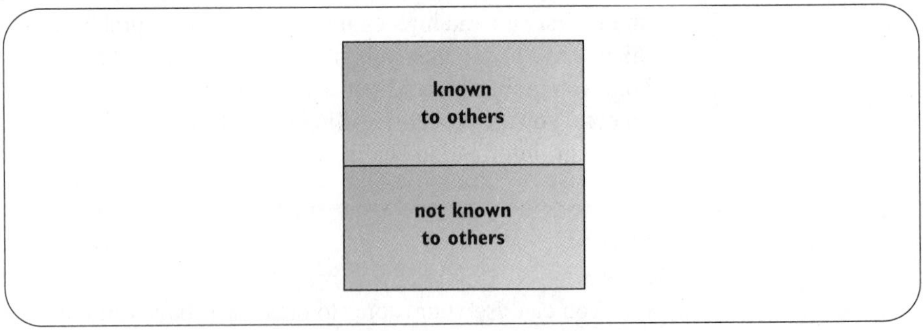

FIGURE 9.3   Everything about Yourself Known and Unknown to Others

If you superimpose the two divided boxes on top of each other, the result is a Johari Window that contains everything there is to know about you, both known and unknown to yourself, and known and unknown to others (Figure 9.4).

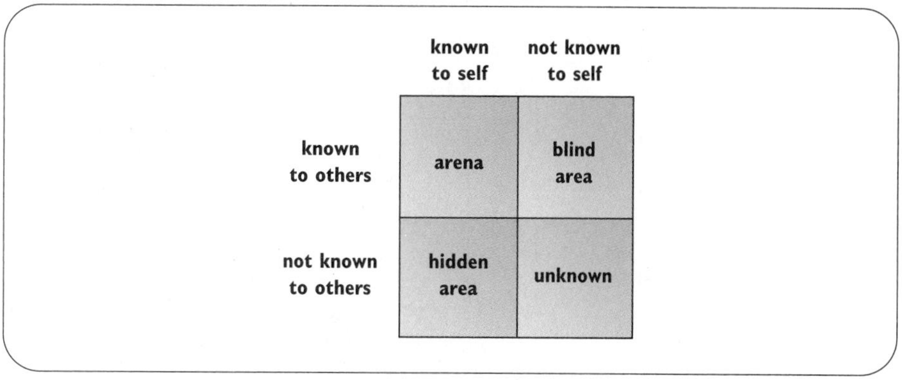

FIGURE 9.4   Johari Window

The upper-left pane of the window, which contains information about you that is known to yourself and others, is called the *open area* or *arena*. Interacting with someone when information is in the arena takes little energy; you do not have to worry about what you say because everything is known by you and your communication partner.

The lower-left area, which contains information about you that is known to yourself but not known to others, is called the *hidden area* because all your secrets are hidden there. Interacting with someone when information in the hidden area is relevant takes a great deal of energy; you have to think carefully about what to say and not to say so the secret stays a secret, while all the time maintaining the conversation in a natural manner.

The upper right-hand area, which contains information about you that is unknown to yourself but known to others, is called the *blind area* because you are blind to the information contained in it. Interacting with someone when information in the blind area is made known to you may trigger an accepting response—"Thanks for telling me that. I didn't know that I have a habit of ending sentences with, 'you know?'"—or, perhaps, a defensive one—"I *do not* say 'you know?' at the end of my sentences!"

Finally, the lower right-hand area, which contains information about you that is unknown to yourself and others, is called the *unknown area* because it contains things about yourself that remain to be discovered. This area may strike you as strange: If you don't know something about yourself, and the other person doesn't know it about you, how do you know it exists? You know it exists because information from this area sometimes becomes known. The therapeutic process, for example, often leads to self-discoveries. And, you may go running one day only to discover you are a much better runner than you imagined. Information from your unknown area that becomes known either enters the arena—you let others know what you learned about yourself—or your hidden area—you keep it secret.

The window in Figure 9.4 has four equal areas, but your own Johari Window would show different-sized areas, depending on the relationship. For example, your open area would likely be larger for a friend than for a stranger. Figure 9.5 presents four different Johari Windows, each representing a different, and exaggerated, interaction style.

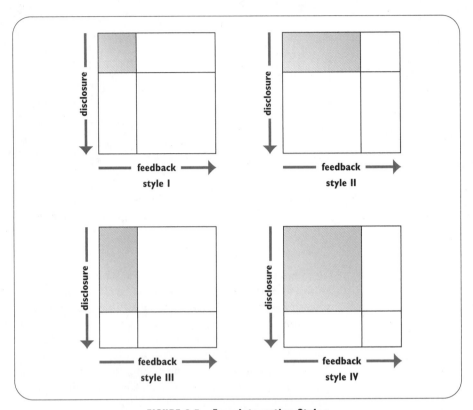

FIGURE 9.5   Four Interaction Styles

Style I, with its small arena, depicts a person who is unwilling either to disclose or to receive feedback. This person takes few risks and often appears aloof and uncommunicative. The largest area is the unknown, indicating that this person has a great deal to learn about herself or himself.

Style II depicts a person who is willing to receive feedback but unwilling to disclose. This person may fear exposure, possibly because he or she perceives others as untrustworthy. Unlike the Style I person, this individual seems friendly and supportive at first—mainly because of a willingness to listen—but after a short time it becomes apparent that this person will not share anything personal, so the initial positive feelings turn to distrust. Style II people, because their largest area is the hidden one, are ultimately perceived as secretive and detached.

Style III depicts the opposite of Style II: this person is willing to disclose but unwilling to seek, encourage, or receive feedback. Unless interacting with a Style II person (who is willing to listen but not talk), a Style III person may be perceived as self-centered and egotistical. Style III people have large blind areas, indicating they have much to learn about themselves that others could provide. Unfortunately, Style III people won't listen.

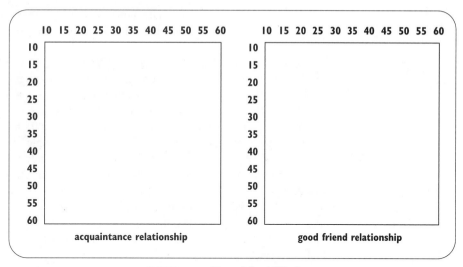

FIGURE 9.6   Your Johari Windows

Style IV people, with their large open areas, are willing to disclose information about themselves and to receive feedback. Although Style IV may seem to be the best of the four possibilities—given that Style IV people have the highest probability of forming close and personal relationships—it is not without drawbacks. For example, a Style IV person may appear aggressive to a Style I person (insisting on interacting on more than a superficial level), demanding to a Style II person (trying to get the Style II person to talk), and egotistical to a Style III person (self-disclosing instead of silently listening to Style III's monologue). Style IV interaction can be intimidating to people who are unwilling to talk, unwilling to listen, or unwilling to do both. Used in moderation, however, beginning with relatively low levels of self-disclosure and requests for feedback and building to higher levels, Style IV is the most successful interaction style for forming personal relationships.

Use Figure 9.6 to draw your own Johari Windows, one for your acquaintance relationship, and the other for your good friend relationship. Plot your "willingness to self-disclose" total score on the vertical axis and your "willingness to receive feedback" total score on the horizontal axis. With the points marked on each axis, draw lines down and across the window so that you have four areas. How do your Johari Windows compare with the four styles in Figure 9.5? Which area of each of your windows is largest? What do your Johari Windows indicate about your interaction with the person you had in mind who is an acquaintance, and the person you had in mind who is a good friend?

Your willingness to self-disclose depends on several things,[30] two important ones of which are your relationship with the other person—whether he or she is a friend or stranger—and the situation—whether you are alone or in a group, and whether the setting is more or less intimate.[31] For example, you might be more willing to self-disclose with your friend when alone in her or his house than when in the library. (Other criteria for choosing whether to disclose include the other person's trustworthiness, sincerity, and warmth.)

Reasons for disclosing to a friend differ from those for disclosing to a stranger, regardless of whether the situation is more or less intimate.[32] For example, primary reasons for disclosing to a friend include relationship maintenance, relationship enhancement, and self-clarification, while those for disclosing to a stranger are reciprocity and impression formation. The reasons for disclosing to friends and strangers reflect the different goals for each type of relationship. For example, the goal of communicating with a friend is to keep and deepen the relationship, while, at the same time, using the other person to help gain self-understanding. Communicating with a stranger has the two-pronged goal of getting the other person to talk (so you can gain information necessary to make decisions about continuing the relationship) while creating a particular, mostly positive, impression of yourself.

When to disclose often is less problematic than *what* to disclose. What you choose to disclose depends on several considerations:

> Does the disclosure suit the relationship? For example, highly intimate disclosure in a nonintimate relationship is inappropriate. Also, in early stages of relationship development, positive disclosures are better liked than either negative or boastful disclosures; indeed, boasters are viewed as least socially competent.[33]

> Is the disclosure relevant to the relationship? Disclosure about your family to your employer, for example, may not be pertinent to your relationship.

> Is the disclosure relevant to the immediate interaction?

> How likely is the other person to treat the disclosure with respect?

> How constructive is the disclosure likely to be for the relationship?

> Can you communicate your disclosure clearly and understandably?

Only you can decide whether your present disclosure and feedback patterns are effective and self-fulfilling. If they are, continue your present patterns. If not, consider making some alterations in your communication behavior. For example, if you scored low on Part 1 of Knowledge Checkup 9.4, consider developing skills to increase your self-disclosing communication. You may have trouble trusting people to respond to your disclosures in ways that are comfortable for you. As you gain experience in self-disclosing, you should become more skilled at knowing what to reveal and when. Also, your assessment of the potential risks should become more realistic.

If you scored low on Part 2 of Knowledge Checkup 9.4, consider developing skills to increase your receptiveness to feedback about yourself. You may doubt that others' comments will be relevant, or you may believe that others' comments can hurt you. Once you realize that feedback *may* be relevant (you can decide whether or not it is) and that *you choose* how to feel (you don't have to feel hurt by what someone says, although you can choose to—you can also choose to feel glad or disappointed), you can begin to open yourself to feedback by not cutting off others' observations and by practicing requests for information. The resulting information will be only as useful as you decide to let it be.

Skill Development 9.4 provides you with a method for increasing the amount of self-disclosure in your communication and for soliciting feedback about your disclosure.

Skill Development 9.4

INCREASING YOUR SELF-DISCLOSURE AND RECEPTIVENESS TO FEEDBACK

With your responses to Knowledge Checkup 9.4 in mind, consider what aspects of yourself you are unwilling or least willing to share in your acquaintance and your good friend relationships.

1. Make a list of some of the information you would keep to yourself, your secrets, in your relationship with the acquaintance and in your relationship with the good friend.

2. Select your *least* threatening secret for each relationship and ask yourself what the most horrible consequences would be if you were to reveal it. What would be the consequences for your acquaintance relationship? What would be the consequences for your good friend relationship?

3. With your *least* threatening secret and its presumed consequences in mind, select either your acquaintance *or* good friend to tell your secret (select the person with whom you would feel more comfortable).

4. Tell your secret.

5. If you do not get feedback concerning your secret, ask for it. Phrases such as "Tell me what you think about what I just said" and "How do you feel about my . . . ?" encourage the other person to provide feedback.

6. Observe what happens. You will probably learn that your secret is more threatening to you than it is to others and that the horrible consequences you imagine rarely come to pass.

7. Continue to think about your secrets and their consequences (for example, your secrets function as a barrier between you and the other person). Remember that you do not have to reveal every secret or even everything about each secret.

Self-disclosure isn't an all-or-nothing proposition; it begins slowly with revealing positive aspects of yourself and progresses, if at all, to greater breadth, depth, and amount. And, in general, openness will wax and wane throughout a conversation as well as an entire relationship.[34] Early disclosures test the situation: Is this person trustworthy? Does this person care about what I say? Each yes bolsters your willingness to self-disclose.

Despite its benefits, self-disclosure is risky. Telling a boss how you feel about the new organizational chart may lead to rebuke, just as telling a friend how you really feel about his new shirt may result in hurt feelings. How will the other person feel after the disclosure? What will happen to your relationship if you disclose your real feelings? You may well have to ask the extent to which you should be honest. Total honesty may not always be the "best policy."

The primary fear associated with self-disclosing for both men and women is the fear of rejection.[35] Many men also fear that disclosing will make them look bad and cause them to lose control over other people: "If you know my weaknesses, I will no longer be powerful." Many women, on the other hand, fear the consequences of disclosure for the relationship: "If I disclose, you might use the information against me" or "Disclosing might hurt our relationship." For the majority of men, control is the primary objective; for the majority of women, the relationship itself is the primary objective. These objectives affect how each gender discloses and the reasons each chooses to avoid disclosure.

Keep in mind that people in some cultures do not feel comfortable revealing personal information. The reasons for this discomfort may not be the same, but the results all mean that you need to be aware of cultural differences. For the Chinese, a preoccupation with talk about the "I" is a sign of selfishness. The German, British, and Japanese cultures value privacy and do not like disclosing to very many people.[36]

Affinity Seeking   Using confirming and supporting behaviors and engaging in positive self-disclosure are ways to present an appealing image to others. The active process used to get other people to like and feel positive toward you is called **affinity seeking.** People who like you are more willing to give you needed information for relational decision making, as well as participate with you in maintaining a relationship.

You probably have developed a variety of strategies to get others to like you, strategies that have met with some success and, therefore, continue to be used. There are a great many strategies available, although some may fit how you see yourself better than others.[37] When you want someone to like you, do you dress a particular way, cooperate more than usual, behave politely? Knowledge Checkup 9.5 provides you with the opportunity to examine some of the many affinity-seeking strategies available to you.

Knowledge Checkup 9.5

ASSESSING YOUR AFFINITY-SEEKING STRATEGIES[38]

Assume you met someone you find attractive and whom you would like to know better. What would you do to get this person to like and feel positive toward you? Below are 25 strategies. Check those you are likely to use.

_____ **4.** I point out that a good person would do what I want.

_____ **5.** I behave in ways to bother my partner until he or she does what I want.

_____ **6.** I try to strike a deal: I'll do what my partner wants if my partner does what I want.

_____ **7.** I tell my partner how doing what I want will benefit her or him personally.

_____ **8.** I tell my partner how doing what I want will benefit me personally.

_____ **9.** I compliment my partner on her or his abilities.

_____ **10.** I criticize my partner on a personal level.

_____ **11.** I remind my partner of things I have done for her or him.

_____ **12.** I simply state what I want without giving any reasons to comply.

_____ **13.** I point out that other people cannot help me or do what is needed.

_____ **14.** I point out that I have no choice but to make the request, and that I do so reluctantly.

_____ **15.** I downplay what I want and try to get my partner to see my request as easy for her or him to comply with.

_____ **16.** I point out that it would be unfair for my partner to refuse my request.

_____ **17.** I point out that other people will view my partner negatively if he or she does not comply.

_____ **18.** I point out that I will view my partner negatively if he or she does not comply.

_____ **19.** I point out that other people will view my partner positively if he or she complies.

_____ **20.** I point out that I will view my partner positively if he or she complies.

_____ **21.** I hint at what I want and hope my partner will figure it out.

_____ **22.** I give my partner logical reasons why she or he should comply.

_____ **23.** I keep repeating my request until my partner complies.

_____ **24.** I try to charm my partner into complying with my request by being very friendly and expressing positive emotions.

_____ **25.** I do nice things for my partner in advance of making my request.

_____ **26.** I promise to do something my partner wants if he or she complies with my request.

_____ **27.** I try to get my partner to see that by not complying she or he will feel bad about herself or himself.

_____ **28.** I try to get my partner to see that by complying she or he will feel good about herself or himself.

_____ **29.** I get someone else to intervene and make my request for me.

_____ **30.** I try to get my partner to think my request is really his or her own idea.

_____ **31.** I tell my partner I will punish her or him if she or he does not comply.

_____ **32.** Other:

1. What, if anything, do the strategies you checked have in common?
2. Why did you reject those strategies you did not check?
3. What do your compliance-gaining strategies tell you about the kind of relationship you have with the other person?

A request for compliance that uses an altruistic approach (like number 2) is more likely to be successful than one that uses threats (like number 31) or guilt (like number 11). Also, aggressive strategies tend to sacrifice long-term goodwill for short-term compliance. Communication in a relationship is more satisfying if compliance-gaining strategies are positive, like being supportive and social as a way to induce cooperation, rather than negative, such as threats of punishment or denials of your partner's future requests. Greater satisfaction with communication relates directly to greater willingness to comply.[42]

Findings from a study comparing compliance-gaining strategies in the United States and Colombia reveal, once again, the importance of taking cultural differences into account when describing communication behaviors. For example, while giving explanations or reasons is an often-used strategy in the United States—implying that anyone given relevant and sufficient information will choose to comply and that whether or not to comply is an individual choice—invoking shared obligations is more powerful in Colombia where relational connectedness and duties are paramount. In Colombia, the obligations of relationships often outweigh the desires of individuals.[43]

Electronic Mail   Because electronic mail (e-mail) is fairly easy to access and use, and because it is free or inexpensive for most people, people are turning to this means of communicating to help begin and maintain their interpersonal relationships. In some instances, this mode of communication is taking the place of telephone and face-to-face interaction as a means of conveying messages. The growth of the Internet—"a globe-spanning web of computer networks, which offer millions of users the opportunity to exchange electronic mail, transfer files, search databases . . . and participate in discussion groups"[44]—has been explosive in recent years and is likely to continue.

E-mail has been a salvation for individuals who are homebound and find that they can use this means to make personal contact with others. It is also a means for forming relationships for those who are communicatively apprehensive in one-on-one, face-to-face situations. By hiding behind the anonymity of a computer screen, they can say things and make contacts that would be emotionally impossible under normal circumstances. E-mail also has become another means for people to meet. "Chat lines" have become the cybergeneration's means of personal advertising. The chat lines open opportunities for persons with varying interests to meet quickly and without concern for the miles that separate them.

Although e-mail offers many advantages, such as (almost) instantaneous sending and receiving of messages from one part of the world to another, there are two disadvantages that make it necessary to use this new means of communicating with caution. First, there are e-mail systems that give you little control over what you send, because they display to the other person everything you type one key at a time, as you type it. This makes it impossible to edit something before you send it off. This can be dangerous, as ill-advised comments can appear for an instant, even though they are erased.[45] More traditional systems allow you to write and edit your comments before you mail them, which gives you more control. Second, be aware that your e-mail messages might have a much larger audience and a much longer lifetime than you think. Simply because your message is not sent out on a physical sheet of paper doesn't mean that it can't be retrieved, copied, and duplicated, or forwarded.[46]

As with any means of communication, certain rules of etiquette have developed for the use of the Internet. If you use e-mail with the same level of concern as you use for other communication, you should be fine. There are, however, a few things of which to be aware:[47]

- It is not a good idea to send highly personal or sensitive messages via e-mail because they may be perceived as "impersonal" and "cold."
- You should not read or forward someone else's e-mail without her or his permission.
- Be as brief as possible—it is likely that the message recipient pays for access to the Internet based on the time she or he is connected. The use of abbreviations can help reduce the length of your messages. For example, AAMOF stands for "as a matter of fact," BBFN stands for "bye bye for now," FITB stand for "fill in the blank." IMHO stands for "in my humble opinion," OTOH stands for "on the other hand," and TYVM stands for "thank you very much."
- Don't send a message with an "urgent" designation unless it truly is.
- You can convey emotions via e-mail by using symbols called "smileys" or "emoticons;" but be careful to use them correctly so that you do not inadvertently send the wrong message. Some smileys include:
  - { } which symbolizes a hug
  - :-) which symbolizes a smile
  - :-(which symbolizes a frown
  - :-D which symbolizes laughing
  - :-P which symbolizes sticking your tongue out
  - :'-(which symbolizes crying
- Capital letters should be used sparingly since they are perceived as "shouting."

ENDING A RELATIONSHIP

Relationships end for a variety of reasons. Goals may be fulfilled and no new goals established. Goals may not be accomplished and there may be little chance of achieving them. The partners may continue to feel lonely despite their relationship. The patterns of interaction may be too fixed, too inflexible, or too boring. The initial attractiveness may fade and nothing new may replace it. New relationships may appear more attractive. Changes in either person may alter the possible rewards. The two may no longer agree on things that were once no problem, and their interests may no longer be compatible. Sexual dysfunction, conflicts with work, financial difficulties, changes in commitment, and endless other possibilities, may plague highly intimate relationships. Relationships are fragile, and the possible threats to their well-being are numerous and powerful.

Reactions to relationship termination may vary from relief to self-recrimination, from happiness to deep depression. Similar to the death of a loved one, the death of a relationship evokes strong responses, strong responses that are often accompanied by heightened defensiveness: denying that the relationship is over, creating logical but untrue explanations for "what went wrong," feeling anger that's generalized to everyone and everything, and presuming that how you feel is how everyone feels.

Terminating a relationship often involves changes in many of your other relationships. New groups of friends may need to be formed and explanations to friends, relatives, and parents may be required. Your relationship termination affects others' relationships, as well as other relationships of your own.

Several of the most common communication strategies for the disengagement process have been studied.[48] Six critical dimensions describe the variations in relationship disengagement. The first three are:

- Was the onset of relational problems gradual or sudden? Most problems emerge gradually, making it difficult to determine their specific causes and the most clearly related consequences.
- Does only one partner want to end the relationship (*unilateral desire*) or do both agree (*bilateral desire*)?
- Is a direct or an indirect strategy used to end the relationship?

If you want to end a relationship and the other person does not, you may confront the other person with your desire—a *direct strategy*. You may also arrange to see the other person less—an *indirect strategy*. If both you and the other person wish to end your relationship, a direct strategy would be to talk it out and an indirect strategy would be to decrease the amount of time you spend together.

Strategies vary not only according to whether they're direct or indirect, but also according to whether they're self-oriented or other-oriented. Strategies that have a self-orientation are *fait accompli* ("I've decided this is over!"), *withdrawal* ("I'm going to be busy all next week"), *cost escalation* ("If you want me to go with you, you'll have to give up going out on Fridays with your other friends"), and *attributional conflict* ("It's your fault, jerk!"). Fait accompli takes control away from the other person, inflicting a blow to the other's self-esteem. Withdrawal also limits the other's control. Cost escalation raises the relationship's costs for the other person, and attributional conflict results in hostile communication of disparaging remarks.

In contrast, *state-of-the-relationship talk* ("Where is this relationship going?"), *pseudo-deescalation* ("I think we should see less of each other for a while"—when no contact really is desired), *negotiated farewell* ("Let's rationally discuss how to end this

TABLE 9.1	Strategies for Relationship Disengagement	

| | | **Desire to Exit** | |
		Unilateral	**Bilateral**
S **T** **R**	**Direct**	1. *fait accompli:* declaration that the relationship is over 2. *state-of-the-relationship talk:* discussion of dissatisfaction, relationship problems, and desire to exit	1. *attributional conflict:* hostile argument focused on why termination is necessary 2. *negotiated farewell:* conflict-free discussion to formally end the relationship
A **T** **E** **G** **I** **E** **S**	**Indirect**	1. *withdrawal:* decrease of intimacy and/or contact 2. *pseudo-deescalation:* false declaration of a desire to reduce closeness when the goal is termination 3. *cost escalation:* increase in costs to the other person to maintain the relationship (for example, treat the other disrespectfully)	1. *fading away:* decrease of contact without any discussion of the relationship 2. *pseudo-deescalation:* mutual false declaration of a desire to reduce closeness when the goal is termination

without fighting"), and *fading away* (seeing the other person less and disclosing less) are more other-oriented. They allow both relationship partners to "save face."

Table 9.1 summarizes various methods of ending relationships in four possible situations: unilateral and bilateral desires to exit using a direct strategy, and unilateral and bilateral desires to exit using an indirect strategy. Except for the bilateral-indirect situation, each describes a self-oriented and an other-oriented strategy. The two indirect strategies for terminating a relationship when both people want it to end are other-oriented.

The final three dimensions on which disengagement processes may be distinguished are:

● Does it take a long time or a short time to break away? Using an indirect strategy is likely to result in a drawn-out disengagement with several rounds of negotiations. Overreliance on indirectness also is likely to lead both partners to regret that they didn't use a more direct strategy to make the break quicker and less complex.
● Are there any attempts to repair the relationship? Partners are more likely to try to repair their relationship if they use an indirect disengagement strategy.
● Is the final outcome termination or a restructured relationship? Restructuring may result in a relationship that is successfully repaired and restored to approximately the same state it was in before problems arose, or it may lead to a different relationship with new goals, structure, or rules, or modified commitment, intimacy, or

For Better or For Worse®   **by Lynn Johnston**

resources. The infrequency with which relationships are successfully restructured demonstrates the difficulty of accomplishing this task to both partners' satisfaction.

The most frequently used disengagement process involves a unilateral desire to exit (one person wants out) coupled with an indirect strategy (the person decreases contact, claims a desire to reduce contact when no contact is really the goal, or makes contact very costly for the other person), with no attempts at repair, which leads to termination without trying to structure a new relationship (the pair say good-bye with no expectation for future contact). For example, Merle wants to break off with Lupe. Merle stops calling Lupe. Lupe calls Merle and asks, "What's wrong?" Merle tells Lupe, "Nothing. I don't want to talk about it. Good-bye." Merle hangs up. (When the goal is a repaired relationship, directness and more involvement in negotiations is a typical pattern.[49]).

The discussion so far about ending relationships makes it seem as though this final stage to relational development is clear-cut, that when a relationship ends, it *ends*. This interpretation, however, is misleading because relationships, in a very real sense, *never end*. Communication is a social activity with consequences, and those consequences often outlive your direct contact with relational partners.

How your parents communicated with you affects how you think and feel about yourself. Although you may no longer live with your parents or interact with them often—in fact, they may no longer be alive—their influence persists and will persist throughout your lifetime.

The teacher who modeled kindness for you and taught you that to be less than perfect is human still influences you although more than a decade may have passed since the relationship "ended."

Someone you loved but who is no longer in your life still affects how you think about friends and friendship.

The on-going influence of your relationships with people with whom you no longer interact attests to the fact that relationships never end—certainly not the important ones, and often not even those that were fleeting or seemingly unimportant at the time. Memory, the symbols we construct to stand for the events and people we experience, persists; so, the relationships we "had" continue to be those we "have."

You may realize from this that communication is an extremely powerful process. Accepting the responsibility of entering into a relationship means (whether you care to or not) accepting the responsibility for influencing and being influenced by another person. Every relationship opens the possibility for change, change that may last a lifetime. In one form or another, you will always be with your relational partners.

In the beginning of our relationship, we learned each other's language
Like over-eager babies
Mouthing unintelligible gaggles and sounds
Unable to articulate
Clumsily tripping on words
Falling into abject frustration
But once we found the common language
Each action and deed, every word and sentence was a joy and an excitement
A tingling of senses
A radiant discovery

Then, as if through osmosis, we used each other's words and expressions
Borrowing shamelessly and
Indeliberately incorporating them into our language
Speaking as one
Thinking as one
Feeling as one
And in the course, we invented new words
Gave existing words new meaning
Redefined and polished our language
Making it a special one of our own
One that we selfishly shared
One that no one could decipher or understand
One that we used in the comfort of each other's arms in quiet evenings

Then we tired of it
Lost interest
Got lazy
Became indifferent
Words gradually lost their meaning and significance
Like drunken dancers, we emphasized wrong accents in words
Sentences led to misinterpretations
Misinterpretations led to misunderstandings
Misunderstandings led to inevitable silence

In the end, we spoke different languages
Even though, we wanted the same thing

Chay Yew, *A Language of Their Own*

BUILDING RELATIONAL AWARENESS

Your relationships are what you make them. This is good news because it underscores your active role. You can begin relationships to meet your goals. You can improve relationships that need improvement. And you can end relationships that are best ended.

Here are some thoughts that might help you achieve more effective, satisfying relationships.

1. Be aware that *relationships have goals.* Understanding your goals, the other person's goals, and your mutual goals should provide a firm foundation for obtaining those goals. At the least, understanding all the goals should help you assess the relationship's possibilities.

2. Be aware that *relationships have structure* and that structure can be changed to meet changing needs. Changing patterns of behavior is difficult, but recognizing the patterns that exist and determining which patterns might be better can help the relationship grow in responsible and beneficial ways.

3. Be aware that *relationships have rules.* The rules coordinate interaction and make it more predictable. You have to know the rules to follow them, so talking about rules and reaching mutual understanding can benefit you and your partner. And if you want to change a rule, recognize that doing so is a slow process, one that requires understanding the reasons for the rule in the first place.

4. Be aware that *relationships are always in process.* Like everything else, relationships change with time. Attempting to freeze a relationship at one moment in time is bound to fail. Relationships change as you and the other person change and as the context for the relationship changes. Although this progression may seem obvious, few people behave as if change is inevitable. The comfort of old habits, old patterns, and old viewpoints can be more powerful than the reality of change. The moment comes when the relationship *as it is* no longer matches what either of the partners *thinks* it is, and the result of their shortsightedness is conflict.

5. Be aware that *relationships require attention.* Creating a supportive and confirming communication climate, appropriately self-disclosing, and using suitable affinity-seeking and compliance-gaining strategies are important ways of attending to your relationship. They ensure the exchange of information necessary for meeting your needs and your partner's as well as the needs of the relationship. Talk about your relationship with your partner and deal directly with relational issues.

Communication Competency Checkup

The goal of this Communication Competency Checkup is to guide you in putting your skills and knowledge about beginning, maintaining, and ending interpersonal relationships to use and to help you summarize the material in this chapter.

Male thinks: We've made eye contact. Now what?
Female thinks: We've made eye contact. Now what?

1. What are the most plausible reasons for these two people to be attracted to each other?

2. Based on the five steps for forming a new relationship, what specific recommendations would you make to each person in response to the question, "Now what?"

3. Assume that your recommendations are good ones and that the two persons begin a relationship. Problems arise, however, because he avoids self-disclosing and she complains that he's too quiet and doesn't seem to care about her. What could each do to help maintain their relationship?

4. The relationship is crumbling. Because you are their friend, they come to you for help. What questions would you ask to gain an understanding of their disengagement?

5. You are aware that the two are from different cultures. What recommendations would you make to them based on this awareness?

6. They are so impressed with your insight that they invite you to address their organization. The title for your talk is, "The Relationship Fairy Is Dead: Your Relationships Are Your Choices!" What would you tell the audience about increasing relational satisfaction?

NOTES

1. Elaine Hatfield and S. Sprecher, *Mirror, Mirror: The Importance of Looks in Everyday Life* (Albany, NY: State University of New York Press, 1986).

2. "Beauty in Diversity," *Science News* (February 12, 1991): 78.

3. Judith Langlois and Lori A. Roggman, "Attractive Faces Are Only Average," *Psychological Science* 1 (1990): 115–21.

4. Bruce Bower, "Facial Beauty May Lie More Than Skin Deep," *Science News* (March 19, 1994): 182.

5. Devendra Singh, "Adaptive Significance of Female Attractiveness: Role of Waist-to-Hip Ratio," *Journal of Personality and Social Psychology* 65 (1993): 293–307.

6. In a series of investigations done in 37 countries and with more than 10,000 women and men, David M. Buss and his colleagues found that mating preferences—what people were attracted to—were the same regardless of the culture studied. For example, both women and men indicated physical attractiveness was important in a short-term relationship, but for a long-term mate, physical attractivness remained important only for men. David M. Buss, "The Strategies of Human Mating," *American Scientist* 82 (May–June 1994): 238–49.

7. A summary of studies concerned with the similarity principle of attraction, what characteristics are perceived as attractive, and the implications of people marrying people with whom they share many similarities is available in David M. Buss, "Human Mate Selection," *American Scientist* 73 (January–February 1985): 47–51.

8. Bruce Bower, "Nice Guys Look Better in Women's Eyes," *Science News* (March 18, 1995): 165.

9. Larry A. Samovar and Richard E. Porter, *Communication between Cultures* (Belmont, CA: Wadsworth, 1991), 188.

10. For a summary of the research on the effects of physical attractiveness, see Mark L. Knapp and Judith A. Hall, *Nonverbal Communication in Human Interaction,* 3rd ed. (Fort Worth, TX: Harcourt Brace Jovanovich, 1992), 94–121; and Dale G. Leathers, *Successful Nonverbal Communication,* 2nd ed. (New York: Macmillan, 1992), 138–44.

11. Vicki Ritts, Miles L. Patterson, and Mark E. Tubbs, "Expectations, Impressions, and Judgments of Physically Attractive Students," *Review of Educational Research* 62 (1992): 413–26.

12. John Thibaut and Harold H. Kelley, *The Social Psychology of Groups* (New York: Wiley, 1959).

13. Michael Sunnafrank, "On Debunking the Attitude Similarity Myth," *Communication Monographs* 59 (1992): 164–79.

14. Elaine Hatfield and Richard L. Rapson, "Similarity and Attraction in Close Relationships," *Communication Monographs* 59 (1992): 209–12; Donn Byrne, "The Transition from Controlled Laboratory Experimentation to Less Controlled Settings: Surprise? Additional Variables Are Operative," *Communication Monographs* 59 (1992): 190–98.

15. Buss, "Human Mate Selection," 48.

16. These six motives were identified by Rebecca Rubin, Elizabeth Perse, and Carole A. Barbato and reported in "Conceptualization and Measurement of Interpersonal Motives," *Human Communication Research* 14 (1988): 602–28.

17. Carl G. Jung, *Two Essays in Analytical Psychology,* R. F. C. Hull (Trans.) (Princeton, NJ: Princeton University Press, 1969).

18. A full explanation of this basis for attraction is provided by Harville Hendrix in his book *Getting the Love You Want* (New York: HarperPerennial, 1988).

19. Susan R. Glaser and Anna Eblen, *Toward Communication Competency: Developing Interpersonal Skills,* 2nd ed. (New York: Holt, Rinehart and Winston, 1986).

20. Daniel D. Pratt, "Conceptions of Self within China and the United States: Contrasting Foundations for Adult Education," *International Journal of Intercultural Relations* 15 (1991): 287.

21. Ronald D. Gordon, "The Difference between Feeling Defensive and Feeling Understood," *Journal of Business Communication* 25 (1988): 53–64.

22. Jack R. Gibb, "Defensive Communication," *Journal of Communication* 11 (September 1961): 604–17.

23. Russell F. Proctor and James R. Wilcox, "An Exploratory Analysis of Responses to Owned Messages in Interpersonal Communication," *ETC: A Review of General Semantics* 50 (1993): 201–20.

24. Kenneth N. L. Cissna and Evelyn Sieburg, "Patterns of Interactional Confirmation and Disconfirmation," in C. Wilder-Mott and J. H. Weakland (Eds.), *Rigor and Imagination: Essays from the Legacy of Gregory Bateson* (New York: Praeger, 1981), 253–82.

25. Dale G. Leathers, *Successful Nonverbal*

Communication: Principles and Applications, 2nd ed., 216–18.

26. Valerian J. Derlega, B. Winstead, P. Wong, and M. Greenspan, "Self-Disclosure and Relationship Development: An Attributional Analysis," in Michael Roloff and Gerald R. Miller (Eds.), *Interpersonal Processes: New Directions in Communication Research* (Beverly Hills, CA: Sage, 1987).

27. Valerian J. Derlega, "Self-Disclosure and Intimate Relationships," in Valerian J. Derlega (Ed.), *Communication, Intimacy, and Close Relationships* (Orlando, FL: Academic Press, 1984), 1–9; Lawrence B. Rosenfeld and Gary L. Bowen, "Marital Disclosure and Marital Satisfaction: Direct-Effect Versus Interaction-Effect Models," *Western Journal of Speech Communication* 55 (1991): 69–84.

28. Lawrence B. Rosenfeld and W. Leslie Kendrick, "Choosing to Be Open: Subjective Reasons for Self-Disclosing," *Western Journal of Speech Communication* 48 (1984): 326–43.

29. The Johari Window was developed by Joseph Luft and Harry Ingham. For a detailed explanation, see Joseph Luft, *Group Process: An Introduction to Group Dynamics,* 2nd ed. (Palo Alto, CA: National Press Books, 1970), 11–20.

30. Sandra Petronio, "Communication Boundary Management: A Theoretical Model of Managing Disclosure of Private Information between Married People," *Communication Theory* 1 (1991): 311–35; Sandra Petronio, Judith Martin, and Robert Littlefield, "Prerequisite Conditions for Self-Disclosing," *Communication Monographs* 51 (1984): 268–73.

31. Gordon J. Chelune, "The Self-Disclosure Situations Survey. A New Approach to Measuring Self-Disclosure," *JSAS Catalog of Documents in Psychology* 6 (1976): 111–12.

32. Rosenfeld and Kendrick, "Choosing to Be Open."

33. Lynn Carol Miller, Linda Lee Cook, Jennifer Tsang, and Faith Morgan, "Should I Brag? Nature and Impact of Positive and Boastful Disclosures for Women and Men," *Human Communication Research* 18 (1992): 364–99.

34. C. Arthur VanLear, "Testing a Cyclical Model of Communicative Openness in Relationship Development: Two Longitudinal Studies," *Communication Monographs* 58 (1991): 337–61.

35. Lawrence B. Rosenfeld, "Self-Disclosure Avoidance: Why I Am Afraid to Tell You Who I Am," *Communication Monographs* 46 (1979): 63–74.

36. William B. Gudykunst and Young Yun Kim, *Communicating with Strangers: An Approach to Intercultural Communication* (New York: McGraw-Hill, 1992), 200–01.

37. F. Scott Christopher and Michael M. Frandsen, "Strategies of Influence in Sex and Dating," *Journal of Social and Personal Relationships* 7 (1990): 89–105.

38. Adapted from Robert A. Bell and John A. Daly, "The Affinity-Seeking Function of Communication," *Communication Monographs* 51 (1984): 91–115; Virginia Richmond, Joan S. Gorham, and Brian J. Furio, "Affinity-Seeking Communication in Collegiate Female-Male Relationships," *Communication Quarterly* 35 (1987): 334–48; and Michael G. Garko, "Perspectives on and Conceptualizations of Compliance-Gaining," *Communication Quarterly* 38 (1990): 138–57.

39. Kathy Kellerman and Tim Cole, "Classifying Compliance Gaining Messages: Taxonomic Disorder and Strategic Confusion," *Communication Theory* 4 (1994): 3–60.

40. The 24 compliance-gaining strategies are from Myron W. Lustig and Stephen W. King, "The Effect of Communication Apprehension and Situation on Communication Strategy Choices," *Human Communication Research* 7 (1980): 74–82; G. Marwell and D. R. Schmitt, "Dimensions of Compliance-Gaining Behavior: An Empirical Analysis," *Sociometry* 30 (1967): 350–64; Alan L. Sillars, "The Stranger and the Spouse as Target Persons for Compliance-Gaining Strategies: A Subjective Expected Utility Model," *Human Communication Research* 6 (1980): 265–79; and Richard L. Wiseman and William Schenck-Hamlin, "A Multidimensional Scaling Validation of an Inductively-Derived Set of-Compliance-Gaining Strategies," *Communication Monographs* 48 (1981): 251–70.

41. The list of strategies is from Kellerman and Cole, "Classifying Compliance Gaining Messages: Taxonomic Disorder and Strategic Confusion."

42. Jo Anna Grant, Paul E. King, and Ralph R. Behnke, "Compliance-Gaining Strategies. Communication Satisfaction, and Willingness to Comply," *Communication Reports* 7 (1994): 99–108.

43. Kristine L. Fitch, "A Cross-Cultural Study of Directive Sequences and Some Implications for Compliance-Gaining Research," *Communication Monographs* 61 (1994): 185–209.

44. Steven G. Jones, *Cybersociety: Computer-Mediated Communication and Community* (Thousand Oaks, CA: Sage Publications, 1995), 90. Also see Malcolm Parks and Kory Floyd, "Making Friends in Cyberspace," *Journal of Communication,* 46 (1996): 80–97.

45. Ed Krol, *The Whole Internet: User's Guide and Catalog* (Sebastopol, CA: O'Reilly and Associates, 1992).

46. Mike Snider, "E-Mail Isn't as Private as You May Think," *USA Today,* October 10, 1995, 6D.

47. Diana K. McLean, "E-Mail Etiquette," *PC Novice,* September 1995, 42–44.

48. The series of studies concerned with relationship disengagement is summarized in Leslie A. Baxter, "Accomplishing Relationship Disengagement," in Steve Duck and Daniel Perlman (Eds.), *Understanding Human Relationships* (Beverly Hills, CA: Sage, 1985), 243–65. More recent research on these as well as additional strategies used to disengage, include John A. Courtright, Frank E. Millar, L. Edna Rogers, and Dennis Bagarozzi, "Interaction Dynamics of Relational Negotiation: Reconciliation versus Termination of Distressed Relationships," *Western Journal of Speech Communication* 54 (1990): 429–53; and Kathy Kellerman, Rodney Reynoldo, and Josephine Bao-Sun Chen, "Strategies of Conversational Retreat: When Parting Is Not Sweet Sorrow," *Communication Monographs* 58 (1991): 362–83.

49. Courtright, Millar, Rogers, and Bagarozzi, "Interaction Dynamics of Relational Negotiation: Reconciliation versus Termination of Distressed Relationships."

COMMUNICATION COMPETENCIES

This chapter examines interpersonal relationships in the family. Specifically, the objective of the chapter is for you to learn to:

- Identify family images, themes, boundaries, and biosocial beliefs, and recognize the influence of families on children's development of social skills and feelings of self-worth.
- Describe the defining characteristics of a family.
- Recognize the importance of the family in society.
- Describe the role of culture in family communication.
- Describe family communication systems and their operation.
- Describe the family developmental cycle.
- Describe cohesion, adaptability, and conflict as characteristics of functional family communication.

KEY WORDS

The key words in this chapter are:

family
two-parent biological
    family
live-in couple
single-parent family
blended family
extended family
family-of-origin
family images
family themes
boundaries
biosocial attitudes
system
functional family
enmeshed family
disengaged family
chaotic family
rigid family

What is your full given name?

Do you know the origins of your name?

What does your name and how you got your name reveal about you?

Your name probably reveals something about your cultural background, family relationships, and family emotional ties. For example, in an interview with his mother, one of the authors of this book learned how he got his first and middle names, Lawrence Bernard. This is what his mother told him. "Grandpa Abe [Lawrence's paternal grandfather] had a wonderful cousin, Lawrence Brightbart, who had died. The Jewish people name after someone who died. The Sephardic Jews—Jews from the Mediterranean—name after the living, but we don't, we name after someone dead. Anyway, this wonderful man died, so I gave you his name, 'Lawrence.' 'Bernard' came from my grandmother, whose name was Brana. And I loved my grandparents very much." The name Lawrence Bernard reveals religious background, cultural origins, and an intricate set of family emotional ties. In this instance, the name reveals many of the roots of the person.

Your name may have been selected from a book of names, revealing the taste of the person or people who named you, or you may have been named after an admired television or movie character, with the hopes, perhaps, that you would be like this person. Whatever its origins, in all likelihood your name placed you in your family, provided you with a glimpse of your family history, and linked you to those with whom you had your earliest and most important interpersonal relationships.

A DEFINITION OF FAMILY

Complete the following sentence: I believe a family is _____.

Did your sentence completion contain reference to blood or legal ties? What about references to children? Did you mention relationship qualities, such as commitment, sharing, mutal support and understanding, and fulfillment of shared needs?

Complete the following sentence: The members of my family are _____.

Did your sentence completion include parents and siblings? What about grandparents, aunts, uncles, and cousins? What about neighbors and friends who are "like family"? What about family pets?

What is a family? Who are members of the family? These are not easy questions to answer. Social scientists, as well as lawyers and judges, have grappled with these questions for a long time. Even members of the same family may have different definitions.[1] Definitions of "family" undergo alterations from generation to generation, and as social needs warrant. As the courts consider cases concerning children being allowed to "divorce" their parents, who the parents should be when there is an egg donor or a sperm donor, the rights of adoptive parents and adopted children, and whether homosexual couples can adopt a child, definitions change.[2]

Early definitions typically stressed common residence, reproduction or adoption of children by different-sexed adults, and a "socially approved sexual relationship."[3] The 1980 census shortened the definition to two or more people related by birth, marriage, or adoption, but included the limiting notion of residing together. No definition of "family" will suit everyone, and certainly not everyone for a long period of time. With this in mind, we define **family** broadly as a system with two or more interdependent people with a common past history, a present reality, and a future expectation of interconnected mutually influencing relationships.[4] *Interdependent* means that every member of the family influences and is influenced by the other members; *common past history* "refers to the shared experiences, images, meanings, and values associated with a family unit as it functions and evolves over time";[5] *present reality* highlights the notion that family members' present interactions are influenced by their shared history; and *future expectation of interconnected mutually influencing relationships* stresses the significance of family members' ongoing interdependence.

This definition includes a variety of family configurations, such as **two-parent biological family,** consisting of two people and their biological offspring; **live-in couples,** heterosexual or homosexual, with or without children, who are unmarried but have a binding relationship; **single-parent family,** in which the parent—married, never married, widowed, or divorced—lives with her or his biological or adopted child; **blended family,** consisting of two adults and their children, all, some, or none of whom may be the offspring from their union; and **extended family,** consisting of groups of relatives, usually thought of as having blood or legal ties, living nearby to each other.

Your **family-of-origin,** the family in which you grew up, provided you with the foundation for your self-concept and communication competencies. Your family-of-origin provided you with your most important lessons in creating, maintaining, and ending interpersonal relationships, and it stands as the primary model for how you will create your own family.[6] From your introduction to language to your ways of expressing love, your family-of-origin is your first and most important teacher.[7] Just reflect for a moment on some of the most significant attitudes, values, and behaviors that are part of who you are. You surely will discover that many of them can be traced to your family-of-origin. A family-of-origin takes us from the womb and begins to teach us self-reliance, how to please and annoy others, responsibility, obedience, dominance, social skills, aggression, loyalty, sex roles, and age roles.

THE IMPORTANCE OF THE FAMILY

Knowledge Checkup 10.1 provides you with the opportunity to review what you know about the contemporary family in the United States.

Knowledge Checkup 10.1

THE CONTEMPORARY FAMILY IN THE UNITED STATES[8]

How much do you know about families in the United States in the 1990's? Fill in the blanks:

_____ percent of first marriages end in divorce.

_____ percent of second marriages end in divorce.

_____ percent of children live in poverty.

_____ percent of married women are in the workforce.

_____ percent of working mothers have children under six-years-old.

_____ percent of working mothers have children under one-year-old.

_____ percent of families fit the "traditional" configuration of a married couple with children or stepparents and children.

As many as 50 percent of first marriages end in divorce; approximately 60 percent of second marriages end this way.

More than half of African-American children and approximately 40 percent of Hispanic children live in poverty; about 20 percent of all children in the United States live in poverty.

Almost 60 percent of all married women are in the workforce; 57 percent of working mothers have a child under age six, and 51 percent have a child under age one.

Although you would think that the "traditional" family configuration would be the most common one, this pattern fits under 20 percent of all families.

As are families, so is society.
WILLIAM THAYER

Modern society in North America has been plagued with a host of problems linked directly to the family. The number of children born to unwed mothers has increased (from 5 percent of the population in 1960 to 30 percent in 1991[9]), and this is paralleled by an increase in the divorce rate (up 700 percent since 1900). The result is a situation in which millions of children are now being raised by a single parent (the number of single-parent families increased from 3.8 million in 1970 to 10.5 million in 1992[10]). These events have caused many social critics to declare that the United States is witnessing a breakdown of the family and, in turn, the unraveling of an important cultural institution.

Single-parent families are five times as likely to be poor as two-parent unions. Broken and unformed homes are the most important root cause of violent crime, drug abuse, and academic failure.

For an anthropologist, the widespread failure to marry is a sign of impending disaster. Cultures differ in many ways, but all societies that survive are built on marriage. Marriage is a society's cultural infrastructure, its bridges of social connectedness. The history of human society shows that when people stop marrying, their continuity as a culture is in jeopardy.[11]

The last paragraph is not meant to broach the topic of family with a moral tone, but rather to amplify the force and importance of the family unit in the study of human communication. Families socialize us, help us mature, and teach us how to be spouses and parents. Our families shape us and determine our future to a far greater extent than any other social institution, including school and the media. Family is "where one has the first experience of love, and of hate; of giving, and of denying; and of deep sadness . . . Here the first hopes are raised and met—or disappointed. Here is where one learns whom to trust and whom to fear. Above all, family is where people get their first start in life."[12]

The responsibility of the family is to transform a biological organism into a human being who spends the better part of her or his life communicating with other people. This communication is the basis for human relationships, and these relationships are the basis for society. "Without the family human society as we know it would not exist."[13]

CULTURE AND THE FAMILY

Culture plays a dominant role in both the development and maintenance of the family.

Families do not develop their rules, beliefs, and rituals in a vacuum. What you think, how you act, even your language, are all transmitted through the family from the wider cultural context. This context includes the culture in which you live, and those from which your ancestors have come.[14]

If you are going to understand how family interaction patterns offer clues to communication patterns outside the family, you must examine the place of culture in the family. The place of culture in the family takes on added significance as cultural diversity increases in the United States. Families from each culture offer their children different messages and, therefore, produce people with specific cultural perceptions and specialized communication styles. Many of these perceptions and styles change very slowly—if at all—as people interact with members of other and perhaps more dominant cultures.

Children born into a family in India or from India may notice women eating after the men have finished, while in other families everyone may eat at the same time. Each culture teaches its own set of gender-role expectations.

Meals served from a common bowl may be usual in Chinese and Chinese-American households, while other families may have separate plates brought to the table for each family member. Each culture teaches its own version of sharing.

In Mexican and Mexican-American families grandparents may live with the family. In other families grandparents may live in their own home or in a retirement community. Each culture teaches its version of the relationship between aging and the family unit.[15]

As cultures differ, so do families. As families differ, so do individual patterns of communication.

WHAT FAMILIES TEACH

Each family, in manifest and subtle ways, teaches countless values, perceptions, and attitudes to its members. It teaches its children what a family is by creating an image or picture of the family and images of each family member. It teaches what is to be valued and what is to be condemned by its recurrent themes. It teaches its children who may be spoken to, and when, and about what, by making clear the boundaries surrounding the family. It teaches what it means to be female or male, old or young, through its expression of biosocial attitudes. It teaches its children how to interact with others as it helps them develop their social skills. And, finally, it teaches its children how to feel about themselves.

In some families these values, perceptions, and attitudes stay the same for genera-tions; while in other families they are in constant flux, paralleling the changes in society. Knowing the lessons taught by the family aids in understanding its communication.

IMAGES

Family images are the perceptions and mental pictures family members hold of the family as a whole and of the individual family members. Although family members may hold similar images of the family, it is more likely that each member will have a different perspective. These images come from interactions with other family members and from watching what roles and functions each family member fulfills. One student described his family with this image: "My family is a basketball team, with my mom the coach, my dad the team owner who pops in on occasion and yells about this or that problem, and my brothers, sisters, and me the players running up and down the floor trying to do what we're told perfectly. To get things done, we all have to watch each other and work together—otherwise the owner might not be happy!" A different family was described with this image: "We're like a confederacy. We each have lots of individ-ual rights and freedom, but we stay together because we enjoy each other's company."

Your image of your family, and your place in it, is affected by your culture. In the dominant culture of North America, for example, children often have an image of their family that describes emotional support and loyalty coming from a limited number of people; in general, the family is isolated from other families.[16] In these types of families children quickly learn to be independent and self-reliant. In many other cultures the image of the family is very different. In the extended families typical of Mexico, Latin America, Africa, parts of Europe, the Middle East, and Asia support and loyalty extend beyond the immediate family of parents and siblings to include grandparents, first, second, and third cousins, aunts, uncles, great aunts and uncles, and even godparents. In the United States, "the black community is oriented primarily toward extended families, in that most black family structures involve a system of kinship ties."[17]

Think of your family and of the members of your family. What is your image of your family—basketball team or confederacy? What is your image of each family member—helper, helpless, dynamic, stable? Knowledge Checkup 10.2 provides you with the opportunity to identify your images by having you look at your family and each family member in an unusual way.

> Family, the dear octopus from whose tentacles we never quite escape, nor in our innermost hearts never quite wish to.
> DODIE SMITH

Knowledge Checkup 10.2

IDENTIFYING YOUR FAMILY IMAGES

1. Complete the following simile for your family: My family is like a _____ .
2. If your mother or female guardian were a musical instrument, which one would she be?
3. If you have siblings, and each were an animal, which one would each be?

4. If your father or male guardian were a machine, which one would he be?

5. If you were a flavor of ice cream, which one would you be?

6. Who, if anyone, plays the martyr—the one who does most of the cooking, serving, and cleaning up?

7. Who, if anyone, plays the pet—the spoiled one who always gets the last spoonful of stuffing and the biggest slice of cake?

8. Who, if anyone, plays the victim—the one who always finds others to blame for any and every problem she or he has?

9. Who, if anyone, plays the rebel—the one who wears old jeans when everyone else is dressed up for the party, then sits back and waits for the fireworks?

10. Who, if anyone, plays the peacemaker—the one who makes sure that everyone stays civil and then is the one to suffer with heartburn?

11. Who, if anyone, plays the smart one—the one who, without even seeing the movie, knows it's rotten? You don't even argue. Why invite the fight you know you'll lose?

Was it easy to identify the images you hold of your family members? Do you think each member of your family would complete this checkup similarly?

FAMILY THEMES

Family themes are "underlying family perspectives or points of view."[18] Family themes are important because they provide clues to the family's meaningful goals, values, and concerns; they provide a focus for the family's thought and energy. Themes may reflect a family's view of the interdependence and cooperation among family members (for example, "We all share the same goals, so we help each other a lot") or the extent to which family members are independent or different (for example, "We believe that each person in the family should take care of himself or herself and not depend on the others," "Jose is the talkative one, and Mary is the one who never says a word," and "John and John Jr. fight like pit bulls").[19] Themes often reflect a family's relationship with the world outside itself: "It's impossible to be successful without a good education," and "It's a tough world that can only be conquered with hard work."

Themes are revealed in a family's special nicknames (for example, "JR," short for "Junior," is the youngest family member and treated like the "baby" of the family) and roles (who does what, such as, "Lori always does the ironing"). They also are revealed by the rules that guide who talks to whom and who does what and when. For example, if a family rule is, "Children should only speak to their parents when they are spoken to," the theme revealed is: "Children should respect their elders and know their place." Even the seemingly simple rule regarding age is touched by culture. Anyone living in the United States probably knows, for example, that in this country, whether intentionally or unintentionally, children learn to value youth over age. In the Arab,

Chinese, Japanese, Mexican-American, and Native American cultures the elderly are viewed as people who should be respected and honored.[20] A similar perception is found in the Filipino culture, where "there is an almost automatic deference of younger to older, both within the family and [in] day-to-day interaction in school, social life, and work."[21]

Through its themes, a family describes its reality and how it deals with that reality. "Family business is kept inside the house—we don't air our dirty linen in public." "It is our responsibility to help others less fortunate than ourselves." "If you're going to do something, do it right." "Life is tough, and then you die." "The family is first."

Knowledge Checkup 10.3 provides you with the opportunity to recognize your family's predominant themes.

Knowledge Checkup 10.3

IDENTIFYING YOUR FAMILY'S THEMES

What are some common themes in your current family or family-of-origin?

1. What, if any, are some common phrases in the family that describe how family members are interdependent and cooperative?

2. What, if any, are some common phrases in the family that describe how family members are independent and different?

3. What, if any, are some common phrases in the family that describe how the family relates to the world outside the family?

4. Describe one family custom that is important for all members to follow.

5. Describe one family story that is repeated over and over at parties, during holidays, and at family get-togethers.

6. Describe one wish that all or most family members repeat over and over.

7. Describe one family belief that restricts or encourages family thinking.

Was it easy to choose themes to describe? Do you think each member of your family would complete this checkup similarly? How do these themes describe your family; that is, what do they tell you about how your family members interact?

BOUNDARIES

Boundaries are the limits a family sets on its members' actions. Within the family, boundaries define who may speak with whom, and under what circumstances—for example, you may talk to Mom after she gets home from work, but only after she changes into her "relaxing clothes." Outside the family, boundaries define who family members may communicate with, including extended family members, friends, and neighbors—for instance, Aunt Jenny may be someone to ignore, whereas Aunt Christy may be the one to call once a month. Boundaries also consider what groups and organizations are open or closed to family members. The Sierra Club may be an organization you are encouraged to support, but calls from one political party or the other for contributions are supposed to be disregarded.

Families create boundaries to regulate their interaction with specific ideas, people, and values. Boundaries may encourage or restrict contact with people outside the family's religious or ethnic group. They may allow or forbid intermingling with certain races or social classes. They may encourage or discourage certain liberal or conservative attitudes. They may dictate what cannot be talked about (death, alcohol, the way money is spent, sex, or weight), what can be talked about, how certain topics can be expressed ("Mommy is sick" versus "Mommy is drunk"), where certain topics can be talked about (around the kitchen table, only in the house, in the bedroom), and who can talk about certain things with whom (parents only, one parent to a particular child).

Boundaries may be clearer in some families than others. *Rigid boundaries* are clearly defined and difficult to ignore or avoid. For example, you may come from a family where dinner conversation was dominated by the head of the household, and you knew not to interrupt or change the topic. On the other hand, *diffuse boundaries* are less clear and, because of this, easier to ignore or avoid. For example, you may come from a family where dinner conversation, although generally dominated by the head of the household, allowed for a free flow of interruptions and topic changes.

Rigid boundaries may be found in a *position-oriented family,* where family roles are based on status and social identities related to sex and age. The child in a position-oriented family, for instance, is expected to communicate in defined ways. Such guidelines as "Honor thy mother and father," "Children are to be seen and not heard," and "Act your age" must be respected. Even when older, if the offspring is still seen as the "child," then she or he must fulfill that role.

A *person-oriented family* has more diffuse boundaries and allows a wide range of communication behaviors related to an individual's needs rather than her or his position in the family. A person-oriented family fosters open communication in which roles are continuously accommodated and the different intents of family members are recognized and dealt with. For example, when a "child" in a person-oriented family grows to adulthood, she or he is treated as an adult and not a child.

Position-oriented families require their children to learn global rules about how to communicate with others, while person-oriented families require children to develop more complex strategies for matching their communication to the intentions of a specific family member. This makes children from person-oriented homes better able to adapt their communication both to members of the family and to those outside the family.

BIOSOCIAL ATTITUDES

Biosocial attitudes concern the way the family deals with male and female identity, authority and power, and the rights of family members. Each of us was brought up with notions of what females and males are allowed to do, supposed to do, and capable of

doing. These gender roles may have included household roles (boys do the cooking and cleaning and girls do the car repairs), occupational roles (girls are mechanics and boys are elementary school teachers), areas of responsibility (women are the principal wage earners and men take care of the home), and emotional roles (girls don't cry and boys don't get angry). (If you were taken aback by some of the role identifications given as examples because you thought they were role reversals, you have identified some of the biosocial roles you learned in your family.)

In cultures such as the Japanese, Chinese, and Korean, attitudes toward gender have their roots deep in Confucianism.[22] In many families the father is the ultimate authority, and all members of the family are subservient to him. In the Indian culture, males are considered the superior sex: Male children are thought to be entrusted to parents by the gods, inheritance is through the male line, and a woman lives in her husband's village after marriage.[23]

Knowledge Checkup 10.4 will alert you to your biosocial attitudes concerning gender roles by having you reflect on what responsibilities should belong to a male and which to a female.

Knowledge Checkup 10.4

IDENTIFYING YOUR GENDER ROLE ATTITUDES[24]

In the first blank space, indicate whether primary responsibility for each task should belong to a male (M) or a female (F). In the second blank space, indicate whether a male or female assumed responsibility for each task in the family in which you were raised.

_____ _____ a. taking out the garbage

_____ _____ b. writing thank-you notes for a family gift

_____ _____ c. initiating sexual activity

_____ _____ d. changing diapers

_____ _____ e. bringing home the major paycheck for household use

_____ _____ f. disciplining the children

_____ _____ g. cooking

_____ _____ h. cleaning the bathroom

_____ _____ i. fixing or making arrangements for fixing the car

_____ _____ j. taking the children to piano lessons

_____ _____ k. taking a child to baseball practice

_____ _____ l. fixing the leaky faucet

_____ _____ m. changing the bed sheets and pillowcases

_____ _____ n. making family investments

_____ _____ o. selecting new furniture for the living room

Research indicates North Americans perceive items a, c, e, i, l, and n to be "male activities," and b, d, f, g, h, j, k, m, and o as "female activities." Give yourself one point for each of your answers that conforms to what was found in the research. A score of 10 or more indicates your biosocial attitudes or biosocial attitudes in your family-of-origin are parallel to traditional societal thinking from the mid-1970s. How much did your results differ from these? If there were differences, why? How stable are biosocial attitudes related to gender roles?

The task of identifying the self as a boy or a girl is apparently not very difficult, given that by age three most children will identify not only which sex they belong to, but also which jobs are done by men and women, what roles mommies and daddies play, and what kind of behavior is allowed for each sex.[25]

In addition to gender roles, biosocial attitudes concern authority and power, that is, the extent to which leadership, decision making, and control are linked to traditional sex, age, and role expectations. Biosocial attitudes in a family are revealed to the extent that answers to the following questions are based on age, sex, or position in the family.

Who is responsible for making decisions regarding money and work, and who is responsible for making decisions regarding the children? (Is the "man of the house" responsible for the former and the "woman of the house" responsible for the latter?)

In a single-parent home, who is responsible for making the important decisions? (Is it the person in the role of parent, or do the children share in decision making?)

How much authority are children allowed, and how does this authority change with age? (Are children allowed to make more decisions and assume more responsibility as they get older? And does it matter whether the child is female or male? In one household we know, the children, both male and female, are treated as if they are mindless and in need of constant care until the age of 18, at which point they are thrown from the "nest" and told to "make it on their own.")

How are responsibilities decided, such as who takes out the garbage and who does the dishes? (Are the decisions based on age? Are they based on sex? Are they based on some combination of age and sex?)

SOCIAL SKILLS

In addition to teaching its members family images, themes, boundaries, and biosocial attitudes, families also instruct their members—explicitly and implicitly—as to the proper ways to use verbal and nonverbal codes. At a very early age, your family taught you basic social skills, including politeness and how to initiate and maintain friendships. Were you taught to say "Ma'am" and "Sir" to anyone older than you? Were you taught to smile at strangers you wanted to meet?

Although all families, regardless of their culture, teach their children basic communication skills, the techniques that are stressed reflect cultural values. Research into Western family life, for example, reveals that parents often encourage, approve, and reward aggressive behavior.[26] On the other hand, in many Mexican and Mexican-American families, children are taught to avoid aggressive behavior and to use "diplomacy and tactfulness when communicating with another individual."[27] In many Chinese and Chinese-American families, children learn the social skills essential for group harmony, family togetherness, interdependence in relationships, respect for their place in the line of generations, and saving face.[28]

CONCEPTS OF SELF

Your self-concept, which is the foundation for how you communicate, develops in your family and is modified by your culture. In adult-centered cultures, such as the English and Indian (not Native American), children are not the center of attention. Feelings of self-worth are often diminished in these cultures. In contrast, Jewish children are usually told that they are very important. In Jewish families parents expend a great deal of energy on the emotional and intellectual development of their children. These behaviors typically create a person with a high level of self-esteem. In Mexican and Mexican-American families, because of collectiveness and impenetrable family ties, children also grow up with strong feelings of self-worth.

Skill Development 10.1 provides you with the opportunity to observe a family and examine its important themes, boundaries, and biosocial attitudes. Also, this skill development provides you with the chance to conjecture on how the observed family may have taught its members particular social skills and helped develop feelings of self-worth in the children.

Skill Development 10.1

OBSERVING WHAT FAMILIES TEACH

Select a family to observe other than your own. This choice could include a family on television or a friend's family.

1. What are some of this family's important images? How do these images affect how the family members communicate?

2. What themes did you have to learn in order to understand the family's interaction?

3. What are some boundaries that guide how members of this family communicate with one another and people and organizations outside the family?

4. How do biosocial attitudes—attitudes regarding gender roles and the influence of age, sex, and position in the family on authority and decision making—affect family interaction?

5. What social skills do you observe that seem to reflect the family and its cultural background?

6. To what extent do the children you observe seem to have feelings of high or low self-worth? Can you conjecture what family interactions may have contributed to these feelings?

Based on your responses to the six questions, how do the images, themes, boundaries, biosocial attitudes, social skills, and concepts of self combine to create the communication pattern unique to this family?

THE FAMILY AS A COMMUNICATION SYSTEM

Family members interact much like characters in a play, movie, or television show. They assume roles, act out events, and share their ideas, thoughts, and beliefs in a coordinated way. Much can be learned about the basic principles of a family's communication by examining the drama they enact, by observing the patterns they follow.

Families, like characters in a play, are organized into systems. A family's **system** is the pattern of interaction it uses as its primary or usual mode of operation. This pattern is based on the family's themes, images, boundaries, and biosocial attitudes, as well as rules concerning how messages should travel through the family. For example, in one family, the father may make the decisions and pass the information to the mother, who relays it to the children. In another family, everyone may get together to discuss and agree upon family matters.

Regardless of the countless ways in which the infinite number of themes, images, boundaries, and biosocial attitudes may come together to form unique families, in North America several characteristics of family systems seem widespread:[29]

1. Any change in one part of the system causes the entire system to change.   Family members are interdependent. The unit creates a *synergy*—that is, the whole is greater than the sum of parts. Much like the pieces of a mobile, if one part moves or changes, all the other parts move and change. If a family member leaves home to go to college, the system is no longer the same. If a parent loses a job, becomes permanently disabled, or becomes angry with another member, the system is no longer in balance. When that happens, new rules are needed to bring the system back into balance. Healthy families are capable of recreating a balance.

2. Family systems are complex, adaptive, and information-processing.   A family system is complex because it is constantly in flux. Because a family is made up of people, and because people change as they gain new experiences, age, and mature, the system continuously modifies itself. A family system is adaptive because it develops in response to interaction among its members. The ongoing interaction is bound to lead to strains and tensions, but a well-developed family system accommodates itself to such difficulties. Systems are information-processing because the basis of a family is the exchange of ideas, attitudes, and beliefs.

3. People act out what is wrong in their family system.   Arguments, physical conflicts, pouting, and isolation of a family member are all clues that something is wrong. But things are not always as they appear. Often what is dealt with is the *presenting problem,* the problem the family members complain about. However, the presenting problem is usually only a symptom of the *underlying problem,* the real issue. For example, a teenager who complains that she is not permitted to stay overnight at a friend's house may really be crying out for a change in the rule-making procedure that will allow her to make her own decisions and be perceived as mature and independent.

4. Factors outside the family affect the system.   Laws, economic changes, and societal pressures constantly influence the family and prevent even the most effective systems from operating efficiently and happily all the time. The family cannot exist in isolation from the society in which it is embedded. No family can protect itself fully from wars, job layoffs, natural disasters, and random acts of violence.

5. A family system creates its children's notions of reality when they are young.   Through its images, themes, boundaries, instruction in social skills, and influence on self-esteem, families in effect determine who each child is and how she or he will interact with others. The family lays the foundation for the child; current relationships reflect early family experiences (unless the child undertakes the difficult task of overcoming the influence of early family-of-origin experiences).

6. There are costs and rewards for belonging to a family system.   It costs a great deal to belong to a family—time, money, emotion, and loyalty. The rewards, however, are the benefits received for being in the family—love, support, caring, refuge, and information. Members of a family system tend to continue their participation, whether they are physically present or not, as long as they feel that the rewards of the relationships are worth the costs. The payback is not necessarily dollar for dollar, kiss for kiss, and thank you for thank you. Rather, individuals remain satisfied and productive parts of a family as long as their needs are met and they don't feel put upon or taken advantage of. If and when the costs exceed the rewards, disengagement may take place and a family member may break ties, either physically, by moving away and cutting off communication, or psychologically, by using drugs or alcohol, or refusing to attend family functions.

To operate successfully within a family system, you must examine and understand the connections between yourself and the other elements of the system. Of particular importance is your understanding of the role you play as a family member. Ask yourself: Who am I in this family? For example, am I the financial provider, the child of a troubled family member who is forcing me to be the parent, the caretaker in a dual-parent working family, the oldest child carrying the burden of success for the entire family, the college student who is an occasional home visitor, or the peacemaker among warring factions? Understanding your role leads you to understand whether you are effectively communicating in your family environment and enables you to assess what changes you may want to make in your role as a family member.

STAGES IN THE FAMILY LIFE CYCLE

Families may go through several identifiable stages of development, the first of which is leaving home—separating from parents and caretakers and accepting responsibility for self—and the last of which may be separation, divorce, or death. Stages could include: (1) establishing a family, which begins when two people form an intimate bond and begin to define themselves as a family; (2) the addition of family members through birth, foster care, kinship care, or adoption; (3) the children's development of independence; (4) launching the children, including the reestablishement of the couple as a couple; (5) post-launching the children and retirement; and (6) couple dissolution through separation, divorce, or death.[30] These stages are based on several assumptions: couples have children, partners live together with their children, children grow up, and children, in turn, establish their own families. These assumptions do not apply to all families; however, regardless of a particular family's individual and unique stages of development, most families approximate the stages outlined here or, at the least, the stages can serve as a point of reference for discussing a particular family's life cycle development.

For many families the order of the six stages may not fit the pattern outlined. For example, a couple may not have a child, a woman may get pregnant and not marry the father, or the parental role may be enacted by a grandparent. One or more children, because of emotional or intellectual problems, may not be capable of developing their independence. Divorce may come before children are launched, and a new, blended family may be formed. Children may not leave their home or, after leaving, return—

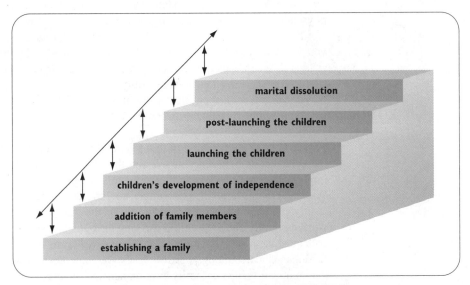

FIGURE 10.1 **Stages in the Family Life Cycle**

perhaps with their own children—to live with their parents. Alternative life cycles are abundant. Figure 10.1 represents the stages as steps that may be climbed in order, or that a family may climb, then step back, and climb again, depending on its own life cycle pattern.[31]

ESTABLISHING A FAMILY

In the mainstream North American culture, beginning a family typically means separating from your family-of-origin, commiting yourself to a new relationship, and establishing new rules and roles. Dating, being engaged, even cohabitation are not the same as a marital relationship.[32]

How is a wife different from a date, from an intimate friend?

How is a husband different from a date, from an intimate friend?

How is cohabitation different from courting and marriage?

How is a marriage different from courting and cohabitating?

The answers to these questions probe your expectations regarding the marital relationship. It is usual for your expectations for this relationship to be different from those for other relationships. For example, while closeness may not be too important an issue before marriage, especially if the relationship partners have separate apartments and work in different places, after marriage it is an important issue to resolve. To what extent should you and your spouse be connected? At one extreme, do you feel you should be very close and dependent, spend a lot of time together, share all your thoughts and feelings, and have few individual friends? And at the other extreme, do you feel you should be emotionally separate, spend little time sharing your thoughts and feelings, pursue independent activities, and have many individual friends? At what point between these two extremes do your expectations fall?

Flexibility, like closeness, is another issue that requires discussion. It is not uncommon for people who are courting to behave in ways that enhance their attractiveness to one another, perhaps as a way to guarantee that the relationship doesn't have problems. This may mean being more cooperative than you really care to be or letting the other person make more decisions than you are really comfortable with.[33] How flexible should you be as a couple with regards to your roles and rules? At one extreme, you may expect that rules will change frequently, that nothing will be stable, and that how you behave at any given moment will be negotiated and dependent on current circumstances. At the other extreme, you may expect each person to adhere strictly to traditional male-female roles—with the male working outside the home and the woman inside, or, at least, if both are working outside the home, the male earning more—and expect clear distinctions regarding who should make what decisions. Where do your expectations fall on this continuum?

ADDITION OF FAMILY MEMBERS

To be considered a "normally functioning heterosexual couple" in the United States has traditionally meant having children, although this is less a requirement in the 1990s than during earlier decades. Voluntarily childless couples are often viewed as selfish, unhappy, lonely, and immature.[34] Organizations exist to help couples who choose not to have children cope with the hostile environment in which they find themselves.[35] Even couples with only one child may be perceived negatively, although not as negatively as those with no children.

With the arrival of the first child, family relationships get very complicated. The family changes from a husband-wife dyad to a husband-wife dyad plus a wife-child dyad, a husband-child dyad, and a wife-husband-child triad. Before, if you wished to study the couple, you could study the influence of the husband on the wife and the influence of the wife on the husband; now you have at least seven influence patterns you could study:

the husband's influence on the wife's interaction with the child (he: "Stop coddling him.");

the wife's influence on the husband's interaction with the child (she: "Give her a kiss good night.");

the influence of the husband-child relationship on wife-child interaction (he yells at the child and the child runs to the mother for comfort);

the influence of the wife-child relationship on husband-child interaction (she teaches the child that his father is mean);

the influence of the husband-child relationship on husband-wife interaction (he takes the child to the football game instead of his wife);

the influence of the wife-child relationship on husband-wife interaction (she talks about her problems with the child instead of with her husband); and

the influence of the husband-wife relationship on husband-wife-child interaction (a conflict between the husband and wife spills over to a conflict with the child).

Imagine the possible number of influence relationships to study if a second child comes into the family, or a third, or a fourth! And this ignores the influence of extended family—grandparents, aunts, uncles, cousins—each of whom has his or her own expectations and influences.

A great deal of the energy that goes into parent-child relationships focuses on the parents' fulfillment of the children's needs. Children have seven basic needs: belonging, nurturance, support, protection, structuring, respect, and observing appropriate attachment. The extent to which these needs are satisfied by the parents determines, to a large extent, how well the child interacts with others when she or he is an adult.

Belonging needs refer to the parents creating a place for the child, both in their home and in their hearts. The child learns that she belongs in *this* home and with *these* parents. Parents communicate that the child belongs with messages such as, "You belong in this home with us" and "We belong together."

Nurturance needs are satisfied by communicating to the child that he is loved and cared for and that the parents are a source of comfort. "We love you" and "No matter what happens, we'll take care of you" are messages that communicate nurturance.

Support has to do with the encouragement and support the child needs as she begins problem solving and risk taking. "Don't worry, we'll catch you if you fall" and "When you need encouragement, we're here for you" are messages that communicate support for the child.

Protection is, perhaps, one of the most basic needs—the need to be safe. "Don't be afraid, we'll protect you" and "We won't leave you without shelter" are messages that communicate to the child that he is safe with his parents and protected by them.

Structuring refers to the child's need for limits. Parents set limits and establish rules to help the child develop good habits and to free her from having to deal with a chaotic environment. "You need to go to bed by 8:00 P.M. to make sure you have a good night's sleep" and "The dinner meal begins with a prayer" help the child learn habits the parents think are important and free her from having to decide certain issues on her own (especially at an early age when such decision making may be difficult).

Respect has to do with the child's need for being valued apart from the parents. By valuing the child's ideas, thoughts, and feelings, and by valuing his differences from the parents, the parents communicate respect. "You are special to me because of your sense of humor" and "I respect your right to come and go as you need" are messages related to respect.

Observing appropriate attachment refers to the child's need to witness a positive, loving relationship. When the parents love and support each other and have more of their needs met through each other than others (including the child), they serve as a model for appropriate attachment. "We love and support each other" and "You are not more important to me than my spouse" provide the child with an opportunity to observe suitable attachment.

Although it was once believed that marital satisfaction decreases as children enter the family, the relationship between having children and marital satisfaction is not so easy to summarize. The relationship is complex.

> The birth of a baby clearly has an impact on marital behavior patterns. Spouses change the way they organize [their work] and leisure time. Wives' day-to-day activities become more home and family centered. Husbands engage in fewer of the leisure activities that they enjoy. The responsibilities that accompany child care limit the amount of time spouses have to spend as a couple.[36]

The arrival of a child—whether by birth, adoption, foster care, or kinship care—represents a big change in a couple's life. For some couples, marital satisfaction decreases, while for others it remains the same. Predicting changes in satisfaction is an uncertain venture. For example, couples with more traditional gender-role attitudes ("The husband should earn the family's money and the wife should care for the children") have an easier time making the transition to having children than couples with more egalitarian gender-role attitudes ("We should share equally in household chores

and in earning money for the family"). Also, although drawing a husband in a dual-earner marriage into child care may reduce the tension he and his wife feel because her workload decreases, often it negatively affects his evaluation of the marriage.[37]

CHILDREN'S DEVELOPMENT OF INDEPENDENCE

Children begin to develop their independence when they enter school. With school comes an increase in autonomy, at least for several hours a day. The child interacts with teachers, children, and school personnel, all without the direct supervision of the parents. These new relationships bring with them new roles (including the role of "student"), competition, judgments, and comparisons. Family boundaries may be challenged as the child learns things the family considers less-than-desirable, such as sex education, and interacts with people the family holds in low regard, such as the children of neighbors with whom the parents are feuding.

The struggle to be independent from the family reaches its highest point during adolescence. This is, perhaps, the most difficult time for the family—as well as for the adolescent. The question, "Who am I?," becomes paramount for the adolescent, and answering it is not an easy task. The method chosen to answer the question commonly requires challenging family rules, themes, boundaries, and biosocial beliefs, establishing powerful non-family relationships, and weakening family bonds. Through this conflict, it is hoped, an answer emerges; then, the adolescent can turn around and reestablish good relationships with the other family members. The adolescent normally needs to break away in order to return.

The families most successful at negotiating this difficult period tend to be those with high flexibility, those, for example, that are able to change how they discipline and how they determine family roles. Adolescents are most likely to be healthy and well-adjusted when rules and roles can be discussed adult-to-adult with their parents, when they can explore alternative identities without excessive criticism, when their caring family relationships do not give way to conflict and abuse, and when they are encouraged to take responsibility for their lives. "The quality of the communication between parents and adolescents is a critical feature of all these tasks."[38]

The parents' need to be needed by the adolescent and the adolescent's need not to need her or his parents come into direct conflict. With leaving the home an inevitable event for most children, the parents' need to be needed is less important than helping the adolescent achieve independence.

LAUNCHING THE CHILDREN

There are three perspectives to be considered when looking at the launching process: the couple and their recoupling, that is, their redevelopment as a couple; the redeveloped family, with and without the launched member; and the launched person's individual development.

Recoupling

There's nothing wrong with teenagers that reasoning with them won't aggravate.
UNKNOWN

After a family's only child or last child is launched, the couple needs to consider what changes in their relationship are likely and how to respond to these changes. Launching typically means the couple has more time together, experiences less stress without the demands of the launched member, has less direct need to talk about the launched child (and this may be an important consideration if the launched child was a main topic of conversation), and enjoys opportunities to restructure their time together and to increase their intimacy. If the launched child served as a link with the community, changes need to be made. For example, it is common for people with same-aged children to become friends, with their discussion of "the children" serving as their main connection. What happens with the children gone?

Recoupling can be very complicated. For example, while most couples develop their intimacy before children are born, couples in blended families need to develop their intimacy with children in the house. Also, if a couple was not very intimate prior to the birth of their children, or if they did not do much to maintain their intimacy during the child-rearing years, there is a high probably they will have problems recoupling. Finally, if the children were why they stayed together in the first place, with the launching of the last child divorce becomes a "simple" solution to the problem of recoupling.

The Redeveloped Family

Launching requires the remaining family members to restructure their relationships. Boundaries need to be renegotiated; for example, if the launched sibling watched over the younger sisters and brothers, new rules may need to be discussed as the parents assume the responsibility of monitoring the younger children's behavior. Roles and obligations need to be redefined; for example, if the launched family member was responsible for taking out the garbage or keeping family members cooperative or baking cookies for family events, who assumes these jobs?

What does the family do with the launched member's clothes, room, seat at the table, and so on?

When the launched member comes home, is he or she a visitor, a member of the family as if he or she never left, or a member of the family with new rights and obligations that need to be negotiated? For example, although the launched member had a Saturday night curfew of 1:00 A.M. when living at home, what's the curfew—if any—when she or he returns home for a short vacation from school or work? If she or he took out the garbage when living at home, should that person be expected to do this task when home for a weekend?

The Launched Family Member

The launched family member has several issues with which to grapple.

"How do I stay connected to my family?" The launched person needs to consider how often to call home, whether to go home or not during vacations, and how to maintain open lines of communication with both parents. (It is common for mothers to get most of the telephone talk-time with launched children, isolating the father.)

"How do I adapt to my new freedom?" The launched person needs to consider what family themes and behaviors to maintain. For example, although she or he may have attended the family's place of worship every week when living at home, she or he needs to consider whether to continue this behavior while away. Family themes regarding sex, drugs, and drinking, as well as cleanliness, need to be considered, and decisions must be made about which themes to embrace and which themes to ignore.

"How do I adapt to adulthood?" Responsibilities once handled by the family, such as shopping, paying bills, and keeping income tax records, now need to be performed by the launched person. Time structuring, once dictated or guided by the family— encouragement to study during certain times, to be in bed by a particular hour, to balance school and work—now needs to be determined by the launched member.

POST-LAUNCHING THE CHILDREN

For many families, the post-launching period of the family life cycle is marked by an increase in freedom for the wife and husband, a decrease in financial worries, less concern with the children (as one person put it, "When they're younger they're always on your mind, and when they're older they're always on your heart"), and increased opportunity to focus on building a new relationship and having new experiences.

In addition to all the positive aspects of the post-launching period, however, there is the potential for problems. For example, retirement may result in feeling unproductive, social relationships may change, income may decrease, identity problems may arise if there was a strong identification with work, and one's spouse may die.

As people live longer, the chances of being a grandparent increase. By age 32, half of African-American parents are grandparents, and by age 56 they are great-grandparents. The age most European-American parents become grandparents is 50.[39] If grandchildren enter the family picture, one must learn how to behave as a grandparent. In the United States, there are at least five different grandparenting styles: *formal,* which requires a clear definiton of the boundaries between the grandparent and parent roles, plus little interaction with the grandchildren, such as babysitting; *fun seeker,* where the primary interaction is play and fun—for both the grandparent and grandchildren; *second parent,* which often occurs when the parents cannot assume all the responsibilities of parenting, perhaps because of heavy work loads (for example, in 1991, approximately 3.3 million children in the United States lived with their grandparents); *family sage,* which requires the grandparent to serve as the repository of the family's wisdom; and *distant figure,* where the grandparent becomes an infrequent benevolent visitor, showing up at holidays loaded with gifts.[40]

Knowledge Checkup 10.5 provides you with the opportunity to analyze the styles used by your grandparents and to consider their influence on you.

Knowledge Checkup 10.5

YOUR GRANDPARENTS' GRANDPARENTING STYLE

1. Which, if any, of your grandparents enacts/enacted a formal grandparenting style? What are/were the boundaries drawn between the grandparent and parent roles? How often do/did you see this grandparent, and what is/was communication like with her or him?

2. Which, if any, of your grandparents enacts/enacted a fun-seeker grandparenting style? What activities do/did you do with this grandparent? What is/was communication like with him or her?

3. Which, if any, of your grandparents enacts/enacted a surrogate- or second-parent grandparenting style? Does/did this grandparent have the full responsibility for raising you or partial responsibility? In what ways is/was this grandparent your surrogate or second parent? What is/was communication like with her or him?

4. Which, if any, of your grandparents enacts/enacted a family-sage grandparenting style? What have you learned from this grandparent that is an important part of who you are? What is/was communication like with him or her?

5. Which, if any, of your grandparents enacts/enacted a distant-figure grandparenting style? How often do/did you see this grandparent, and what is/was communication like with her or him?

What do your grandparents' grandparenting styles have to do with how you see yourself and how you communicate? What kind of style do you think you will enact if you are a grandparent?

Interaction with their grandchildren is only one part of the communication in which elderly parents engage. What is communication like between elderly spouses, between elderly spouses and their children, and between the children?[41] Elderly spouses who are relatively satisfied with their marriages often become disengaged, talking less with each other than earlier in the family life cycle. The lower levels of communication bring lower levels of conflict, but also lower levels of self-disclosure. Many thoughts and feelings go unexpressed.

Communication between elderly parents and their children is contingent on a number of things. For example, more parent-child contact is likely when the child is a daughter (who often phones, visits, helps out with transportation, household tasks, and shopping), when the child lives nearby, and when the parent likes the child. Also, a married daughter who has her own children is more likely than her brothers or sisters to be her parents' confidant.

Communication between children of elderly parents often focuses on reminiscences—talk about "old times." When aid, such as daily care, is an issue, unmarried sisters are more likely than brothers or brothers-in-law to provide it. Also, African-American siblings, in general, are more likely to provide assistance than European-American siblings.

MARITAL DISSOLUTION

Divorce

As many as half the marriages in the United States end with divorce. Divorce is typically a process that occurs in several stages. The divorce process usually begins with *denial,* a lack of willingness on the part of either spouse to admit that there may be a problem. Denial is followed by *loss and depression,* when the two people realize that being together is, itself, a problem. Whether they like or dislike each other, the realization that something is very wrong with the marriage often creates a feeling of loss, of "unattachment." Loss and depression are followed by *anger and ambivalence.* Anger toward the spouse and ambivalence about ending the marriage characterize this stage, as do last attempts to save the marriage. Anger and ambivalence are followed by a *reorientation of lifestyle and identity.* The divorcing partners spend less time looking backward and more time looking forward—forward to an identity without the marital partner. Since marriage affects each partner's personal, professional, social, and sexual identity, the exploration of a "new" identity without the partner is often difficult and stressful. Finally, reorientation is followed by *acceptance* and a new level of functioning—acceptance of the divorce, reorientation, and moving on to new relationships, including a new relationship with the ex-marital partner.[42]

In the United States, communication between divorced individuals depends on whether the decision to divorce was mutual or not and how much anger is still present. When the decision to divorce is mutual and the ex-partner is perceived as a caring and responsible parent, the two people may plan activities together for their children and, in many ways, be "perfect pals." A small number of divorced couples have this relationship. If the ex-spouses cannot be friends, they at least may be "cooperative colleagues." Many ex-partners have this type of relationship, in which they have different ideas about parenting and probably do not like each other, but are able to compromise for the sake of their children. When anger, resentment, and bitterness characterize the post-divorce relationship, the ex-spouses may become "angry associates" who conflict with each other openly and use the children as players in their drama—as message-carriers, perhaps, or as objects to "win over" in the fight against the ex-partner. When anger is so great that the ex-spouses cannot even tolerate each other's presence, they become "fiery foes" for whom co-parenting is impossible. In this situation, one parent often sees the children less and is excluded from celebrations, such as birthdays and weddings, where the other parent may appear. Finally, many couples become "dissolved duos," for whom there is little post-divorce contact. The parent with the children establishes what is essentially a single-parent home.[43]

Family reconfiguring after divorce can become very complicated.[44] Although the most common thing for people in the United States to do after a divorce is to remarry (approximately two-thirds of divorced people remarry within three years), they may live without a partner, cohabitate, engage in serial monogomy (where they go from divorce to cohabitation to marriage to divorce to cohabitation to marriage, and so on), or begin a committed gay or lesbian relationship (25 percent of gay men and probably an equal percent of lesbian women were in heterosexual marriages at one time). Each new configuration brings additional considerations, including stepchildren, brothers and sisters with one parent in common, and brothers and sisters with both parents in common, all living in the same household or in close proximity.

Although there may be expectations for how first-time married people should interact and what two-parent biological or adoptive families should be like, there are few guidelines for the multiple types of families that actually exist—and the matter becomes even more perplexing as divorce and remarriage are taken into consideration.

Death

In the typical family life cyle, death occurs when the wife and husband are elderly. At this point, death may be less stressful than divorce because, in many ways, it is final: Contact with the former spouse is over, and there is no constant reminder of a "failed marriage" or "poor choice of mate." There is no ambiguity when a marriage ends because of the death of a spouse; the role of spouse is terminated, and the role of parent, although requiring readjustment, does not necessitate negotiation and coordination with an ex-spouse. (Of course, if the death of a spouse occurs early in the developmental cycle, as when the children are young, the stress it creates is extremely intense and the effect is different.)

The average age at which someone is likely to become a widow or widower in the United States increases with each new generation. In 1900 a woman could expect to be a widow around the age of 50; by 1980 the age increased to 68. Because women tend to marry older men and to live longer, they are more likely than men to care for ailing spouses, to be widowed earlier, and to spend a larger portion of their life after the death of a spouse.[45] However, whether the death of a spouse is expected (as after a long illness) or not does not seem to affect the length of the adjustment period of the surviving spouse. The death of a spouse is so great a trauma that it hardly allows for preparation.

The likelihood of remarriage declines with age; indeed, women over the age of 50 whose spouses die are unlikely to remarry. In general, the remarriage rate is about seven times higher for men than it is for women.

LESS FUNCTIONAL VERSUS MORE FUNCTIONAL FAMILIES

Determining whether a family is more or less functional is not easy. Although each of us could generate a list of the requirements for a family to be considered functional, each list would be biased according to the unique cultural and family-of-origin experiences of its creator. From research in the United States, however, some commonalities among the lists can be found, and a **functional family** may be defined as one that creates an appropriate environment for supportive and caring interactions, encourages open and accepting communication, and enables children to grow and achieve suitable independence.[46] Aspects of family life that determine whether the family is likely to be functional or not are its cohesion and adaptability and how it handles conflict.

COHESION AND ADAPTABILITY

Two issues that families need to address are *cohesion*—the degree to which family members are bonded to one another—and *adaptability*—the ability of the family to alter itself in response to changes in the family life cycle and other stresses. The extent to which a family is able to avoid demanding too high or low a level of cohesion and to avoid having too high or low a level of adaptability largely determines how functional it is.[47]

Knowledge Checkup 10.6 will help you assess the levels of cohesion and adaptability in your family-of-origin or your current family. With this information, you can begin to look at one aspect of your family's functioning.

Knowledge Checkup 10.6

COHESION AND ADAPTABILITY IN YOUR FAMILY[48]

With either your current family or family-of-origin in mind, respond to each item using the following scale:

If the description is never or almost never true for your family, rate it **1.**

If the description is true for your family once in a while, rate it **2.**

If the description is sometimes true for your family, rate it **3.**

If the description is frequently true for your family, rate it **4.**

If the description is always or almost always true for your family, rate it **5.**

_____ 1. Family members feel closer to people inside the family than outside the family.

_____ 2. Family members are not afraid to say what is on their minds.

_____ 3. Our family does things together.

_____ 4. Each family member has input in major family decisions.

_____ 5. Family members know each other's close friends.

_____ 6. It is hard to know what the rules are in our family.

_____ 7. Family members feel very close to each other.

_____ 8. Our family tries new ways of dealing with problems.

_____ 9. Family members share interests and hobbies with each other.

_____ 10. We shift household responsibilities from person to person.

_____ Total your score for items 1, 3, 5, 7, and 9. This is your *cohesion* score.

_____ Total your score for items 2, 4, 6, 8, and 10. This is your *adaptability* score.

Scores of 20 and higher on the cohesion scale are high, scores of 10 and lower are low, and scores between 10 and 20 indicate moderate levels of cohesion. Scores of 17 and higher on the adaptability scale are high, scores of 10 and lower are low, and scores between 10 and 17 indicate moderate levels of adaptability.

When cohesion is moderate, family members are able to be independent from each other while still remaining dependent on, loyal to, and connected to the family. When cohesion is too high, the family may be **enmeshed,** indicating there is too much consensus, too little independence, and a very high demand for loyalty. At the other extreme, when cohesion is too low, the family may be **disengaged,** indicating there is limited attachment or commitment to the family and an overall lack of loyalty.

When adaptability is moderate, a family has the ability to change three important features of its organization in response to situational stress, such as the loss of a parent's job or a child's dropping out of school, and life cycle stress, such as that encountered when a child reaches adolescence. First, *the family can adapt its power structure*—for example, parents' levels of assertiveness and control can decrease as their child reaches adolescence, and methods of discipline, effective when the child was younger, can be adjusted to suit a more adult-like family member. Second, *the family can adapt its role relationships*—for example, if the role of the husband requires that he function as the sole wage earner and he loses his job, the wife and children can change their own roles and work to support the family. Third, *the family can adapt its rules*—for example, the rule that "we don't talk about the family to strangers" can be altered to include "unless the stranger is a therapist helping the family or one of the family members."

When adaptability is too high, the result may be a **chaotic** family which has erratic leadership or no leadership at all, dramatic shifts in roles, unclear roles, and impulsive decision making. When adaptability is too low, the result may be a **rigid** family which has authoritarian leadership (usually in the hands of one person, the mother or father), strict discipline, roles that are inflexible, and unchanging rules.

"Balanced" families are those that have moderate levels of both cohesion and adaptability, "mid-range" families are those that are moderate on one dimension and high or low on the other (moderate cohesion and chaotic or rigid adaptability, or moderate adaptability and enmeshed or disengaged cohesion). "Extreme" families are those that are high on both cohesion and adaptability (enmeshed and chaotic), low on both (disengaged and rigid), or high on one and low on the other (a family that is enmeshed and rigid, or disengaged and chaotic).

Balanced families and mid-range families generally function more adequately than extreme families. For example, extreme families appear to have more emotional problems, such as neurotic and schizophrenic family members; these problems were found in only 9 percent of the balanced families studied and in 47 percent of the extreme families. They also seem to have more alcoholism: Whereas 20 percent of families with alcoholism were an extreme type, only 3 percent of nonalcoholic families were an extreme type. In addition, they may have more sex offenders—50 percent of the families-of-origin of sex offenders were an extreme type, only 19 percent of non-offender families-of-origin were an extreme type. And, finally, they seem to have more juvenile offenders; looking at female-headed single-parent homes, half with juvenile offenders and half without, 93 percent of the families with a juvenile offender were an extreme family type, while 69 percent of the families without a juvenile offender were balanced.[49]

Members of balanced families have more positive communication skills than do members of extreme families. In comparison to extreme families, they exhibit more supportive communication, provide each other with clearer and more explicit information, and display more positive emotions. Communication in a balanced family is likely to create a supportive and caring environment in which communication is open and accepting—in other words, a functional family.

FAMILY CONFLICT

Conflict is natural. When different people with different ideas come together, conflict is inevitable. When considering how functional a family is, the question is not whether the family does or does not have conflict, but how family members conflict with each other.

Family conflicts often center on *power struggles* in the family (for example, how rules are set up, who enforces them, and how biosocial issues are handled), *differences in intimacy needs* (showing levels of caring, physical and emotional touching, and sexual activity), and *interactional difficulties* (how to resolve conflicts, make decisions, and interact with each other).

In most North American families, conflicts invariably arise about the exercise of power—the amount of control the family should be allowed to have over individual members' lives.[50] Do one or two people control all or most of the actions of the others? How are decisions made? Can you make some, any, or all decisions about matters that are important to you? The ideal balance should enable each person within the family to be most effective in gaining access to what he or she wants.

Family members make varying claims on each other for love, affection, recreational companionship, and understanding. Intimacy plays a role in matters such as feeling loved or unloved; inflicting and submitting to sexual, physical, or verbal abuse; getting praise or being ignored; and being included or left out of family activities.

In addition to conflicts concerning power (who's on the top and who's on the bottom) and intimacy (how emotionally close or how far family members should be from each other), there may be conflicts about how to handle conflicts. The next chapter of this book contains information regarding various conflict strategies that apply to all relationships, regardless of whether they are among family or non-family members. Specific to families, however, are parent-child conflicts. These conflicts are different from other types of conflicts due to the unique role relationship of the combatants.

How a parent conceives of his or her authority determines to a large extent how he or she approaches parent-child conflict. Knowledge Checkup 10.7, which focuses on parental authority, provides you with the opportunity to assess your tendency to use one of two ways for exercising control. If you are a parent, respond to the items based on how you act. If you are not a parent, imagine yourself as a parent and indicate how you would act.

> Govern a family as you
> would a small fish—very
> gently.
> CHINESE PROVERB

Knowledge Checkup 10.7

USE OF PARENTAL AUTHORITY

Here are some typical things parents do in their relationships with their children. For each statement, mark the column that tells how you as a parent act or would act.

L   = likely to act that way

UL = unlikely to act that way

?   = uncertain how I would act

L	UL	?	
_____	_____	_____	1. I would physically remove my child from the piano if he refused to stop banging on it after I told him it was disturbing me.

———— ———— ————   **2.** I would praise my child for consistently being prompt in coming home to dinner.

———— ———— ————   **3.** I would scold my six-year-old if she demonstrated poor table manners in front of guests.

———— ———— ————   **4.** I would praise my adolescent when I saw him reading literature I approved of.

———— ———— ————   **5.** I would punish my child if she used swear words.

———— ———— ————   **6.** I would reward my child if he showed me a chart indicating that he had not missed brushing his teeth even once in the past month.

———— ———— ————   **7.** I would make my child apologize to another child that she treated rudely.

———— ———— ————   **8.** I would praise my child if she remembered to wait at school for me to pick her up.

———— ———— ————   **9.** I would make my child eat almost everything on his plate before being allowed to leave the table.

———— ———— ————   **10.** I would require my daughter to take a bath each day and give her a reward for not missing a single day for a month.

———— ———— ————   **11.** I would punish my child if I caught him telling a lie.

———— ———— ————   **12.** I would offer my teenage son some kind of reward to change his hair style to one I approved of.

———— ———— ————   **13.** I would punish my child for stealing money from my wallet.

———— ———— ————   **14.** I would promise my daughter something she wanted badly if she would refrain from using too much makeup.

———— ———— ————   **15.** I would insist that my child play the piano for relatives or guests.

———— ———— ————   **16.** I would promise my child something I knew he wanted if he would practice his piano lessons for thirty minutes each day.

———— ———— ————   **17.** I would make my two-year-old remain on the toilet as long as necessary if I knew that she had to go.

———— ———— ————   **18.** I would set up a system whereby my child could earn a reward if he regularly did his household chores.

———— ———— ————   **19.** I would punish or threaten to punish my child if she ate between meals after I told her not to.

———— ———— ————   **20.** I would promise a reward to encourage my teenager to come home on time after dates.

Count the L's checked before the ODD numbers: _____

Count the L's checked before the EVEN numbers: _____

Add the two sums of L's: _____

The *odd-numbered* L's indicate the degree to which you do use or would use *punishment* or the *threat of punishment* to control your child or to enforce your solutions to problems. The *even-numbered* L's indicate the degree to which you do use or would use *rewards* or *incentives* to control your child or to enforce your solutions to problems. The total number of L's indicates the degree to which you do use or would use both sources of your parental power to control your child. Use the following scale to indicate your power level.

USE OF PUNISHMENT	USE OF REWARD	USE OF BOTH KINDS OF POWER	RATING
0-3	0-3	0-5	Anti-authoritarian
4-5	4-5	6-10	Moderately authoritarian
6-8	6-8	11-15	Considerably authoritarian
9-10	9-10	16-20	Very authoritarian

Through Knowledge Checkup 10.7, you explored one very important aspect of your attitudes toward being a parent—how you use or would use your parental authority. There is no ideal level of authoritarianism. Some situations, such as when physical danger exists (for example, the teenager wants to borrow the family car during an ice storm), may call for a very authoritarian approach; on the other hand, responses to conflicts over issues such as room cleaning, curfews, and taking out the garbage, depend solely on the extent to which these things are important to you. The more important an issue is to you as a parent, the more likely you will behave in an authoritarian manner.

Family conflicts—whether parent-child, spouse-spouse, or among siblings— often revolve around one erroneous thought: "If only you were more like me or could see that I'm right and you're wrong, I wouldn't have to be upset." Family members, however, are not identical, and no family member has a corner on the truth; therefore, conflict erupts.

Family members participate in conflict because they get something out of it. If not, they wouldn't participate in it. Constructive family conflicts—which indicate a more functional than dysfunctional family—provide new information, excitement and stimulation, and the resolution of mutual problems. Destructive family conflicts— which indicate a more dysfunctional than functional family—also have payoffs, such as gaining control over others, placing the blame on someone else in order to get oneself off the hook, and feeling superior to those who are seemingly wrong or inferior. Unfortunately, the benefits of destructive conflict sow the seeds for relational dissatisfaction.

Physical and Verbal Aggression in Families

A serious problem with conflict in families is that it may turn into physical and/or verbal aggression. *Aggression,* sometimes referred to as a type of abuse, is the taking of actions that advance personal goals without concern for the harm they may cause others. Physical aggression, such as hitting, is common among siblings—a disturbing finding since sibling aggression seems to be related to aggression outside the home.[51]

Verbal aggression includes the use of words to attack another person: nagging, yelling, insulting, attacking character, accusing, rejecting, refusing to talk to, and swearing. Verbal abuse against children and spouses is extremely common in North America. Studies indicate that more than two out of three North American children, and more than three out of four spouses, are victims of verbal aggression. Swearing and attacking character are the two most common specific acts of verbal aggression against spouses and children.[52]

Verbal aggression strongly affects people. For example, the more verbal aggression a child suffers, the greater the probability that the child will be physically aggressive, become delinquent, or have interpersonal problems. In addition, the more verbal aggression a spouse endures, the higher the probability that he or she will experience psychosomatic symptoms, poor health, depression, and suicidal thoughts. Conflict between parents is particularly stressful to a child when it is frequent, intense, involves physical aggression, remains unresolved, and concerns the child's behavior.[53]

Verbal aggression often leads to physical violence. Contrary to the claim that verbal venting releases pent-up anger and thus avoids physical aggression, it has been found that verbal venting contributes to higher levels of physical attack and violence.[54]

Family Conflict Should Be Confronted

Physical and verbal aggression are inappropriate responses to conflict; however, the other extreme, ignoring a conflict, may be equally as destructive to the family. Families can improve their communication by recognizing that family conflict should be confronted. Placing conflict on the back burner, attempting to ignore it, smoothing it over, or denying that it exists create tensions. The key to resolution lies in how the conflict is dealt with. General principles of conflict management in the family include:

- *It is better to focus on conflicts over small rather than large issues.* Small issues can generally be resolved within a reasonable amount of time and with a reasonable amount of effort. Large issues need planning and, sometimes, outside help for resolution.
- *It is better to recognize the differences in power and ability among participants than to ignore or minimize them.* If the family system is based on the dominance of one person, disagreements about his or her use of power may be difficult or impossible to resolve unless lines of authority are clear. Similarly, differences in ability,

whether because of age and experience, physical attributes, knowledge background, or some other reason, also need to be clear to members of the family to help them participate effectively in constructive conflict.

- *It is better to avoid solutions that fail to address important concerns of the participants.* A dictated solution, such as, "As long as you live in this house, you will do what I tell you," will not allow all participants to leave the scene feeling satisfied. Strong feelings that are not resolved in one conflict will probably resurface later in another.

OPENING FAMILY LINES OF COMMUNICATION

Why is it that at some time in every person's life she or he wished to belong to a different family? "In Shane's family, they discuss everything before a decision is made." "Taylor's parents would never force her to tell them what happened on a date." The truth is, most families have both healthy and unhealthy communication patterns. The question is one of degree rather than "healthy" or "unhealthy." "To what degree is a family's communication system healthy?" is a better question than, "Is the family's communication system healthy?"

One way to improve family functioning is to open lines of communication among family members. In order to communicate support, care, and acceptance and to create an environment in which children can learn to become independent, spouses need to communicate, parents and children need to communicate, and children need to communicate with each other.

A useful approach to helping a family open its lines of communication and make appropriate changes in both its structure and how family members communicate is the *workshop process of change.*[55] With this process, family members get together and generate a list of important family rules that guide them both individually and as a family. Then, they discuss the rules to see if some are changeable. Once possible changes are identified, a plan of action is developed. The plan may require someone to take some difficult or upsetting risks, but these often are necessary to improve the family system. Family members must be honest in dealing with themselves and others, and this means they must be willing to see and correct their mistakes.

For example, consider a family with the following rule: "Your bedroom should be neat, with all clothes hung away every day." The parents and younger daughter follow the rule, but the older daughter does not. Rather than continue the battle over the child's not keeping her bedroom neat, family members get together to discuss the rule. First, they talk about the rule and discuss whether change is possible. The parents need to accept that old techniques, such as constant threats, have not worked, and that new approaches need to be explored. Through discussion they decide that the rule needs to be changed. What the discussion revealed was that (1) getting the eldest daughter to obey the rule was more trouble than the rule was worth, (2) the problem was not so much the clothes not being hung up, but *seeing* the clothes not hung up, and (3) the real problem was a fear on the part of the parents that if there were food in the room it would bring in insects. So, the old rule was changed from "keep the room neat" to "keep your door closed and do not bring food into the room." The hard part of this solution, of course, is not slipping back into the old and useless patterns, such as opening the child's door and yelling at her because her clothes aren't hung up.

Skill Development 10.2

APPLYING THE WORKSHOP PROCESS OF CHANGE

Assume you and your family are applying the workshop process of change. Complete steps 1 and 2 as if you were actually participating in the process. Then, picture your family going through the remaining steps.

Step 1: Each family member lists two family rules that she or he feels enhances family functioning (for example, "It's a rule that we all eat dinner together.").

Step 2: Each family member lists two family rules that she or he feels causes her or him personal difficulties (for example, "My curfew is too early.")

Step 3: Each person reads aloud her or his "enhancing rules."

Step 4: Each person reads aloud her or his "difficulty rules."

Step 5: A discussion is held during which family members acknowledge the "enhancing rules" and talk about the "difficulty rules" with respect to why the rules exist, whether the rules are appropriate, and what changes could be made, if any.

How successful do you anticipate the workshop process of change to be for your family? What did you learn about your own desire for changing the family rules?

In some instances, families or some members of a family are unable to make needed changes by themselves and require outside help. One-on-one counseling, family counseling, and support groups are often helpful in solving the problems of dysfunctional families.[56]

Keeping in mind that each family represents a complex set of relationships that evolve over time—as children are added, grow, become independent, leave, and form families of their own, and as the parents confront adjustments to their roles, responsibilities, and capabilities—provides a good foundation for developing useful expectations. Change is possible, but it is slow and often very difficult. A family's levels of cohesion and adaptability and its method of handling conflict are ingrained patterns that may require a great deal of effort to alter.

Communication Competency Checkup

The goal of this Communication Competency Checkup is to guide you in putting your skills and knowledge about interpersonal relationships in the family to use and to help you summarize the material in this chapter.

Calvin and Hobbes

by Bill Watterson

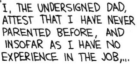

The interaction between Calvin and his father displays many of the family communication principles discussed in this chapter.

1. Given the agreement that Calvin wrote for his father to sign, what do you think Calvin includes in his definition of what a family is? Would Hobbes, Calvin's stuffed-animal tiger companion, be a "member of the family"? What definition of "family" would this require?

2. Calvin's family is a "traditional" two-parent biological one. How common is this family?

3. What is Calvin's image of his father? What do you think the father's image is of Calvin?

4. What family themes are displayed in the interaction between Calvin and his father? (Consider what Calvin is attempting to do and what the result is for him.)

5. What rules does Calvin have concerning how his father should behave? What rules does his father have concerning how Calvin should behave? What do these rules "tell you" about family boundaries?

6. Given Calvin's initiation of this particular interaction with his father, what would you estimate his self-esteem is?

7. What evidence does this cartoon present that Calvin's family may best be described as a system?

8. Does Calvin's family appear more position-oriented or person-oriented with respect to its roles?

9. Calvin's family is in the "addition of family members" stage of the family life cycle. What are Calvin's basic needs, and what parent-child communication might help fulfill these needs? What would you predict subsequent stages might be like, for example, the "children's development of independence" and "launching the children" stages?

10. What are cohesion and adaptability probably like in Calvin's family?

11. How does Calvin's family, at least in the interaction in the cartoon, handle conflict?

12. If Calvin and his family wanted to, how could they employ the "workshop process of change"?

NOTES

1. J. Jorgenson, "Where Is the 'Family' in Family Communication?: Exploring Families' Self-Definitions," *Journal of Applied Communication Research* 17 (1989): 27–41.

2. Frank Cavaliere, "Society Appears More Open to Gay Parenting," *American Psychological Association Monitor* (July 1995), 51.

3. George P. Murdock, *Social Structure* (New York: Free Press, 1965), 1.

4. For a discussion of issues regarding the definition of family, see Kathleen M. Galvin and Bernard J. Brommel, *Family Communication: Cohesion and Change,* 3d ed. (New York: HarperCollins, 1991), 2–11; Judy C. Pearson, *Communication in the Family: Seeking Satisfaction in Changing Times,* 2nd ed. (New York: HarperCollins, 1993), 13–19; and Janet Yerby, Nancy Buerkel-Rothfuss, and Arthur P. Bochner, *Understanding Family Communication,* 2nd ed. (Scottsdale, AZ: Gorsuch Scarisbrick, 1995), 13–17.

5. Yerby, Buerkel-Rothfuss, and Bochner, *Understanding Family Communication,* 16.

6. C. Arthur VanLear, "Marital Communication Across the Generations: Learning and Rebellion, Continuity and Change," *Journal of Social and Personal Relationships* 9 (1992): 103–23.

7. Virginia Satir, *The New Peoplemaking* (Mountain View, CA: Science and Behavior Books, 1988), Chapter 2.

8. P. Day, E. Cole, M. Ramiu, A. Shotton, F. Gutterman, L. Graber, and P. Pratski, *Keeping Families Together: Resources in Cross-Sector Training on Reasonable Efforts* (Washington, DC: Child Welfare League of America, 1991).

9. David W. Murray, "Every Society is Threatened by the Disappearance of Legitimate Marriage," *Chronicle of Higher Education* (July 13, 1994), B5.

10. Sara Martin, "Today's Families are in Transition, Not Decline," *American Psychological Association Monitor* (October 1994), 18.

11. Murray, "Every Society is Threatened by the Disappearance of Legitimate Marriage."

12. Amy Swerdlow, Renate Bridenthal, Joan Kelly, and Phyllis Vine, *Families in Flex* (New York: The Feminist Press, 1989), 64.

13. F. Ivan Nye and Felix M. Berardo, *The Family: Its Structures and Interaction* (New York: Macmillan, 1973), 3.

14. Monica McGoldrick, "Ethnicity, Cultural Diversity, and Normality," in F. Walish (Ed.), *Normal Family Process* (New York: Guildford Press, 1973), 331.

15. Larry A. Samovar, Richard E. Porter, and Nemi C. Jain, *Understanding Intercultural Communication* (Belmont, CA: Wadsworth, 1981), 99–101.

16. Fathali M. Moghaddam, Donald M. Taylor, and Stephen C. Wright, *Social-Psychology in Cross-Cultural Perspective* (New York: W. H. Freeman, 1993), 98.

17. Jualyyne Dodson, "Conceptualizations of Black Families," in Hariette Pipes McAdoo (Ed.), *Black Families,* 2nd ed. (Newbury Park, CA: Sage, 1988).

18. Galvin and Brommel, *Family Communication: Cohesion and Change,* 109.

19. Alan L. Sillars, Cynthia S. Burggraf, S. Yost, and P. H. Zietlow, "Conversational Themes and

Marital Relationship Definitions: Quantitative and Qualitative Definitions," *Human Communication Research* 19 (1992): 124–54.

20. Larry A. Samovar and Richard E. Porter, *Communication between Cultures,* 2nd ed. (Belmont, CA: Wadsworth, 1995), 98.

21. Theodore Gochenour, *Considering Filipinos* (Yarmouth, ME: Intercultural Press, 1990), 19.

22. Samovar and Porter, *Communication between Cultures,* 130.

23. Serena Nanda, *Cultural Anthropology,* 5th ed. (Belmont, CA: Wadsworth, 1994), 137.

24. Based on questions from an activity developed by Thomas Gordon, in *Parent Effectiveness Training* (New York: New American Library, 1975).

25. Deborah Tannen, *You Just Don't Understand: Men and Women in Conversation* (New York: William Morrow, 1990), 44.

26. Moghaddam, Taylor, and Wright, *Social-Psychology in Cross-Cultural Perspective,* 125.

27. Nathan Murillo, "The Mexican Family," in Charrol A. Hernandez, Marshall J. Hang, and Nathaniel N. Wagner (Eds.), *Chicanos: Social and Psychological Perspectives* (Saint Louis, MO: C. V. Mosby, 1976), 19.

28. McGoldrick, "Ethnicity, Cultural Diversity, and Normality," 341.

29. Galvin and Brommel, *Family Communication,* 27–40; S. R. Marks, "Toward a Systems Theory of Marital Quality," *Journal of Marriage and the Family* 51.1 (1989): 15–26.

30. Different models of family development are available, each making different assumptions about what is "typical," and each taking into account different influencing variables, such as poverty and culture. See Pearson, *Communication in the Family: Seeking Satisfaction in Changing Times,* 171–268; Jack M. Richman, *Family Systems* (Chapel Hill, NC: North Carolina Family and Children's Resource Program, 1993); and Roy H. Rodgers and James M. White, "Family Development Theory," in Pauline G. Boss, William J. Doherty, Ralph LaRossa. Walter R. Schumm, and Suzanne K. Steinmetz (Eds.), *Sourcebook of Family Theories and Methods: A Contextual Approach* (New York: Plenum Press, 1993), 225–54.

31. Figure 10.1 is adapted from Richman, *Family Systems.*

32. John D. Cunningham and John K. Antill, "Current Trends in Nonmarital Cohabitation: In Search of the POSSLQ," in Julia T. Wood and Steve Duck (Eds.), *Under-Studied Relationships* (Thousand Oaks, CA: Sage, 1995), 148–72.

33. For a discussion and demystification of four myths regarding courtship—courtships follow similar pathways to marriages, courting partners idealize their relationship, people are naive about why they get married, and relationships begin anew at marriage—see Catherine A. Surra, Michelle L. Batchelder, and Debra K. Hughes, "Accounts and Demystification of Courtship," in Mary Anne Fitzpatrick and Anita L. Vangelisti (Eds.), *Explaining Family Interactions* (Thousand Oaks, CA: Sage, 1995), 112–41.

34. Darryl E. Owens, "Couples Who Are Childless by Choice Face Questions, Pressure," *Herald-Sun* [Durham, NC] (June 25, 1995): E2.

35. For example: Childless by Choice, a national network with a quarterly newsletter offering practical advice on the childless lifestyle; and The Childfree Network, a national support organization for couples childless by choice or by chance, which publishes a bimonthly newsletter.

36. Ted L. Huston and Anita L. Vangelisti, "How Parenthood Affects Marriage," in Mary Anne Fitzpatrick and Anita L. Vangelisti (Eds.), *Explaining Family Interactions* (Thousand Oaks, CA: Sage, 1995), 147–76.

37. Huston and Vangelisti, "How Parenthood Affects Marriage," 172.

38. Patricia Noller, "Parent-Adolescent Relationships," in Mary Anne Fitzpatrick and Anita L. Vangelisti (Eds.), *Explaining Family Interactions* (Thousand Oaks, CA: Sage, 1995), 106.

39. Mary-Louise Mares, "The Aging Family," in Mary Anne Fitzpatrick and Anita L. Vangelisti (Eds.), *Explaining Family Interactions* (Thousand Oaks, CA: Sage, 1995), 359.

40. B. Neugarten and K. K. Weinstein, "The Changing American Grandparent," *Journal of Marriage and the Family* 26 (1964): 119–204. In a more recent study, Cherlin and Furstenberg found that the most common activities grandparents engaged in with their grandchildren were joking, providing money, and watching television together. See A. J. Cherlin and F. F. Furstenberg, *The New American Grandparent: A Place in the Family, a Life Apart* (New York: Basic Books, 1986).

41. For a summary of studies on communication in the aging family, see Mares, "The Aging Family," 344–74.

42. Much of the material for this section is drawn from the Orange County (North Carolina) Task Force on Divorce, *Parenting After Divorce Workshop* (Orange County, NC: Author, 1991).

43. The typology comes from research summarized in C. R. Ahrons and R. H. Rodgers, *Divorced*

Families: A Multidisciplinary Developmental View (New York, W. W. Norton, 1987). Also see C. R. Ahrons and R. B. Miller, "The Effect of the Post-divorce Relationship on Parental Involvement: A Longitudinal Analysis," *American Journal of Orthopsychiatry* 63 (1993): 441–50.

44. Marilyn Coleman and Lawrence H. Ganong, "Family Reconfiguring Following Divorce," in Steve Duck and Julia T. Wood (Eds.), *Confronting Relationship Challenges* (Thousand Oaks, CA: Sage, 1995), 73–108; Sandra Metts and William R. Cupach, "Postdivorce Relations," in Mary Anne Fitzpatrick and Anita L. Vangelisti (Eds.), *Explaining Family Interactions* (Thousand Oaks, CA: Sage, 1995), 232–51.

45. Mares, "The Aging Family," 348–49.

46. Galvin and Brommel, *Family Communication,* 282–89.

47. David H. Olson, "Circumplex Model VII: Validation Studies and FACES III," *Family Processes* 25 (1986): 337–51.

48. The questionnaire is adapted from an early version of David H. Olson's FACES (Family Adaptability and Cohesion Evaluation Scales) instrument. For more information on the full instrument, as well as its validity and reliability, see Olson, "Circumplex Model VII: Validation Studies and FACES III"; and D. H. Olson, H. I. McCubbin, H. L. Barnes, A. S. Larsen, M. J. Muxen, and M. A. Wilson, *Families: What Makes Them Work* (Beverly Hills, CA: Sage, 1983).

49. Olson, "Circumplex Model VII: Validation Studies and FACES III."

50. Gail G. Whitchurch, "Linkages in Conjugal Violence and Communication: A Review and Critical Appraisal," paper presented at the third national Family Violence Conference for Researchers, Durham, NH, July 1987.

51. Noller, "Parent-Adolescent Relationships," 96.

52. Murray A. Straus, Stephen Sweet, and Yvonne M. Vissing, "Verbal Aggression Against Spouses and Children in a Nationally Representative Sample of American Families," paper presented at the annual meeting of the Speech Communication Association, San Francisco, November 18, 1989. This research is part of the Family Violence Research program of the Family Research Laboratory, University of New Hampshire, Durham, NH 03824, funded by the National Institute of Mental Health.

53. Susan Gano-Phillips and Frank D. Fincham, "Family Conflict, Divorce, and Children's Adjustment," in Mary Anne Fitzpatrick and Anita L. Vangelisti (Eds.), *Explaining Family Interactions* (Thousand Oaks, CA: Sage, 1995), 206–18.

54. Teresa Chandler, "Perceptions of Verbal and Physical Aggression in Interpersonal Violence," paper presented at the meeting of the Eastern Communication Association, Baltimore, April 1988.

55. This approach was developed by psychologist Michael Popkin in a video, "Active Parenting." For a summary of this approach, see Barbara Burtoff, "Family Pow-Wows," *Chronicle-Telegram* [Elyria, Ohio] (October 1985), B1.

56. There are many local and national organizations that offer families help. Calling a local social service agency, a mental health facility, city mental health departments, or consulting the yellow pages of a telephone book can lead to discovering resources. College campus student counseling centers, as well as hotlines, are additional resources. For an extended discussion of the procedures such help sources provide, see Galvin and Brommel, *Family Communication,* Chapter 14.

CHAPTER 11

MANAGING RELATIONAL DISCORD

COMMUNICATION COMPETENCIES

This chapter examines the process of managing relational discord. Specifically, the objective of the chapter is for you to learn to:

- Describe the three distinguishing features of conflict situations and use them to analyze your own conflicts.

- Recognize cultural differences in interpersonal conflict.

- Analyze the characteristics of your conflicts: your frustration, your interdependence with the person with whom you are in conflict, and the sources of your conflicts.

- Recognize the role that family, educational institutions, and the media play in forming views of conflict.

- Analyze the constructive and destructive consequences of your conflicts.

- Describe your conflict strategies and assess their advantages and disadvantages.

- Respond assertively in conflict situations.

- Describe gender differences in responses to conflict.

- Describe types of difficult people and how to deal with them.

- Describe general rules for conflict resolution with people from cultures different from your own.

- Assess the extent to which the process and outcomes of a conflict are functional.

KEY WORDS

The key words in this chapter are:

conflict
interpersonal conflict
intrapersonal conflict
avoidance
compromise
smoothing over
dominance
integration
win-lose conflict
    management
lose-lose conflict
    management
win-win conflict
    management
nonassertive behavior
indirect aggression
passive aggression
direct aggression
assertion
A*S*S*E*R*T formula
sexual harassment

Kevin and Serena, who are in their early twenties, have been married for nine months. Serena's parents were against the marriage, because they felt Kevin was immature. Kevin is aware of their feelings.

Kevin: Let's go out Friday night.

Serena: Where do you want to go?

Kevin: How about going to a movie?

Serena: OK, but I don't want to see one of your usual choices—a flick with lots of killing.

Kevin: What's the matter with action movies?

Serena: You're just trying to act macho by going to that kind of film.

Kevin: You think I have to act at being macho?

Serena: I didn't say that.

Kevin: I'm not man enough for you? You never complained before. I'm more a man than your wimpy father.

Serena: Of all the . . . why are you making nasty cracks about my dad?

Kevin: And your mother is no better, she's always nagging. I guess that's where you get it from!

Serena: You can just go out by yourself Friday night, and maybe forever, you jerk!

CONFLICT

When you think of the word *conflict,* what metaphors do you think of? If you are typical, you probably conjure up: "Conflict is war," "Conflict is explosive," or "Conflict is a game in which no one wins."

A **conflict** is any situation in which you perceive that another person, with whom you're interdependent, is frustrating or might frustrate the satisfaction of some concern, need, want, or desire of yours. The source of the conflict could be your perception of a limited resource (such as money) or an individual difference between you and the other person (such as differences in gender or differences in how you and the other person define your relationship).

You may believe that even better than a conflict that ends happily is no conflict at all. You may wish for, hope for, and even work for peace between nations, between groups within a nation, between individuals, and in your own relationships. How successful are you? Is peace—*real* peace, not merely a cease-fire—possible?

If you think about it, you'll probably see that the basic outline of a conflict situation—you want or need something, and you believe someone could keep you from getting what you want or need because his or her wants or needs are in opposition to yours—characterizes a great many interactions. Knowledge Checkup 11.1 will help you grasp the basic outline of all conflict situations by providing you with the opportunity to analyze the dialogue between Kevin and Serena.

Reread the Serena and Kevin scenario presented at the beginning of this chapter. Assuming you are Kevin, complete the following, using the information presented in that interchange.

1. I (Kevin) *want* (Kevin's concern, need, want) _____ *but* Serena (the other person) *wants* (Serena's concern, need, want) _____.
2. Describe how Serena and Kevin are interdependent in ways that affect the conflict.
3. Describe the possible sources of their conflict.

We boil at different degrees.
R. W. EMERSON

Complete the "I want . . . but . . . wants" for one of your important relational conflicts.

1. I *want* _____,
    but _____
    wants _____.
2. Describe the possible sources of the conflict you just related.

Your own experiences probably confirm that a conflict-free relationship between normal human beings is unlikely. Interpersonal problems are inevitable whenever two individuals participate in an ongoing relationship. The inevitability of conflict, however, shouldn't disturb you. In fact, conflict can play a positive role in healthy and growing relationships. And though conflict may be impossible to eliminate, it can be managed successfully with appropriate communication skills.

What do you do when you're involved in a conflict? Do you scream, cry, call names, throw things, hit walls or people? Do you stop talking, withdraw, glare at the other person, mutter hostile remarks under your breath? Do you try to reason things out, discuss the problem, seek solutions that satisfy both your needs and the needs of the other person? Do you behave differently in different conflicts?

CONFLICT AND CULTURE

Not all cultures perceive conflict in the same manner or employ the same methods for dealing with it. While "French and Arab men (not women) find argument stimulating,"[1] many Asians find it distasteful. In most of the Middle Eastern and Mediterranean

SALLY FORTH HOWARD & MACINTOSH

SALLY FORTH copyright © Howard & MacIntosh. Distributed by King Features Syndicate. Reprinted with special permission of King Features Syndicate.

cultures conflict is accepted as an important part of life. These cultures take great delight and pleasure in haggling and arguing. These arguments are often very heated and, if they don't take place, one or the other person may feel cheated. Haggling, for example, is expected when purchasing goods in many South American and Arabic cultures. North American tourists traveling to these areas have found that this haggling is so imbued in the interpersonal communication process that attempting to purchase something from a shopkeeper without negotiating may well lead to the person not selling them the desired item.

On the other hand, there is a Chinese proverb that states, "The first person to raise his voice loses the argument." People from conflict avoidance societies believe that the best way to deal with conflict is to handle it on their own without confronting the other person. They embrace the philosophy that face-to-face confrontations are to be avoided.[2] So strong is the notion of self-restraint in dealing with conflict that the Japanese have a word in their language (*wa*) that reminds their members that interpersonal harmony is essential. The Japanese believe that each of us comes to an encounter with this feeling of *wa* (harmony) already inside of us and that communication between people should foster this harmony, not disrupt it. This concept pervades nearly every aspect of Japanese life. People often wear surgical masks in public to keep from giving their colds to others. The words, "I am very sorry" (*soo-mee-mah-sehn*) are heard with great regularity. This aversion to conflict is even manifested in the Japanese legal system. In general, Japanese feel such distaste for using the court because of its combative nature that they try to resolve disputes without lawyers. In fact, it is estimated that the Japanese only have one lawyer for every 10,000 people, while in the United States, a culture that values assertive behavior, there is one lawyer for every 50 people.

CHARACTERISTICS OF CONFLICT

Although types of conflicts and responses to conflict vary, they all share, at least in North American culture, some common characteristics.[3]

Frustration

Conflict is a process that begins when you perceive that someone else has either frustrated some concern of yours, such as obtaining a goal, or is going to frustrate some concern of yours. For example:

I want *to borrow money,*
but *my friend* doesn't
want to *lend it to me.*

I want *to switch jobs with a coworker,*
but *the supervisor*
wants *people to stay in the jobs they were hired to do.*

I want *to go to a comedy club Friday night,*
but *my companion*
wants *to go to a concert.*

I want *my relationship partner and me to date each other exclusively,*
but *my relationship partner*
wants *to date other people.*

If you communicate your concern to the other person, you have an **interpersonal conflict,** a conflict between people. You tell your friend that you want to borrow money; you request the job swap from your supervisor; you tell your companion you want to go to the comedy club; you inform your relationship partner that you want the two of you not to date other people.

If you decide to resolve the conflict on your own, you have an **intrapersonal conflict,** a conflict within a person. Without talking to your friend, you may decide that your friend wouldn't lend you the money even if you asked for it. You may decide that the supervisor is too inflexible and that it wouldn't pay to ask about switching jobs. You may decide to keep your frustration about not being able to go where you want to go on Friday night because you fear you'll harm your relationship if you say something. You avoid telling your relationship partner about not dating other people because it may lead to a discussion about the nature of your relationship, and you fear that you will disagree with each other. However, in each situation, you are likely to communicate your frustration by being sarcastic with your friend, curt with your supervisor, withdrawn from your companion, or melancholy with your relationship partner. Recognizing that being sarcastic, curt, withdrawn, or melancholy does not resolve the problem (and is likely to add more problems) may motivate you to resolve the conflict interpersonally.

Interdependence

You and the other person in your "I want . . . but . . . wants . . ." example are *interdependent;* that is, you depend on each other and need each other in some way. Parents and children, workers and supervisors, and partners in a relationship all depend on each other for something, whether it's care, affection, goods, or services. Without interdependence, there is no interpersonal conflict.

If you need money and your friend has money, together you need to resolve the problem of scarce resources. If you were not friends, or if both of you had the money you needed—if you were not interdependent—there would be no conflict.

You and your supervisor need each other to solve the problem of how you can swap jobs with a coworker. If you both saw the job change in the same way, there would be no conflict.

You and your companion need each other to solve the problem of how to satisfy your control needs. If you did not care whether you spent the evening together or not, there would be no conflict.

You and your relationship partner need to resolve your differences in how you define your relationship. If you both defined your relationship the same way—as casual and non-exclusive or as serious and exclusive—there would be no conflict.

How are you and the other person in Knowledge Checkup 11.1 interdependent?

Sources of Conflict

The frustration that triggers your conflict has a source. Five common sources of conflict are limited resources, individual differences, cultural differences, differences in defining your relationship, and competition.[4]

Limited Resources   Limited resources are a widespread source of conflict. You may feel that any problem could be solved if there were more money (for example, selecting a college to attend would not be a source of conflict with your parents if there were unlimited funds available), time (you and your spouse would not have to argue about whether to see movie A or movie B if there were enough time to see both), space (storing last semester's books would not be a source of conflict with your roommate if your dormitory room were larger), equipment (you and your brother would not have to argue about who gets to use the telephone if there were two of them), or people to help (you and your boss would not have to argue about a job deadline if there were more people available to help). Money, time, space, equipment, and people are common limited resources that may trigger interpersonal conflicts.

Individual Differences   Individual differences are probably the most common and least often acknowledged source of conflict. Each person's perceptions of the world are uniquely her or his own, based on her or his past experiences, background, history, and interpretations of and responses to events. No two people view the same object or event in exactly the same way, and these perceptual differences may initiate conflicts.

Among the typical sources of frustration are individual differences in gender, attitudes, beliefs, values, experiences, upbringing, and education. For example, your supervisor may believe that not rocking the boat is an important goal and has little experience with training methods that differ from how he or she was trained ("You get a job and stay in it"). You might enjoy taking risks and have training in a variety of positions in the organization. The differences may not matter under most circumstances, but when you request to swap positions with a coworker, the stage is set for conflict.

Cultural Differences   Having just highlighted the possibility of individual experiences as a source of conflict, it is fitting to call your attention to the fact that cultural differences also can bring about conflict. Try to imagine the potential for conflict in a meeting where someone from the United States, who believes that "we should clear the air by getting everything off our chests," is interacting with someone from the Chinese culture who holds the belief that "social harmony is preserved when all the people in the social situation behave in a seemly manner."[5] Or what about a situation that finds some African Americans, whose communication style is "emotional, intense, dynamic, and enthusiastic,"[6] trying to communicate with a group of very reserved white North Americans? Again, the potential for conflict is present because of cultural differences.

Differences in Defining Your Relationship   The third general source of conflict stems from your view of your relationship: You and the other person may define your roles in the relationship differently, or you may define the relationship itself differently. For example, you may want to socialize with other people because you see your current relationship as unable to fulfill your needs; you view yourselves as steady but not serious or long-term partners. The other person may define the relationship as serious, and define your roles as intimate friends and prospective spouses. Under these circumstances, your desire to see other people triggers a conflict, one born of your different definitions of the relationship.

Competition

Competition is an inescapable fact of life. From the nursery to the nursing home, from the bedroom to the boardroom, in politics and business and school and sports and everyday conversation, human beings are in constant competition with each other. We compete for jobs, grades, social position, sex, friendship, money, power, even love. So pervasive is the competitive urge that it frequently governs our behavior even when we are unaware of its influence. From the time we were very small, it is a fundamental aspect of the process by which we develop our self-esteem, social assurance, our very identity.[7]

Not all cultures perceive conflict arising out of the same situations. An examination of "competition" is a vivid illustration of how culture and perception are linked. In cultures that do not value competition with the same intensity as North Americans do, there is less likelihood of conflict when competition does arise. In the Native American and Mexican cultures, for example, people seldom compete with the same aggressive attitude as do members of the predominant North American culture. People from these cultures are apt to withdraw rather than stand toe-to-toe and "slug it out." In fact, "assertive speech and behavior are a sign of discourtesy, restlessness, self-centeredness, and a lack of discipline."[8] This is one of the historical factors that caused the Native Americans, unlike their image as portrayed in old Hollywood cavalry movies, to be taken advantage of. The same is true of the Indian tribes in Mexico, especially the kind and trusting Mayans, as they met and dealt with their European invaders. This does not mean to imply that these cultures avoid conflict, but rather it underscores the notion that conflict and competition are defined differently by different cultures.

Look back at Kevin and Serena's interaction described at the beginning of the chapter, in which their conflict about going out on a Friday night ended when Serena told Kevin to go by himself, and consider what the source(s) of their conflict might be. Is the source limited resources (for example, there may be few choices of movies to see), individual differences (one may like action movies, and one may not), cultural differences (one may come from a culture that shuns violence, and the other may come from a culture that glorifies it), differences in defining their relationship (one may see their relationship as equal, and the other may see it as dominant-submissive), or competition (their interaction may be part of a game they play to see who can get the other person to give in)? Or is it some combination of sources that triggers their conflict?

What about the sources of the conflict you described in Knowledge Checkup 11.1? What are the sources of this conflict? Why did you select these causes?

PERCEPTIONS OF CONFLICT

Can you think of a situation in which limited resources, individual differences, cultural differences, differences in definitions of the relationship, or competition do not exist? Such a situation would require individuals who were identical in their concerns, wants, needs, desires, attitudes, beliefs, values, cultures, goals, and perceptions of the other person and the relationship. Even identical twins raised in the same household are not that similar.

Given that no two people are identical, it follows that conflict is natural and inevitable. A comic strip expressed the normality of conflict this way: Cathy (in the syndicated cartoon of the same name), talking to several of her coworkers, says, "I want just one normal week. Is that so much to ask? Just one normal week where I have normal non-hysterical work days, and come home to normal non-crisis-point relationships." One of her coworkers tells her, "I've *never* had a week like that," and another says, "Me neither." She responds, "Me neither" and, addressing the reader, adds: "Why does the one experience no one has ever had keep seeming like the normal one?"[9]

The answer to Cathy's question requires a look at three main socializing agents: the family, educational institutions, and the media.

FAMILY

Perceptions of conflict are based on your early experiences with your family. How was conflict between your parents treated? Was it something to do openly, in front of you and your siblings, or was it something to be hidden behind closed doors late at night? Was it handled in productive ways so that the outcomes were positive, or were most conflicts screaming bouts followed by periods of cool silence? "Don't fight in front of the children" may be a norm in many families, but the message it communicates is that conflict is wrong, unfit for children.

As conflicts rage around you (whether conducted quietly or not), you may have been taught: "Don't fight with your sister/brother!" "If you don't have something nice to say, don't say anything at all!" "Don't talk back!" "Real friends don't fight!" The intended point of these messages is the same: Conflict is unnatural, something that good people who like each other don't do. But these messages are pitted against reality: People who love each other *do* fight, just as siblings and spouses who really care for each other do.

"And they lived happily ever after" is a phrase common to fairy tales, not real relationships between real people. Adopting the fairy tale version of life can create frustration for yourself and your partner. Yet people are inclined to ask, "What's wrong with us that we fight?" rather than reject the unrealistic and unattainable fairy tale ending.

EDUCATIONAL INSTITUTIONS

The message about conflict that you learn in educational institutions probably is similar to the one you learned at home: Conflict is bad. In elementary grades, a fight with a classmate may mean being sent to the principal and possibly having your parents called in for a conference. Instead of teaching youngsters how to deal constructively with their conflicts—how to define their problems and communicate their feelings and needs to each other to find mutually satisfactory resolutions— schools typically punish children for perfectly understandable and predictable behavior.

Because open conflicts between teachers and students are forbidden, more subtle expressions of discord prevail. Instructors and students and bosses and workers often exchange *bristle statements,* comments that each knows probably will trigger the other's anger. For example, an instructor may tell a student, "It's in the book—try reading it," or "No one forced you to take this course," while a student may ask, "Are we doing anything important in class today?" or "Do spelling and grammar count?" A boss may tell a worker, "You've been working here long enough to know that," or "We don't do it that way here," while a worker may say, "My last boss gave me a lot of useful feedback," or "If I had the right equipment I could do the job right." Each attacks the other in ways that sidestep the issue. Educational institutions teach students to fight dirty when conflicts are perceived as dirty.

MEDIA

Conflict is dramatic. Because of this, it has inherent excitement and interest value. It is not surprising (indeed, it could hardly be otherwise without risking boring the audience) that movies and television programs present us with both subtle and not-so-subtle conflicts. Obvious and violent conflict is available for viewing in war movies, science fiction, and movies about families, such as *The War of the Roses* (in which, under the guise of a comedy, we get the opportunity to watch a married couple, the Roses, battle each other to death). Television programs, even when not violent, present conflicts over scarce resources (for example, the ever-popular "cattle ranchers versus sheep herders in the quest for grazing land"), cultural differences (a familiar plot device on *Star Trek* and its many spin-offs), differences in defining the relationship (a common theme in almost every plot and subplot of every soap opera), and competition (a popular subject on all dramas, including *Saved by the Bell,* aimed specifically at young school-age children). Of course, there are more conflicts to watch in a few hours of Saturday morning cartoons than most people experience personally in a lifetime.

How many movies have you seen in your life (in the movie theaters, on videocassette, on television)? How much television do you watch now, and how much did you watch when you were younger? You may have spent more hours watching television than you have spent in school, and you probably have learned more about day-to-day life from the tube than from your teachers. What are conflicts like in most of the programs you watch? In half-hour programs, you see complex problems being solved in twenty-four minutes plus commercials. In one-hour programs, even more complex problems get resolved in about fifty minutes plus commercials. But real life is not made up of half-hour and one-hour segments. Nor is real-life made up of what happens in movies, comic books, and Saturday morning cartoons.

Your own life is not realistically portrayed on television, so when your conflicts fail to conform to television-style conflicts and resolutions, you probably assume that something is wrong with you. "What's wrong with me, and what's wrong with us, that our conflicts last for a long time, rarely end neatly, and aren't as glamorous or as gloriously dramatic as the conflicts on TV?" Television may embody the modern fairy tale that, in the end, everybody but the villain lives happily ever after, but is this reality?

CONSEQUENCES OF CONFLICT

Your early experiences no doubt introduced you to many of the negative consequences of conflict, and they may have persuaded you that conflict is something to be avoided. But conflict also may have positive consequences that benefit your work, your relationships, your personal life, and your health.

EFFECTS ON WORK

Conflict is dysfunctional when it keeps you from doing your work. It takes time and energy to engage in or avoid a conflict. Also, an unresolved conflict requires a great deal of thought about who said what, when, and how, as well as what caused the conflict and what can be done about it. When you have a conflict on your mind, reading one page of a textbook may take an hour, concentrating on a lecture may be difficult, and dealing with a customer may be almost impossible.

Conflict also may be dysfunctional when it forces conformity. If you fear that open conflict may lead to public ridicule, blame, or harsh punishment, you are likely to accept

whatever happens and keep your frustrations to yourself in order to avoid the harassment.

In contrast, conflict is functional when it increases your motivation to interact with the person causing your frustration, to discuss the areas of conflict, and to arrive at new and better solutions to the problem. Conflict often yields results when heightened excitement and interaction get channeled into communication that focuses on resolution.

EFFECTS ON RELATIONSHIPS

Conflicts are dysfunctional when they threaten the integrity of a relationship. Given that as many as half the marriages in the United States end in divorce, conflicts obviously threaten and destroy relationships.[10] If two persons perceive that an important problem cannot be resolved within the confines of their relationship, they may terminate the relationship. Indeed, even if a relationship is not terminated, research has found that wives and husbands who believe that conflicts and disagreements are healthy report greater marital satisfaction than those who view them as unhealthy.[11]

Conflicts are functional when they promote relationship growth, which can happen in two ways. First, *conflicts require negotiation about how to negotiate.* How will you and your partner communicate your thoughts and feelings? How will you agree on a solution? As you answer these questions you develop new strategies for interacting with each other.

Second, *conflicts require the exchange of new information about the subject of the dispute.* Information about each person's needs, wants, desires, and goals is necessary to generate and select a mutually satisfactory solution to the problem. Acquiring and using new strategies for interacting, plus gaining and using new information, equal relational growth.

PERSONAL EFFECTS

A conflict is dysfunctional when it leaves you feeling foolish, inadequate, or cruel. Insults such as "You're stupid," whether you say them or someone says them to you, are personally destructive. If you say them, they testify to your cruelty; if someone says them to you, they prompt self-doubt and feelings of inadequacy, or possibly fury.

Think about conflicts you have had with your parents, siblings, companions, and friends. Which of these phrases (or similar ones) did you use? Which of these phrases did they use?

"You're stupid!"

"I hate you!"

"You're just like your father/mother/sister/brother!"

"I wish you were dead!"

"If you loved me you wouldn't . . ."

"You think that's a problem? That's nothing!"

"If you'd do it my way . . ."

"I told you so!"

"Your problem is easy to trace: poor toilet training!"

"Why do you always . . . ?"

"Can't you ever do anything right?"

"For an idiot, that's a good answer!"

"That's ridiculous!"

"You're ridiculous!"

In contrast, functional conflicts increase your self-understanding and feelings of self-worth. You learn about yourself, how you view certain issues, and how strongly you feel about them. You also increase your ability to see life through someone else's eyes, to understand how others think and feel about issues that are important to them.

HEALTH EFFECTS

Conflicts are dysfunctional when they endanger your health. From personal experience you most likely have learned that your body, as well as your mind, suffers when the conflict is vehement and fierce (for example, conflict between parents is most stressful to a child when, among other things, it is frequent and intense[12]). The link between conflict and health, while complex in medical terms, is really quite simple. Your immune system is burdened with the momentous task of keeping you healthy by recognizing and destroying foreign material, such as bacteria, viruses, fungi, and tumors. When an unpleasant stimulus, such as conflict, is perceived, your body chemistry is altered. Your immune system, instead of keeping your body in balance, is effected. Your lungs, heart, and stomach are not independent, autonomous organs. Your entire body is interconnected. Consequently, when your emotions are upset, so is your whole body. Dysfunctional conflict floods your body with adrenaline, speeds up your heart, and activates the immune system, opening you up for illnesses such as ulcers, heart disease, and the common cold.

Conflicts that are functional can actually contribute to your health. The freedom to express yourself in a nonantagonistic and nonhostile manner can often keep you from brooding over an issue until it makes you ill. In the United States, "clearing the air" often has a positive and therapeutic effect.

Knowledge Checkup 11.2 will help you recognize the work, relationship, personal, and health consequences of a conflict with which you are familiar.

Knowledge Checkup 11.2
CONFLICT CONSEQUENCES

Choose a novel you've read or a movie or television show you've seen that focuses on personal or family relationships.

1.   Describe one of the major conflicts portrayed.

2. Describe the negative consequences of the conflict on:
   a. work
   b. relationships
   c. personal feelings of adequacy
   d. health

3. Describe the positive consequences on:
   a. work
   b. relationships
   c. personal feelings of adequacy
   d. health

4. What conclusions could you draw from your analysis of conflict portrayed in this one novel, movie, or television program?

CONFLICT STRATEGIES

You learned early in life how to respond to conflicts. The strategies you now use developed during your interactions with parents and siblings, teachers and classmates, and friends and enemies. Your responses to conflict are probably automatic, which poses a problem: Automatic responses are difficult to recognize, yet you must recognize them before change is possible.

When your needs seem incompatible with other people's needs, how do you react? What strategies do you use to resolve your conflicts? Knowledge Checkup 11.3 will help you increase your awareness of the conflict strategies you use.

Knowledge Checkup 11.3
YOUR CONFLICT STRATEGIES[13]

Think of a relationship you have with someone with whom you interact regularly (for example, a parent, sibling, roommate, close friend, wife, husband, or lover), and with whom you engage in conflict. How do you usually respond to your conflict with this person? In each pair below, circle the **A** or **B** statement which is most characteristic of your behavior. In some cases, neither answer may be very typical of your behavior. If this happens, select the response which you would be more likely to use.

1. A. There are times when I let others take responsibility for solving the problem.
   B. Rather than negotiate the things on which we disagree, I try to stress those things upon which we both agree.

2. A. I try to find a compromise solution.
   B. I attempt to deal with all of the other person's and my concerns.

3. A. I am usually firm in pursuing my goals.
   B. I might try to soothe the other's feelings and preserve our relationship.

4. A. I try to find a compromise solution.
   B. I sometimes sacrifice my own wishes for the wishes of the other person.

5. A. I consistently seek the other's help in working out a solution.
   B. I don't worry about my own concerns if satisfying them means damaging the relationship.

6. A. I try to avoid creating unpleasantness for myself.
   B. I try to win my position.

7. A. I try to postpone the issue until I have had some time to think it over.
   B. I give up some points in exchange for others.

8. A. I am usually firm in pursuing my goals.
   B. I attempt to get all concerns and issues immediately out in the open.

9. A. I feel that differences are not always worth worrying about.
   B. I try to integrate my concerns with the other person's concerns.

10. A. I am firm in pursuing my goals.
    B. I try to find a compromise solution.

11. A. I attempt to get all concerns and issues immediately out in the open.
    B. I might try to soothe the other's feelings and preserve our relationship.

12. A. I sometimes avoid taking positions which would create controversy.
    B. I will let the other person have some of his or her positions if the person lets me have some of mine.

13. A. I propose a middle ground.
    B. I press to get my points made.

14. A. I tell the other person my ideas and ask for his or hers.
    B. I try to show the other person the logic and benefits of my position.

15. A. I might try to soothe the other's feelings and preserve our relationship.
    B. I try to do what is necessary to avoid tensions.

Scoring

For question 1, circle the **A** or **B** according to your answer; for question 2, circle the **A** or **B** according to your answer. Repeat the process for all fifteen questions.

	D	**I**	**C**	**A**	**S**
1.				A	B
2.		B	A		
3.	A				B
4.			A		B
5.		A			B

	D	I	C	A	S
6.	B			A	
7.			B	A	
8.	A	B			
9.		B		A	
10.	A		B		
11.		A			B
12.			B	A	
13.	B		A		
14.	B	A			
15.				B	A

Number of **A**s and **B**s circled in column D (**D**ominance) _____

Number of **A**s and **B**s circled in column I (**I**ntegration) _____

Number of **A**s and **B**s circled in column C (**C**ompromise) _____

Number of **A**s and **B**s circled in column A (**A**voidance) _____

Number of **A**s and **B**s circled in column S (**S**moothing Over) _____

On which of the five strategies did you score highest and on which did you score lowest? You may use different strategies in different situations, and you may start a conflict with one strategy and use another if it fails (for example, if you start with a dominance strategy, you may switch to a compromise strategy if the dominance strategy fails to help you achieve your goals), but the odds are that you have a favorite strategy that you use whether or not it is most appropriate for the situation. In order to understand and evaluate your conflict strategies, you need to know your typical responses to conflict so that you can examine their appropriateness and make decisions about their use. If you understand which strategy is best for a given conflict, you can increase the range of your responses and, therefore, react more effectively.

Each of the five conflict strategies balances differing amounts of self-satisfaction and concern for the other person (see Figure 11.1). Being too concerned with the other person's welfare may leave your own needs unsatisfied, while concern only for yourself may seem self-aggrandizing, even if you do get what you want. Each strategy has advantages and disadvantages that must be weighed against the demands of the situation: No one strategy suits every situation.[14]

Your strategies for dealing with conflict echo both your individual personality and your cultural background, as well as characteristics of your relationship, such as its intimacy.[15] These strategies are reflected in the manner in which you communicate. For instance, in Asian cultures, where people seek to avoid direct face-to-face conflict,

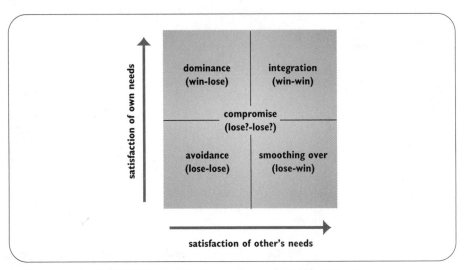

FIGURE 11.1 **Conflict Strategies and Need Satisfaction**

communication strategies usually include cautious and indirect speech, taking time to sense another's mood before venturing an opinion, and avoiding disagreement in the presence of other people.[16]

AVOIDANCE AND COMPROMISE

Avoidance, also called *denial* or *withdrawal,* is a strategy based on the assumption that a conflict will just go away if it is ignored. Only rarely, however, does a conflict permanently go away, so people who use this strategy must worry that their conflict will recur.

What was your avoidance score on Knowledge Checkup 11.3? Was it your highest or lowest score of the five conflict strategy scores? A high score, in comparison to the others, indicates that this is your typical strategy, and a low score indicates that this is an atypical strategy for you.

The biggest problem with avoidance strategy is that neither your needs nor the other person's needs are satisfied. Though you may be able to persuade yourself that your needs are unimportant, you will likely find out differently in time. You can intellectually reject the issue as trivial, but your body may respond with stress-related disorders, such as headaches and ulcers.

Of course, avoidance sometimes is an appropriate response to a conflict. If neither the conflict issue nor your relationship with the other person is very important to you, withdrawal may be a reasonable strategy (but don't fool yourself about the true importance of these two variables). Also, it may be appropriate when the odds of satisfying your concerns are very low. In addition, this strategy can usefully reduce tension in a conflict long enough for a different, more productive and longer-lasting approach to be found.

Avoidance is a popular technique for dealing with conflict in many cultures. The Japanese and Chinese cultures, for example, encourage avoidance instead of confrontation. And they are not alone in their disdain for conflict: Research indicates that Mexican and Mexican-American individuals also tend to avoid conflict or deny that it exists.[17]

While no satisfaction of anyone's needs is the usual outcome of avoidance, some satisfaction of each person's needs is the goal of compromise. **Compromise,** also called *bargaining* or *negotiating,* is a sharing strategy designed to satisfy everyone's concerns to some extent. The aim is to give up something to gain something. Compromise usually does not permanently resolve conflicts, but it may be useful as a stop-gap measure.

What was your compromise score on Knowledge Checkup 11.3? A high score, in comparison to the others, indicates that this is your typical strategy, and a low score indicates that this is an atypical strategy for you.

Compromise is a popular conflict strategy because people generally believe that something is better than nothing. If the odds of getting your needs fully satisfied are slight, or if the end result may be no satisfaction at all, a little satisfaction may seem a worthy goal. The problem with compromise, however, is that people rarely negotiate in good faith. Because they assume that they'll have to give in a little, they inflate their demands. And because they assume that something is better than nothing, they are willing to compromise on matters that are truly important to them and thus should not be conceded. If both persons operate on the assumption that honesty may not be the best policy, they try to deceive each other by arguing for irrelevant issues that they can later relinquish as bargaining chips. For example, union negotiators often include extraneous items in their list of demands so that they can seem to be giving something up when they withdraw those items from negotiation.

Finally, working out a fair compromise requires communication skills that may be too advanced for many people. For example, you need to communicate exactly what your concerns are and what you are and are not willing to give up. You also need to listen actively to determine how the other person's concerns do and do not conflict with your own.

If your goal and your relationship are both moderately important to you, compromise may be an appropriate conflict strategy, but the importance of these two variables and the level of both individuals' communication skills are crucial determinants.

Avoidance and compromise are **lose-lose** approaches to conflict: Neither your goals nor the other person's goals are fully satisfied. There may be some gain, but often something important is also lost. Of course, if, with compromise, needs are satisfied enough, the lose-lose approach turns into a lose?-lose? one. For example, a couple arguing about whether to dine at a Mexican restaurant or a Chinese one may compromise and eat Italian food, although neither really was in the mood for it; however, if the couple enjoys the Italian food enough, "lose-lose" turns into "lose?-lose?"

SMOOTHING OVER AND DOMINANCE

A **smoothing over** strategy, also called an *obliging* or *self-suppression* strategy, shows concern for the other person but not for yourself. This strategy aims to satisfy the other person's concerns to the neglect of your own. It grows out of the notions that "nice people don't fight" and "if you don't have something nice to say, then don't say anything."

What was your smoothing over score on Knowledge Checkup 11.3? A high score, in comparison to the others, indicates that this is your typical strategy, and a low score indicates that this is an atypical strategy for you.

Smoothing over is often used as a delaying tactic, to keep things peaceful until the conflict goes away. However, because your needs have been subverted, the conflict does not go away. Just like people who avoid open conflict or achieve unsuccessful compromises, people who smooth things over must always worry that the problem will recur.

A smoothing strategy does suit some conflicts. If your concern is really unimportant to you and if maintaining your relationship with the other person is very important, smoothing over may be effective (but once again, an honest assessment of the importance of these two factors is crucial).

Dominance, also called *power* or *forcing,* is the reverse of smoothing over: It focuses on your own needs at the expense of the other person's. Your ability to dominate the other person may come from your position (you may be the supervisor, the parent, or the person with the needed information), your physical size or strength, or your control of rewards and punishments. "Do what I want or else!" is a common threat from those who try to use dominance to solve their problems.

What was your dominance score on Knowledge Checkup 11.3? A high score, in comparison to the others, indicates that this is your typical strategy, and a low score indicates that this is an atypical strategy for you.

The primary problem with this strategy is that, while your own needs may be satisfied, those of the other person remain unsatisfied, which will likely breed resentment, hostility, and a desire for revenge. For example, a mother who refuses to give her teenage son the car when he needs it may satisfy her need to use the car herself or her need to confirm that she's in charge, but her son is likely to retaliate by refusing to cooperate in some future situation.

There are times when a dominating strategy is appropriate. For example, an emergency situation may call for quick and decisive action, and discussion may make matters worse. When a small child runs into a busy street, you must return her to the sidewalk quickly. You and the child may have incompatible goals and both feel frustrated, but the circumstance requires a dominating strategy to avoid disaster.

On the whole, however, a dominating strategy is rarely the best one. It should be used only if your goal is very important to you and if your relationship with the other person is of little or no importance. Remember that once you create a situation with you as the winner and the other person as the loser, you probably also create an enemy.

Both smoothing over and dominance are **win-lose** approaches to conflict, where one person wins and the other loses. If your goal is to win and have the other person lose, you use a dominance strategy, and if your goal is to lose and have the other person win, you use a smoothing over strategy.

People often use the win-lose approach to conflict management even when it isn't necessary. Most of the conflicts you observed or participated in while growing up were probably treated as win-lose. For example, television programs stress the hero-villain conflict, with the hero almost always winning. Sports stress the bottom line: The team that scores the most points wins. Promotions at work may be limited to a select few: Some get ahead, some don't. At home, conflicts with siblings and spouses are often win-lose: You get to watch the television program you want and your brother doesn't, you turn down your radio so that your roommate can study, though you don't want to, and the cookie you want goes to your guest. Even our political system, majority rule, is a win-lose approach to conflict management. One candidate wins, the other loses; one party comes into power, the other waits in the wings until it wins.

The unequal power that distinguishes win-lose conflicts tends to damage relationships. Power may take the form of physical force, control over rewards and punishments, or cunning. For example, if you want to study but your friend wants to watch television, you might threaten physical violence: "Shut that off or you're dead meat"; threaten the loss of a reward: "You're not going to get any help from me when you're short of time on your project"; threaten a nonphysical punishment: "Shut it off or I'll watch television the next time you want to study"; or use cunning to get your way: "It's okay if you watch television while I study—it doesn't distract me too much [sigh]."

In some cases—when resources are limited and only one person or group can succeed, for instance—a win-lose approach to managing conflict is appropriate. For these situations, the interaction is competitive, not cooperative. For example, only one person can get the newly purchased computer.

A win-lose approach is also appropriate when the person with whom you're in conflict chooses it. Sometimes another person ignores your repeated invitations to approach a conflict cooperatively and instead insists on being competitive. You must then decide whether to accept the win-lose approach and attempt to win, to be the loser, or to change the situation so that your needs will be met in another way. For example, when you pull into a gas station, if someone pulls in alongside you and takes the pump you planned on using, you can argue over your right to use the pump because you pulled in first, you can brood while you wait for the latecomer to finish using the pump, or you can use another pump.

Finally, a win-lose approach is appropriate when the other person is clearly behaving improperly. Few would disagree that drunk drivers, people trying to carry weapons aboard planes, and child abusers should all be restrained.

Usual Outcomes of Lose-Lose and Win-Lose Conflicts

Win-lose and lose-lose approaches to managing relationship discord are more common than an approach in which everyone wins. As a result, the outcomes of most conflicts are dysfunctional and negative.

In a typical conflict, *people rarely give in since their egos are at stake.* Rather than admit that the other person may be right, they try to reconceptualize the problem or the issues. By saying, "Oh, that's what you mean. Well, that's different," people can save face by claiming that there really was no conflict in the first place. In the absence of such face-saving devices, the conflict may rage on indefinitely.

In a typical conflict, *biases are obvious and selfishness predominates.* You see yourself as "good" and the other as "bad," yourself as "trustworthy" and the other as "deceitful," yourself as "open" and the other as "sneaky." Even if one person tries to be cooperative (and in almost every conflict, each person makes bids for cooperation), the other person ignores the attempt. Cooperative behavior from a "bad, sneaky, deceitful" person is not deemed credible.

In a typical conflict, *tactics become more coercive* as the discord persists. Because you see the other person as bad, your trust decreases and your suspicion increases. You tell yourself, "The only way to deal with this untrustworthy sneak is to force him to do what I want."

In a typical conflict, *the original issue gets lost and the conflict spreads to other issues.* Although the source of the problem gets lost in the struggle, new issues, such as hurt feelings and resentment, arise; the conflict spreads to new areas: "If I can't trust you to file the papers when I ask you to [the original issue], how can I trust you to organize the files [a seemingly related issue] or type the necessary letters [an unrelated issue]?"

In a typical conflict, *you and the other person grow apart as human beings,* lose the ability to communicate with each other as individuals, and see each other only as roles or symbols. A police officer who stops you after you go through a red light may change from "Officer Long," a unique individual (whom you met when he came to your house to investigate a break-in), to "officer," a role; to "cop," a negative term for the role; and, finally, to "pig," an animal symbolizing disrespect for law enforcement officials. Of course, you can't reason with a "pig," so productive communication ceases.

At the end of a typical lose-lose or win-lose conflict, *neither you nor the other person gets exactly what you want* (even though it may seem so in the short run), the possibility for a continuing relationship is damaged, and neither of you has positive self-feelings. A more productive way to managing relationship discord is the win-win approach.

INTEGRATION

Unlike the lose-lose strategies avoidance and compromise, and the win-lose strategies dominance and smoothing over, **integration,** also referred to as *collaboration* and *problem solving,* has as its goal the full satisfaction of your own and the other person's concerns. By definition alone, this strategy may seem to be the best one, but it has limited usefulness. If the goal and the relationship are both very important, integration may be the most appropriate strategy to employ. However, in most cases, either the concern or the relationship is not very important, or both are of only moderate importance.

What was your integration score on Knowledge Checkup 11.3? A high score, in comparison to the others, indicates that this is your typical strategy, and a low score indicates that this is an atypical strategy for you.

Besides taking the most time, an integrating strategy requires the widest range of well-developed communication skills. For example, you must be able to self-disclose openly and honestly about your own needs and to listen actively to the disclosures of the other person. You must be able to see the problem from the other person's perspective and integrate that perspective with your own. You must integrate your needs with the other person's needs to be able to generate creative and mutually satisfying solutions. You must also realize that the issues at stake in the conflict are more important than the contestants' egos.

Integration is a **win-win** approach to conflict that recognizes the importance of both the issue and the participants; neither person gives up something crucial and neither one feels that the relationship was damaged by the conflict management process or its outcomes. Success hinges on dedication to the win-win process and to the other person, mutual respect, and strong communication skills. Although true win-win conflict management is sometimes difficult to carry out, the results justify the effort.

The steps in win-win conflict management follow.

STEP 1: Define the conflict for yourself before approaching the other person.   This requires some self-analysis: What is your concern? Who or what is frustrating you? What is the source of conflict?

Once you understand the conflict from your perspective, approach the other person and agree on a time to talk. Don't spring the conflict on the other person without warning or bring it up when there isn't enough time to deal with it. If the other person feels attacked, he or she may become defensive, which will make it difficult for you to establish a supportive climate. Also, agree on an appropriate place for your discussion. Certain locations may inhibit open and honest interaction. Attempting to deal with conflict in a public place, such as a restaurant, virtually assures failure.

STEP 2: Communicate your understanding of the problem assertively to the other person.   This approach includes describing the other person's behaviors as they affect you in a direct, clear, nonjudgmental way. You must also communicate your interpretation of the situation and your feelings.

Once your own concerns are clear, invite the other person to express her or his concerns. Listen carefully to the content of the message and try to perceive the feelings that accompany it. Share your perceptions of the other person's point of view without labels ("That's stupid!") or insults ("You're crazy!"). Be sure you can state your partner's perspective to her or his satisfaction. Then reverse the process and encourage your partner to reiterate your point of view to your satisfaction.

When you complete this step, both you and your partner will have defined the problem specifically, described your feelings, and recounted the actions that led to the conflict and perpetuated it.

STEP 3: Based on your understanding of your own and the other's perspective, arrive at a mutual, shared definition of the problem and a mutual, shared goal.   Consider your areas of agreement and disagreement; figure out how you're dependent on one another. Discuss the consequences of the conflict for each of you.

STEP 4: Communicate your cooperative intentions.   Let your partner know that your aim is to satisfy the needs of both of you and to achieve your shared goals and that you do not want to win either by being competitive or by simply giving in. If you can (and it may

---

When all think alike, then no one is thinking.
WALTER LIPPMANN

be difficult under stressful conditions), communicate your intention in a calm, firm voice and invite your partner to join you in being cooperative.

Successful conflict resolution is impossible unless both you and your partner are motivated to behave cooperatively. If your partner is reluctant to cooperate, you may want to discuss what each of you gets out of continuing the conflict. Perhaps the conflict gives you something to complain about or an excuse to end the relationship. Or perhaps you feel threatened because a solution to your shared problem will require changes in your behavior. Whatever the reasons, they must be recognized and overcome before you can proceed.

STEP 5: Generate solutions to your shared problem.   Avoid discussing or evaluating each solution as it is generated; instead, generate as many ideas as you can. If you and your partner agree to defer evaluation, the number of possible solutions should be high. Be spontaneous and creative and build on each other's suggestions. Remember that even a foolish-sounding solution may contain a shred of useful information.[18]

STEP 6: After you've suggested all the solutions you can think of, evaluate them and select the best one.   How might each solution satisfy the shared goal? How easy or difficult would each be to implement?

STEP 7: Implement the solution.   First, be sure that you and your partner truly agree on which solution to implement. Make sure that you both agree fully and that you're not agreeing because you're tired, because you want to please your partner, or for some other reason that will later undermine the solution.

Second, agree on who does what, when, and how. If you don't specify the particulars, the groundwork may well be laid for the next conflict.

Third, do what needs to be done.

STEP 8: Plan to check on how the solution is working.   You may have to adjust your plan or scrap the solution and generate a new one. The need for modification is a predictable consequence of changes brought on by time and an inability to foresee all possible outcomes during the initial problem-solving stage.

Although this eight-step procedure takes a great amount of work, it pays off: in the end, both you and your partner will get what you want, strengthen your relationship, and feel good about yourselves. Furthermore, in the long run, the win-win approach takes less effort than do the lose-lose or win-lose approaches. Most importantly, the win-win approach lets you productively confront the problem—you don't have to let it fester unresolved. Win-lose and lose-lose approaches require repeated attempts to resolve the problems they themselves create, while the win-win approach usually gets at the problem and eliminates it.

NONASSERTION, DIRECT AGGRESSION, AND ASSERTION

The five conflict resolution strategies—avoidance, compromise, dominance, smoothing over, and integration—differ in the extent to which you make your concerns known to the other person. With avoidance and smoothing over strategies you may fail to communicate your concerns at all; with a dominance strategy you are sure to communicate your concerns, but in a way that will probably hurt your relationship; and with an integration style you communicate your concerns—and listen to the other person's concerns— with respect. A useful framework for looking at conflict strategies considers if and how each relationship partner's concerns are communicated.

NONASSERTION

Reluctance to communicate your feelings and thoughts characterizes **nonassertive behavior.** Linked with avoidance and smoothing over conflict strategies, nonassertive behavior virtually ensures that your concerns go unsatisfied, unless you are lucky or the other person takes pity on you. A nonassertive person will fail to take action or will take action with someone completely uninvolved in the conflict. For example, you would be nonassertive if you received an incorrect bill from the gas company but, instead of demanding a correction, you paid the bill and said nothing or complained to a friend about the unfairness of big business. Neither course of action informs the gas company that there is a problem.

Nonassertive communicators often defend their behavior by saying, "It wasn't the best time [or place] to talk," or "I didn't think the other person was ready to hear what I wanted to say," or "They won't like me if I say what's on my mind." Such excuses normally have nothing to do with the actual situation; they merely justify avoiding an unpleasant exchange or a possible confrontation.

Several nonverbal cues tend to accompany nonassertiveness, including rapid eye blinking, avoiding eye contact, squinting, repeated swallowing, throat clearing, tightening or pursing the lips, tensing and wrinkling the forehead, covering the mouth while speaking, shifting weight from foot to foot, nervous giggling, and preening behaviors, such as hair smoothing, beard stroking, and fingernail cleaning. All of these are the body's way of displaying nonverbal signs of internal distress.

Some theorists divide nonassertiveness into two categories: nonconfrontation and indirect aggression. In this approach, *nonconfrontation* is the same as what has been described as nonassertion, while **indirect** or **passive aggression** is the expression of concerns in a disguised way. Rather than stating the real issue, you attack or embarrass the other person or attempt to manipulate the situation in various ways. These include:

- Attacking the other person directly but avoiding the real issue (you receive a grade of D on a paper and, bursting into the professor's office, tell her, "I think you're a lousy teacher!");
- Attacking the person indirectly ("What was your curve for the grades on the last set of papers?");
- Lying about your real feelings ("I've thought about the D you gave me, and I really think I deserved it.");
- Manipulating the situation ("I know you don't believe in extra credit assignments, but if I do another paper on the same topic, will you read it and give me your comments?");

- Embarrassing the person ("My lack of ability to write reflects your lack of ability to teach!");
- Hinting about the problem ("Do you think I can still get an A in your course?");
- Withholding something from the other person—some service, compliance with a request, or courtesy ("I forgot to pick up the papers that you wanted to give out in class today");
- Inviting the person to feel guilty ("No, no, it's okay if you give me a D and I lose my scholarship"[19]);
- Using sarcasm ("You want me to write better papers? Great advice coming from a teacher with ten typos on a two-page exam!").

Indirect aggression is risky for several reasons. First, because you communicate your concerns indirectly, the other person may miss the point. Second, even if the other person understands your message, she or he may decide to ignore it because your indirectness offers a ready excuse: "I didn't know what you wanted." Third, indirect aggression is risky because people who feel manipulated often respond angrily. Even if the other person does what you want, the relationship may be damaged and future conflicts may be more difficult to resolve.

Be aware that there are many cultures that employ nonassertive behaviors as their primary means of defusing conflict. While it might seem like a trivial example, reflect for a moment on the subtle differences toward conflict in how two cultures deal with the posting of signs that carry potentially antagonistic messages. In the United States a sign would read NO DOGS ALLOWED. In England, a reserved culture that does not relish outward displays of conflict, the same sign would read WE REGRET THAT IN THE INTEREST OF HYGIENE DOGS ARE NOT ALLOWED ON THESE PREMISES.

Signs, of course, are not the only way the English seek to avoid harsh disagreements. Disputes often begin with phrases such as, "I may be wrong, but, . . ." or "There is just a very minor point in what you are saying that worries me a little."

The British are not the only ones who employ indirect methods to deal with conflict. Cultures such as the Chinese and Japanese have a strong faith in intuition and highly value collectivism and the indirect approach; some even believe at times that the other person will sense feelings of anger or conflict without a single word having to be spoken.[20]

AGGRESSION

Linked with a dominance conflict strategy, direct aggression, unlike nonassertiveness and indirect aggression, is easy to recognize. **Direct aggression** is the open expression of feelings, needs, wants, desires, and ideas, at the expense of others. People who use direct aggression try to dominate and possibly humiliate the other person by acting self-righteously, certain of themselves, as if they're superior, and as if they know what's best for everyone. For example, in response to the request to use the family car, the teenager's mother may say: "No, I want to use it, and I don't care that you need it to go see your friends. I have to go to the store and that's more important!" In this way, the mother clearly declares that her needs will be satisfied at the expense of the teen's, as well as clearly indicating the power structure of the relationship.

Direct aggression may get you what you want, but the costs are high. Initial hurt and humiliation may fade, but a loser is often left feeling angry, resentful, and vengeful and is apt to retaliate in kind. Direct aggression begets further direct aggression, ensuring continued hostility and lack of cooperation.

ASSERTION

Linked with compromise and integration, **assertion** is the direct statement of needs and wants. Because it is direct, assertion is more closely related to direct aggression than to either indirect aggression or nonassertiveness. Assertive communication lacks an important element of direct aggression, however; it expresses thoughts and feelings directly and clearly *without judging or dictating to others.* It is honest and has as its goal the resolution of conflict. Unlike direct aggression, assertiveness does not mean winning at the other person's expense—it attacks the problem, not the person.[21]

An assertive style has several advantages over other conflict styles. It increases the probability that your concerns will be satisfied and that you'll feel good about yourself. In addition, others are more likely to understand your needs and, possibly, work with you in managing the conflict. Relationships often are improved when assertiveness is used because the participants know exactly what they are in conflict about.

Assertive communication is useful in both simple and complex situations. The way you assert yourself will depend on who you are in conflict with and how involved the problem is.

Assertive Skills for Simple Situations

A conflict situation is simple when the problem is narrow and well-defined and you are not emotionally close to the other person. Such conflicts can be handled by stating your perception of the facts. For example, if you receive a bill from your school charging you for a class you did not sign up to take, you could assert yourself in three different ways. You could call the business office and say:

1. "Hello, this is _____. I received my tuition bill today and I'm being charged for a class I'm not taking."

2. "Hello, this is _____. I know you're probably not the person who's responsible, but I received my tuition bill today and I'm being charged for a class I'm not taking."

3. "Hello, this is _____. I received my tuition bill today and I'm being charged for a class I'm not taking. I would like the overcharge removed."

All three assertive comments are variations on the same theme—stating your perception of the facts. In the first instance, you simply present the facts with the assumption that once the other person knows them, he or she will resolve the problem. The advantage of this assertion is that it does not accuse the other person of anything, states exactly what's frustrating you, and does not back the other person into a corner.

The second assertion takes into account the role of the other person in the conflict situation. This recognizes his or her needs and softens the impact of the message.

The third assertion goes one step further. You not only state the facts, but you also specify what needs to be done to satisfy your concerns.

In none of these three assertions do you tell the person *how* to do what you feel needs to be done, which forestalls a defensive response. Defensiveness is common when you command someone to do something, when you overstate your case, when you don't clearly state what's wrong, or when you implicitly communicate, "I know more about your job than you do."

Skill Development 11.1 will help you practice assertive communication in simple, straightforward problem situations.

Skill Development 11.1
STATING SIMPLE ASSERTIONS

Tyler and you are from the same hometown. Tyler has a car and the agreement you made at the beginning of the semester was that if you did Tyler's laundry, Tyler would drive you home for Thanksgiving vacation. It's the Monday before vacation and Tyler tells you that the two Wednesday classes Tyler is in have been canceled and the new plan is to go home Tuesday. You have an exam on Wednesday. Your instructor has stated that there will be no makeup exams given, no matter the excuse.

Write three statements, each reflecting a different type of assertion that may be used in this conflict situation:

1.

2.

3.

Assertive Skills for Complex Situations

A conflict situation is complex if it has one or more of the following characteristics: It is a long-term dispute, it involves people with whom you're emotionally close, there is a strong possibility of physical or verbal violence, and there are differences in power. Such cases require more detailed assertive responses.

A complex assertive message can be expressed by using the **A*S*S*E*R*T** **formula:**

A: Describe the *action* that prompted the need for the assertive message. Your description should be behavioral; that is, it should focus on who is involved, the circumstances that are relevant, and the specific behaviors that are the source of your frustration and that trigger the assertive message. The expression of a descriptive message is clear and objective—for example, "When we discuss a serious matter, you joke around."

S: Express your *subjective interpretation* of the action. Using "I" language, offer your interpretation of the behavior you describe. Separate this subjective interpretation from the objective description. For example, "When you joke around, I think you want to avoid talking about the serious issue under discussion."

S: Express your *sensations* related to the action. Say how you feel about the behavior as precisely as possible even if you are somewhat confused. Try to include the intensity of your feelings. Does the joking make you thoughtful, sad, or grief-stricken? Are you distracted, surprised, or amazed? Are you apprehensive, fearful, or filled with terror? Are you annoyed, angry, or enraged? For example, "I feel angry when you don't stop kidding around. I also feel frustrated because I don't know what to do to get you to take what we're talking about seriously."

E: Indicate the *effects* of the action. Effects can focus on you ("I want to avoid discussing serious matters with you because you joke around"), on the other person ("I think you're missing out on some good discussions that might improve our relationship"), or on others ("I think people misinterpret the importance of our relationship when they see you joke around about serious matters").

R: Make your *request*. Indicate what specific behaviors you want. For example, "When we discuss a serious matter, I would like you to stop telling jokes and kidding around." (Note that the request ends with a period, not an exclamation point—it is a statement, not a command.)

T: *Tell* your intentions: "If we can't resolve this problem, I'll avoid discussing serious issues with you."

Skill Development 11.2 will help you practice using the A*S*S*E*R*T method.

Skill Development 11.2

A*S*S*E*R*T YOURSELF

Early in the semester a friend, Val, asked to copy your completed accounting homework. Throughout the semester the requests continued, each time with an apology from Val and a promise not to ask again. But there's always another excuse why the homework needs to be copied, including "no time," "don't understand," "forgot to write down the assignment." Last night you told Val you won't give out your homework again. Today Val asks for it again, pleading this is the last time, and, "Anyway, that's what friends are for." You've had it! Use the A*S*S*E*R*T formula to present your view of the situation to your friend.

A:

S:

S:

E:

R:

T:

Be aware that many cultures feel uncomfortable with assertive behavior and, therefore, offer their members a communication style that is almost opposite to the one found in the United States. For example, in the Filipino culture few things are as important as smooth interpersonal relationships. The aversion to assertive behavior is strong there because they value people who appear to be timid, submissive, humble, and modest. Hence, your attempts to be assertive to a Filipino or a person of other cultures with a similar orientation may not yield the results you had in mind. Patience and understanding are what is needed to resolve conflicts with people of cultures other than your own. If possible, adjust your communication to fit the style of the culture of the person with whom you are communicating.

GENDER DIFFERENCES AND CONFLICT

"No close relationship, no matter how ideal for both partners, maintains uniformly high satisfaction; no close relationship is without its ups and downs."[22] Of the many factors that potentially affect the process and outcome of relational conflict, gender is especially important. Gender appears linked to what comprises discontent, how dissatisfaction is expressed, managed, and resolved, and how both processes and outcomes are regarded by the relationship partners.

As shown in Table 11.1, females and males differ in their responses to conflict. Because of the different ways men and women are socialized, the ways they each perceive and respond to conflict vary. Males tend to want to retain their independence and distance in a relationship, while females want interdependence, cooperative sharing, intimacy, and caring.[23] Because of these differences in wants, men and women tend to communicate, express, and deal with conflict in different manners. Women are inclined to recognize conflicts and make active efforts to identify, discuss, and work toward resolution—that is, they have a greater tendency than men to use an integration ap-

TABLE 11.1	Female and Male Tendencies in Responses to Conflict

Female	Male
orientation: equity and caring; connections with and responsibility to the other person	orientation: equality of rights and fairness; adherence to abstract principles and rules
the goal of interaction is to achieve closeness and interdependence	the goal of interaction is to solve a problem or complete a task; what is sought is distance and autonomy
it is important to attend to the interpersonal dynamics of a relationship to assess its health	awareness of the interpersonal dynamics of a relationship is not very important
encourage mutual involvement	protect self-interest
a relationship crisis is caused by problems in the relationship	a relationship crisis is caused by problems external to the relationship
relationship-centered; concern is with the impact of the relationship on personal identity	neither relationship- nor self-centered
response to conflict focuses mainly on the relationship	response to conflict focuses mainly on rules and being evasive until a unilateral decision is reached

proach to conflict; also, they tend to smooth over and compromise more than men in conflict situations.[24] Men, on the other hand, tend to deny, avoid, or run away from conflict, or to deal with the problem by stating what they think should be done and assuming that the matter is taken care of—that is, they have a greater tendency than women to use avoidance and dominance approaches to conflict.[25] Women tend to respond to crises by attending to the processes of communication and encouraging mutual involvement, whereas men respond by protecting their self-interests.[26]

SEXUAL HARASSMENT

Although there are many similarities in the ways North American women and men initiate sexual contact and talk about sexuality, there are also a great many differences—and these differences can serve as an important source of conflict and misunderstanding. **Sexual harassment,** the "unwelcome sexual advances, requests for sexual favors, and other verbal and physical conduct of a sexual nature,"[27] affects individuals' personal, social, and professional lives, whether it is a man sexually harassing a woman, a woman harassing a man, or someone harassing a same-sex individual.

Sexual harassment can be real, and not just a matter of two people perceiving the same behavior differently. However, differences in perception are often a part of the problem of sexual harassment. For example, testimony given during the William Kennedy Smith trial, in which he was charged with the date rape of Patricia Bowman, highlights differences in perceptions of the "same" event. Ms. Bowman reported that she "bumped into" Mr. Smith and that this event led to their talking and, eventually, the development of a relationship in which she needed to use direct strategies to avoid a sexual encounter (she told him to "stop" and that "she did not want to have intercourse"). Mr. Smith reported the initial encounter—ostensibly the same event—with different words, and these words reflected his different perception. He reported she "brushed up against him" and "stood very close" to him. Along with other behaviors, Mr. Smith reported that he "thought we were going to have sex." Her "bump" was his "brush," and their encounter was off on the road to conflict.[28] Similar misunderstandings seem to have been present in the interactions between Clarence Thomas and Anita Hill, who accused the now Supreme Court Justice of sexual harassment in the work environment.[29]

What was the basis for these differences in the interpretation of what happened? First, many men and women view casual social interaction differently: Men, more than women, typically consider that these interactions have the potential to develop into sexual encounters. Women, by contrast, tend to regard interactions as the bases for friendship and possibly a relationship. Second, men view flirtatious behavior as somewhat sexual, whereas women are more likely to distinguish between "friendly" and "sexual" flirtatious behavior. Third, whereas women are more likely than men to use touch to express support, affection, and comfort, men are more likely to use touch to assert their authority or express sexual interest—differences that add to the confusion inherent in interpreting nonverbal tactile behavior. Fourth, the traditional stereotype of women as sex objects—people perceived exclusively in terms of their sexuality (a problem also encountered by lesbian women and gay men)—devalues women. And finally, a cultural norm seems to exist in the United States that suggests men are supposed to initiate sexual encounters and women are supposed to avoid them—a norm that ensures miscommunication and conflict as men and women try to determine what the other person "really" means.[30]

Sexual harassment does not always target the woman as victim. Though not as commonly reported, men also may be the victims of sexual harassment by women as well as by other men. In addition, there are cultural differences regarding sexual harassment. Because of the variances in some cultures regarding the roles and the expectations of females, sexual harassment, as understood in Northern American culture, is an alien concept because of what is expected of each gender.

DEALING WITH DIFFICULT PEOPLE AND DIFFERENT CULTURES

Two particularly troublesome conflict situations involve difficult people and people from different cultures. The former situation presents familiar types—the complainer, the know-it-all, the hostile-aggressor, the clam, the wet blanket, and the agreeable person—that trigger automatic and often ineffective responses from others. The latter situation presents unfamiliar people that leave you wondering how to respond. What are some useful strategies in both situations, strategies that can help you get your needs and wants satisfied and, at the same time, help you build and maintain effective and satisfying relationships?

DEALING WITH DIFFICULT PEOPLE[31]

Sometimes conflicts occur when we encounter difficult people. These people tend to fall into prescribed categories: The *complainer* gripes constantly, but does nothing to improve the situation except complain. The *know-it-all* has all the right answers and, therefore, never has to listen to anyone else. The *hostile-aggressive* person bullies his or her way through life and, when that doesn't work, throws a tantrum, while the *clam* never participates and you have no way of knowing how she or he feels or thinks. The *wet blanket* believes that nothing not completely in her or his control will work and that others don't care about her or his feelings. The *agreeable person* wants to please so much that he or she will agree to take on tasks that can't possibly be handled.

How can these people be dealt with in a constructive conflict resolution style?

Since *complainers* feel powerless to determine their own fate, complaining seems their only choice of behavior. So, listen with attention to the complaints, even if you feel impatient or annoyed, and allow the person to blow off steam. Acknowledge that you've heard the complaint by paraphrasing it. Make the complainer take responsibility for doing something about the complaint so it is more than just whining. Get the complainer to come up with a specific solution to the problem that is realistic and, if possible, encourage him or her to take on the task of carrying out the solution.

Know-it-alls are often difficult to deal with since they believe they are right. They behave arrogantly because they need to ensure that their understanding and perspective is the prevailing one in an argument and that others' perceptions are seen as irrelevant. In a chaotic world, knowledge is power, and know-it-alls like to feel powerful. Normally, know-it-alls are excellent debaters. In dealing with a know-it-all, make sure you've done your homework and are prepared: Ask questions rather than make statements, and try to direct the conversation from concepts and theories to more concrete points. Acknowledge the know-it-all's input and try to get specific action. For example, "Yes, I agree that's how things should be done. Now, how do we go about it?" It does no good to get as arrogant as the know-it-all.

One of the most difficult things to do when confronting a *hostile-aggressive person* is to avoid shouting back. Since the hostile-aggressive person tends to have a strong sense of the way things should be done and an incredible capacity for feeling hurt or wronged, he or she is often an insecure person whose bluster is an effective but thin defense. When hostile-aggressive people shout, let them vent. Let them wind down. Ask them to sit down (most people are less aggressive when seated) and then present your point of view after paraphrasing the hostile-aggressive person's argument. Maintain direct eye contact. If the person continues to rant, calmly repeat your point of view over and over.

The *clam* uses silence. She or he hides fears or strongly felt emotions by withdrawing and not communicating. If you want to get along with a clam, first give up trying to understand what the silence means. Instead, work toward opening the person up by asking open-ended questions, questions requiring more than one-word answers. Ask, "What do you think about that?" or "What can we do to solve the problem?" You will have to be patient. Wait for the response. If, after a reasonable period the person doesn't answer, ask the question again.

Wet blankets can sap your strength since they believe that they must be involved in every step of any action or it won't work. They also believe that those in power are incapable or don't care. Be careful not to get dragged down into their despair. Make optimistic but realistic comments about the situation or past similar situations; don't try to talk wet blankets out of their negativism—it just won't work. Don't offer solutions until the problem has been fully discussed. When a solution is discussed, raise the question of the negative events that might occur.

The *agreeable people* of the world have a strong desire to be liked. To do this they often make commitments they can't fulfill. They volunteer for impossible tasks, take on more than they can handle, accept deadlines they can't meet. Keep agreeable people from making unrealistic commitments. Encourage them to be realistic and remove the fear that they have that you won't like them if they don't do everything.

Skill Development 11.3 will help you practice communicating with difficult people.

Skill Development 11.3

DEALING WITH DIFFICULT PEOPLE

Situation: The University Social Committee is meeting.

1. Miguelle always comes up with the first suggestion and then goes on to prove adamantly he is right. Miguelle: "There is only one theme for the party. We should have a toga blast. According to the report from last year's social committee, it was the most popular event held. Besides, before I transferred here I was in charge of a toga party on the other campus, and it was great."
   What type is Miguelle and what is an appropriate action?

2. Bill—who is nearly failing school because he is taking a full academic load, holding a part-time job, serving on three university committees, and acting as treasurer of his fraternity—immediately agrees with Miguelle and says, "I'll volunteer to get the togas, order the food, and decorate."
   What type is Bill and what is an appropriate action?

3. Regina: "That's a lousy idea. Nothing we ever do around here is any fun. This is going to be another flop. Why can't we ever do something that isn't dumb?"
   What type is Regina and what is an appropriate action?

4. Ariel (jumps out of his chair and screams): "This is totally stupid! Everyone is always giving in to Miguelle just because he transferred here from a Big Ten

school. What a bunch of wimps! You always get led around by your noses! You never listen to my ideas or anyone else's, only Miguelle's!"
What type is Ariel and what is an appropriate action?

5. Mika just sits there, saying nothing, as usual.
What type is Mika and what is an appropriate action?

CONFLICT RESOLUTION WITH PEOPLE FROM DIFFERENT CULTURES

Throughout this chapter we have pointed out how culture influences both the perception and resolution of conflict. We noted that some cultures, such as the Arab, typically do not mind disputes and arguments, while others, like the Filipino, Chinese, and Japanese, usually find verbal aggression distasteful. How do you adapt your communication behavior to people from other cultures when there is a potential for conflict? While there is no easy answer to this question, there are a few general rules you can follow when you are face-to-face with someone who deals with conflict in a manner that is foreign to you.[32]

First, recognize that in many Asian and East Asian cultures conflict is in direct violation of a number of key cultural values. For example, interpersonal harmony, pride, shame, and honor are often under attack when one engages in direct and hostile conflict. Be sensitive to these deep-seated cultural values and try to adapt your conflict style to meet the needs of your communication partner.

Second, "be proactive in dealing with low-grade conflict situations (such as by using informal consultations or the 'go between' method) before they escalate into runaway, irrevocable mutual face-lose episodes."[33] A go-between is a third person brought in to negotiate and mediate the conflict as a means of avoiding direct conflict and possibly causing the other person to "lose face."

Third, if your communication partner dislikes direct confrontation, you should reject propelling him or her into a situation where there is no room to save pride and honor. This is particularly important if the conflict is taking place in the presence of others. For example, being embarrassed in public produces a very humiliating experience for many Asians.

Fourth, learn to be serene, calm, and patient. In many cultures, silence is used to think and be mindful. So, "use deep-level silence, deliberative pauses, and patient conversational turn-taking in conflict interaction processes."[34]

Finally, learn to accept the idea that in many instances you may be dealing with individuals who simply do not want to (or have never been taught how to) act on their feelings. Although avoidance, by Western standards, may seem like a form of denial, it is a very popular conflict response style in many Asian cultures. The motivation driving this approach is that the loss of respect and the disruption of harmonious relationships are consequences more negative than enduring the original conflict.

On the other hand, in dealing with people who have been taught by their culture to be aggressive and to appreciate direct conflict, be aware that backing off or giving in too quickly may result in a lack of respect for you and a less-than-satisfactory resolution to the conflict.

For Better or For Worse® by Lynn Johnston

FOR BETTER OR FOR WORSE copyright © Lynn Johnston Prod., Inc. Reprinted with permission of UNIVERSAL PRESS SYNDICATE.

OPTIONS FOR RESOLVING CONFLICT

In resolving conflict, at least three options for change seem available: change the other person, try to alter the conflict conditions, or try to change your own behavior.

Trying to change the other person is nearly impossible.   People don't change unless they want to do so. Most people have a way of responding to conflict that seems to work for them, or at least that they have tried and feel comfortable using, for whatever reasons. To lecture or point out the problems with their conflict style is often an exercise in futility. Also, lecturing often escalates the conflict. This does not mean that no change is possible, but you have to have the other person agree to a change if there is going to be any lasting alterations in behavior.

Altering conflict conditions is a more hopeful solution.   By increasing the resources available, altering your and the other person's interdependency, or changing each person's perceptions of the other person or the goals, there may be some hope of altering the conflict. For example, sufficient resources are not available—such as money, or time, or other people to help out—and supplying these needed resources may be the way of dealing with the problem. Hiring help to clean the house or take care of the children may be the solution to giving a married couple the time they need to relax together. This action could relieve the pressures of all work and no play that resulted in the stress they experienced.

Changing interdependency may be more difficult. If you are in school, for example, and need extra money, you can reduce your dependency on your parents by getting a job on weekends.

Changing perceptions or goals also is difficult. For example, changing your perceptions of your parents and your parents' perceptions of you, or changing the goals of the conflict may help resolve your antagonism over money. If you can get your parents to see you as a hard-working student who deserves some extra money, as opposed to how they see you now, as "having too good a time in college," you may get what you need. Similarly, if you and your parents could redefine the goals of the conflict (yours is to get money, and theirs is not to increase expenditures for college) to the mutual goal of reducing your stress so you can perform better as a student, you both may be happy with a resolution that provides you with greater funds and them with the understanding that they are helping you succeed.

Changing your own behavior can be positive if you really want to make a change and you have the experience or ability to do what is necessary.   Some people really want to change the way they deal with conflict but lack the skills. One way to change already discussed in this chapter is to recognize the strategies you use in a conflict and to decide whether they are more or less appropriate than other strategies.

If you tend to use an avoidance strategy, reconsider how important the issue is (is it really that unimportant?) and how important your relationship with the other person is (is it really that unimportant?).

If you tend to use a dominating strategy, reconsider how important the issue is (is it really that important?) and how important your relationship with the other person is (is it really that unimportant?).

If you tend to use a smoothing over strategy, reconsider how important the issue is (is it really that unimportant?) and how important your relationship with the other person is (is it really that important?).

If you tend to use a compromise strategy, reconsider how important the issue is (is it really only of moderate importance?) and how important your relationship with the other person is (is it really only of moderate importance?).

If you tend to use an integrating strategy, reconsider how important the issue may be (is it really that important?) and how important your relationship with the other person is (is it really that important?).

You may decide, based on your answers to the questions, that a change in strategy is called for. You may decide that communicating assertively will increase your chances of satisfying your needs and maintaining your relationship.

ASSESSING CONFLICT PROCESSES AND OUTCOMES

Assessing the process and outcomes of a conflict can help you understand its constructive and destructive consequences. Are your communication skills effective for managing relationship discord? What can you do to improve your conflict management strategies?

Skill Development 11.4 provides you with a method for assessing the process and outcomes of a conflict. Developing this analytical skill provides you with a way to gain a more objective view of your own conflicts, a view that can serve as the basis for determining your conflict strengths and weaknesses. The first part of the skill development presents nine questions that, together, create a Conflict Process Profile. This profile assesses the constructive and destructive aspects of the process of your conflict. The second part of the skill development presents five questions that, together, create a Conflict Outcomes Profile. This profile assesses the constructive and destructive aspects of the outcomes of your conflict.

Skill Development 11.4

ASSESSING THE PROCESS AND OUTCOMES OF YOUR CONFLICTS

Think of a recently resolved conflict in which you and another person were involved.

Building a Conflict Process Profile

Using the answers below each question, circle the word or phrase that best describes the process of the conflict.

1. To what extent did each person agree that there was a problem?
   strongly agreed   agreed   disagreed   strongly disagreed

2. To what extent did each person agree on what the problem was?
   strongly agreed   agreed   disagreed   strongly disagreed

3. How did each person appear to enter into the discussion?
   cooperatively   somewhat cooperatively   somewhat competitively   competitively

4. How were possible solutions generated?
   cooperatively   somewhat cooperatively   somewhat competitively   competitively

5. How were the possible solutions evaluated?
   cooperatively   somewhat cooperatively   somewhat competitively   competitively

6. How committed was each person to the selected solution?
   very committed   committed   somewhat committed   uncommitted

7. To what extent did each person agree on how to implement the solution?
   strongly agreed   agreed   disagreed   strongly disagreed

8. How were feelings and ideas expressed?
   openly   somewhat openly   guardedly   not at all

9. To what extent did each person perceive the problem from the other's perspective?
   totally   moderately   somewhat   hardly at all

After you have answered the nine questions, join your circled answers with a line going from the first question to the last. This line graphically represents your Conflict Process Profile. If the line stays mainly to the left, your conflict process was constructive, but if it stays mainly to the right, your conflict process was probably dysfunctional. If your circled answers form a jagged line, you can pinpoint your weak areas by looking at the items for which your responses fell to the right side.

1. What were the constructive aspects of your conflict process?
2. What were the dysfunctional aspects of your conflict process?
3. What did you learn about yourself as a participant in this conflict that you can apply to future conflicts?

Building a Conflict Outcomes Profile
Based on the same situation that you used to complete your Conflict Process Profile, circle the word below each question that best describes the outcomes of your conflict.

1. How effective was the solution in dealing with the problem?
   effective   somewhat effective   somewhat ineffective   ineffective

2. How did you feel about yourself and your behavior while you were working toward conflict resolution?
   positive   somewhat positive   somewhat negative   negative

3. How did you feel about the other person and her or his behavior while you were working toward conflict resolution?
   positive   somewhat positive   somewhat negative   negative

4. How did you feel about your and the other person's relationship before the conflict?
   positive   somewhat positive   somewhat negative   negative

5. How did you feel about the relationship after the conflict was resolved?
   positive   somewhat positive   somewhat negative   negative

Join your circled answers with a line going from the first response to the last. This line graphically represents your Conflict Outcomes Profile. A line that stays predominantly to the left represents a constructive conflict, while a line that stays predominantly to the right suggests a dysfunctional conflict. Questions for which your circled responses fall to the right indicate your trouble spots.

1. What were the constructive aspects of your conflict outcomes?
2. What were the dysfunctional aspects of your conflict outcomes?
3. What did you learn about yourself as a participant in this conflict that you can apply to future conflicts?

Every conflict has the potential to be constructive—to help you, the other person, and your relationship. Your understanding of conflict and how to manage it can increase your ability to communicate effectively and, therefore, increase the probability of your having constructive conflicts.

Communication Competency Checkup

The goal of this Communication Competency Checkup is to guide you in putting your skills and knowledge about managing relational discord to use, and to help you summarize the material in this chapter.

"Harrison, we never fight.
I've heard that people who really love each other fight."

1. Is the woman correct in her assessment of conflict being a normal part of relationships? Assume this interchange followed the statement made in the cartoon:

   He: You're always looking for trouble, leave well enough alone.

   She: Why do you always change the subject and not want to talk about things that bother either of us?

   He: You sound just like your mother. She always wanted to talk things to death. She would start fights so she could be the winner. That woman had a nasty mouth.

She: That is the stupidest thing I ever heard. That's ridiculous. Why are you always saying nasty things about my mother?

He: There you go again, calling me stupid and ridiculous. You asked whether people who love each other fight? Well, I usually just keep quiet, but if you want to fight, I'll give you a good one!

She: All I did was tell you what I heard.

2. Describe the conflict between him and her with respect to their interdependence and the sources of their conflict.

3. Describe the relational discord using the "I want . . . but . . . wants" formula.

4. What are the possible consequences of this conflict?

5. What are the possible effects of this conflict on the couple's relationship?

7. Which conflict strategy did she describe that he used?

8. Which conflict strategy does he describe her mother using?

9. Give an example of direct aggression used in this conflict.

10. What simple assertion could he have made, rather than his opening statement, in order to avoid the confrontation?

11. Assume that she has "bated" him before about the same issue. Write an A*S*S*E*R*T script that he could have used rather than the approach he took.

12. "How can I assess what the results of the conflict are?" he asks you. Describe a procedure he can use to assess whether the conflict process and the conflict outcomes were functional or not.

13. If these people were Asian or English, would this type of conflict probably take place? Why or why not? Write a statement to put under the cartoon that would represent either of those cultures.

14. If one person was from an Arab culture and the other from an Asian culture, what recommendations would you make to them about how to engage in interpersonal conflict?

NOTES

1. Lennie Copeland and Lewis Griggs, *Going International* (New York: Random House, 1985), 109.

2. Diana Rowland, *Japanese Business Etiquette* (New York: Warner Books, 1985), 5.

3. Joyce Hocker and William W. Wilmot, *Interpersonal Conflict,* 3d ed. (Dubuque, IA: Wm. C. Brown, 1991).

4. Hocker and Wilmot, *Interpersonal Conflict.*

5. Hu Wenzhong and Cornelius L. Grove, *Encountering the Chinese: A Guide for Americans* (Yarmouth, ME: Intercultural Press, 1991), 116–17.

6. Michael L. Hecht, Mary Jane Collier, and Sidney A. Ribeau, *African American Communication: Ethnic Identity and Cultural Interpretation* (Newbury Park, CA: Sage, 1993), 113.

7. Harvey L. Ruben, *Competing, Understanding, and Winning the Strategic Games We All Play*

(New York: Lippincott & Crowell, 1980), as quoted in John W. (Sam) Keltner, *Mediation—Toward a Civilized System of Dispute* (Annandale, VA, Speech Communication Association, 1987), 5.

8. Larry A. Samovar and Richard E. Porter, *Communication between Cultures* (Belmont, CA: Wadsworth, 1991), 108.

9. Cathy Guisewite, *Cathy,* Universal Press Syndicate, April 18, 1985.

10. P. Day, E. Cole, M. Ramiu, A. Shotton, F. Gutterman, L. Graber, and P. Pratski, *Keeping Families Together: Resources in Cross-Sector Training on Reasonable Efforts* (Washington, DC: Child Welfare League of America, 1991). Also see Kathleen M. Galvin and Bernard J. Brommel, *Family Communication: Cohesion and Change,* 4th ed. (New York: HarperCollins, 1996), 9–17.

11. Susan E. Crohan, "Marital Happiness and Spousal Consensus on Beliefs About Marital Conflict: A Longitudinal Investigation," *Journal of Social and Personal Relationships* 9 (1992): 89–102.

12. Susan Gano-Phillips and Frank D. Fincham, "Family Conflict, Divorce, and Children's Adjustment," in Mary Anne Fitzpatrick and Anita L. Vangelisti (Eds.), *Explaining Family Interactions* (Thousand Oaks, CA: Sage, 1995), 206–18.

13. Adapted from a handout, *Thomas-Kilmann Conflict Mode Instrument,* developed by Joyce L. Hocker and William W. Wilmot, "Teaching a College Course on Conflict and Communication," paper presented at the meeting of the Western Communication Association, Tucson, Arizona, February 1986.

14. Daniel Canary and William R. Cupach, "Relational and Episodic Characteristics Associated with Conflict Tactics," *Journal of Social and Personal Relationships* 5 (1988): 305–25; Hocker and Wilmot, *Interpersonal Conflict;* David W. Miguelleson, *Human Relations and Your Career,* 2nd ed. (Englewood Cliffs, NJ: Prentice-Hall, 1987), Chapters 9 and 10.

15. Karen J. Prager, "Intimacy Status and Couple Conflict Resolution," *Journal of Social and Personal Relationships* 8 (1991): 505–26.

16. Stella Ting-Toomey, "Managing Intercultural Conflicts Effectively," in Larry A. Samovar and Richard R. Porter (Eds.), *Intercultural Communication: A Reader,* 7th ed. (Belmont, CA: Wadsworth, 1994), 360–72.

17. William B. Gudykunst, Stella Ting-Toomey, Sandra Sudweeks, and Lea P. Steward, *Building Bridges: Interpersonal Skills for a Changing World* (Belmont, CA: Wadsworth, 1995), 437.

18. Alex F. Osborn, *Applied Imagination,* rev. ed. (New York: Scribners, 1957).

19. Anita Vangelisti, John A. Daly, and Janine Rae Rudnick, "Making People Feel Guilty in Conversation: Techniques and Correlates," *Human Communication Research* 18 (1991): 3–39.

20. William B. Gudykunst and Stella Ting-Toomey, *Culture and Interpersonal Communication* (Newbury Park, CA: Sage Publications, 1988), 158.

21. Dominick Infante and C. J. Wigley III, "Verbal Aggressiveness: An Interpersonal Model and Measure," *Communication Monographs* 53 (1986): 61–69.

22. Caryl E. Rusbult, "Responses to Dissatisfaction in Close Relationships: The Exit-Voice-Loyalty-Neglect Model," in Daniel Perlman and Steve Duck (Eds.), *Intimate Relationships: Development, Dynamics and Deterioration* (London: Sage, 1987), 209.

23. For a discussion of male-female differences in conflict behavior, see Carol Gilligan, *In a Different Voice: Psychological Theory and Women's Development* (Cambridge, MA: Harvard University Press, 1982); Deborah Tannen, *You Just Don't Understand: Women and Men in Conversation* (New York: Morrow, 1990); and Julia T. Wood, *Gendered Lives: Communication, Gender, and Culture* (Belmont, CA: Wadsworth, 1994).

24. Julia T. Wood, *Relational Communication: Continuity and Change in Personal Relationships* (Belmont, CA: Wadsworth, 1995), 263.

25. Caryl E. Rusbult and J. Iwaniszek, "Problem-Solving in Male and Female Homosexual and Heterosexual Relationships," unpublished manuscript, University of Kentucky, Lexington, 1986.

26. Lawrence B. Rosenfeld, "Sex Differences in Response to Relationship Crises: A Case Study of the Hill-Thomas Hearing," in Paul Siegel (Ed.), *He Said, She Said, We Listened: A Communication Perspective on the Hill/Thomas Hearings* (New York: Hampton Press, in press).

27. G. L. Mastalli, "Appendix: The Legal Context," *Harvard Business Review* 59.2 (1981): 94–95.

28. Ann L. Darling, "Talking About Sex in the Classroom: What Can We Learn from the William Kennedy Smith Trial?," paper presented at the meeting of the Speech Communication Association, Chicago, November 1992.

29. Rosenfeld, "Sex Differences in Response to Relationship Crises: A Case Study of the Hill-Thomas Hearing."

30. C. L. Muehlenhard and L. C. Hollabaugh, "Do Women Sometimes Say No When They Mean Yes? The Prevalence and Correlates of Women's Token Resistance to Sex," *Journal of Personality and Social Psychology* 54 (1988): 872–79; Michael R.

Semonsky and Lawrence B. Rosenfeld, "Perceptions of Sexual Violations: Denying a Kiss, Stealing a Kiss," *Sex Roles,* 30 (1994): 503–20; Julia T. Wood, "Defining and Studying Sexual Harassment as Situated Experience," in Gary L. Kreps (Ed.), *Communication and Sexual Harassment in the Workplace* (Cresskill, NJ: Hampton Press, 1993); and Wood, *Gendered Lives: Communication, Gender, and Culture.*

31. Based on materials from Robert Bramson, *Coping with Difficult People in Business and in Life* (New York: Dell, 1988); G. Corey, *I Never Knew I Had A Choice* (Pacific Grove, CA: Brooks-Cole, 1990); and Michael Doyle and David Straus, *How to Make Meetings Work* (New York: Jove Publishing, 1986).

32. Ting-Toomey, "Managing Intercultural Conflicts Effectively," 360–72.

33. Ting-Toomey, "Managing Intercultural Conflicts Effectively," 369.

34. Ting-Toomey, "Managing Intercultural Conflicts Effectively," 369.

CHAPTER 12

CREATIVITY, POWER, AND INTERPERSONAL SATISFACTION

COMMUNICATION COMPETENCIES

This chapter examines the relationship of creativity and power to interpersonal satisfaction. Specifically, the objective of the chapter is for you to learn to:

- Recognize the differences between creative and more usual ways of thinking.
- Specify the relational benefits of being creative.
- Recognize cultural and personal obstacles to creativity.
- Develop your creativity by learning how to form new associations, apply the technique of analytic breakdown, and manipulate the details of objects.
- Recognize the consequences of feeling both powerful and powerless.
- Determine your sources of power in particular relationships.
- Develop strategies for enhancing your power.
- Choose the most appropriate sources of power in particular circumstances.
- Increase the extent to which your language reflects feelings of powerfulness.

KEY WORDS

The key words in this chapter are:

creative thinking
power
expert power
referent power
associative power
reward power
coercive power
legitimate power
powerful language
powerless language
hedges
qualifiers
hesitations
tag question
disclaimers

What happens when you and a partner in a relationship have a problem? What do you do to resolve your differences? Circle the number of those responses that best describe how you go about solving problems in your relationships.

1. I look for a method and a plan for solving the problem.
2. I think a lot about how I'm approaching the problem while trying to resolve it.
3. I discard alternatives quickly and try to identify the best solution.
4. I conduct an orderly search for additional information.
5. I redefine the problem as I proceed.
6. I rely on my hunches.
7. I consider a number of alternatives and options simultaneously.
8. I jump from one step to another and back again as I analyze the situation.

The first four statements describe people's usual thinking about problem solving, whereas the second four define a less typical, more creative approach. If you circled more in the second group than the first, you may be a creative problem solver.

CREATIVITY

In modern North American thinking, to be creative is to be valued—even if the creative person may sometimes be labeled as an eccentric, a nonconformist, or a troublemaker. We value creativity because it affords us the ability to produce things that are new and different and to think in unusual ways—and the new and the unusual are what make

© Jefferson Communications, Inc. Distributed by C J N T N S.

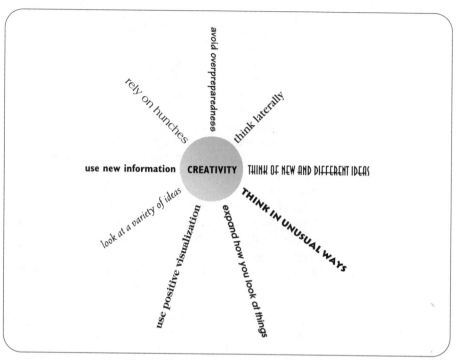

FIGURE 12.1   Characteristics of Creativity

life exciting! Ironically, we may label creative people negatively because they force us to think in different modes, approach typical problem-solving techniques from new perspectives, and, in general, decrease our feeling secure.

Creative thinking, also called *lateral* or *divergent* thinking, parallels the mind's process of scanning laterally, looking for alternatives and ideas, and expanding and diverging as it continues (see Figure 12.1). *Usual* thinking, also called *vertical* or *convergent* thinking, is more linear, concerning itself with one alternative or idea at a time, building one thought on the other, vertically, in a process that converges as it proceeds, narrowing in on fewer and fewer ideas and alternatives.[1]

Are you more comfortable with creative or usual thinking? Usual thinkers are more comfortable with creating a well-developed plan for solving a problem, understanding how to approach a problem, and conducting an orderly search for information. They often ignore hunches, refrain from redefining a problem, and avoid considering several alternatives simultaneously.

In contrast, creative thinking requires a "looseness" that includes relying on hunches, avoiding overpreparedness, allowing a problem to be redefined as new information arises, and simultaneously looking at a variety of ideas and alternatives. Creativity calls for faith in yourself—faith that you can do what needs to be done by expanding how you look at things instead of narrowing your focus.

Creativity offers many benefits, all of which can contribute to the quality of your communication and your relationships.

- Creativity is essential if you hope to solve difficult mutual problems that conventional approaches usually can't settle.
- Creativity can keep you out of ruts. When you can predict the contents of a ten-minute dialogue that you and another person will have, you are in a well-worn rut, one that could increase feelings of dissatisfaction and boredom. It is common for couples, after knowing each other for a long time, to avoid certain topics altogether because each knows what both will say and how each will react. The end result can be a stifled, though safe, relationship.
- Creativity is important if you hope to discover alternatives that are potentially easier and more satisfying ways of doing things—whether dividing up household chores, deciding where to go on a night out, or completing a group assignment.
- Creativity is important if you want to discover new ways for your relationships to develop.
- Creativity is useful if you are to adapt effectively to the many and diverse cultures you will be facing.

The potential benefits of being creative have a common goal: more satisfying, exciting, developing relationships and communication.

OBSTACLES TO CREATIVITY

Imagination is the highest
kite one can fly.
LAUREN BACALL

Small children tend to be naturally creative, probably because no one has yet told them to "think logically" or to "stay in the lines when you color." They think of unique methods of reaching the cookie jar on top of the refrigerator, novel ways of putting unconnected thoughts together (a child we know was told to "look at the car being towed," which he converted to "look at the Carbine Toad," a two-gun-carrying, ten-gallon-hat-wearing frog), and poetic ways to use language (referring to "smashed" rather than "mashed" potatoes, a "rubbish" rather than "rummage" sale, and the sink "overfloating"). Guess the age of the author who, upon seeing a sunset, declared: "I'd love to go for a ride on the rays and go to bed in sheets made of clouds."[2]

A four-year-old made that unique and creative statement. Before the age of four, a child spends as much as half the time dreaming, having hundreds of unconnected thoughts; from about three to five years of age, he or she spends half the time engaged in poetic thinking, intuitively making associations and using metaphors and similes; and from about age four to age six, half the time is spent inventing, putting the poetic similes to practical use, such as by turning a stool, a drawer, and a counter top into "steps" to climb to some desired cookies.[3]

You may have trouble remembering your own creative acts as a child because of the obstacles that parents and teachers raised in your path—obstacles that said, "Don't be creative." Most of us heard do's and don'ts that included, "Don't make a fool of yourself," "Follow the rules," and "That's not the right way to do this."

Creative people are often difficult to understand, cope with, and be around. While people speak of creativity with respect, they often prefer that it belong to someone else's

offspring. (Few parents would wish their child to write poetry like Emily Dickinson if it also meant that the child be a social isolate, as she was.)

Obstacles to creativity may be classified as either cultural or personal barriers.

Cultural Obstacles

Cultural obstacles stem from the values and attitudes that our society considers important. For example, where on the one hand, the high value that North American society places on individuality and competition should encourage the risk taking required for creative problem solving, the high value it also places on logic and practicality may inhibit solutions requiring feelings and imagination. Adults learn that to be other than serious and humorless—except during specified times—is to risk being perceived as frivolous. For example, although teachers may say they like students who are creative, challenging, and assertive, they really seem to prefer students who are pleasant, compliant, and obedient.[4]

Personal Obstacles

There are three *personal obstacles* to creativity: habitual ways of doing things, beliefs about how things are, and fear of failure. Examining these three obstacles can make you aware of their negative effects.

Habitual Ways of Doing Things   "Habit," as playwright Samuel Beckett put it, "is a great deadener." Habits curb the natural urge to be creative. As a brief experiment, try the following: Fold your arms across your chest. Note which arm is on top. Now, put your arms at your side and, once again, fold them across your chest—only this time change which arm is on top. How does this feel?

Most people feel uncomfortable changing their customary way of doing things, and some find it difficult to do at all. When crossing their arms in an unaccustomed way, some people, for example, wind up holding an elbow without realizing it; others must give the task some strong concentration; and still others keep rotating their arms, unable to decide when to stop.

What habits determine your interaction when you meet someone for the first time? Do you always say the same things in the same order, such as, "Hi, my name is _____," followed by, "How are you?," followed by, "Hardly anyone in this area was born here, so where are you from?" Do you automatically ask where the person is from, even though a different question would be more appropriate? What happens when the answer to your first question is, "I just got out of the hospital"? How ingrained is your meeting-new-people habit?

Not all habits are harmful, of course. Most habits, in themselves, are helpful, such as when a task is easily performed or done very often. These tasks do not require reflection or the development of "new and improved ways" of doing them. However, not all tasks can or should be accomplished while on "automatic pilot." When you fail to question the "why" of these habits, you hinder your effectiveness in solving new problems and interacting with people.

Most habitual ways of behaving are easy to recognize once they're pointed out. Habitual ways of looking at things are more difficult to recognize and they inhibit creative thinking. People often believe that solutions and ideas can be found in comfortable, usual ways of looking at things, and often they fall into the habit of presuming that a problem has only one solution—especially after they have found the solution.

Look at the droodles (a droodle is a drawing that appears meaningless until it is given a title) in Figure 12.2. One possible title for the first illustration is "Two Corpuscles Who Loved in Vein." A possible title for the second illustration is "Three Degrees below Zero." Can you think of other titles for the two droodles?

Because the problem of what the drawings mean is solved by the titles, you may find it difficult to come up with other titles. Similarly, if you yourself had generated

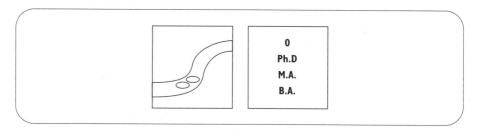

FIGURE 12.2 Droodles

titles, instead of being given them, coming up with other titles also might be trouble-some. Once you know the given titles, you may accept them as the only solutions and have difficulty devising other choices.

The first step to overcoming such a limited viewpoint is to recognize your habits, and the second step is to break away from them. To be creative and develop new ideas, you must stop your customary ways of behaving and looking at things. And to change your typical responses, you must reject the comfortable answers that habits automatically provide. Knowledge Checkup 12.1 provides you with the opportunity to examine a habit many people share: saying no before imaginatively thinking of what the answer actually is.

Knowledge Checkup 12.1

EXAMINING THE HABIT OF SAYING NO

Do you think you could recognize at least twenty-five varieties of dogs? If you're a dog enthusiast, you probably would answer yes. You may have answered yes even if you were not. But most people answer no, even though they probably know most, if not all, of these thirty-six breeds:

Boxer	Dalmatian	St. Bernard	Bloodhound
Great Dane	Beagle	German Shepherd	English Setter
Pointer	Labrador Retriever	Scottish Terrier	Fox Terrier
Pekingese	Dachshund	Collie	Boston (Bull) Terrier
Pomeranian	Schnauzer	Dingo	English Springer Spaniel
Irish Setter	English Bulldog	Spitz	Doberman Pinscher
Chow	French Poodle	Afghan Hound	Golden Retriever
Greyhound	Basset Hound	Sheep Dog	Siberian Husky
Chihuahua	Cocker Spaniel	Alaskan Malamute	Jack Russell Terrier

You probably know more about almost anything than you give yourself credit for. The mental habit of saying no to a question rather than making the effort to figure out the answer curtails thinking and stifles creativity. You are probably more creative than you realize! In fact, you could probably generate another long list of breeds of dogs to add to the one in the knowledge checkup—or did you automatically say, "No, I can't"?

Beliefs A second obstacle to your creativity is your beliefs about the world, about how things "are." Although reality is based only on perception, people usually create beliefs about the world around them and then fail to think any further. *The belief becomes the reality.* The six blind men of Hindustan each examined a different part of an elephant and described the whole elephant based on that part. They missed the reality of the elephant by accepting the belief that "What I perceive is all there is to perceive."

Do you believe that married couples should live happily ever after, that men should work outside the home and "bring home the bacon," and that women should stay home and take care of the children? If you mistake your beliefs for reality, how do you begin to respond to marital arguments (your own or others) or other people's differing definitions of their roles in relationships?

Creativity requires open-mindedness, the willingness to receive new information, perspectives, assumptions, beliefs, and opinions. Recognize that your beliefs are merely beliefs—not reality—and you can begin to stimulate your creativity, to think in new and exciting ways. Knowledge Checkup 12.2 will provide you with some practice in examining your beliefs associated with dating, and then provide you with the opportunity to overcome those beliefs.

Knowledge Checkup 12.2
OVERCOMING BELIEFS

What are some beliefs you have about heterosexual first dates? For each belief, answer two questions: (1) What does a person who has the belief miss out on? and (2) What is needed to overcome the belief? The first belief is presented as an example.

Belief: For a first date, the man needs to ask the woman out, not the other way around.

A person with this belief misses out on: A person with this belief misses out on a lot of dates! A woman with this belief may miss out on dates she could initiate. A man with this belief may not call a woman who might be interested in going out with him (he may not realize she is interested in dating him), or he may, in general, avoid calling for dates because he is shy.

To overcome this belief: To overcome this belief, an individual needs to realize that anyone can call anyone for a first date (or any date, for that matter).

Belief: For a first date, a woman can't date a man shorter than she is; a man cannot date a woman taller than he is.

A person with this belief misses out on:

To overcome this belief:

Belief: For a first date, the man has to pay for everything.
A person with this belief misses out on:

To overcome this belief:

Belief: For a first date, the man needs to drive.
A person with this belief misses out on:

To overcome this belief:

Belief: For a first date, it is important to remember that women don't like action movies, and men don't like love stories.
A person with this belief misses out on:

To overcome this belief:

Fear of Failure   When people have creative thoughts, they often hesitate to share them. What are some of your own reasons for keeping new ideas to yourself?

I was afraid.

It sounded stupid.

It seemed impractical.

It was too odd.

It was too abstract.

People would think I was crazy.

It was too personal.

It was hard to express.

It wasn't like other people's ideas.

People would make fun of me.

I was taught to be seen and not heard.

I wanted to agree with what others had to say.

It was foolish.

At the root of all these reasons for avoiding sharing creative thoughts is the fear of failing at something, whether it is failing at being a "strong person" (who is fearless and sane), an "intelligent person" (who is smart and practical), a "good communicator"

(who is agreeable and able to put complex ideas into understandable words), or some other type of person.[5]

Like most people, you might be anxious about expressing your ideas. This often prevents you from offering or even considering all the ideas you think up. You may have been taught—and believe—that new ideas are ridiculed, that your ideas don't count for much, that you need to be perfect, or that people want agreement, not creativity. In short, your fear of failure may keep you from trying new and innovative ideas; it also may prevent you from engaging in unique and original behaviors. This attitude can rob you of your creativity. An old Yiddish proverb says, "He that lies on the ground cannot fall far." We would add, he also will not develop his creativity.

DEVELOPING YOUR CREATIVITY

Regardless of the many obstacles to creativity, the situation is not hopeless: No one is doomed to be unimaginative, dull, and boring. There are simple ways to exercise your mind back into shape—mental aerobics—that include forming new associations, using analytic breakdown, and manipulating details. As a result of mental aerobics, you will be capable of handling relationships and confronting daily problems with energy and creativity.

Forming New Associations

Many of the associations people make stem from fixed ways of looking at things that they learned as children and never bothered to change. For example, consider your automatic responses to these word combinations:

bread and _____

ham and _____

hot and _____

short and _____

What color is wind?

ZEN KOAN

If you said "butter," "eggs" or "cheese," "cold," and "tall" or "fat," you made habitual responses. Such associations are made almost by reflex. Skill Development 12.1 provides you with several opportunities for breaking old habits and forming new associations.

Skill Development 12.1

FORMING NEW ASSOCIATIONS[6]

Part I

Pick two words at random from the following list. Combine them to invent a new product or something that improves on either of the two original items. (For example, an "apple suitcase" can be a suitcase in the shape of an apple, a suitcase made especially to transport apples or an Apple computer, or maybe a suitcase made of apple skins.) Do this for two pairs of words.

apple	suitcase	glass	basket
bottle	hook	shoe	pen
hand	star	phone	wax
chair	magazine	band	comb
tar	disk	clip	typewriter

Association 1:

Association 2:

Part II

Write two rhyming words that apply to each of the following definitions. For example, "boob tube" is a pair of rhyming words that together define "television."

1. A feline rug

2. A useless musical percussion instrument

3. An ill person brought up in the "back woods"

4. An angry young male

5. A person who murders for the fun of it

Part III

Find one word that ties together each group of three words. For example, the words "base," "meat," and "bearing" all have the word "ball" in common (as in baseball, meatball, and ball bearing).

1. night, bulb, and sky

2. ever, bean, and light

3. down, over, and through

Activities such as these help you develop skills that expand how you perceive things. If you have the opportunity, share your responses with your classmates. Sharing perceptions expands your perceptual frame and enriches your way of looking at things. What word combinations struck you as unique and imaginative? How did your rhymes compare with those created by others? Did you all agree that a feline rug is a "cat mat," a broken percussion instrument a "bum drum," an ill person from the "back woods" a "sick hick," an angry young male a "mad lad," and a person who murders for the fun of it a "thriller killer?" And did you think of "light," "green," and "run" as possible tie-ins?

The only way to form new associations is through conscious effort. The more you set aside habitual associations and practice making new connections, the higher the probability that you will be creative in other aspects of your life, including your relationships.

Analytic Breakdown

When you've exhausted all possibilities, remember this: you haven't!
ROBERT SCHULLER

A second technique for increasing your creativity is *analytical breakdown.* Analytical breakdown begins with reducing a complex problem into its individual components, then listing as many alternatives as possible for each component, and then combining the alternatives to create new variations. Assume, for example, that you wanted to improve staff meetings in an office. This is a complex problem that can be broken down into several key issues. For example, one issue is *when* to have a meeting, a second is *where* to have it, a third is *who* should attend, and a fourth is *what* to discuss. As you consider the situation, you note that "when" includes (at least) before opening, morning, lunch time, afternoon, and after closing; "where" includes (at least) your office, someone else's office, the coffee room, a restaurant, someone's house, and a nearby park; *who* includes (at least) everyone, managers only, staff only, managers and staff,

TABLE 12.1	Analytic Breakdown: How to Improve Staff Meetings		
When	**Where**	**Who**	**What**
before opening	my office	everyone	office procedures
morning	another office	managers	interface: public
lunch time	coffee room	staff	salary
afternoon	house	managers and staff	new personnel
after closing	restaurant	one department	scheduling
	park	two+ departments	new products
			productivity

personnel from one office, and personnel from two or more departments; and "what" includes (at least) discussion of office procedures, dealing with the public, salary concerns, new personnel issues, scheduling, new product possibilities, and improving productivity.

By placing one key issue at the top of a column and generating a list of alternatives for each heading, you can begin to see possibilities that you may not have thought of before (Table 12.1). When the information is laid out in columns, you can visualize the various combinations that will lead to a variety of potential meeting formats.

How many alternative ways can you think of to spend a weekend with a friend? Skill Development 12.2 will help you practice using the technique of analytic breakdown for generating a large number of possible weekend activities.

Skill Development 12.2

DOING AN ANALYTIC BREAKDOWN

Problem: Jointly planning activities with a close friend for the upcoming weekend to ensure the greatest amount of fun.

1. Divide the problem into its component parts. (For example, one component might be *who* could join you and your friend over the weekend, a second might be *where* you could go, a third might be *when* you could plan to do something, and a fourth might be *what* you could do.)
2. Divide a sheet of paper into as many columns as you have components and head each column with the name of a different component (you may use the four components suggested here and add to them).

3.   Generate as many alternatives as possible under each heading.

4.   Select the combination of choices from each column that solves the problem in the most satisfactory way. To find the best solution, you may want to develop several combinations and compare and contrast them.

Manipulating Details

A third method for increasing creativity is *manipulating the details* that you notice about an object. For example, you can change something by enlarging it, making it smaller, dividing it, rotating it, stretching it, coloring it, hardening it, softening it, flattening it, flipping it, squeezing it, freezing it, heating it, rearranging it, shortening it, fluffing it up, and patting it down.

Consider that dollhouses, midget racers, and the many items made for travel, such as hair dryers, resulted from applying the verb *minify*. Large-print books resulted from applying the verb *enlarge*. Frozen food and other forms of packaging all came from attempts to manipulate the details of an object. In Skill Development 12.3, you will manipulate details to find a creative solution to a common problem: what to get a friend for a gift.

Skill Development 12.3

CREATING NEW GIFT IDEAS

Create ten unique gifts for friends by manipulating the details of a fork. (Assume you can create anything that you think of.) For example, you may *enlarge*—and give one friend a ten-foot sculpture of a fork to put in front of her new restaurant, or you might wish to *extend*—and give a very busy friend a fork with a one-foot handle so he can eat while standing. Be creative!

Create ten unique gifts for friends by manipulating the details of a brick. (Again, assume you can create anything you can think of.) For example, you may make it smaller and present it to a friend as a paperweight, or you might paint it your school colors and give it to a friend as a door stop.

As you gain experience with forming new associations, doing analytic breakdowns, and manipulating the details of objects, you will stretch your mind and increase your capacity for creativity. The benefit to be gained—more satisfying relationships—is well worth the effort.

Just as being more creative increases the satisfaction and enjoyment you can experience in all your relationships, so does being more powerful. And there are a variety of creative ways for increasing your power—your influence and your feeling of being in control—in your relationships.

POWER

Consider the following four questions: Is your answer to each a *definite yes* (Y), a *possible yes* (PY), a *tentative no* (TN), or an *unequivocal no* (N)?

_____ 1. Do you have confidence in yourself, trust your feelings, and maintain a sense of personal worth regardless of the reactions of others?

_____ 2. Do you like yourself, including your perceived faults?

_____ 3. Do you remain optimistic even when someone finds fault with something you've done?

_____ 4. Do you feel self-confident enough to encourage the people around you to develop their abilities even though they may surpass your own?

The extent to which you responded positively to each question reflects your feelings of being powerful, of being in control of your options. People who feel powerful, as compared to people who do not, are more likely to be happy with themselves and their relationships, to enjoy physical and emotional health, to savor their work and play, and to feel self-satisfied.

A DEFINITION OF POWER

Power is the ability to control what happens—to cause things you want to happen and to block things you don't want to happen.[7] To put it simply, power is the ability to choose. Roget's Thesaurus lists these synonyms for *powerful: potent, capable, strong, competent, energetic, influential,* and *productive.* In contrast, the synonyms for *powerless* are *impotent, incapable, weak,* and *incompetent.*

Defining power as the ability to control what happens and to make choices clarifies several preconceptions. First, the power to choose is not bad, but rather something that is exercised in every human transaction. The view of power as bad may stem from its abuse (often in the form of winning at someone else's expense), from its contradiction of the belief that all humans should be equal, or from its waste (as when there's really no opportunity to gain anything and large amounts of resources are thrown away in the process, such as spending time and money on a former romantic partner who does not intend to begin a new relationship with you). In fact, power, the ability to make choices, is desirable, not bad.

Based on this definition, it is also simplistic to say that one person is "more powerful" than another or that someone is "powerless." Every person may be more or less powerful or powerless, depending on the situation, its dimensions, and its participants. Thus, you have power and you are powerful—maybe not with everyone, at all times, and in every circumstance, but certainly with some people, at some times, and in particular settings. And, you always have power over yourself—the power to change your attitudes, beliefs, values, and behavior.

People who feel powerless often lack the willingness to make choices about their relationships, such as which to maintain and which to terminate. Because they may feel that they don't have the ability to make choices, they settle for unsatisfying relationships. Also, people who feel powerless in one situation may take out their hostilities and frustrations in other situations. For example, a parent having problems with his or her boss at work—and who feels powerless to do anything about it—may be unusually harsh with his or her children.

Powerlessness, not power, often destroys relationships. People who are empowered are aware of their resources, their strengths, their weaknesses, and their uniqueness as individuals. They also are clear about what they want to accomplish and, most importantly, optimistic about their ability to achieve their goals. The powerless feel less well equipped and less qualified to make choices that affect their relationships.

Many people in North American culture are raised to believe that they have great power over their lives and even the lives of others, that they are "masters of their own fate," "captains of their ships," and that they "pull themselves up by their bootstraps." Not only do they want power, and think they deserve it, they do not want other people to have power over them. They often leave home at an early age so their parents will not have power over them, and they make teachers, police, and bosses the brunt of jokes because they do not like the power these people have or are given. They hear cries of black power, gray power, and gay power. Women and minority groups ask for power so that they can have freedom from internal and external restraints. In short, persons are taught in North America not to be powerless.

This, of course, is not the case with all cultures. Most of the world, in fact, believes that an outside source or fate, be it "God," "the gods," "reincarnation," or "nature," controls their lives. Power, for these cultures, is a basic fact of society. It is not something they feel they want or need. Muslims use the phrase "it is Allah's will" and Hindus believe that their karma is being acted out. In both instances, these people do not feel powerless, per se, but instead believe in a philosophy of "what will be, will be." It is not their mission to seek power, nor in most instances do they rebel against the fact that they do not have power. In most instances, they hold the view that the legitimacy of power is irrelevant.[8]

Knowledge Checkup 12.3 will help you assess your own feelings of empowerment.

Knowledge Checkup 12.3
HOW POWERFUL DO YOU FEEL?[9]

Think of one of your important relationships and keep it in mind as you respond to the questionnaire. Each item has two alternatives. Your task is to divide 10 points between the two alternatives according to how well each describes you. You may give all 10 points to one alternative and none to the other, split the points evenly, 5 and 5, or assign any other combination of 10 points that seems appropriate.

1. When the other person says something with which I disagree, I

    _____ a. assume my position is correct.

    _____ b. assume what the other person says is correct.

2. When I get angry at the other person, I

    _____ a. ask the other person to stop the behavior that offends me.

    _____ b. say little, not knowing quite what to do.

3. When something goes wrong in the relationship, I

    _____ a try to solve the problem.

    _____ b. try to find out who's at fault.

4. When I participate in the relationship, it is important that I

    _____ a. live up to my own expectations.

    _____ b. live up to the expectations of the other person.

5. In general, I try to surround myself with people

    _____ a. whom I respect.

    _____ b. who respect me.

Scoring

Add all of your a responses. a = _____

Add all of your b responses. b = _____

The two totals, a and b, indicate how powerful you feel in the relationship you chose. The total number of points is 50, so one score could be 50 and the other zero, although that is unlikely.

If your b score is greater than your a score by 10 or more points, you probably feel somewhat powerless in your relationship because you see the other person's choices as more important than your own.

If your two scores are within 10 points of each other, you are probably unsure of your own power and your potential to influence others.

If your a score is greater than your b score by 10 or more points, you most likely feel quite powerful and in control of the choices you make in the relationship.

Once you understand your own feelings of empowerment and the importance of feeling empowered, you can take two further steps to increase your feelings of power: (1) determine your power bases, or sources of power; and (2) develop strategies for enhancing your power.

SOURCES OF POWER

What are your sources of power, that is, how are you able to get other people to behave in ways you would like? Are you seen as an expert? Are you well-liked? Are you seen as able to reward people if they do what you ask? Knowledge Checkup 12.4 is designed to help you assess these and other possible sources of your power.

Knowledge Checkup 12.4

ASSESSING YOUR SOURCES OF POWER[10]

With two relationships in mind—one with a close friend and one with a work partner who is not a close friend—indicate the extent to which each statement is true of you. Use the first column to mark answers for the close friend and the second column for your work partner. Use the following scale:

Write **5** if the statement is true.

Write **4** if the statement is sometimes true.

Write **3** if the statement is neither true nor false.

Write **2** if the statement is sometimes false.

Write **1** if the statement is false.

———— ———— 1. I try to set a good example for the other person.

———— ———— 2. The other person considers me an expert.

———— ———— 3. Because of the nature of our relationship, I carry a great deal of authority with the other person.

———— ———— 4. I can help the other person achieve his or her goals.

———— ———— 5. The other person is impressed by people I know.

———— ———— 6. I can keep the other person from achieving his or her goals or satisfying his or her wants.

———— ———— 7. The other person sees me as having a lot in common with her or him.

———— ———— 8. The other person knows I have no trouble handling my responsibilities in the relationship.

———— ———— 9. The other person respects my authority.

———— ———— 10. I have something the other person wants or values, and I can make it available to her or him.

———— ———— 11. I can find someone else to influence the other person if I so wish.

———— ———— 12. I can hurt the other person.

Scoring

Add your responses to items 4 and 10. This is your reward power score.

Close Friend: _____   Work Partner: _____

Add your responses to items 6 and 12. This is your coercive power score.

Close Friend: _____   Work Partner: _____

Add your responses to items 3 and 9. This is your legitimate power score.

Close Friend: _____   Work Partner: _____

Add your responses to items 2 and 8. This is your expert power score.

Close Friend: _____   Work Partner: _____

Add your responses to items 1 and 7. This is your referent power score.

Close Friend: _____   Work Partner: _____

Add your responses to items 5 and 11. This is your associative power score.

Close Friend: _____   Work Partner: _____

Scores of 8 to 10 for a category are high; you perceive that this is a very important source of power for the relationship. Scores of 5 to 7 for a category are moderate; you perceive that this is a potentially important source of power for the relationship, but is not particularly significant right now. Scores of 2 to 4 for a category are low; you perceive that this is an unimportant source of power for the relationship.

The six sources of power measured in Knowledge Checkup 12.4 and outlined in Table 12.2, fall into two broad categories, formal and informal. *Formal power bases* reflect your role (boss versus coworker) or the nature of the relationship (friend versus

TABLE 12.2	Informal and Formal Power Bases
Informal Power Bases	**Source of Power**
Expert Power	Person is perceived as having knowledge and skills relevant to the particular task or activity.
Referent Power	Person is perceived as loyal, friendly, and trustworthy.
Associative Power	Person is perceived as knowing others who are influential.
Formal Power Bases	**Source of Power**
Reward Power	Person is perceived as the best or only source of something desired.
Coercive Power	Person is perceived as capable of producing a negative outcome.
Legitimate Power	Person's role or relationship is perceived as granting certain rights and privileges.

acquaintance), while *informal power bases* relate to perceptions of your abilities, qualities, and traits.

The three informal bases of power are *expert power*, your perceived skill and knowledge; *referent power*, how well you are liked; and *associative power*, which is based on who you know. The three formal bases of power are *reward power*, your perceived ability to reward others; *coercive power*, your perceived ability to punish; and *legitimate power*, your perceived right to make requests because of your relationship with the other person.

Is your formal power a stronger base than your informal one? Or is the opposite true? Do you have one or two particular sources of power with your close friend? What sources of power do you have with your coworker? Do both persons perceive you as having the same sources of power? And which sources of power do you lack, if any?

If you perceive yourself as having little, or very limited sources of power, you can remedy the situation. Each of the six sources of power can be developed through the use of particular strategies.[11]

Expert Power

Expert power is your capacity to influence another person because of the knowledge and skills you are presumed to have. Note that *being* an expert and being *perceived* as an expert are two different things and that to use your expertise, you must be perceived as an expert. To build expert power, you need to communicate your expertise to the other person. You can do this by mentioning your background and training, demonstrating that you are well informed on topics that are important to the other person, and accomplishing tasks competently and noticeably. In other words, you need to call attention to yourself. For example, telling your friend that you had experience cooking when you worked for a local restaurant should help gain you expert power in the kitchen.

People telling others about their power is not a universal trait. You will be in contact with people who, because of their cultural background, will not tell you about their expert power. There are two reasons for this. First, there are cultures, such as in parts of Asia, in which people do not talk about themselves. Too much self-focus is considered a form of bragging or boasting. Individuality is "systematically repressed."[12] Second, cultures that have a nonverbal rather than a verbal tradition believe that people possess an intuitive feeling about each other and, as such, do not have to state what is "known" by both parties. If they have power, you will just know it. In these cultures there is a belief that, "It is the heart always that sees, before the head can see."

Referent Power

Referent power is probably the most important source of power because it's based on personal loyalty, friendship, affection, and admiration. The key to securing this power base is to demonstrate your friendliness and trustworthiness. For example, emphasize the similarities between yourself and the other person, such as background, goals, attitudes, and values. The more similarities the better. It also helps to communicate your support for the other person, give her or him the benefit of the doubt, and create symbols that bind you together, such as in-jokes and a special language. If you smile frequently, encourage and support the other person, and share secret handshakes and expressions, you will increase your chances of having referent power.

As you would suspect, it is very difficult to use referent power in an intercultural setting. This technique is based on your stressing any similarities that exist between you and your communication partner. When the other person's culture is different from your own, it might be hard to locate key similarities. There are, of course, similarities between all people and all cultures, such as wanting relational satisfaction, having as a goal a good life, and seeking the meaning of life. But, the task of locating these similarities is compounded when past experiences are quite different, and you are each unfamiliar with the other person's customs.

Associative Power

Associative power is based on your acquaintance with people the other person holds in high esteem. For example, if you worked in the White House and had opportunity to talk with the President, making a statement such as, "While working in the White House, the President told me . . ." is likely to bring attention to your ideas. Referring to acquaintances is often risky because the name you mention may be irrelevant or unfamiliar to the other person and because you may be perceived as a snob or a name-dropper. Nonetheless, if you pick an appropriate name, you have a good chance of increasing your influence. To benefit from associative power, make sure the name you choose is known by the person you want to impress, and avoid name-dropping too often.

Reward Power

Expert and referent power are based on your perceived abilities and traits. Associative power stems from whom you know. By contrast, reward, coercive, and legitimate power are related to your relationship with the other person. **Reward power** requires that you be perceived as the best or only source of desired rewards. To possess reward power, you must (1) know what the other person wants, (2) amass the objects of desire, (3) communicate that you have the desired objects, and (4) specify what the other person must do to get them. For example, you know that your friend wants a place to hold an end-of-term party and you have access to a private cabin. You communicate that the cabin is yours to give and then you spell out what the other person needs to do to get it.

Be careful! If the object is seen as a bribe, or if you dangle rewards too often, you're likely to meet resistance or seem manipulative.

Coercive Power

In contrast to reward power, which is based on positive outcomes, **coercive power** is based on negative outcomes that are used as weapons. To exercise coercive power, you need to (1) know what weapons the other person fears most, (2) acquire them,

THE FAMILY CIRCUS BIL KEANE

"Instead of spankings, my Mom imposes economic sanctions."

(3) communicate that you have them, and (4) persuade the other person that you're willing to use them. For example, when you originally split a project, even though your co-worker's typing skills are poor and yours are well-developed, you agreed that your partner would do the final typing. You can make it clear that if he or she does not comply with your requests, you will refuse to work with her or him on another project.

Because people tend to resist coercive power, whether by punching the power broker in the nose or by slowly withdrawing from contact, it is best to avoid its use. There are times, however, when you have no option but to act coercively. During these times, be as calm and reasonable as possible, and act only if you are certain that it's the most effective power base at your disposal. The goal is to be perceived as fair—even if you're using a source of power that's disliked.

Legitimate Power

Legitimate power stems from one person perceiving that another person has the right to make requests because of the position that the other person occupies or because of the nature of the relationship. For example, in a parent-child relationship, children perceive that parents have the right to make requests of them; in a military relationship, lieutenants perceive that generals have the right to make requests of them; in a work relationship, workers perceive that the boss has the right to make requests of them; and in a committed relationship, companions often feel that their partners have the right to ask them favors. To increase your legitimate power, you must either move into a new position or role that has more authority (for example, become the boss), change the nature of the relationship (from acquaintance to friend), or persuade the other person that you have more authority by changing the expectations of your position. Call yourself an "administrative assistant" instead of a "secretary," and others' views of your power may change.

CHOOSING YOUR POWER BASE

Which power base should you use?[13] The answer depends in part on the kind of influence you desire—whether you want *commitment* or *compliance* from the other person. When people are committed to a request, they feel enthusiastic about it, agree that it is a good idea, and believe that it's the right thing to do. When they merely comply with a request, they obey reluctantly, without believing in the goodness of the idea.

The choice of a power base also depends on how much time you have: Some sources of power are likely to get quicker action. If you want to get things done quickly, with little or no discussion, and if others need not feel committed to your request, you may find that reward and coercive power work best. But both sources of power have drawbacks.

If you plan to use coercive power, you must expect to be disliked. In addition, the more you use coercive power the less effective it tends to become, so your threats must escalate. For example, to get children to eat their vegetables, parents may first threaten them with no dessert, then with no television, and ultimately with grounding for longer and longer periods of time. Finally, because coercive power causes so much resentment, you'll need to develop a strategy for ensuring that your request is obeyed and watch the outcomes. (A child can devise a hundred ways to make it seem as if the vegetables have been eaten and can retaliate in a variety of stressful ways, including crying, tantrums, poor grades, and embarrassing conduct in public.)

> And the trouble is, if you don't risk anything, you risk even more.
> ERICA JONG

Reward power raises some of the same problems. For example, a reward often needs to be increased regularly to maintain the same effect. Bringing home flowers once a week ceases to be a reward as soon as it is expected that you'll bring them home. And if you skip a week, it may be perceived as punishment. Also, when you use reward power routinely, you're likely to get results only if you keep an eye on the other person to make sure what you request is done.

Using legitimate power in combination with small doses of reward and coercive power can be effective; however, the best you can usually hope for is compliance without enthusiastic support.

If your request is very important and if you want commitment, expert and referent power are the most productive. An expert who communicates a request without arrogance or insult is more likely to get commitment than compliance, as long as others truly perceive her or him as an expert.

Because it has the highest probability of obtaining commitment on the widest range of requests, referent power is perhaps the most useful source of power. Unlike expert power, which inspires commitment to the *request,* referent power inspires commitment to *you.* An expert can only make requests that relate to her or his perceived area of expertise, but someone with referent power can make requests in any area.

The primary drawback of referent power is that it takes a great deal of time to develop. Relationships need to move from the stranger stage through the acquaintance stage before a low level of friendship is established and referent power can begin to gain strength.

In North American culture most sources of power are enhanced through communication. Communicating to others that you are knowledgeable and skillful enhances your expert power. Communicating to others that you are their friend enhances your referent power. Communicating to others that you know people they hold in high esteem enhances your associative power. Communicating to others that you are the best or only source of their rewards enhances your reward power. Communicating to others that you have and will use weapons they fear enhances your coercive power. As you communicate both verbally and nonverbally, you signal how powerful (or powerless) you feel.

POWERFUL AND POWERLESS LANGUAGE

Powerful language often creates an impression of strength, capability, and control. **Powerless language,** on the other hand, often creates a perception of being incompetent and passive. Several language habits contribute to perceptions of powerlessness. For example, **hedges**—words that limit your responsibility for what you say—and **qualifiers**—words that modify what you say—detract from the certainty of a statement. For instance, "kind of," "I think," and "I guess" may indicate that you are unsure of yourself. Consider the degree of assertiveness in "I guess I'll leave work today at 5:00" versus "I'll leave at 5:00." Hedges, more than other forms of powerless language, decrease perceptions of authoritativeness; on the other hand, hesitations decrease perceptions of both authoritativeness and sociability.[14]

While North Americans often equate hedging with a lack of power, other cultures take a somewhat different view of language. Because they do not wish to offend, the Japanese intentionally use language that is characterized by hedge words, qualifiers, and ambiguity. Being too blunt in the Japanese culture can cause others discomfort; hence, language is used to moderate instead of assert. In fact, in most Japanese sentences the verb comes at the end of the sentence so the "action" part of the statement can be postponed. The Mexican culture, with its strong emphasis on cooperation, also uses hedging to smooth over interpersonal relationships. By not taking a firm stand with their spoken language, Mexicans believe they will not make others feel ill at ease. The Korean culture represents yet another group of people who prefer "indirect" (for example, "perhaps," "could be") over "direct" speech.[15]

Hesitations, like hedges and qualifiers, also suggest uncertainty. If you add "um," "er," or "well" to your speech, you may create the perception that you are unsure about what you are saying. Compare "I . . . well . . . er . . . want you to know that . . . well . . . I'll be leaving today at . . . uh . . . 5:00" to "I want you to know I'll be leaving at 5:00."

Tag questions, unnecessary questions added to statements, signal that you may lack confidence in what you're saying or are unwilling to take a stand. For example, "right?" or "OK?" at the end of a statement requests approval or agreement. Note the difference between "I'm leaving today at 5:00, right?" and "I'm leaving today at 5:00."

Disclaimers, expressions that excuse what you're saying or ask another person to bear with you while you make a point, indicate uncertainty and communicate subservience. For instance, compare "I probably shouldn't say this, but I'm leaving at 5:00" or "If you'll just let me tell you one more thing, I want to say I'm leaving at 5:00" to "I'm leaving at 5:00."

If you use a great many aspects of powerless language and you are interacting with people from North America, you probably will be perceived as incompetent and passive, as opposed to competent and dynamic. You will not be considered as attractive as someone who uses powerful language.[16] And because you will be perceived as less competent, dynamic, and attractive, you will not be as influential as someone who uses powerful speech.

Remember, you will be in contact with people from cultures that do not apply the same yardsticks for the measurement of competence and attractiveness as you might. These cultures also have a different definition for the so-called "dynamic" person. They find the person who is still, modest, reserved, thoughtful, and careful with words to be the most powerful, credible, and attractive. In the Japanese, Indonesian, and Chinese cultures, for example, people who speak too well are often perceived as having low credibility. In addition, "a person who is quiet and spends more time listening than speaking is more credible."[17] Think of the advice contained in the Japanese proverb, "He who speaks has not knowledge and he who has knowledge does not speak," or the Indonesian proverb telling people that "Empty cans clatter the loudest." In short, be careful of your own ethnocentrism when you use powerful language with people of other cultures. Those messages might be construed in quite a different way than would be the case if you were speaking to someone from your culture.

With this in mind, to be perceived as powerful in North American society, eliminate, as much as possible, the use of hedges, qualifiers, hesitations, tag questions, and disclaimers. This is not to imply that every hedge, qualifier, hesitation, tag question, and disclaimer should be eliminated—that the more powerful speech you use the better. Actually, the best way to influence others and maintain good relationships is through the use of a combination of powerful and polite speech.[18]

Can you recognize powerless speech when you hear it? Do you know how to change your powerless speech into a powerful form? Skill Development 12.4 will help you recognize and eliminate powerless language from your messages.

RECOGNIZING AND ELIMINATING POWERLESS LANGUAGE

Rewrite the following paragraph by substituting powerful language for powerless language.

> I was like, uh, hoping that, uh, if you'd like we could go out this weekend, you know? Gee, I'd understand if you're busy—sometimes I am, too, but, well, uh, I thought that, well, if you're not busy or doing anything you'd like maybe to go out with me. Yes? I'm having a hard time expressing myself.

The most powerful way this could be rewritten is as follows:

> I would like you to go out with me this weekend.

This straightforward statement eliminates the hedges ("I was hoping" and "I thought"), qualifiers ("maybe"), hesitations ("uh" and "well"), tag questions ("you know?" and "yes?"), and the disclaimer ("I'm having a hard time expressing myself"). Also, it increases perceptions of power by changing the question, "I was like, uh, hoping that, uh, if you'd like we could go out this weekend, you know?" to a statement.

Depending on the situation, some form of language more powerful than the first example and less powerful than the second example may be most appropriate. This leads to the following possibility:

> I would like you to go out with me this weekend if you're not busy.

Powerful and powerless speech reflect some differences in male and female verbal language. For example, women's speech tends to be more "tentative" than men's speech.[19] By including tag questions, "That was a good meal, right?" and qualifiers, "I think that . . . ," in their speech, women may forego looking powerful in lieu of opening up the lines of communication between them and their relational partners. Men's speech, on the other hand, tends to be "more forceful, direct, and authoritative."[20] Although this language may increase perceptions of powerfulness, it also may close lines of communication and decrease the possibility of an ongoing dialogue.

Communication Competency Checkup

The goal of this Communication Competency Checkup is to guide you in putting your skills and knowledge about creativity, power, and interpersonal satisfaction to use and to help you summarize the material in this chapter.

FOR BETTER OR FOR WORSE copyright © Lynn Johnston Prod., Inc. Reprinted with permission of UNIVERSAL PRESS SYNDICATE. All rights reserved.

Assume you are listening in on the conversation between the mother and daughter. Also assume that they see you listening in and approach you. You tell them you are a student of communication and that you were listening to their conversation. They ask for your help: How can they improve their communication? Help the mother and daughter to understand how they can use creativity and power to improve their relationship.

1. What relational benefits might the mother and daughter obtain from creatively solving their problem?

2. What cultural and personal obstacles to solving their problem creatively might the mother and daughter encounter? For example, is it possible the daughter might say, "No matter what idea I come up with, it'll be stupid"?

3. The mother tells you, "I'm tired of pretending that I understand what 'I dunno' means when I don't!" The daughter then tells you, "Why do I have to keep explaining myself? She should know what I mean when I say 'I dunno.'" Explain three techniques the mother and daughter can use to develop their capacity for creative problem solving.

4. "I want more influence with her, especially when it comes to discussing things about buying clothes," the mother tells you. What questions could you ask to help her assess the power bases she has in her relationship with her daughter?

5. What techniques could the mother employ to increase the odds her daughter perceives her as powerful?

6. How could the mother determine which sources of power might be best to use in her relationship with her daughter?

7. How could the daughter reduce the extent to which her language makes her appear powerless (for example, "I dunno") and increase the extent to which it makes her appear powerful?

NOTES

1. For an extensive discussion of creative thinking, see Daniel Goleman, *Emotional Intelligence: Why It Can Matter More Than IQ* (New York: Bantam Books, 1995).

2. Stephen Lehane, *The Creative Child* (Englewood Cliffs, NJ: Prentice-Hall, 1979).

3. Lehane describes the stages of creative growth children go through and provides strategies for helping children develop and maintain their creativity.

4. Sarah Trenholm and Toby Rose, "The Compliant Communicator: Teacher Perceptions of Appropriate Classroom Behavior," *Western Journal of Speech Communication* 45 (1981): 13–26.

5. Kathryn Dindia, "The Intrapersonal-Interpersonal Dialectical Process of Self-Disclosure," in Steve Duck (Ed.), *Dynamics of Relationships* (Thousand Oaks, CA: Sage, 1994), 27–57; Sandra Petronio and Dawn Braithwaite, "I'd Rather Not Say: The Role of Privacy in Small Groups," in M. Mayer and N. Dollar (Eds.), *Issues in Group Communication* (Scottsdale, AZ: Gorsuch Scarisbrick Publishers, 1987); John Powell, *Why Am I Afraid to Tell You Who I Am?* (Miles, IL: Argus, 1968); Lawrence Rosenfeld, "Self-Disclosure Avoidance: Why I Am Afraid to Tell You Who I Am," *Communication Monographs* 46 (1979): 63–74.

6. These exercises are adapted from those developed by Noller, Parnes, and Biondi. For more information and other exercises designed to develop creativity, see Ruth B. Noller, Sidney J. Parnes, and Angelo M. Biondi, *Creative Actionbook* (New York: Scribner's, 1976).

7. Robert A. Barraclough and Robert A. Stewart, "Power and Control: Social Science Perspectives," in Virginia P. Richmond and James C. McCroskey (Eds.), *Power in the Classroom* (Hillsdale, NJ: Lawrence Erlbaum, 1992), 1–4.

8. George A. Borden, *Cultural Orientation: An Approach to Understanding Intercultural Communication* (Englewood Cliffs, NJ: Prentice-Hall, 1991), 116.

9. Adapted from Pamela Cuming, "Empowerment Profile," *The Power Handbook* (Boston: CBI, 1981), 2–5.

10. Adapted from Pamela Cuming, "Determining Your Power Bases," *The Power Handbook* (Boston: CBI, 1981), 57–59; D. L. Dieterly and B. Schneider, "The Effect of Organizational Environment on Perceived Climate and Power," *Organizational Behavior and Human Performance* 11 (1974): 334–35. Also see Barraclough and Stewart, "Power and Control: Social Science Perspectives"; and John R. P. French, Jr. and Bertram Raven, "The Bases of Social Power," in Dorwin Cartwright (Ed.), *Studies in Social Power* (Ann Arbor, MI: Institute for Social Research, 1959).

11. John A. Daly and Pamelo Kreiser, "Affinity

in the Classroom," in *Power in the Classroom,* 121–44; Timothy G. Plax and Patricia Kearney, "Teacher Power in the Classroom: Defining and Advancing a Program of Research," in *Power in the Classroom,* 67–84.

12. Jan Servaes, "Cultural Identity in East and West," *Howard Journal of Communication* 1 (Summer 1988), 64.

13. Gary A. Yukl, *Leadership in Organizations,* 2nd ed. (Englewood Cliffs, NJ: Prentice-Hall, 1989), 43–49.

14. In addition to the findings for hesitations and hedges, Hosman found that extensive use of any one of the powerless language forms was enough to be perceived negatively; that is, it did not require the use of several in combination. Lawrence A. Hosman, "The Evaluative Consequences of Hedges, Hesitations, and Intensifiers: Powerful and Powerless Speech Styles," *Human Communication Research* 15 (1989): 383–406. Also see James J. Bradac and Anthony Mulac, "A Molecular View of Powerful and Powerless Speech Styles: Attributional Consequences of Specific Language Features and Communicator Intentions," *Communication Monographs* 51 (1984): 307–19; Charles Conrad, "Communica-

tion, Power and Politics in Organizations" in *Strategic Organizational Communication,* 3rd ed. (Fort Worth: Harcourt Brace, 1994), 265–97; and Craig E. Johnson, "An Introduction to Powerful and Powerless Talk in the Classroom," *Communication Education* 36 (1987): 167–72.

15. Larry A. Samovar and Richard E. Porter, *Communication between Cultures,* 2nd ed. (Belmont, CA: Wadsworth, 1995), 158–59.

16. S. H. Ng and James J. Bradac, *Power in Language: Verbal Communication and Social Influence* (Newbury Park, CA: Sage, 1993).

17. Larry A. Samovar and Richard E. Porter, *Communication between Cultures* (Belmont, CA: Wadsworth, 1991), 106.

18. D. Geddes, "Sex Roles in Management: The Impact of Varying Power of Speech Style on Union Members' Perception of Satisfaction and Effectiveness," *Journal of Psychology* 126 (1992): 589–607.

19. Julia T. Wood, *Gendered Lives: Communication, Gender, and Culture* (Belmont, CA: Wadsworth, 1994), 143.

20. Wood, *Gendered Lives: Communication, Gender, and Culture,* 145.

GLOSSARY

acculturation   The transfer of culture from one group to another, commonly a process of change experienced by members of a minority group as they adapt to a majority group's culture.

active listening   Listening for main and supporting ideas, acknowledging and responding, giving appropriate feedback, and paying attention to a speaker's total communication, including the content, the intent, and the feelings expressed.

actual self   An image of self that conforms to one's capabilities and the restrictions of one's environment.

adaptation   To adjust a message based on feedback.

adaptation to stress   The second stage of the stress process during which a person adapts to a situation by accepting it and adjusting his or her behavior to meet its demands, or resists it by denying or ignoring it.

adapters   Body movements performed by habit, often to satisfy physical and psychological needs.

affect displays   Body movements that express emotions.

affinity seeking   The active process a communicator uses to get other people to like and feel positive toward him or her.

alarm stage   The first stage of the stress process, during which a body's systems are alerted to a potential threat.

allness   The assumption that when a person says something, she or he has said all there is to say on the subject.

androgynous   Communicating or behaving in ways that are both highly masculine and highly feminine.

approachability cues   Indications that an individual is available for conversation.

A*S*S*E*R*T formula   A method for developing assertive statements in complex situations.

assertion   A conflict strategy in which a direct statement of needs and wants is made so that one's needs are met without taking away another person's rights.

associative power   A source of power based on an individual's acquaintance with people others hold in high esteem.

attacking behavior   A message that communicates the other person is not acknowledged, understood, or accepted.

avoidance   Also called denial or withdrawal. A conflict strategy based on the assumption that a conflict will just go away if it is ignored.

biosocial family attitudes   A family's perspective of male and female identity, authority, and power, and the rights of individual family members.

blended family   Two adults and their children, all, some, or none of whom may be the offspring from their union.

boundaries, family   Limits a family sets on its members' actions. Within the family, boundaries define who may speak with whom, and under what circumstances. Outside the family, boundaries define who family members may communicate with, including extended family members, friends, neighbors, groups, and organizations.

buffering stress   Associated with a response to stress; takes place when a stressor is anticipated and a plan is developed that helps a person deal with a situation before experiencing distress.

burnout   Physical, emotional, and mental exhaustion resulting from continuous and high levels of stress.

bypassing   When a communicator incorrectly assumes that his or her meaning for his or her message is the same as another person's.

channel   The medium a speaker chooses, such as writing a letter, talking on the telephone, using electronic mail.

chaotic family   A family that has erratic leadership or no leadership at all, dramatic shifts in roles, unclear roles, and impulsive decision making.

chunking   Grouping together of bits of information insofar as they share a particular relationship.

clichés   Trite expressions that convey a common or popular thought.

coercive power   Power associated with an individual's being perceived as able to ensure negative outcomes.

collective cultures   Cultures in which individuals are subjugated to the group.

combating stress   Associated with a response to stress. Reducing or eliminating the stress through self-help techniques or techniques requiring others.

commitment   A pledge to the continuation of a relationship, including each person's commitment, each person's perception of the other's commitment, and what it is each person is committed to.

communication anxiety   The fear of engaging in communicative interactions.

communication   The process of sending and receiving messages through a channel. Seven elements can be included: senders, receivers, messages, a context, a purpose, feedback, and adaptation.

complementary relationship   A relationship structure in which one partner's behavior complements or

completes the other's—the behaviors seem to go together. Based on differences which, when they come together, form a stable relationship.

compliance gaining   The active process a communicator uses to direct and influence his or her communication partner's behavior.

compromise   Also called bargaining or negotiating. A sharing strategy designed to satisfy everyone's concerns to some extent.

confirming behavior   See **supportive behavior.**

conflict   Any situation in which an individual perceives that another person, with whom she or he is interdependent, is frustrating or might frustrate, the satisfaction of some concern, need, want, or desire of her or his.

connotation   The secondary associations for a symbol that are more personal and may not be shared by every member of a language community.

context   The characteristics of a situation in which a communication takes place, such as the physical environment and the other people present.

controlling stress   Associated with a response to stress. Takes place when the stress is not strong enough to require combat, but action is taken to ensure that it does not increase.

conversational turn taking   A nonverbal indication that it is the other person's turn to talk.

creative thinking   Also called lateral or divergent thinking. Type of thinking that parallels the mind's process of scanning laterally, looking for alternatives and ideas and expanding and diverging as it continues.

cultural obstacles   Obstacles to communication that result from people's differences in background and experience.

culture   The deposit of knowledge, experience, beliefs, values, attitudes, meanings, hierarchies, religion, timing, roles, spatial relations, concepts of the universe, and material objects and possessions acquired by a group of people in the course of generations through individual and group striving.

denotation   The usual associations that members of a particular language community have for a symbol.

dialectical tensions   Incompatible and opposing communication goals that exist simultaneously.

direct aggression   The open expression of feelings, needs, wants, desires, and ideas at the expense of others.

disclaimers   Expressions that excuse what a speaker is saying or ask another person to bear with the speaker while he or she makes a point.

disconfirming behavior   See **attacking behavior.**

disengaged family   A family with limited attachment or commitment and an overall lack of loyalty.

distorted language   Attempts to exaggerate or to minimize the value, importance, or worth of something.

distress   Stress perceived as being negative.

dominance   Also called power or forcing. A conflict strategy in which an individual's own needs are satisfied at the expense of the other person's.

ectomorph   Person with a body type characterized as being thin and frail-looking.

egospeaking Jumping into a communicative transaction because one has something to say or because one feels that what one has to say is more important or more interesting than what the other person is saying.

emblems Body movements, used intentionally, that have direct verbal translations in a given culture.

emotional challenge support A type of social support that involves encouraging someone to evaluate her or his attitudes, values, and feelings.

emotional support A type of social support that involves being on the other person's side whether or not you agree with what he or she is doing.

emotions Feelings accompanied by physiological changes and overt nonverbal manifestations.

emotive words Words that seem to be descriptive but actually communicate an attitude toward something or someone.

empathy One's ability to experience the world as others do; seeing things from the other person's point of view.

endomorph Person with a body type characterized as being fat and round.

enmeshed family A family with too much consensus, too little independence, and a very high demand for loyalty.

environmental obstacle Something in the physical surroundings that impairs a communicator's ability to send or receive messages.

ethics Rules for conduct that distinguish right from wrong.

ethnocentrism The tendency to put a person's own culture and societal patterns at the core of all evaluations.

euphemisms Inoffensive words or phrases that are substituted for possibly offensive language.

eustress Stress perceived as being positive.

exhaustion stage After surviving a stressful situation, the stage at which a person typically feels physically and mentally drained.

expert power An individual's capacity to influence another person because of the knowledge and skills he or she is presumed to have.

extended family Groups of relatives, usually thought of as having blood or legal ties, living nearby to each other.

external distraction People, objects, or events in the environment that divert a communicator's attention from the communication partner.

fact-inference confusion The tendency to respond to something as if it were observed when, reality, it was merely suggested by observations; associated with the lack of grammatical distinction between facts and inferences in the English language.

facts Statements based on observations; they relate directly to what is seen, heard, touched, tasted, or smelled.

family A social system with two or more interdependent people with a common past history, a present reality, and a future expectation of interconnected mutually influencing relationships.

family-of-origin The family in which an individual is raised.

feedback The process of sending information about the effect of a message.

flexibility skills Skills that enhance one's versatility and resourcefulness.

free information Elaborations a communicator provides that may be used to find new topics of conversation.

functional family A family that creates an appropriate environment for supportive and caring interactions, encourages open and accepting communication, and enables children to grow and achieve suitable independence.

generalized others What an individual thinks people in general consider correct or proper.

green flag A word or phrase that stirs up positive feelings that may interfere with listening.

hearing The biological act of receiving sounds.

hedges Words that limit an individual's responsibility for what he or she says.

hesitations Words or nonverbal vocal utterances, like "um," "er," or "well," that suggest uncertainty.

idealized self A person's perception of self as "perfect." Elements of this image emerge when a person says, "If I were _____, then everything would be OK."

illustrators Unintentional body movements used to add to or support what is said.

images, family The perceptions and mental pictures family members hold of the family as a whole and of the individual family members.

impression management One's strategies to influence how others view him or her.

indirect aggression   The expression of concerns in a disguised way.

indiscrimination   The failure to see people, objects, ideas, or concepts as unique and individual.

individual cultures   Cultures that stress the importance of being identified as an individual rather than as a member of a group.

inferences   Conclusions that are suggested by observations.

insulated listening   Avoiding listening to ideas with which one disagrees and avoiding topics perceived as unpleasant, uninteresting, or controversial.

integration   Also referred to as collaboration and problem solving. A conflict strategy that has as its goal the full satisfaction of each person's concerns.

interactive process model of communication   A characterization of communication as a two-way event in which senders and receivers exchange messages in response to one another. Adds the notions of feedback and adaptation to the linear process model.

internal distractions   Processes within a communicator that divert his or her attention from the communication partner.

interpersonal communication   A type of communication based on communicators' recognition of each other's uniqueness and the development of messages that reflect that recognition.

interpersonal communication competency   The ability to use one's knowledge, skills, and motivation to achieve her or his interpersonal goals appropriately and effectively.

interpersonal conflict   A conflict between people.

intimacy   A quality of a relationship based on detailed knowledge and deep understanding of the other person.

intimate distance   From touching to 18 inches. Reserved for intimate activities, including passing secrets, making love, and having confidential conversations.

intrapersonal conflict   A conflict within a person.

Johari Window   A model that illustrates how a communicator's willingness to self-disclose and receive feedback operate in her or his relationship.

labeling   A verbal declaration of feelings being felt or displayed.

language obstacles   Obstacles to communication that result from different meanings people give to words and the way they organize those words.

legitimate power   Power associated with an individual's being perceived as having the right to make requests because of the position that she or he occupies.

linear process model of communication   A communication model that characterizes communication as a one-way event, from sender to receiver, taking place within a context.

listening support   A type of social support that involves listening without offering advice, asking penetrating questions, or making judgments.

listening   The active process of receiving, attending to, and assign-

ing meaning to sounds, and of remembering.

live-in couples   Also referred to as couplehood. Two people, heterosexual or homosexual, with or without children, who are unmarried but have a binding relationship.

lose-lose conflict   Linked with avoidance and compromise conflict strategies. An approach to conflict is one in which the conflict outcome results in neither person's goals being fully satisfied.

mesomorph   Person with a body type characterized as being muscular and well-proportioned.

message   The information a sender devises for someone to achieve a purpose.

nonassertive behavior   Reluctance to communicate feelings and thoughts; linked with avoidance and smoothing-over conflict strategies.

nonemotive words   Words that do not communicate an attitude toward an object.

nonfluencies   Vocal behaviors that interrupt or disturb the flow of messages, such as "uh," "you know," and "stuff like that," unnecessary repetition of words, stuttering, incomplete sentences, and corrections.

nonverbal communication   Actions and attributes of people other than words and aspects of the environment that convey meaning.

ordering   Arranging of bits of information into a systematic sequence.

oxymorons   Self-contradictory phrases.

paralanguage   Also referred to as vocalics. Refers to variations that give an individual's vocal cues their unique character: loudness, pitch , rate, quality, articulation, duration, and pronunciation.

parallel relationship   A relationship structure in which complementary and symmetrical aspects are combined. One partner may be dominant and the other submissive at times; other times, the partners may reverse roles; and sometimes, both partners may be dominant or both may be submissive. The expression of feelings depends on the situation.

paraphrasing   When a communicator restates a speaker's message in her or his own words.

passive aggression   See **indirect aggression.**

perception   The process of becoming aware of objects and events, including oneself and others.

personal assistance support   A type of social support that involves providing someone with services or help, such as running an errand.

personal distance   From 18 inches to 4 feet. Used for discussing personal topics.

personal obstacles   Obstacles to communication that result from one's likes and dislikes, what one thinks is important and unimportant, and what one does and does not want.

personal space   An invisible bubble of space a person carries around himself or herself. Sometimes called a body buffer zone, it is larger in front than in the back, and varies in overall size depending on the communication context.

polarization   The tendency to describe people, ideas, and events in either-or terms.

positive visualization   Associated with communication anxiety reduction. A process in which a person prepares for the anticipated unpleasant experience by picturing the situation being carried out successfully.

power   The ability to control what happens; to make choices.

powerful language   Language that creates an impression of strength, capability, and control.

powerless language   Language that creates a perception of being incompetent and passive.

pragmatic rules   Rules that concern how verbal language is actually used. Pragmatic rules guide a communicator's interpretation of messages by drawing attention to the relationship she or he has with the communication partner and the context in which the messages are sent.

private language   Language whose meanings are agreed upon by one segment of a larger language community; may consist of both specialized words and specialized meanings for common words.

privately anxious people   People who mentally resist active communication, but will participate by forcing themselves. In public, they seldom display the outward physical reactions of stress, such as fingernail biting, sweaty palms, or dry mouth, but still feel discomfort.

proactive process   Responding to a message based on one's total history.

pseudolistening   Acting like one is listening when one really is not.

public distance   Twelve feet and beyond. Usually used for small group meetings and for hailing people. Dis-

tances farther than 25 feet limit communication to shouts and broad nonverbal gestures.

publicly anxious people   People who are strongly hesitant about communicating with others and who display their anxiety through such outward signs as avoiding eye contact, blushing, perspiring, and speaking in a quavering voice when forced to communicate in public settings.

purpose, communication   The goal of a communication transaction.

qualifiers   Words that clarify or limit the meaning of an idea.

qualifiers   Words that detract from the certainty of a statement.

racist language   Language that expresses stereotyped racial attitudes or feelings of superiority of one race over another.

reality confirmation support   A type of social support that involves confirming a person's perceptions and perspectives of the world.

receiver   The person who takes in and decodes a message.

red flag   A judgmental word or phrase that evokes strong negative emotions and interferes with a communicator's willingness and ability to listen.

referent power   A source of power based on personal loyalty, friendship, affection, and admiration.

reflected appraisal   A perspective on self-concept development which argues that one's self-concept is consistent with the view others hold of him or her, and that one comes to view oneself as he or she does because of the views of others.

regulators Nonverbal behaviors used intentionally that influence who talks, when, and for how long.

relational obstacles Obstacles to communication that result from differences in status and power, differences in the ways people define their roles in a relationship, and differences in the ways people perceive their relationships.

relationship The connection that exists when (1) the interactants are aware of each other and take each other into account, (2) there is some exchange of influence, and (3) there is some agreement about what the nature of the relationship is and what the appropriate behaviors are given the nature of the relationship.

relative words Words that gain their meaning by comparison and clarification; unless the point of comparison is specified, relative words lack clarity.

reordering Changing of an existing system of organizing information so that a new or different sequence is developed.

resistance See **adaptation.**

reward power Power associated with an individual's being perceived as the best or only source of desired rewards.

rigid family A family that has authoritarian leadership, strict discipline, roles that are inflexible, and unchanging rules.

rules The regulations that govern actions in a relationship; necessary to make predictions about another person's behavior.

selective interpretation A communicator's choice for how to explain the

information he or she selectively perceives and selectively organizes.

selective listening Paying attention only to topics in which one is personally interested.

selective organization The process of fitting together the information one selectively perceives to form a whole.

selective perception Perceiving what one chooses to perceive.

self-concept The totality of one's thoughts about herself or himself concerning who she or he is.

self-esteem How one feels about who she or he is.

self-fulfilling prophecy When what a communicator believes about herself or himself and others has a tendency to come true.

self-serving bias The tendency to judge oneself less harshly than others.

semantic differential A method to measure a person's reactions to an object or concept by marking spaces between a pair of adjectives, one positive and one negative, with each space representing an attitude position.

semantic rules Rules that govern the relationship between words and the meaning assigned them.

sender A person who devises and encodes a message.

sexist language Language that expresses stereotyped sexual attitudes or a sense that one gender is superior to another.

sexual harassment Unwelcome sexual advances, requests for sexual favors, and other offensive verbal and physical actions of a sexual nature.

shared language Language whose meanings are agreed upon by members of a language community.

should self An image of self that contains all the "oughts" and "shoulds" that serve as one's moral guidelines.

significant other A person whose opinion matters or whose judgment is trusted.

single-parent family One parent—married, never married, or divorced—who lives with her or his biological or adopted child.

smoothing-over Also called an obliging or suppression strategy. A conflict resolution strategy that shows concern for the other person but not for oneself.

social comparison A perspective on self-concept development which argues that one's self-concept is based on one's comparative evaluation of self to others.

social distance From 4 to 12 feet. Requires a louder voice than intimate or personal distance and is thus used for impersonal conversations, such as business transactions.

social identity The groups or categories to which one belongs or aspires.

static evaluation The inability of the English language to account for constant change.

stress A body's reaction to any event that pushes it out of what is considered, for it, to be normal; a body's preparation to respond to the unusual.

stressor A source of stress.

stuffing   The process of pushing emotions inside rather than confronting and expressing them.

supportive behavior   A message that communicates to an individual that he or she is acknowledged, understood, and accepted.

symmetrical relationship   A relationship structure in which the partners contribute equally to their relationship, that is, both are dominant or submissive, loving or hostile.

syntactic rules   Also called grammar. Rules that govern how words can be arranged.

system, family   The pattern of interaction a family uses as its primary or usual mode of operation.

systematic desensitization   Associated with communication anxiety reduction. A process by which a person gains control over his or her anxiety by learning to recognize his or her stressors and to use relaxation techniques to combat their effects.

tag questions   A type of tentative language in which questions are added onto the end of statements.

technical appreciation support   A type of social support that involves acknowledging a person for a job well done.

technical challenge support   A type of social support that involves urging a person to think about a task or an activity in new ways so as to motivate and stretch the person and to increase her or his creativity, excitement, and involvement.

territorial contamination   Occurs when a person makes someone else's territory "impure," "dirty," or "unclean."

territorial invasion   Occurs when someone tries to take over another person's territory and dislodge him or her.

territorial violation   Occurs when someone uses another's territory without her or his permission.

territoriality   Feelings of ownership toward some fixed area.

themes, family   Underlying family perspectives or points of view that provide clues to a family's meaningful goals, values, and concerns. Themes provide a focus for a family's thought and energy.

time management   A method for setting priorities for the use of an individual's time by deciding what to do when and for how long.

transactive communication process   Building on the interaction process model, this characterization of communication stresses that messages are simultaneously sent and received, messages cannot be erased or taken back, communicators respond to messages proactively, the meaning of any message depends on the situation, communicators can only infer what their partners are thinking or feeling, the messages that are received have a consequence, and communicators are self-reflective.

two-parent biological family   Two people and their biological offspring.

values   The importance one attaches to different ways of behaving, such as being honest, as well as the goals to which one aspires.

verbal language   The words and grammatical system of a particular society.

vocalics   See **paralanguage.**

win-lose conflict   Linked with smoothing over and dominance conflict strategies. Approach to conflict resolution in which one person wins and the other loses.

PHOTO CREDITS

LITERARY CREDIT

A

acculturation 13
acquaintance relationships 255–56
active listening 110, 126–30
actual self 48
adaptability 356–58
adaptation 6
adapters 169
affect display 169
affinity seeking 312–14
Affinity-Seeking Strategies, Assessing
     Your (Knowledge Checkup 9.5)
     312–13
allness 202
Analytic Breakdown, Doing an (Skill
     Development 12.2) 425
androgyny 39
Appearance Satisfaction (Knowledge
     Checkup 5.1) 140–41
approachability cues 294–95
arena (open area; Johari Window) 307
argot 184
A*S*S*E*R*T formula 396–98
A*S*S*E*R*T Yourself (Skill
     Development 11.2) 397–98
assertion 395–98
associative power 434
attachment needs, child's 348
attacking behavior 300–03
attitudes, self-defeating 225–29
attraction 286–94
Attraction, Your Bases of (Knowledge
     Checkup 9.3) 293–94
attractiveness 286–88
avoidance 386–87

B

Becall, Lauren 416
Beliefs, Overcoming (Knowledge
     Checkup 12.2) 420–21
belonging needs, child's 347
Bem Sex-Role Inventory (Knowledge
     Checkup 2.2) 38–39
biosocial attitudes, family 338–41
blind area (Johari Window) 307
body image 140
body movements 168–72

types of 169–70
uses of 170–72
body shape 140
boundaries, family 337–38
bristle statements 379
burnout 223
bypassing 203

C

CAGC: Communication Apprehension in
     Generalized Contexts
     Questionnaire (Knowledge
     Checkup 7.4) 241–42
channel 5
chaotic family 358
chunking 121
Chunking, Ordering, and Reordering (Skill
     Development 4.2) 122
clichés 206
Clothing Preferences (Knowledge
     Checkup 5.2) 142–43
clothing 142–44
coercive power 435
cohesion 356–58
Cohesion and Adaptability in Your Family
     (Knowledge Checkup 10.6)
     356–57
collective culture 160–61
commitment 272–274, 436
Commitment Probe (Knowledge Checkup
     8.4) 272–73
communication, culture and 10–14
     definition of 5–10
     elements of 5–10
     ethical 27–28
     goals for 52–53
     interactive process model of 6–7
     linear process model of 5–6
     obstacles to effective 26–27
     transactive model of 7–10
communication anxiety (shyness), causes
     of 244–45
     dealing with 245–49
     definition of 243
     effects of 245
     private 243–44
     public 243–44

situational 244
communication skills training 246–47
communicator, definition of 8
     qualities of a competent 23–27
Comparing Your Preferences with the
     General Population (Knowledge
     Checkup 9.2) 291
complementarity, attraction and
     289–90
complementary relationship 262
compliance 436
compliance gaining 314–16
Compliance-Gaining Strategies, Assessing
     Your (Knowledge Checkup 9.6)
     314–16
compromise 387–88
confirming behavior 300–03
conflict, assessment of 405–08
     characteristics of 374–78
     consequences of 380–83
     culture and 373–74, 394, 403
     definition of 372–73
     educational institutions and 379
     family and 358–63, 379
     gender and 398–400
     media and 379–80
     outcomes of 389–90
     perceptions of 378
     resolution options for 404–05
     sources of 376–78
     strategies of 383–92
Conflict Consequences (Knowledge
     Checkup 11.2) 382–83
Conflict Strategies, Your (Knowledge
     Checkup 11.3) 383–85
connotation 191–92
contamination, territorial 153–54
context 5
convergent thinking 415
Coping Responses to Self-Defeating
     Attitudes, Developing (Skill
     Development 7.1) 228–29
Creating New Gift Ideas (Skill
     Development 12.3) 426–27
creativity, benefits of 416
     definition of 415
     developing 422–27

creativity (*continued*)
  obstacles to 416–21
culture, aggression and 340–41, 362
  attractiveness and 287
  avoidance and 387
  characteristics of 12–14
  clothing and 142
  collective 34–35, 160–61
  communication and 10–14
  communication goals and 53
  conflict and 373–74, 377–78
  conflict resolution and 403
  definition of 11
  emotion and 86–88, 94–95
  empathy and 82
  extroversion-introversion and 40
  eye contact and 147
  family communication and 333–34
  family images and 335–36
  gender roles and 339
  idealized self and 48
  individualistic 34, 160–61
  interpersonal distance and 155
  intimacy and 275
  listening and 100, 108, 128
  nonassertion and 394, 398
  nonverbal communication and 137, 139
  perception and 67, 69, 72
  power and 428–29, 434
  powerful language and 437–38
  relationship rules and 269–70
  relationships and 257–58
  self-esteem and 57
  should self and 49
  time and 172–73
  touch and 157, 160–61
  verbal language and 183, 193

D
Darwin, Charles 142
death 355
deception, nonverbal cues to 174–75
denotation 190–91
Dietrich, Marlene 255
Differences, Communicating (Skill
    Development 6.2) 199–200
Difficult People, Dealing with (Skill
    Development 11.3) 402–03
dialectical tension 24
direct aggression 394–95
disclaimers 438
Disclosure and Feedback in Two
    Relationships (Knowledge
    Checkup 9.4) 304–05
disconfirming behavior 300–03

disengaged family 357
distance, intimate 155
  personal 155
  public 156
  social 155–56
distortions 207
distress 218
divergent thinking 415
divorce 354–55
dominance 387–89
dominance/submission 261–68

E
ectomorph 140
egospeaking 112
electronic mail 316–17
Elements and Characteristics of Human
    Communication, Recognizing the
    (Knowledge Checkup 1.1) 15–16
emblems 169
Emerson, Ralph Waldo 35, 36, 373
emotion, definition of 84–85
  expressing 90–93
  failure to express 86–89
  gender and 89–90
  helping others express 93–95
Emotional Reactions, Identifying Your
    (Knowledge Checkup 3.4)
    88–89
emotional challenge support 237
emotional support 236
Emotions Effectively, Expressing Your
    (Skill Development 5.3) 165–66
Emotions, Identifying Your (Knowledge
    Checkup 3.3) 85–86
emotive words 206–07
empathy 26, 82–84, 102
Empathy in Friendship, Assessing
    (Knowledge Checkup 3.2) 83
empowerment 429–30
endomorph 140
enmeshed family 357
Environments, Assessing Two (Skill
    Development 5.2) 151
ethnocentrism 14
euphemisms 205–06
Euripides 172
eustress 218
expert power 433
exercise, stress and 233
external distractions 115
eye behavior 144–49

F
facial expressions 144–49

Facial Expressions, Increasing Your Skill
    at Interpreting (Skill Development
    5.1) 148–49
fact 200
fact-inference confusion 200–01
Facts from Inferences, Distinguishing
    (Knowledge Checkup 6.1)
    200–01
Families Teach, Observing What (Skill
    Development 10.1) 341–42
family, adaptability of 356–58
  addition of members to 346–49
  biosocial attitudes 338–41
  boundaries 337–38
  cohesion in 356–58
  configurations of 331
  conflict and 358–63
  culture and 333–34
  definition of 330–31
  dissolution of 354–55
  establishment of 345–46
  functional 355–63
  images 335–36
  importance of 331–33
  launching from 349–50
  post-launching and 352–54
  stages 344–55
  systems approach to 342–44
  themes 336–37
Family Images, Identifying Your
    (Knowledge Checkup 10.2)
    335–36
Family in the United States, The
    Contemporary (Knowledge
    Checkup 10.1) 332
Family's Themes, Identifying Your
    (Knowledge Checkup 10.3) 337
family-of-origin 331
  attraction and 292–93
feedback 6, 122
Feedback to Indicate You Are Listening,
    Providing (Skill Development 4.3)
    123–24
Feelings, Expressing Your (Skill
    Development 3.3) 93
flexibility skills 25
free information, beginning relationships
    and 296
friend relationships 256
functional family 355–63

G
gender, biosocial attitudes and 338–41
  communication anxiety and 243
  emotion and 89–90

eye contact and 147
    intimacy and 277
    language differences and 194–97
    listening response styles and 127
    powerful language and 439
    stress and 223–24
Gender Role Attitudes, Identifying Your
        (Knowledge Checkup 10.4)
        339–40
gender roles, families and 338–39
    culture and 339
generalized other 45–46
gestures 171
good friend relationships 256
Goodman, Ellen 81
grandparenting styles 352
Grandparents' Grandparenting Style,
        Your (Knowledge Checkup 10.5)
        353
green flag words 114

H
Habit of Saying No, Examining the
        (Knowledge Checkup 12.1) 419
Hazlitt, William 303
hearing 101
hedges 437
hesitations 438
hidden area (Johari Window) 307
Hodgson, Ralph 75
hostility/love 261–68
How Competently Do You Communicate?
        (Knowledge Checkup 1.2) 20–22
How Powerful Do You Feel? (Knowledge
        Checkup 12.3) 429–30
Huxley, Aldous 4

I
idealized self 48
illustrators 169
images, family 335–36
impression management 52–53
Impression, Creating a Favorable (Skill
        Development 9.2) 298–99
independence, child's development of
        349–50
indirect (passive) aggression 393–94
indiscrimination 198–200
individualistic culture 160–61
inference 200
information, cultural 17
    psychological 17
    sociological 17
Information, Probing for (Skill
        Development 9.1) 297

Inge, W. R. 245
insulated listening 112–13
integration conflict style 390–92
internal distractions 115–16
interpersonal communication, definition of
        16–18
    obstacles to 26–27
interpersonal communication competency,
        components of 18–23
    definition of 18–19
    knowledge and 19
    motivation and 22–23
    skills and 19–22
interpersonal conflict 375
interpretation, selective 74–77
Interpretations, Developing Alternative
        (Skill Development 3.1) 75
intimacy 275–77
Intimacy Probe (Knowledge Checkup 8.5)
        276–77
intimate distance 155
intimate experience 275
intimate relationships 256–57
intrapersonal conflict 375
invasion, territorial 153–54

J
jargon 192–93
Johari Window 305–10
Jong, Erica 436
Joubert, Joseph 188
Jung, Carl 55

K
Kennedy, John F. 218
Kipling, Rudyard 204
Krishnamuriti 114, 235

L
labeling 85
ladder of abstraction 188–89
Ladder of Abstraction, Constructing a
        (Skill Development 6.1) 189–90
language, feminine 194–97
    masculine 194–97
    nonsexist 209–211
    power and 437–39
    private 192–94
    racist 211
    sexist 209
    shared 192–94
    unclear 204
launching, child's 350–51
learning styles, listening and 106–108

Left/Right, Linear/Global Brain
        Dominance (Knowledge Checkup
        4.2) 107–08
legitimate power 435–36
Lippman, Walter 391
listening, barriers to effective 110–16
    definition of 100–01
    feedback and 122–24
    learning styles and 106–08
    levels of 108–10
    patterns of 103–05
    principles of 105–06
    reasons for 102–03
    response styles 124–28
    stages of 101
    techniques to improve 116–22
Listening Responses, Assessing Your
        (Knowledge Checkup 4.5) 124–26
listening support 235–36
listening to help 128–30
Long-Term, Intimate Partner, Desired
        Characteristics in a (Knowledge
        Checkup 9.1) 285–86
Lord Chesterfield 13
lose-lose conflict 387
love/hostility 261–68

M
meditation 233–35
mesomorph 140
message 5
Milton, John 24

N
New Associations, Forming (Skill
        Development 12.1) 423–24
Nimoy, Leonard 296
nonassertion 393
nonfluencies 164
Nonlistening Signals, Your (Knowledge
        Checkup 4.3) 110
nonsexist language 209–10
nonverbal communication, body
        movements and 168–72
    characteristics of 138–39
    context and 149–56
    culture and 137, 139, 142, 147, 155,
        157, 160–01, 172–03
    deception and 174–75
    definition of 136
    eye behavior and 144–49
    facial expressions and 144–49
    functions of 137–38
    physical appearance and 139–44
    time and 172–74

nonverbal communication (*continued*
   touch and 156–63
   voice and 163–68
nurturance needs, child's 348

O

Ogden, C. K. 204
organization, selective 69–74
oxymorons 207–08

P

pace of life 173–74
parallel relationship 264
paraphrasing 118
Paraphrasing, Recognizing Effective (Skill
   Development 4.1) 118–19
Parental Authority, Use of (Knowledge
   Checkup 10.7) 359–61
Paying Attention? Take This Listening
   Self-Evaluation Test and See
   (Knowledge Checkup 4.1) 104–05
perception, culture and 67, 69, 72
   definition of 66–67
   increasing accuracy of 79–84
   problems in 78–79
   selective 67–69
Perception Process, Analyzing Your
   (Knowledge Checkup 3.1) 76
person-oriented family 338
personal assistance support 237
personal distance 155
personal space 154–55
physical context 150–52
polarization 197–98
position-oriented family 338
positive visualization 247–48
post-launching 352–54
posture 171
Power, Assessing Your Sources of
   (Knowledge Checkup 12.4)
   430–31
power, associative 434
   coercive 434
   culture and 428–29, 434, 437–38
   definition of 428–30
   expert 433
   language and 437–39
   legitimate 435–36
   referent 433–34
   reward 434
   sources of 430–36
power bases, choosing 436–37
   formal 431
   informal 431

Powerless Language, Recognizing and
   Eliminating (Skill Development
   12.4) 439
pragmatic rules 187
presenting problem 343
proactive 8
Process and Outcomes of Your Conflicts,
   Assessing the (Skill Development
   11.4) 406–07
prom queen syndrome 288
protection needs, child's 348
proximity, attraction and 288–89
pseudolistening 113
psychological context 152–56
public distance 156
punctuality 173
purpose 5

Q

qualifiers 207, 437

R

racist language 211
reality confirmation support 237
receiver 5
Red and Green Flags, Sending Up Your
   (Knowledge Checkup 4.4) 114–15
red flag words 113–14
referent power 433–34
reflected appraisal 43–45
regulators 169
Reid, John 226
Relational Structure Analysis (Knowledge
   Checkup 8.2) 264–66
relationship, definition of 254
Relationship Discord, Analysis of
   (Knowledge Checkup 11.1) 373
Relationship Goals, Ascertaining Your
   (Skill Development 8.1) 260–61
Relationship Goals?, What Are Your
   (Knowledge Checkup 8.1) 258–59
Relationship Interpersonalness, Assessing
   (Skill Development 1.1) 18
Relationship Rules, Your (Knowledge
   Checkup 8.3) 271–72
relationships, attraction and 286–94
   beginning 284–99
   commitment and 272–74
   complementary 262
   conditions of 254–55
   culture and 257–58
   ending 317–21
   goals for 258–61

intimacy and 274–77
   maintaining 299–317
   parallel 264, 268
   qualities and resources of 271–78
   rules for 268–72
   structure of 261–68
   symmetrical 263–64
   types of 255–57
relative words 204–05
respect needs, child's 348
Rich, Adrienne 174
Richards, I. A. 204
rigid family 358
role relationships 255
role taking 26
Roosevelt, Eleanor 58
Roshi, Yasutani 78

S

Sapir-Whorf hypothesis 184
Sawyer, Diane 101
Schuller, Robert 424
selective listening 112
self-concept, actual self and 48
   culture and 34–35, 40, 48–49
   definition of 37
   dimensions of 35–53
   family and 341
   idealized self and 48
   organization of 47–48
   personality characteristics and 38–41
   physical characteristics and 43
   reflected appraisal and 43–45
   should self and 49–50, 57–58
   social comparison and 46
   social identity and 37
   sources of 43–46
   stress and 223
   values and 41–43
   verbal language and 184
Self-Disclosure and Receptiveness to
   Feedback, Increasing Your (Skill
   Development 9.4) 311
self-disclosure, definition of 303
   fear of 312
   functions of 303
   Johari Window and 305–10
   touch and 160
Self-Esteem, Analyzing Your General
   (Knowledge Checkup 2.7) 53–54
Self-Esteem, Analyzing Your Specific
   (Knowledge Checkup 2.8) 55–56
self-esteem, attraction and 292
   culture and 57

definition of 53
enhancing 57–60
self-fulfilling prophecy 77–78
self-presentation, influences on 50–53
self-serving bias 78–79
semantic rules 187
sender 5
Sense Awareness and Sense Imagination,
    Increasing (Skill Development 3.2)
    80
Sexist Language, Eliminating (Skill
    Development 6.4) 210–11
sexist language 209
sexual harassment 399–400
Should Messages, Confronting Your (Skill
    Development 2.1) 58
should self 49
"Should" Statements, Identifying Your
    (Knowledge Checkup 2.6) 49–50
shyness see communication anxiety
Significant Others and Their Appraisals of
    You, Identifying Your (Knowledge
    Checkup 2.4) 44–45
significant other 44–45
similarity, attraction and 290–91
Similarity, Increasing Perceptions of (Skill
    Development 5.4) 172
Simple Assertions, Stating (Skill
    Development 11.1) 396
Smith, Dodie 335
smoothing over 387
snap judgment 69
social comparison 46
Social Comparison Groups, Identifying
    Your (Knowledge Checkup 2.5) 46
social distance 155–56
social identity 37
social support 235–39
Social Support, Providing (Skill
    Development 7.3) 237–39
Space in a Common Setting, Analyzing
    the Use of (Knowledge Checkup
    5.4) 156
St. Jerome 145
static evaluation 202–03
Static Evaluation, Eliminating (Skill
    Development 6.3) 203
stereotypes 199
stress, adaptation stage of 223
    alarm stage of 222–23
    definition of 218
    exhaustion stage of 223

nonverbal indicators of 221–22
responses to 225–40
social support and 235–39
stages of 222–23
verbal indicators of 218–21
Stress Analysis, Your (Knowledge
    Checkup 7.3) 224–25
Stress Reactions, Self-Assessment of Your
    (Knowledge Checkup 7.1) 220–21
Stress, Your Nonverbal Signs of
    (Knowledge Checkup 7.2) 221–22
stressor 218, 223–25
structuring needs, child's 348
stuffing 87
submission/dominance 261–68
support needs, child's 348
Supportive and Confirming Responses,
    Giving (Skill Development 9.3)
    302–03
supportive behavior 300–03
symbols, abstract 187–89
    concrete 187–89
symmetrical relationship 263–64
syntactic rules 187
systematic desensitization 247

T
tag questions 196, 438
technical appreciation support 236
technical challenge support 236
territorial contamination 153–54
    invasion 153–54
    violation 153–54
Territorial Defense, Analyzing Your
    (Knowledge Checkup 5.3) 154
Thayer, William 332
themes, family 336–37
Thoreau, Henry David 127, 164
Tillich, Paul 275
time 172–74
    culture and 172–73
time management 229–32
Time Management Model (Skill
    Development 7.2) 230–32
Tomlinson, H. M. 67
touch 156–63
    culture and 157, 160–61
    expectations for 160–63
    uses of 160
    violations of 161
Touch Avoidance, Assessing Your
    (Knowledge Checkup 5.5) 159

Touch Behavior, Analyzing Your
    (Knowledge Checkup 5.6)
    161–63
turn taking, conversational 147

U
Unclear Language, Recognizing
    (Knowledge Checkup 6.2) 208
underlying problem 343
unknown area (Johari Window) 307

V
values 41–43, 47–48
Values, Discovering Your (Knowledge
    Checkup 2.3) 41–42
verbal communication, barriers to
    successful 197–203
    characteristics of 185–87
    connotation of 191–92
    culture and 183, 193
    definition of 182
    denotation of 190–91
    effective use of 203–11
    gender and 194–97
    importance of 182–85
    meaning and 187–90
    nonverbal communication and
        137–39
    private 192–94
    self-concept and 184
    shared 192–94
    stress and 218–21
violation, territorial 153–54
Visualization, Practicing Positive (Skill
    Development 7.4) 248
Vocal Cues to Regulate Conversations,
    Using (Knowledge Checkup 5.7)
    167–68
voice (paralanguage; vocalics) 163
Vonnegut, Kurt 50
vultures, psychological 59–60

W
Who Am I? (Knowledge Checkup 2.1)
    36–37
Whyte-Melville, George 260
Willkie, Wendell 198
win-lose conflict 388–89
win-win conflict 391–92
Winfrey, Oprah 382
Workshop Process of Change, Applying
    the (Skill Development 10.2) 364

Every exit is an entry somewhere else.
Tom Stoppard